Covering Immigration

Covering Immigration

Popular Images and the Politics of the Nation

Leo R. Chavez

University of California Press
Berkeley • Los Angeles • London

#4561833 5

University of California Press
Berkeley and Los Angeles, California

University of California Press, Ltd.
London, England

© 2001 by
The Regents of the University of California

Library of Congress Cataloging-in-Publication Data

Chavez, Leo R. (Leo Ralph)
    Covering immigration : popular images and
the politics of the nation / Leo R. Chavez.
        p.   cm.
    Includes bibliographical references and index.
    ISBN 0-520-22435-3 (cloth : alk. paper)—
    ISBN 0-520-22436-1 (pbk. : alk. paper)
    1. United States—Emigration and immigration—
Public opinion.   2. United States—Emigration
and immigration—Government policy.
    3. Immigrants—United States—Public opinion.
    4. Public opinion—United States.   I. Title.
JV6455.C44   2001
325.73—dc21   00-069090

Printed in the United States of America

10 09 08 07 06 05 04 03 02 01
10 9 8 7 6 5 4 3 2 1

The paper used in this publication meets
the minimum requirements of ANSI/NISO
Z39.48-1992 (R 1997) (*Permanence of Paper*).♾

For Cathy Ota, and Koji and Andrea Chavez
because they make it all worthwhile.

Contents

Illustrations and Credits

          World Report, 21 March 1983. Courtesy Maggie Stebe
          and Mark Perlstein/© 1983 *U.S. News and World Report.*   60
4.5.   "Los Angeles." *Time,* 13 June 1983. Courtesy Time-Life
          Syndication.   61
4.6.   "The New Face of America." *Time,* fall 1993 special
          issue. Courtesy Time-Life Syndication.   63
4.7.   "The Immigrants," *Business Week,* 13 July 1992. Cour-
          tesy *Business Week.*   66
4.8.   "The Triumph of Asian Americans," *New Republic,*
          15–22 July 1985. Courtesy *New Republic.*   67
4.9.   "Will U.S. Shut the Door on Immigrants?" *U.S News
          and World Report,* 12 April 1982. Courtesy Superstock
          International.   68
4.10.   "Open the Floodgates?" *New Republic,* 1 April 1985.
          Courtesy *New Republic.*   72
4.11.   "Ready to Talk Now?" *Time,* 5 September 1994.
          Courtesy Time-Life Syndication.   75
4.12.   "The World's Poor Flood the U.S." *Business Week,* 23
          June 1980. Courtesy *Business Week.*   76
4.13.   "The Immigrants." *New Republic,* 27 December 1993.
          Courtesy *New Republic.*   78
5.1.   "A Ray of Hope." *U.S. News and World Report,* 6
          August 1979. Courtesy Corbis-SYGMA.   88
5.2.   "The Cuban Influx." *Newsweek,* 26 May 1980. Cour-
          tesy Mario Ruiz/© 1980 Newsweek, Inc. All rights
          reserved. Reprinted by permission.   102
5.3.   "Still the Land of Opportunity?" *U.S. News and World
          Report,* 4 July 1983. Courtesy Stephen R. Wagner.   115
6.1.   "The New Refugees." *U.S. News and World Report,* 23
          October 1989. Courtesy Image Works.   135
6.2.   "America's Changing Colors." *Time,* 9 April 1990.
          Courtesy Time-Life Syndication.   137
6.3.   "Racial Rifts." *New Republic,* 10 June 1991. Courtesy
          New Republic.   141
6.4.   "The INS Mess." *New Republic,* 13 April 1992. Courtesy
          New Republic.   145
6.5.   "Tired? Poor? Huddled? Tempest-Tossed? Try Australia."
          National Review, 22 June 1992. © 1992 National Review,
          Inc. Reprinted by permission.   146
6.6.   "Blacks vs. Browns." *Atlantic,* October 1992. Courtesy
          Atlantic and Karen Barbour.   156

TABLES

GRAPHS

Preface and Acknowledgments

Humans have long noted the power of visual images, as witnessed by the exquisite cave paintings, carved bone, and engraved rocks produced by our ancestors long before they created writing. In the contemporary world, the quantity of visual images is staggering and growing in conjunction with incredible advances in technology to create and disseminate images. Everywhere we turn, in our homes, on television, computers, movies, magazines, billboards, and walls, images are there, speaking to us. There is practically nowhere in the world today where one can escape the inundation of visual images. Although particular societies and cultures produce images for consumption by their own members, images can also travel rapidly across national and cultural borders.

A puzzling thing about living in a world so permeated with visual images is how little time we spend contemplating the meanings the images have for us as individuals and as members of a society. We rarely pause to ask, "What are the images trying to say?" Seldom, if ever, do we form groups to discuss the images on the magazines we casually examine while buying our groceries. Most of the visual imagery in our daily lives we treat as the flotsam and jetsam of modern life.

In a way, this book is an attempt to improve my own visual literacy. I became hyperaware of the images of immigrants after I began conducting research on the topic in the early 1980s. I began to casually collect magazine covers, cartoons, newspaper articles, and documentaries about immigration. But what caught my eye were magazine covers.

These one-page visual operas sang out the stories they vividly told. Here in artistic form were messages about not just immigration but something much greater: who we are as a nation. By nation I do not mean simply a geographic space with defined political borders. Rather, these covers dwelled on the idea of who we are as a people and on the place of immigrants in that conceptualization. I came to realize that the story of America, both its past and its imagined future, was being constructed, debated, and contested on these magazine covers. This was a story worth examining.[1]

The decision to turn this interest in magazine covers into a book developed slowly. I began to formulate the project during my first fellowship at the University of California Humanities Research Institute, on the Irvine campus, in 1994, and the analysis matured during my subsequent stay at the institute in 1998. I am indebted to both the Humanities Research Institute for an excellent place to think and work and to the two convenors, Norma Alarcon and Gwen Kirkpatrick, for organizing intellectually stimulating seminars.

I would also like to acknowledge the contributions of many of the people who made this book possible. The University of California Chicano/Latino Research Committee provided research funds that allowed me to pursue this work. My colleagues at the Chicano/Latino Studies Program provided forums at which I could present early versions of my analysis of the magazine cover images. My colleagues in the Department of Anthropology at UC Irvine also listened to my colloquia presentations and provided important feedback and insights toward the reading of the images, from which I gained much. I am particularly indebted to Lisbeth Haas for her insightful observations on the images. I also learned a great deal from the students in my anthropology class who shared with me some of their thoughts on the magazine covers. Carlos Velez-Ibañez undertook an insightful reading of the manuscript, and Pauline Manaka provided invaluable assistance with computer searches of library holdings. Although acknowledgments for reproduction rights appear separately, I would like to mention here that I am most grateful to the magazines, artists, and photographers for allowing me to reproduce the covers.

Finally, I am particularly grateful to Michelle Madsen Camacho, Juliet McMullin, and Jonathan Xavier Inda. Michelle assisted me in locating demographic data from the U.S. Census Bureau and the Immigration and Naturalization Service. Juliet provided an alternative eye to the coding of the images, and she was always willing to serve as a sounding board on early drafts. Jonathan spent many hours helping me locate magazine covers and scanning the covers into the computer. He also shared his insights and knowledge concerning textual analysis and provided a critical reading of some of the chapters. Their assistance in all these important areas helped make this book possible. I must emphasize, however, that I alone am responsible for any errors in fact or judgment associated with this work.

CHAPTER I

Introduction

Discourses on Immigration and the Nation

A national culture is a discourse—a way of constructing
meanings which influences and organizes both our actions
and our conception of ourselves. National cultures construct
identities by producing meanings about "the nation" with
which we can identify; these are contained in the stories
which are told about it, memories which connect its present
with its past, and images which are constructed of it.

Stuart Hall, "Question of Cultural Identity"

Americans are not a narrow tribe, our blood is as the flood
of the Amazon, made up of a thousand noble currents all
pouring into one.

Herman Melville

On 5 July 1976, *Time* magazine published an issue celebrating the nation's bicentennial birthday. The cover image was a mosaic of words
printed in red, white, and blue, with the bold text "The Promised Land"
forming a protective semicircle above the text "America's New Immigrants." Inside the magazine was another mosaic of images made from
photographs of immigrants from different periods in U.S. history and
from different countries. *Time*'s 1976 birthday issue was an affirmative
rendition of "the nation of immigrants" theme that is a central part of
the story America tells about its history and national identity.

On 17 October 1994, the cover of the *Nation* told a different story
about immigration. Its cover text proclaimed "The Immigration Wars."
The cover is a collage of overlapping images. The central image appears
to be the western border of the United States on the circular globe of the
earth as seen from space. To the left of the continental border, where the
Pacific Ocean would normally fill in the rest of the globe, is a multitude

1.1.   *Time,* 5 July 1976. "America's New Immigrants."

of people, a mass of heads and partial bodies, many wearing hats and scarves, evoking the mass movement of refugees or migrants. Walking north across the globe, with one foot on the border of the North American continent, is a man with a knapsack on his back and a Mexican sombrero on his head. A barking dog pulls tightly on its leash, right above the Statue of Liberty, which has an upside down American flag sticking out of her head. In the background is another line (border?) with grass beyond it and a rectangular frame that appears to be engulfed in flames.

The *Nation*'s cover used images that evoked a sense of the prevailing climate toward immigrants at the time, a climate filled with a sense of alarm about the perceived negative impact of immigration on the nation. The sentiments clearly elicited by the cover's image did not necessarily represent the editorial stance of the magazine itself, and in this case the

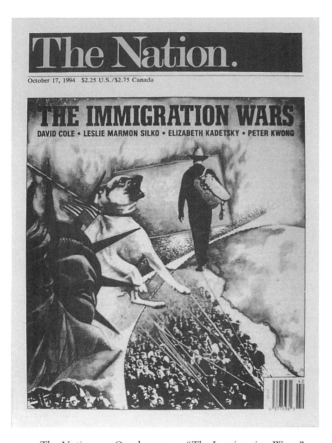

1.2.   The *Nation*, 17 October 1994. "The Immigration Wars."

Nation offered up such an image in critique of what it perceived as pervasive anti-immigrant views in U.S. society. But the point is that the *Nation*'s cover stands in marked contrast to *Time*'s affirmative rendering of immigration and the nation on its cover of almost twenty years earlier. These two magazine covers reflect the demonstrable shift to an increasingly anti-immigrant public debate and public-policy initiatives that occurred during the last quarter of the twentieth century. Moreover, they represent two opposing and yet interlocked views of immigration, a double helix of negative and positive attitudes that have existed throughout America's history. Immigrants are reminders of how Americans, as a people, came to be, and immigration is central to how we view ourselves as a nation. As Oscar Handlin once wrote, immigration *is* the history of the nation. But immigrants are also newcomers whose difference and "otherness" do not go unquestioned or unremarked upon. Their very presence raises concerns about population growth, economic competition, and various linguistic and "cultural" threats. These polarized views constitute the immigration dilemma in American society.

My goal for this book had been to provide a culture history of contemporary discourse about immigrants and immigration. In doing so, however, I came to the realization that what I was actually undertaking was an examination of the politics of the nation. Two fundamental questions drive this politics: Who are Americans as a people? And how do today's immigrants fit into that self-conception? There are, as this analysis will show, competing answers to these questions. The political struggle is over which answers will win out. Or, in the terminology of social theory, which view of "America" will gain hegemony.

Magazine covers serve as entry points into the national discourse on immigration. They serve this purpose in two ways: they punctuate salient moments in the flow of historical events and thus mark those moments for analysis. Magazine covers are also sites of discourse. What they say about immigrants and the nation, as well as how they say it, are open to critical readings. Magazines, through their covers, attempt to encapsulate an issue or issues that will draw in potential consumers or interest existing consumers. In doing so, they rely on symbols, both visual and textual, to represent the nation, its people, its history, and "the immigrant." Magazines are not apolitical in this endeavor; theirs is a struggle over the representation of these categories. Attention to these representations suggests the ways "the immigrant" and "the nation" are discursively constituted.

I am interested in interpreting the messages about immigration conveyed on the covers of *American Heritage, Time, Newsweek, U.S. News and World Report,* the *New Republic,* the *Nation,* the *National Review,* the *Atlantic Monthly, Business Week,* and the *Progressive* for thirty-five years, beginning in 1965, a watershed year in American history. A number of general questions guided my reading of the magazines and their covers. What images and representations of immigrants do the magazine covers use in their discourse about immigration? How does this discourse relate immigrants and immigration to issues of American "identity," "culture," and the "nation"? Answering these questions entailed identifying the basic visual strategies, symbols, icons, and metaphors in the magazines' discourse about immigration. Exploring these questions also demanded a discursive analysis of the magazine covers and their accompanying articles, which occupies most of the space of this book. Finally, the questions lead me to explore how students at the University of California, Irvine, read the magazine covers. The students' readings provided an important counterpoint to my own interpretation of the magazines' discourse on immigration and the nation.

1965: A WATERSHED YEAR

I begin this investigation with 1965 because that was the year the U.S. Congress passed monumental immigration reform that radically changed the criteria used to admit immigrants to the United States (Reimers 1985). Anti-immigration sentiments crystallized in the 1924 immigration law, which instituted the national origins quotas and virtually shut off immigration from eastern and southern Europe. The quota for each nation was defined as 2 percent of the number of foreign-born persons for each nationality present in the United States in 1890 (changed to 1920 in 1929). Because of the composition of the U.S. population in 1890 and 1920, this quota system was heavily weighted in favor of immigration from northern Europe. For example, after 1929, 82 percent of the visas for the Eastern Hemisphere were allotted to countries in northwestern Europe, 16 percent to southeastern Europe and 2 percent to all others (Pedraza 1996, 8). Asians had little to no chance of obtaining a visa.[1] By the 1950s, Europeans still dominated the flow of immigrants to the United States. Europeans accounted for 52.7 percent of all immigrants between 1951 and 1960. Relatively few Asian immigrants (6.1 percent) came during that time. Latin Americans accounted for 22.2 percent of the immigrants during that decade (Pedraza 1996, 4).

The 1965 immigration law abolished national origins quotas. David Reimers (1985) has called this a "cautious reform" with unintended consequences. Instead of national origins quotas, the new law allotted immigrant visas on a first-come, first-served basis within a system of preferences. The law established seven preferences, five for close relatives of U.S. citizens and legal residents and two for immigrants with professions, skills, occupations, or special talents needed in the United States (Reimers 1985, 72). The preference system was built on the principle of family unification, a principle that few policy makers at the time believed would lead to a change in the composition of the immigrants since it was assumed that close relatives would come from the same parent countries as the citizens (Reimers 1985, 75). The "unintended" consequence of the preference system was an increase in the proportion of Asian and Latin American immigrants. Between 1981 and 1990, Asians (37.3 percent) and Latin Americans (47.1 percent) accounted for 84.4 percent of all legal immigrants (Pedraza 1996, 4). In addition to these changes, the number of legal immigrants coming to the United States has increased from 2.5 million between 1951 and 1960 to 7.3 million between 1981 and 1990. During the 1990s, about 800,000 legal immigrants came to our shores each year. When undocumented immigrants (popularly called "illegal aliens") are added, the total number of newcomers was over one million a year. That about equals the number of immigrants that came during the peak years of immigration during the early 1900s.

It must be emphasized here that even though these numbers and proportions show dramatic changes, their relative impact on the nation is somewhat tempered by the large size of the U.S. population in general. Although the total number of immigrants has grown, it must be seen as relative to general population growth. One way to consider this is the proportion of foreign-born residents in the total U.S. population. In 1960, the foreign born accounted for 5.5 percent of the U.S. population. In 1970, they actually went down to 4.7 percent of the population. In 1980, the foreign born accounted for 6.2 percent of the total population, and in 1990 they were 7.9 percent. These numbers are proportionally smaller than in earlier decades of this century, when immigrants made up much larger proportions of the total population. In 1910, for example, the foreign accounted for 14.7 percent of the U.S. population (Rumbaut 1996, 25; U.S. Immigration and Naturalization Service, 1990–93).

Although the year 1965 marks the beginning of a major demographic shift in immigration patterns, not all of these changes can be blamed on alterations in the nation's immigration laws. Since 1965, the nation has received refugees and unauthorized immigrants from various regions of the world. Southeast Asian refugees began migrating to the United States after its military withdrawal from the region in the mid-1970s. Cubans began fleeing the Castro regime in the 1960s, with various moments of increased refugee movements, such as the infamous Mariel boat exodus in 1980, when more than 125,000 Cubans made their way to Florida's coast (see chapter 5). Central Americans fleeing conflict in the region migrated to the United States throughout the 1980s and early 1990s. Eastern Europeans came, escaping the economic collapse of their countries in the post-Cold War era. Undocumented immigration has also contributed to the flow of immigrants both before the 1965 law and after. All of these factors contributed to demographic shifts not just in the national origins of today's immigrants, but also to changes in the ethnic and racial makeup of the nation generally.

At the same time that the total number of immigrants has grown, the native white population in the United States has aged demographically. Relatively young immigrants and an aging (less fertile) white population has meant that immigration's impact on the nation's population growth rate has increased proportionately. In the 1951–60 decade, net immigration accounted for 10.6 percent of the nation's population growth. Between 1961 and 1970, immigrants still accounted for only 16.1 percent of population growth. There was little change between 1971 and 1980 in immigration's relative impact on population growth (it was still only 17.9 percent). But between 1981 and 1990, immigration's net impact on population growth rates doubled from previous decades, accounting for 39.1 percent of the nation's population growth. Moreover, the composition of the immigrants had also changed. Europeans, who accounted for almost 53 percent of legal immigrants between 1951 and 1960, accounted for only 12.5 percent of the immigrants between 1981 and 1990. Asians (37.3 percent) and Latin Americans (47.1 percent) were the major immigrant populations in the 1981–90 decade (Rumbaut 1996, 25; Pedraza 1996, 4). As these statistics suggest, demographic changes related to immigration became more evident during the 1980s and 1990s, at least compared to the previous two decades.

Given immigration trends and fertility rates, Latino and Asian American populations will experience significant growth over the next fifty years (Martin and Midgley 1994). Latino growth should increase from about 11 percent of the nation's population to about one quarter. Asian populations will more than quadruple in size, or grow from about 3.5 percent to about 16 percent. Whites will decrease from about 75 percent to about half of the U.S. population, and African American growth will remain fairly constant in relative numbers. As we shall observe, the implications of these demographic trends inform much of the debate over immigration and the nation.

America was once viewed as a great "melting pot" that blended many immigrant strains into a single nationality. While we may now assert that ethnic identities and traditions are not so easily lost by immigrants, and that becoming American is not always a simple linear process, the melting pot continues to retain its narrative power as a metaphor for American society, if only, for some, to parody. The power of America to absorb immigrants is both marveled at and questioned, but continues to be an important story we tell about ourselves as a people and as a nation. That we can call ourselves "a nation of immigrants" depends on the power of this common narrative about our history.

During the later decades of the twentieth century, the American public was noticeably uneasy with both undocumented and legal immigration and with the melting pot narrative (see Mills 1994). Tensions revolved around the way we think of ourselves as a nation and as a people. As historian David Hollinger (1995) might put it, who is included in "the circle of we" is increasingly debated and narrowed as immigrants, both legal and unauthorized, are targeted as belonging outside the "we." The "rhetoric of exclusion" embedded in contemporary discourse on immigration runs the risk of arousing nativism (Perea 1997a; Stolcke 1995). In his classic book, *Strangers in the Land*, John Higham (1985 [1955], 4) defined nativism as "intense opposition to an internal minority on the ground of its foreign (i.e., 'un-American') connections." Higham argued that nativism gets much of its energy from modern nationalism and that "nativism translates broader cultural antipathies and ethnocentric judgments into a zeal to destroy the enemies of a distinctively American way of life." Indeed, the proponents of restricting immigration often view today's immigrants as a threat to the "nation," which is conceived of as a singular, predominantly Euro-American, English-speaking culture. The "new" immigrants—the *trans*nationalists—threaten this singular vision of the "nation" because they allegedly bring "multiculturalism" and not assimilation (Martinez and McDonnell 1994).[2] From this perspective, the pot no longer has the capacity to melt.

It must be emphasized that attitudes toward immigration are not uniform across the political spectrum (Muller 1997). The ranks of liberals and conservatives often split in their views over immigration, forming surprising alliances across political persuasions in the process. While the governor of California, Pete Wilson, was whipping up anti-immigrant sentiment during the 1994 elections, Texas governor George W. Bush Jr., also a Republican, downplayed the problems wrought by immigration to his state. In well publicized retreats from the then-Republican position on immigration, William Bennett and Jack Kemp argued that California's Proposition 187 (the 1994 ballot initiative to deny undocumented immigrants social services, medical services, and education) was mean-spirited and not a political issue that Republicans should support. The conservative newspaper, the *Wall Street Journal,* espouses a liberal immigration policy because of the continued economic benefits provided by immigrant workers (Muller 1997, 113).

On the other hand, demographic changes wrought in part by immigration, led Arthur Schlesinger Jr., the archetype of a social liberal, to warn America of an impending "disuniting" (Schlesinger 1992). The editor of the conservative *National Review* has argued against high levels of immigration because the social costs are high and the economic benefits minimal (O'Sullivan 1994; Muller 1997, 113). The senior editor of the *New Republic,* a liberal magazine, has taken liberals to task for ignoring the alleged negative effects of immigration on low-income African and white Americans (Muller 1997, 113). Thomas Muller (1997, 113) has noted that "Immigration may well be the only subject on which the views of the two editors converge."

Even immigrants can turn against other immigrants. Peter Brimelow (1995), himself an immigrant from Great Britain, has painted a dark picture for a future of continued immigration. America's problems, according to Brimelow, are due to immigrants who lack the cultural background of earlier European, especially British, immigrants. He also argues that America needs a "time out" from immigration. Failure to restrict immigration, Brimelow warns, will lead America on the road to becoming an "alien nation" (Brimelow's views are further scrutinized in chapter 6).

CONTEMPORARY RESEARCH ON IMMIGRANTS

What does recent academic research indicate about immigrant behavior? Although an exhaustive review of this voluminous literature would extend beyond the confines of this book, some findings are pertinent because they contribute to a quite different narrative about immigrants than that generally found in public discourse.

THE COST OF IMMIGRANTS

Numerous studies have attempted a cost-benefit analysis of immigrants' use of social services compared to their tax contributions. The findings suggest that the problem is not that immigrants do not pay taxes, because they do, but where those taxes go. The cost of providing education, health care, and other social services falls on local and state governments and yet the lion's share of taxes go to the federal government. In Los Angeles County, for example, recently arrived immigrants paid an estimated $4.3 billion in taxes in 1991–92 (P. Martin 1994, 33). The county spent an estimated $947 million for health and justice services for these immigrants, but received only about 3 percent of the immigrants' taxes, leaving the county with a deficit of $808 million. The federal government received about 60 percent of those tax revenues. These differ-

ences underlie the tension between state and local governments on the
one hand, and the federal government on the other hand, over who will
pay for social services provided to immigrants.

A 1997 report by the prestigious National Research Council and the
National Academy of Sciences, "The New Americans: Economic, demographic, and fiscal effects of immigration," found that immigrants'
impact on the economy is relatively modest, and the costs and benefits
for native-born workers are small. In the short run, immigrants have costs,
especially in states such as California that receive inordinate numbers of
immigrants (National Research Council 1997). "But in the long run,"
as *U.S. News and World Report* noted, the report indicates that "when
the bills for baby boomers' retirement come due, immigrants are likely
to prove a tax blessing" (Glastris 1997, 20). The unique aspect of the
National Academy of Sciences/National Research Council report is that
it attempts to assess the lifetime impact of an immigrant on state and local treasuries (-$25,000) and the federal treasure (+$105,000) to arrive
at a total lifetime impact (+$80,000). As is clear, the positive economic
contribution of immigrants to government revenues accrues mainly at
the federal level. In addition, the report found that economic competition from immigrants depressed by about 5 percent the wages of native-
born Americans who are high school dropouts, but that other, better educated Americans benefited.

Immigrants often contribute to the overall economy in ways other than
through their labor. For example, when immigrants become citizens, they
become homeowners at a rate similar to native-born citizens. According
to 1996 data, the U.S. Census Bureau reported that 66.9 percent of foreign-born citizens owned homes, just under the 67.4 percent of native-
born citizens (Gray 1997). Among Latinos, foreign-born citizens (57 percent) are more likely than native-born citizens (48 percent) to own their
own home. Among all immigrants, about one-third of noncitizens owned
homes. A point emphasized in the *Los Angeles Times* about this report
was that "These immigrants are saying loud and clear, by purchasing a
home, that they want to be a part of their local communities" (Gray
1997).

Since most immigrants live in cities, home ownership among immigrants is said to contribute to urban renewal at a time when native-born
citizens are moving out of cities. However, this observation stands in
sharp contrast to popular wisdom on immigrants as contributing to a
decline of cities in which they reside or that they increase the burden on
local citizens, as suggested by the National Academy of Sciences/National

Research Council study cited above. A study by Stephen Moore (1997) for the conservative Hoover Institution examined these two versions of immigration's impact on the nation's cities. Moore examined the nation's eighty-five largest cities. He found that "On a whole range of variables measuring the prosperity of cities—from population growth to poverty rates to income growth to crime to taxes—cities with large foreign-born populations fare better than cities with few immigrants" (Moore 1997, 29). This difference between cities with high and low levels of immigration was also reflected on all the study's quality-of-life measures, except unemployment. Cities with large numbers of immigrants tended to have higher unemployment rates. The study also indirectly suggests that African Americans did better in cities with immigrants than in cities with few immigrants. Rather than causing urban decline, the presence of immigrants, according to this study, is associated with urban growth and renewal.

IMMIGRANTS AND USE OF ENGLISH

Research suggests that the acquisition of English proficiency among Mexican migrants is an ongoing process. As Espinosa and Massey (1997, 44) conclude from their analysis of data acquired from Mexican migrants: "Like most prior research [census-based and survey-based], moreover, we find clear and unambiguous evidence that English proficiency rises sharply with exposure to U.S. society. . . . If Spanish is increasingly spoken in the United States, it is because a large number of Spanish-speaking immigrants arrived in a short time, not because there is any perceptible resistance on the part of Mexican migrants to learning English per se." Research also suggests that the children of immigrants learn English quickly. Portes and Rumbaut (1990) found that the well-established pattern of increasing English dominance with each succeeding generation in the United States continues among today's immigrants and their children. In a longitudinal study of school-age immigrant children in San Diego, California, Rumbaut found that 90 percent spoke a language other than English at home, and yet between 1992 to 1995, the proportion of these youths who preferred English grew from 66 percent to 82 percent (Rumbaut 1997). The U.S.-born children of immigrants went from 78 to about 90 percent preferring English over that three-year period. The growth in English preference was true even for Mexican-origin youth. Among U.S.-born Mexican American students with at least one parent born in Mexico, their preference for English grew from 53 percent to 79 percent over the same time. Among Mexican-born students, their rate of preference for English increased from 32 percent to 61 percent. Rumbaut noted that "contrary to nativist alarms about the perpetuation of foreign language enclaves . . . English easily remains the language of the land" (Woo 1997).

Rumbaut (1995) also examined the perception that knowledge of a foreign language depressed school achievement. Among the students in San Diego, he found that for all ethnic groups, students who were monolingual English-speakers (who tended to be U.S.-born) had significantly lower grade point averages (GPAs) than their bilingual co-ethnics (who tended to be immigrants). Surprisingly, Rumbaut (1995, 37) noted that "One important implication of these findings is that educational achievement, at least as measured by GPA, appears to decline from the first to the second and third generations." This negative effect of assimilation on school achievement and motivation has been supported by other research (Suarez Orozco and Suarez Orozco 1995).

Academic research on the cost of immigrants and their acquisition of English, while important, is incidental to a national discourse concerned with immigration's impact on the nation's identity and racial composition.

COVERING IMMIGRATION

This study of the way immigration has been portrayed on popular magazine covers since 1965 suggests that public anxiety over immigration and related issues of multiculturalism, race, and national identity did not suddenly burst forth in the 1990s. Rather, these issues received increasing attention and formulation over the last thirty-plus years. There are, of course, important questions about the role of the popular press in all of this (German 1994). In covering immigration, do popular magazines merely reflect the American public's increasing anxiety about immigration? Or, by playing to the fears and concerns of the public, do they incite anti-immigrant sentiments? This is an old issue and ultimately perhaps unresolvable (Parenti 1986). However, this examination of the coverage of immigration by popular magazines raises new questions about the media's role in the public's increasing concern about immigration (Simon and Alexander 1993).

I examine seventy-six magazine covers that were published by ten popular national magazines between 1965 and the end of 1999.[3] The ten magazines included: *American Heritage,* the *Atlantic Monthly, Business*

Week, the *Nation,* the *National Review,* the *New Republic, Newsweek,* the *Progressive, Time,* and *U.S. News and World Report.* These magazines suited my purpose since they were "popular" (rather than obscure), national in distribution, and varied as to their place in the political spectrum.

Brief profiles of the ten magazines underscore their coverage of a wide political spectrum. The *American Heritage* magazine began publication in 1954 and targets an audience interested in American history; it publishes eight times a year. The *Atlantic Monthly* was founded in 1857 as a literary magazine directed toward a limited but influential audience of business and political leaders, a direction it has continued to pursue (R. Simon 1985, 57; Wood 1971; Peterson 1956; Mott 1938). *Business Week* began publication in 1929, the year of the Great Depression. It began with an emphasis on business and has continued to examine most issues from an economic viewpoint (Wood 1971, 386). The *Nation* is a weekly magazine that was founded in 1865. Although always a magazine of relatively low circulation, the *Nation*'s liberal voice had an inordinate influence on policy makers during the 1920s, 1930s, and 1950s (R. Simon 1985, 58; Wood 1971, 188; Tebbel 1969).

The *National Review* began publication in 1955 and targets a politically conservative audience that is college educated and relatively affluent. It publishes biweekly, twenty-five times a year. The *New Republic* was founded in 1914 and has been a socially and politically liberal magazine. It is described as "a journal of opinion" that has sought to "goad public opinion into being more vigilant and hospitable, into considering its convictions more carefully" (Wood 1971, 191). The *Progressive* began publication in 1909 as the *Lafollette's Magazine* and then changed the title to the *Progressive* in 1925, publishing monthly. From its inception, the *Progressive* has been a liberal voice committed to "peace, individual freedom, and economic justice" (*Progressive* 1984).

Time magazine was founded in 1923 and sought to present the week's news in a format that could be easily and quickly read. Its readers have been characterized as middle class and well educated (R. Simon 1985, 62; Elson 1968). *Newsweek* was first published in 1933 and, like *Time,* sought to present the week's news in a magazine format. The readership of *Newsweek* has consisted primarily of college graduates and people in business. *U.S. News and World Report* was originally published as two independent magazines. *United States News* began in 1933 and followed *Time* magazine's style. *World Report* began in 1946, covering international news. The two magazines merged in 1948 to become *U.S. News and World Report* (R. Simon 1985, 63; Ford 1969). Although the magazine's circulation is less than *Time*'s or *Newsweek*'s, it has a readership that is influential in business and government (R. Simon 1985, 63).

Table 1.1 presents the magazines and the dates of publications with covers related to immigration. *U.S. News and World Report,* with twenty-one, had the most covers, followed closely by *Time* magazine, with sixteen covers. *Newsweek* had nine covers, the *Atlantic Monthly* had seven covers, the *New Republic* had six covers, the *Nation* and the *National Review* had five covers, the *American Heritage* had three covers, and *Business Week* and the *Progressive* had two covers each. The higher frequency of covers for the big three weeklies—*Newsweek, Time,* and *U.S. News and World Report*—is perhaps expected, given that they have more covers to fill than the monthlies. Most of the magazines displayed immigration-related issues in the central part of their covers, devoting much if not most of the cover's space to the topic. Eight magazines presented the topic in a sidebar, typically in a triangular section in one of the cover's two top corners.

The next chapter presents patterns in the frequency and timing of the magazine covers. Magazine covers dealing with immigration are not uniformly distributed across time. Since 1965, coverage of immigration and related issues has followed patterns influenced by both the particularities of changing attitudes toward immigrants and cultural assumptions about the nation's identity as a nation of immigrants. The month of July, the nation's birthday month, also surfaces as an influence on the subject matter of covers dealing with immigration.

Chapter 3 develops the theoretical framework guiding the reading of the magazines and their covers. Magazines construct messages through their use of symbols, images, and text. To interpret these messages, the reader must move beyond the elementary level, what Barthes calls the "denotive level" and try to understand what the images connote about the society and culture in which they were produced. It is at this level that the magazines actively contribute to a national discourse on immigration. They become sites on which to examine the struggle over the way the nation is to be conceptualized and the place of immigrants in that conceptualization.

In chapter 4, I identify the basic lexicon of images, symbols, and icons used by the magazines to convey messages about immigration and the nation. Nine visual techniques are elaborated upon: directionality of movement, the power of news photographs, assemblages of images, the Statue of Liberty icon, imaging multitudes and masses, woman-child imagery,

TABLE I.I
MAGAZINE COVERS RELATED
TO IMMIGRATION 1965–99

Magazine	Date	Image
American Heritage	Dec. 1978	Neutral
American Heritage	Feb. 1992	Affirmative
American Heritage	Mar. 1994	Alarmist
Atlantic Monthly	Nov. 1983	Alarmist
Atlantic Monthly	May 1992	Alarmist
Atlantic Monthly	Oct. 1992	Alarmist
Atlantic Monthly	Feb. 1994	Alarmist
Atlantic Monthly	Nov. 1996	Alarmist
Atlantic Monthly	July 1998	Alarmist
Atlantic Monthly	Aug. 1998	Alarmist
Business Week	23 June 1980	Alarmist
Business Week	13 July 1992	Affirmative
Nation	25 Jan. 1975	Alarmist
Nation	24 May 1975	Affirmative
Nation	2 Sep. 1978	Alarmist
Nation	7 Oct. 1994	Alarmist
Nation	3 Feb. 1997	Alarmist
National Review	22 June 1992	Alarmist
National Review	21 Feb. 1994	Alarmist
National Review	11 July 1994	Neutral
National Review	16 June 1997	Alarmist
National Review	31 Dec. 1997	Alarmist
New Republic	10 Feb. 1979	Alarmist
New Republic	1 Apr. 1985	Alarmist
New Republic	15 July 1985	Affirmative
New Republic	10 June 1991	Alarmist
New Republic	13 Apr. 1992	Alarmist
New Republic	27 Dec. 1993	Neutral
Newsweek	4 July 1977	Affirmative
Newsweek	2 July 1979	Affirmative
Newsweek	26 May 1980	Alarmist
Newsweek	7 July 1980	Affirmative
Newsweek	1 Feb. 1982	Neutral
Newsweek	17 Jan. 1983	Alarmist
Newsweek	25 June 1984	Alarmist
Newsweek	July 1986	Affirmative
Newsweek	9 Aug. 1993	Alarmist
Progressive	Oct. 1993	Alarmist
Progressive	Sep. 1996	Neutral
Time	5 July 1976	Affirmative
Time	24 July 1978	Affirmative
Time	16 Oct. 1978	Affirmative
Time	9 July 1979	Affirmative

TABLE I.I *(continued)*

Magazine	Date	Image
Time	19 May 1980	Alarmist
Time	23 Nov. 1981	Alarmist
Time	13 June 1983	Alarmist
Time	25 June 1984	Alarmist
Time	2 July 1984	Alarmist
Time	8 July 1985	Affirmative
Time	4 May 1987	Neutral
Time	3 July 1989	Alarmist
Time	9 Apr. 1990	Alarmist
Time	1 Feb. 1993	Neutral
Time	Oct. 1993	Affirmative
Time	5 Sep. 1994	Alarmist
US News and WR	22 July 1974	Alarmist
US News and WR	3 Feb. 1975	Alarmist
US News and WR	13 Dec. 1976	Alarmist
US News and WR	25 Apr. 1977	Alarmist
US News and WR	4 July 1977	Alarmist
US News and WR	20 Feb. 1978	Affirmative
US News and WR	29 Jan. 1979	Alarmist
US News and WR	9 July 1979	Affirmative
US News and WR	6 Aug. 1979	Affirmative
US News and WR	13 Oct. 1980	Alarmist
US News and WR	9 Mar. 1981	Alarmist
US News and WR	22 June 1981	Alarmist
US News and WR	12 Apr. 1982	Alarmist
US News and WR	7 Mar. 1983	Alarmist
US News and WR	21 Mar. 1983	Alarmist
US News and WR	4 July 1983	Affirmative
US News and WR	19 Aug. 1985	Alarmist
US News and WR	7 July 1986	Affirmative
US News and WR	23 Oct. 1989	Neutral
US News and WR	21 June 1993	Alarmist
US News and WR	23 Sep. 1996	Alarmist

water-flood imagery, the U.S. flag icon, and border images. My concern is with *how* the visual and textual languages on magazine covers convey meaning about immigration and the nation, what Hall (1997a, 6) refers to as the "semiotic approach." The covers rely on metaphors, tropes, and allusions to grand narratives of the nation to draw on shared, but often taken-for-granted understandings of American identity, history, and characteristics of various immigrant groups. In other words, I am making explicit some of the codes, conventions, and rules that are typically implicit during the practice of reading magazine covers, what

Spurr (1993), in another context, referred to as "rhetorical features" of a discourse.

Chapter 5 begins a discursive approach to reading the magazine covers. Taking passage of the monumental 1965 changes to the nation's immigration law as a starting point, a chronological reading of magazine covers emphasizes the historical specificity of the period between 1965 and 1985. The magazine covers mark significant moments for examining the otherwise relentless flow of history. For an issue to become immortalized on the cover of a magazine, it must have had an important resonance with the public at that particular time. What were the issues prompting such special treatment? How do the covers and the accompanying articles combine in the construction of knowledge/truth that is central to the discourse on immigration and the nation?

Chapter 6 continues the discursive analysis of the covers and the accompanying articles beginning in 1986, the year the U.S. Congress passed the Immigration Reform and Control Act (IRCA), and continuing to 1993. During the years immediately following IRCA's passage, immigration waned as a cover story. In the 1990s, however, immigration reemerged as a hot topic of debate. Coming to the fore of the debate over competing visions of the nation were issues of race and multiculturalism. Is America defined by its racial/national origins—British and northwestern European—which must be kept demographically dominant through restrictive immigration laws? Or is America still a nation of immigrants that is defined more by the principles that guide it and are learned by immigrants? These two simplified encapsulations of the positions reflect divergent theories of culture. In the former vision, culture is fixed, and the cultural differences of immigrants pose a danger to its continuance. In the latter, culture is transformative; it changes in response to new stimuli such as that introduced by immigrants. Both of these positions, however, adhere to a process of assimilation-acculturation in which all members of society, despite their differences, share some part of a common national culture. There is less acceptance in either position of a postmodern vision of society as one in which there is a multitude of fluidly constructed identities.

Chapter 7 begins in 1994, the year anti-immigrant attitudes found expression in practice, for example, California's ballot initiative popularly known as "Save Our State," and more formally known as Proposition 187, and ends in December 1999. During this period, alarmist images and views concerning immigration continued to be central to the public debate over immigration's contribution to national breakdown, demographic change, and radical multiculturalism. It must be emphasized that the debate cut across traditional political groupings. From within the ranks of both conservatives and liberals, differences in opinion emerge on these issues. Following Proposition 187 and the national welfare and immigration reforms of 1996, the number of covers on immigration declined, at least in comparison to the frenzy of coverage up to that time. Toward the end of this period an interesting trend emerges. The immigrant as a victim of business interests and government collusion with those interests surfaces as important themes on the covers.

Chapter 8 examines the way the magazines have represented the specific case of Mexican immigration since 1965. Mexican immigration has not followed the same pattern as the coverage of immigration more generally. Mexican immigration is not referenced on magazine covers using affirmative imagery. Beginning in the mid-1970s, a discourse develops based on images of Mexicans as an external threat. They are repeatedly represented as invading the nation and as occupying, or challenging, the sovereign territory of the United States (Link 1991). Mexicans also become the "enemy within" due to their growing numbers and ability to reproduce themselves as an allegedly separate community or nation within a nation.

Chapter 9 examines 298 University of California, Irvine, students' responses to eleven of the magazine covers. Magazine covers may construct messages, but what are the messages that are received? Although magazine covers may, in Gramscian terms, move toward construction of a hegemonic world view, consumers of images add their own histories, their own perceptions of American history and identity and their place in that history and identity. The students whose views are examined here are socially diverse. Indeed, white students are a minority of students on campus. Many of the students were immigrants themselves or the children of immigrants. Their readings often reflected resistance to the discourse on immigration on the magazine covers. Their challenges and critiques of the representations of immigrants were based, in part, on a sensitivity to issues of race, class, the privileging of one group (whites) as "Americans," and the singling out of any particular group. They often held America up to its principle of equality and challenged any representation of immigrants that did not meet that ideal. What do the students' views mean for a nation that is rapidly becoming ethnically and racially diverse? Perhaps their critical views of the representations of immigrants found on the magazine covers portend changes in society in general.

CHAPTER 2

Developing a Visual Discourse on Immigration

To produce images is to produce identity.

Octavio Getino, La tercera mirada

Culture is the material site of struggle in which active links
are made between signifying practices and social structure. . . .
Because culture is the contemporary repository of memory,
of history, it is through culture, rather than government, that
alternative forms of subjectivity, collectivity, and public life
are imagined.

Lisa Lowe, Immigrant Acts

Images on popular magazine covers provide an excellent window into
issues of importance in a society. As artifacts of popular culture, magazine covers are ubiquitous yet seldom thought about, especially in a systematic way.[1] We casually glance at them in their neatly ordered rows as
we shop for groceries or browse through them in bookstores and news-
stands or choose among them as we wait in a doctor's or dentist's office.
We often pause for a moment when a magazine cover catches our attention, then plunge quickly into the interior articles. And yet, despite
our lack of attention, the images on magazine covers are not empty of
meaning.

This analysis begins with a search for preliminary patterns in the material under study. The state of the economy appears to have influenced
a pattern of timing and frequency of immigration-related magazine covers. As graph 2.1 indicates, periods of economic recession somewhat fore-
shadow a concern with immigration (Cornelius 1980). There have been
five economic recessions of various lengths since 1965.[2] The first recession occurred between December 1969 and November 1970, as the Vietnam War–related inflation, taxes, and credit rates all went up. Between

November 1973 and March 1975 another recession was ushered in by rising inflation as wage and price controls were lifted and OPEC quadrupled the price of crude oil. Oil prices and inflation soared again between January 1980 and July 1980. Then, between July 1981 and November 1982, the nation was gripped by a major recession as inflation rates rose steeply, and the money supply was tightened in response. Between July 1990 and March 1991, another recession hit the country, from which some states, particularly California, would take many years to fully recover. Except for the 1969–70 period, each of these periods of economic recession was followed by an increase in the number of magazine covers devoted to the topic of immigration, a concern that then receded until the next recession. Indeed, the focus on immigration as a cover story begins in 1974, during a period of recession.

Graph 2.1 also presents the annual fluctuations in the rate of national unemployment over the same period.[3] Following the 1974 recession and the peak high unemployment rate of 1975, the unemployment rate fell each year until 1979. In spite of this downward trend, however, unemployment generally stayed above the pre-1975 highs. The post-1974 rise in the number of magazine covers on immigration occurs during this downturn in the unemployment rate. The number of magazine covers fell in 1980, 1981, and 1982, as the rate of unemployment began to rise again. The peak high unemployment years of 1982 and 1983, and the still relatively high levels of unemployment for 1984 through 1986, are matched with an increase in coverage of immigration-related issues. As the unemployment rate fell in 1988 to 1989, so too did magazine coverage. Rising unemployment and the recession of 1991 were followed by high numbers of magazine covers on immigration-related issues. As the unemployment rate dropped to new lows in 1995 and beyond, the number of covers on immigration also dropped.

Public opinion on immigration and the frequency of magazine covers on the topic are also intertwined (graph 2.2).[4] In 1980, attitudes favoring less immigration reached an all-time high. This occurred during a recession, but also following three years of increasing media attention to immigration as cover stories. Public opinion favoring reduced immigration declined after passage of the 1986 immigration law (IRCA), just as the number of magazine covers declined. The percentage of the nation's public favoring reduced immigration rose to almost 70 percent during the early 1990s, corresponding to both an economic recession and the rise in the number of covers devoted to immigration. Both public opinion and the number of magazine covers fall in the postrecession, post-

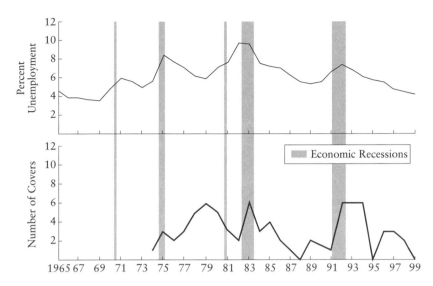

Graph 2.1. Number of magazine covers per year and annual unemployment rates, 1965–99. *Sources:* Espenshade and Hempstead 1996; U.S. Bureau of the Census, *Statistical Abstracts of the United States;* Rosenblatt 1997; Walsh 1999.

1995 part of the decade. The state of the economy, public opinion, and media coverage appear to be engaged in a tightly choreographed dance, each leading and following at various times.

IMAGES AS AFFIRMATIVE OR ALARMIST ABOUT IMMIGRATION

In order to explore other patterns, I classified the magazine covers based upon their use of images that were affirmative, alarmist, or neutral toward immigration. Affirmative covers use images and text in a way that celebrates immigrants, typically tying them to the nation's identity (e.g., America as a nation of immigrants) or present images that appeal for compassion, especially for refugees. Covers raising an alarm about immigration typically use images and text to suggest problems, fears, or dangers raised by immigration, such as population growth, demographic changes, a lack of assimilation, a breakup of the nation, or the death of the nation. Alarmist covers may also feature words such as "invasion," "crisis," and "time bomb" that characterize immigration as a threat to the nation or that appeal to fears and anxieties about immigration. Neu-

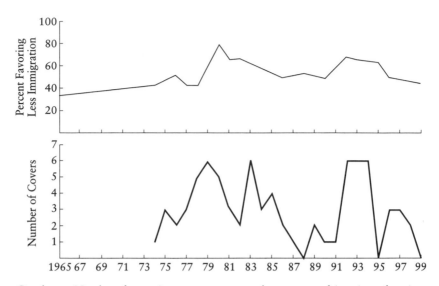

Graph 2.2. Number of magazine covers per year and percentage of Americans favoring less immigration. *Sources:* Espenshade and Hempstead 1996; Simon and Lynch 1999; *U.S. News and World Report* 13 October 1980, 7 July 1986, 23 June 1993; *Business Week* 13 July 1992; *Newsweek* 9 August 1993; *Time* Fall 1993; CBS/*New York Times* Poll September 1995; Gallup Poll 1995, 1999.

tral covers do not make an obvious statement of affirmation or alarm or were seemingly balanced in their message. Whenever it was not obvious if a cover was affirmative or alarmist, it was assigned to the neutral category, the logic being that it is better to be conservative when in doubt. This classification is admittedly subjective. However, the classification was also undertaken independently.[5] The issue of how other readers interpreted the message of the covers is further discussed in chapter 9, which examines reactions from 298 students at the University of California, Irvine, to the covers.

This exercise suggests a "first impression" or "quick message" about immigration issues suggested by what Barthes calls the denotive level of the message on the covers. An initial read, however, may change with more in-depth analysis that expands on the interpretation to the connotive level of meanings about the larger society and culture (see chapter 3 for a discussion of denotive and connotive levels of analysis). Magazine covers are often made up of layers of images and text that express complex messages, juxtaposing affirmative and alarmist messages, or underlying an alarmist message below an ostensibly affirmative message. The result is a complex message alluding to narratives (Barthes's "mythologies" or even ideologies) of the nation, its people, its values, and its identity.

In addition, it must be emphasized that this initial classification is not meant to suggest that "affirmative" means that the magazine's editorial position was pro-immigration or that the use of alarmist images means that the magazine was anti-immigration. Alarmist imagery and text, for example, can be used to send a message about the perils of continued immigration or as a critique on the economic system that "exploits" immigrant workers, suggesting sympathy for immigrants. Presenting such issues may be guaranteed to raise the interest of readers—and thus possibly increasing the number of the magazine's consumers—regardless of, or even because of, their personal stand on immigration policies. It must be stressed that these preliminary classifications are for heuristic purposes only; they need to be judged against deeper interpretations. Before moving to a fuller reading of the images, however, I need to address the general patterns suggested by this initial reading of the magazine covers.

Seven magazine covers (9 percent) conveyed neutral or balanced messages about immigration (see table 1.1). Nineteen magazine covers (25 percent) used affirmative images and text to present issues related to immigration, and fifty covers (66 percent) used alarmist imagery, metaphors, adjectives, or other symbols. Alarmist covers, in this sense, were two-and-a-half times as common as affirmative covers. Even if neutral covers were included with affirmative covers, alarmist covers would still be about double their number. Most of the magazines published covers that at times were affirmative and at other times were alarmist. In terms of the "big three," *Newsweek* and *Time* magazines were about balanced in their presentations; alarmist covers did not exceed the number of affirmative and neutral covers combined. *U.S. News and World Report,* with 71 percent of its covers classified as alarmist, relied more on alarmist imagery and text than the other two magazines. The use of alarmist and affirmative imagery did not generally follow a pattern based on conservative or liberal ideology of the magazine. *Atlantic Monthly,* the *New Republic,* the *Nation,* and the *Progressive* more often used alarmist than affirmative or neutral images and text on their covers dealing with immigration. The *Progressive* and the *Nation* used alarmist imagery as a way of raising critiques of existing anti-immigrant attitudes and policies, as will be discussed later.

An important pattern that emerges from the survey has to do with the timing of the covers that portray immigration with affirmative or alarmist images and text. An examination of the ten magazines for the thirty-five-year period after 1965, reveals a pattern of increasingly alarmist portrayals of immigration. Ten of the nineteen magazine covers (53 percent) conveying an affirmative image were published during the 1970s, compared to six (32 percent) published in the 1980s and three (16 percent) between 1990 and the end of 1999.

This downward trend from the 1970s for affirmative covers stands in marked contrast to the decidedly increasing trend in magazine covers to use alarmist images and text. Only nine (18 percent) of the forty-eight magazines with alarmist covers were published in the 1970s, compared to nineteen (38 percent) in the 1980s and twenty-two (44 percent) between 1990 and 1999. In addition, alarmist covers are not evenly distributed across time. They appear in cycles. For example, all but one of the nineteen alarmist covers that appeared in the 1980s were published between 1980 and 1985. In 1986, President Reagan signed into law the Immigration Reform and Control Act, which was to reduce undocumented immigration. It was not until 1989 that another alarmist cover was published by one of these ten magazines. After 1989, there followed a number of alarmist covers leading up to the passage of the 1996 immigration and welfare reform laws (discussed in chapter 7), and then a precipitous drop off in frequency occurred between 1995 and 1999.

THE NATION'S BIRTHDAY AND THE MAGAZINE COVERS

The linear unfolding of historical time is not the only way events can be ordered. Cultures also have ritual cycles that repeat season after season (Bloch 1989). National holidays are examples of rituals that are imbued with cultural rules concerning the appropriate ways to honor them and the meanings they are intended to convey about society. National magazines appear to consciously or unconsciously follow those rules. Thirteen of the nineteen affirmative covers (68 percent) appeared in the month of July. Only one neutral (14 percent) and four alarmist (8.5 percent) magazine covers appeared in a July issue of one of the magazines surveyed. Or put another way, 68 percent of the covers appearing in July were affirmative of immigration.

July 4th, of course, is the day the United States celebrates its birthday. The nation of immigrants narrative as a founding narrative is fundamental to the identity of the nation. It takes on quasi-religious stature during the month of July, as it becomes associated with patriotism, the birth of the nation, and the subsequent peopling of the continent. July, therefore, becomes a time to speak affirmatively of immigrants and to show compassion for the plight of immigrants, especially refugees. It is a "feel good" moment.

For example, *Newsweek*'s 4 July 1977 cover featured a portrait of a white family wearing clothing that suggests the late 1800s to early 1900s. The family appears to include a grandmother carrying the youngest child of the central family in the picture. Their ethnic background appears to be southern or eastern European. The portrait is three-quarters framed with stars evocative of those on the American flag. The text reads: "Everybody's Search for Roots." This image captures an immigrant history narrative that is affirmative in its romanticization of past immigration as family oriented, working class, and European. To be efficacious, the cover relies on the pervasive cultural stereotype of the European immigrant family, a stereotype that is now seen in the positive light of the distant past. This affirmative reading of past immigration does not reflect the often alarmist view of the immigrants at the time of their arrival. Nonetheless, the image works in the contemporary period because it now carries an important message about America's identity. It is a comfortable reminder that the nation is a united family with an immigrant history and identity. The cover also comes on the heels of the extremely popular television show "Roots," about an African American family's history from slavery to emancipation. Consequently, this cover can also be read as a not-so-subtle reminder that the nation's immigrant history has been collectively imagined as having white or European roots, largely ignoring the mostly forced immigration of Africans.

The use of the photographic portrait of a family is an important part of the cover's success in conveying the nation and its past in terms that are easily understandable and reassuring. With the invention of photography, the family portrait has become the key image used by families to tell the world about themselves, as whole, integrated, and enduring, even when the everyday reality may not be as rosy as the photograph. It was in relation to family portraits that Pierre Bourdieu commented, "Photography itself is most frequently nothing but the *re*production of the image that a group produces of its own integration" (Bourdieu 1965, 48; quoted and translated in Krauss 1990, 19). *Newsweek*'s cover takes this symbol of family unity to the level of the nation.

July is also a time to appeal to America's compassion for the downtrodden and less fortunate, especially those "huddled masses yearning

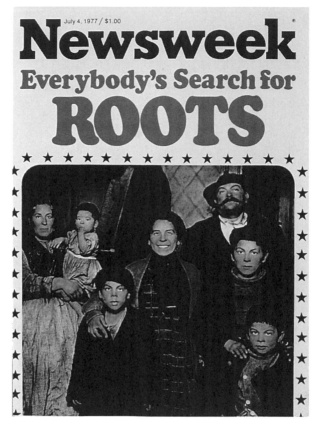

2.1.   *Newsweek,* 4 July 1977. "Roots."

to breathe free." Five of the affirmative covers appearing in July had
refugees on their covers. For example, on 2 July 1979, *Newsweek*'s cover
dealt with the "Agony of the Boat People." The image is of Vietnamese
men, women, and children who appear to be waiting, huddled together,
with tired expressions on their faces. Some children and men wear no
shirts. There is no background, just faces and bodies of people that appear poor and weary. *Time* magazine's cover of that same year (9 July
1979) also pictured a multitude of refugees in the upper right-hand corner. The caption read "Refugees: Tragedy of the homeless." *U.S. News
and World Report* (9 July 1979) weighed in with its July feature on
refugees. Its cover text expressed "America: Still the Promised Land" as
a boatload of Asians stared longingly at the Statue of Liberty.
    The self-congratulatory nature of July magazine issues dealing with

2.2.   *U.S. News and World Report,* 9 July 1979. "America: Still the Promised Land."

immigration is readily apparent in headlines such as "Still the Land of Opportunity?" which appeared on *U.S. News and World Report*'s cover on 4 July 1983 (see fig. 5.3). Although framed as a question, the image of the American flag flowing in the wind with sunlight radiating from behind it left little doubt that the answer was a resounding "Yes!" In similar fashion, *U.S. News and World Report*'s 7 July 1986 cover proudly claimed "Only in America" above a beautiful multicolored painting of the Statue of Liberty's head. The cover suggests that the nation still beckons immigrants and offers them opportunities for success, which is then detailed in the magazine's feature article. On this birthday, America's generosity toward immigrants is celebrated. Immigrants can easily become enveloped in the spirit of patriotism and as a symbol of

2.3.   *Newsweek*, 7 July 1980. "The New Immigrants."

America at her best: a nation that takes in all people and allows them to
make a place for themselves and their families.

Newsweek magazine's 7 July 1980 cover captured these sentiments.
The cover text announcing "The New Immigrants" is printed on a birthday ribbon that also includes white stars on a red, white, and blue background. The ribbon frames the picture of an Asian woman carrying her
baby on her back. The woman, a Hmong living in Providence, Rhode
Island (we learn inside the magazine), smiles pleasantly at the camera.
An American eagle perches atop the picture and text. The woman's happy
expression, the ribbon, and the colors all converge in an overall image
of birthday exuberance and optimism; the "nation of immigrants" is alive
and well as the new, multicultural immigrants are happily becoming
Americans.

2.4. *Time*, 8 July 1985. "The Changing Face of America."

Multiculturalism was also affirmatively represented on *Time* magazine's 8 July 1985 cover of a special issue on the topic. The cover text
read, "The Changing Face of America." A mosaic of faces of different
racial and ethnic backgrounds fills the entire cover. The faces look quietly but expectantly to the right, as if perhaps looking toward the future, wondering what it will bring. They do not appear demanding or
aggressive; they simply wait, hopefully, but seriously. Their position also
suggests that they could be standing just outside a door, waiting to be
invited in, metaphorically raising the question: Will they be accepted
into the nation's "imagined community?" All but one of the twenty-
six heads has black or dark hair. One woman is blond. The changing
face of America is decidedly nonwhite, in the European sense of the
word. While this may be a subtle message about the changing demo-

graphics resulting in increasing minority populations, especially Asians and Latinos, it is not overtly alarmist in its depiction of these "new faces." America as the nation of immigrants, as the country that will somehow continue to function as a melting pot, still exudes from this birthday issue. This is the future, the image suggests, for which these immigrants longingly wait.

The dark side of multiculturalism can also be suggested implicitly, even when the surface image is affirmative. For example, *American Heritage* magazine's cover of February/March 1992 has a photograph of men, women, and children dressed in dark, serious clothing gazing up at a figure of the Statue of Liberty with a statue of President Abraham Lincoln standing next to her. At the foot of the statues is a sign that reads "The Wanderer Finds Liberty in America." Behind and above the people is an American flag. The clothing, the room, and the photograph itself all suggest that these are European immigrants who came to America in the late 1800s or early 1900s. In other words, this is a romantic vision of past (white European) immigrants gazing at two of America's grandest icons. The immigrants, the image suggests, look affirmatively toward becoming American. The text reads: "What Should We Teach Our Children about History? Arthur Schlesinger, Jr., on the multiculturalism furor." The "history" in the text refers us immediately to the old "historical" photographic image. Here is history, and the message the image and text convey is that past immigrants longed to become American rather than maintain their cultural differences, that is, rather than pursue multiculturalism. Although affirmative in its ostensible portrayal of immigrants, the cover suggests that history and the contemporary "furor" over multiculturalism are not in agreement; in fact, they collide. Multiculturalism is counter to the romanticized historical narrative of assimilation and the melting pot. And, indeed, this is exactly Schlesinger's message in the accompanying article (see chapter 6).

The issue of multiculturalism can be raised in a seemingly neutral way and yet convey implicit undertones that suggest that certain immigrant groups lack a will to assimilate. The simple and beautiful photograph on the cover of *American Heritage* magazine's December 1978 issue captures a Chinese man in ethnic dress walking down an urban street, in front of a store with vegetables in woven baskets. The text reads: "San Francisco, 1900." Ostensibly, the cover is neither affirmative nor alarmist, simply a historical photograph that accompanies an article on the photographer and the photographs. However, the image can also be read as capturing not just a historical moment but as raising ques-

2.5.   *American Heritage,* December 1978. "San Francisco, 1900."

tions about assimilation and cultural retention by Chinese immigrants. The clothes and the street scene make the geographic context ambiguous. Is it China or America? Only the text defines the geographic location of the pictured event. Once the location is established, the image suggests that China has been plopped down, intact and immutable, in San Francisco.

The image captures the "Otherness" of Chinese immigrants at the turn of the century. It also says something about 1978, which was the time Asian immigration was on the rise. In a way, this cover is the opposite of the previous cover, which used a historical image of European immigrants to convey a romanticized assimilation/melting pot narrative. In this image, the foreignness of the Chinese man in America suggests that his goal is not to blend into the melting pot and that society will have a difficult task assimilating him. His portrayal is that of the classic Chinese "sojourner," as described by Paul Siu (1987) in his account of the Chinese in Chicago during the early decades of the twentieth century. Sojourners were immigrants whose orientation remained faithful to life and memories of their native homes and who therefore eschewed acculturation into American life.

GENDER AND RACE

There is also a nonrandom pattern of gender representations on the magazine covers. Males account for 225 (79 percent) of the 284 immigrants whose gender was decipherable on the covers with photographic images.[6] Males also accounted for fourteen (70 percent) of the twenty nonimmigrants on the magazine covers. Nonimmigrants were mostly INS or other governmental agents. Illustrations and cartoons were counted separately and only when gender was clearly observable. Males accounted for fifty-five (73 percent) of the seventy-five illustrations of immigrants, and fifteen (100 percent) of the fifteen nonimmigrants. While there may be a margin of error due to the difficulty of counting people in some images, the majority representation of males on the covers is clear.

The breakdown of the people represented on the covers by race and ethnicity is also interesting. Whites accounted for twenty-six (10 percent) of the 266 immigrants for whom race was clear (once again illustrations were counted separately). Most of these were in photographs taken of European immigrants early in the twentieth century. Whites accounted for twelve (71 percent) of the seventeen nonimmigrants, mostly government officers, on the covers. None of the fifty-five illustrations was of white immigrants, but eight (69 percent) of the thirteen illustrations of nonimmigrants were white. There were sixty African Caribbean immigrants (23 percent) found on the covers, but most of these (fifty-four) were on one cover, which featured a long line of black immigrants waiting in an open-air detention area to be processed by INS agents. Two of the nonimmigrants were African Americans. African Caribbeans accounted for twenty-five (46 percent) of the fifty-five illustrations of immigrants, but all of these were on one cover, that of the Statue of Liberty drowning in a sea of immigrants with black figures in boats floating around her. There was only one African Caribbean among the illustrated nonimmigrants.

Asians accounted for 106 (40 percent) of the immigrants on the magazine covers. The large number of Asians is related to the frequent image of a mass of people when depicting refugees. This visual technique is discussed in chapter 4, but suffice it to say that the large frequency of Asians on the covers is directly related to their association with refugee flows. Two (12 percent) of the seventeen nonimmigrants were Asians, and only five (9 percent) of the illustrations of immigrants and none of the illustrations of nonimmigrants were Asians. There were sixty-nine (26 percent) Latin American, mostly Mexican, immigrants on the covers. Only one (7 percent) of the nonimmigrants appeared to be Latin American. Twenty-five (45 percent) of the fifty-five illustrations of immigrants and three of the twelve nonimmigrants were Latin American.

In sum, magazine covers dealing with immigration since 1965 have followed two basic patterns. First, magazines have increasingly used alarmist images, issues, and implications of immigration on their covers to communicate a message to consumers. This pattern supports Harvey's (1989) argument that as social and economic conditions change, so, too, does the way society represents the world and itself to itself. While this pattern is one that could be said to be sensitive to historical changes that society is experiencing, the same could not be said of the second pattern, which is one that is sensitive to deeply embedded cultural assumptions about the nation and our identity as a people. The emergence of July as the month with many affirmative representations of immigration, immigrants, and refugees suggests the unconscious power of culture to influence behavior. I imagine that there is no explicit rule that says "Thou shalt not speak ill of immigrants in July" on a placard in the editorial offices of the nation's popular magazines, and yet this is a pervasive pattern in the thirty-five-year period I have examined.

While the month of July is the repository for most affirmative portrayals of immigration on the nation's popular magazine covers, alarmist treatments of immigration can be found during the remaining eleven months. Many of the same themes—multiculturalism, demographic change in America's racial and ethnic makeup, the nation as melting pot—raised in the affirmative presentations of immigration reappear, but with a decidedly alarmist take. Additional issues, images, and metaphors also become increasingly prominent on the covers. In particular, the survival of the "nation," the U.S.-Mexico border, "illegal" immigrants, and national sovereignty emerge as key issues. Before proceeding to a closer reading of the magazines and their covers, it is important to first elaborate the theoretical framework that informs my reading, which is the topic of the following chapter.

CHAPTER 3

Toward a Framework
for Reading Magazine Covers

History decomposes into pictures, not stories.
Walter Benjamin, Gesammelte Schriften

To read (to listen to) a narrative is not merely to move from
one word to the next, it is also to move from one level to the
next.
Roland Barthes, Image—Music—Text

Chapter 2 initiated a reading of the magazine covers, the images of which
include a great deal of subtext. Unpacking the underlying meanings involves clarifying the relations between the images and society, and it is
therefore necessary to clarify a framework for reading these images. Such
a framework is essential for laying out the theoretical assumptions that
guide this reading and from which the basic research questions emerge.
In addition, it can suggest a method for undertaking such a reading and
a structure for the chapters and analysis that follow.

IMAGES AND THE CONSTRUCTION OF MEANING

Moving forward in the development of a framework for reading magazine covers requires an elaboration of the elementary relation between
symbols and meaning. Humans are culture-bearing animals, and as such
we have the ability to communicate our ideas and the material world
through symbols. We produce meaning through representation. We use
symbols to communicate, or represent, what we want to say about our
feelings, beliefs, concepts, plans, etc. The symbols we use are "signs,"
which "stand for or represent our concepts, ideas and feelings in such a
way as to enable others to 'read,' decode or interpret their meaning in
roughly the same way that we do" (Hall 1997b, 5).

Language is considered the example par excellence of how we use symbols to communicate about our identities, our community, and those whom we set ourselves against. However, as Stuart Hall (1997b) notes in his excellent discussion of cultural representations and signifying practices, we are not limited to words, spoken or written, as the medium through which we communicate meaning about the world. We can communicate through body decoration, clothing, drawings, photographs, and a vast array of technologically assisted visual images. All of these ways of communicating are languages in a broad sense of the word. They communicate because members of a culture group to a very real extent share an understanding of the meaning attached to these symbols and signs.

Importantly, the meanings attached to symbols are not inherent in the symbols themselves. They are arbitrary in that their meanings come from the culture itself; they are constructed through the practices of communication engaged in by members of a social group. A red light, for example, does not have to be the color used to stop traffic. It could be any color (Hall 1997b). But we imbue the symbol of the "red light" with the meaning "stop." As members of a social group, we learn the codes and rules of the language that allows us to decode the message or meaning carried by the sign. Hall (1997b, 15) refers to this as the "social constructionist approach." However, by saying that members of a group share some basic understandings of the world and meanings attached to symbols used to communicate about the world, I am not claiming that all members of a social group interpret symbols in exactly the same way. Interpretation is not a mechanical process. The give and take of communication leaves a great deal of room for the person receiving the message to take away a meaning different from that intended by the sender. To give a simple example that continues with the stop-light analogy, for most drivers a yellow light means "caution—slow down," but for some drivers it means "speed up before the light changes to red."

To read magazine covers one must interpret signs, both in images and texts. This process of interpretation is dependent upon a shared understanding of the mental maps or constructs that underlie the meaning attached to the signs and the codes for relating the signs to the conceptual maps (Hall 1997b, 21). We learn these codes as members of a social group, but they are typically part of our unconscious communication system. The signs speak to us and refer us to broader systems of ideas (e.g., narratives of the nation), but they vary in their openness to interpretation. Varied interpretations are possible because the meanings conveyed by signs are context sensitive. They are subject to history in that what is signified by a sign in one time may shift to a different meaning in another time. Hall refers to this variability in meaning as "play" or "slippage" that opens up meaning to new constructions and interpretations (1997b, 32). This point is particularly important when we (by whom I mean the readers of this book, the students whose readings I examine in chapter 9, and myself) consider that our reading of the covers that are presented here are from our always-contemporary vantage point.

In addition, variability in interpretation is especially important to take into consideration when examining symbols or icons that represent "core" values or issues of identity in a society. Such key symbols may be universally recognized within a society but the meanings attached to a symbol may be subject to contestation, reformulation, or refraction by the reader. In the interpretive act, the reader must complete the dialogue initiated by the sender by giving meaning to what is produced. As such, any meaning intended by the creator of an image may be reinterpreted by the reader in a different historical moment, or even within the same historical time, because readers bring with them different histories and power positions in society. Issues of gender, class, race, age, language, immigration history, and citizenship status all frame the give and take that forms the process by which meaning is communicated. Gabriele Schwab (1996, 9) refers to the act of reading as a "border operation that requires negotiations across boundaries marked by cultural, historical, or aesthetic difference." The metaphor of culture contact, as Schwab applies it to the act of reading, entails an encounter with Otherness and a negotiation and movement across the culture of the text (image) and the culture of the reader.

The process of interpretation, therefore, can lead to differences in meaning even though communication is based on an assumption of shared conceptual maps, signs, and codes. This may be magnified in multicultural societies. For immigrants, especially, one might ask to what extent they share in these basic understandings. Since these shared meanings are acquired through a process of learning and practice as members of a social group or society, immigrants are often at a disadvantage. Anthropologists refer to this as "culture shock." For example, dogs in American culture primarily signify pets. However, dogs can also signify food in the cultures of some immigrant groups. Such divergent cultural codes can lead to problems and tensions between immigrants and the larger society. On the other hand, immigrants are, as shown in chapter 9, often aware of the principles associated with key symbols of the nation.

The practice of interpretation has significance for the discourse about immigrants and the nation that magazines produce and reproduce. Even though magazines may play to, and even reaffirm, a hegemonic world-view, there is always room for counter readings and interpretations in a society with socially constructed differences among its members. After all, in a society such as the United States, magazines are engaged in representing the world, as they interpret it and help to define it, to audiences that are composed of "multiple positions and multiply positioned people" along the lines of ethnicity, race, gender, and class (Devereaux 1995, 3). Doreen Massey (1994, 165) alerts us to being in a position different from that assumed as the one experiencing global change or the new realities of a "postmodern" world. What about those who are not part of the dominant group from whose vantage point change (i.e., dislocation, invasion, and a loss of control) is being considered?[1] Such multiple positions in a society have practical implications. As Catherine Lutz and Jane Collins (1993, 6) have noted, "While culture industries seek to purvey dominant ideologies, the people to whom their messages are directed sometimes struggle to appropriate, subvert, and use the commercially produced images to their own ends. At the least the works remain subject to their consumers' interpretations."

DENOTING AND CONNOTING MEANING

The cover art of popular magazines consists of two general types of images. First, there are images produced specifically for the magazine using the techniques of the plastic arts: drawing, painting, sculpting, and computer images. The other is the photographic image, that is, the journalistic or news photograph. These images comprise two types of messages, which Roland Barthes (1977, 17) describes as the denoted message and the connoted message. The denoted message derives from the fact of the image's analogical reproductions of reality. The image denotes reality. In a photograph, for example, the reader often assumes that the image "captures reality" rather than viewing the image as a fabricated reproduction of reality. The images of photographs and the other imitative arts have messages that derive from the reality they appear to capture and reproduce (discussed further in the following chapter).[2]

The connoted message derives from the treatment of the image by the image's creator(s).[3] What is signified or connoted by the image, "whether aesthetic or ideological, refers to a certain 'culture' of the society receiving the message" (Barthes 1977, 17).[4] The signs and symbols found in the images on magazine covers have meanings that are embedded in a particular culture and historical period. As Stuart Hall (1973, 176) has explained, "Connotative codes [messages] are the configurations of meaning which permit a sign to signify, in addition to its denotative reference, *other, additional implied meanings.* These configurations of meaning are forms of social knowledge, derived from the social practices, the knowledge of institutions, the beliefs and the legitimations that exist in a diffused form within a society, and which order the society's apprehension of the world in terms of dominant meaning-patterns." The interplay of denoted and connoted messages conveys meanings that can be read from the magazine covers.

Although already mentioned in passing, let me emphasize here that images are not the only structural elements of importance found on the covers of popular magazines. Images are in communication with text. As Walter Benjamin has noted, the relationship between image and text is dialectical and reciprocal (Seyhan 1996).[5] At least two elements of text inform the message of the image: the caption accompanying the image on the cover and the related article or articles inside the magazine. The text or caption often suggests a preferred message among the many possible messages for a specific image (Hall 1997c, 228). Magazines often use captions and headings to fix or anchor their intended message to the image in an attempt to narrow the range of imaginable interpretations. The text can agree with the image's message or contradict it (even mock it), thus setting up an ironic message, but in both cases the text and the image share in the production of the overall message or messages (Hunter 1987). In some cases, as the analysis that follows will demonstrate, the text does not merely explain, label, or describe the image. The text itself is rendered as the image. The text/image thus becomes central to the visual narrative of the overall image. As Mitchell (1994, 91) observed: "The real question to ask when confronted with these kinds of image-text relations is not 'what is the difference (or similarity) between the words and the images?' but 'what difference do the differences (and similarities) make?' That is, why does it matter how words and images are juxtaposed, blended, or separated?"

LEVELS OF MEANING

Returning to the two aspects of meaning discussed above, denotive and connotative, it is possible to break an image's message into two hierarchical, but always interrelated, parts (Hall 1997b, 39; Barthes 1977, 1972). A simple, literal meaning can be derived from an initial reading of an image's denotive message. For example, the *Nation*'s cover presented at the beginning of chapter 1 (fig. 1.2) has a number of signs on it that suggest the following simple denotation: man walks across image of globe with North American continent outlined on it, under the caption "The Immigration Wars." This simple reading tells us about the signs on the cover. But to derive a fuller message it is necessary to interpret what the image and text combine to connote. This takes us to a level where what is signified is beyond the image itself, referring to themes, narratives, and what Barthes (1972) refers to as "mythologies," that are an important part of the larger social and cultural system. Often these mythologies are ideological constructions that obscure underlying relationships, for example, the relationship of immigrants to the economic functioning of the society. To try and understand this higher level of meaning is to attempt an understanding of the discourse that the magazine cover both is a part of and helps to construct.

Magazines and their covers do not exist in a vacuum. They are central to the construction of a discourse on immigration and the nation. Hall (1997a, 6) has defined discourse in the following way:

> Discourses are ways of referring to or constructing knowledge about a particular topic of practice: a cluster (or *formation*) of ideas, images and practices, which provide ways of talking about, forms of knowledge and conduct associated with, a particular topic, social activity or institutional site in society. These *discursive formations,* as they are known, define what is and is not appropriate in our formulation of, and our practices in relation to, a particular subject or site of social activity; what knowledge is considered useful, relevant and "true" in that context; and what sorts of persons or "subjects" embody its characteristics.

Michel Foucault (1980), who also was interested in how meanings come to be shared in a culture during different historical periods, heavily influences Hall's definition of discourse. A major contribution of Foucault's (1979) for the framework developed here is his idea of the direct relationship between the power and the construction of knowledge and truth. Each society, according to Foucault, constructs a discourse that functions as a "regime of truth." As Hall (1997b, 49) explains, "Knowledge linked to power not only assumes the authority of 'the truth' but has the power to *make itself true*. All knowledge once applied in the real world, has real effects, and in that sense at least, 'becomes true.'"

Popular national magazines play an important role in the construction of a discourse about immigrants and their relationship to the nation. In their role as a source of information on immigrant behavior and

immigration's effect on the nation and its people, magazines help construct the public's image of immigrants, the public's perceptions of the
benefits provided by immigrants, and their concerns for alleged dangers
associated with immigration. Any attempt to understand contemporary
public policies aimed at immigrants must begin by examining the discourse and the "knowledge/truth" it produces about immigrants and immigration's impact on the nation that emerged during the specific historical period of the post-1965 era. What we think we know about
immigration in the post-1965 period has a bearing on how we regulate,
control, constrain, and punish immigrants. A number of questions arise
out of this perspective for an attempt to decode the connotated message
of magazine covers examined here: What position is ascribed to the
reader? How are immigrants characterized as subjects? What actions toward immigrants are possible based on these characterizations?

COMMUNICATING MESSAGES THROUGH MAGAZINE COVERS

At this point it is useful to turn to a discussion about how messages are
communicated through magazines. As Roland Barthes (1977, 15–16) has
noted, messages are formed by a "source of emission, a channel of transmission and a point of reception." The production staff at the magazines
is the source of emission. They plan the cover, take the photograph, select the photo, do the artwork, and write a caption to accompany the
cover art. These productive activities raise the issue of the role of the "author." Relevant here are the arguments of the structuralists and post-
structuralists concerning the "disappearance of the author" (Vaillancourt
Rosenau 1992; Giddens 1987, 104–5). An author is historically, socially,
and culturally situated at the intersection of various discourses. Therefore, an author does not simply produce something that is purely au-
tonomous in meaning; the meaning that is produced is societal in origin.
Analogously, the meaning of images on magazine covers derive from their
position at the intersection of discourses in which they were produced.
Moreover, a magazine cover is not the product of a single hand, but of
many "hands": artists, photographers, editors, and any number of other
staff members. There is no single "author" of the product. But the intention to communicate still exists. The important work of the authors
of the magazine covers occurs during the production process, when they
construct the messages that are there for the taking by the reader.

   The magazine and its cover constitute the channel of transmission.
The magazine cover can be questioned as to its meaning, or commu-

nicative intent, because it relies on implied forms of mutual understanding between itself and its readers. It is exactly those forms of mutual understanding that require investigation. The public that reads the magazine is the targeted point of reception. Reading is an interpretive practice in which meanings, or the messages, taken by the reader may not be exactly as intended by the sender. The sender may also transmit meanings unintentionally. Each of these parts of the message, then, is suitable for investigation, although they call for different methods.[6] I am concentrating here on the magazines and their covers and the messages they convey to the consumers of the images. An examination of the possible messages requires an informed reading of the images portrayed on the covers.

In order to read these images it is necessary to understand how their meaning is socially and culturally constructed. By social, I refer to the meaning that is created in a social context. Anthony Giddens (1987) has theorized about how meaning is conveyed through cultural products, such as those found in the media, that are produced for mass consumption. He has emphasized the importance of the "contextuality of action" for understanding meaning, or "signification," which is "saturated in the settings of practical action" (Giddens 1987, 99). As he has argued, "Contexts form 'settings' of action, the qualities of which agents routinely draw upon in the course of orienting what they do and what they say to one another. Common awareness of these settings of action forms an anchoring element in the 'mutual knowledge' whereby agents routinely make sense of what others say and do" (Giddens 1987, 99).

The cultural construction of meaning has to do with the "mutual knowledge" relied upon, quite often unconsciously, by readers of magazine covers and the producers of the covers. The communication carried out by cultural objects relies on the same mutual knowledge as talk, or the casual conversations carried out in the everyday settings of social life. When people talk to each other, they are connected culturally by the setting and mutual interaction. Communication is "worked upon," as Giddens (1987, 101) puts it, by participants in a conversation as they reflexively monitor their talk. But cultural objects such as magazine covers are freed from contexts defined by face-to-face conversation. They have, Giddens (1987, 100) notes, "extended forms of signification." Because of the distance between the producer and the consumer, the "reader" receives priority over the producer in the interpretation of cultural objects and "More defined and explicit hermeneutic tasks have to be undertaken in order to forge the communicative link between the cultural object and its interpreter" (Giddens 1987, 101–2).[7]

Giddens's plea for explicit interpretive tasks guides this analysis of magazine covers. It is an attempt to move beyond the limitations of an analysis that focuses principally on the internal codes and the play of signifiers in texts, by seeking the "recovery of meaning" in a social and historical context (Giddens 1987, 102). The approach developing here follows Giddens's push toward a "post-postmodern" method for reading artifacts of popular culture, which would include the images on magazine covers. Such an approach draws on the work of critical scholars (e.g., Williamson 1978, Barthes 1977, and Goffman 1976) who have examined images used in advertisements and postmodern theorists reflecting on such images (e.g., Jameson 1983, Williams 1980). Douglas Kellner (1988, 1992) has proposed that "reading images critically" incorporates, but at the same time is critical of, some postmodern approaches toward the image, especially that of Baudrillard (1983). In Kellner's (1992, 146) view, a pervasive postmodern attitude has characterized the postmodern image as fundamentally flat and one-dimensional. The search for substance and meaning (a hermeneutics) in such flat images becomes fruitless, a view he posits to Fredric Jameson (1983). Once again, Kellner (1992, 146) observes: "Postmodernism thus signifies the death of hermeneutics . . . in place of . . . the polysemic reading of cultural symbols and texts there emerges the postmodern view that there is nothing behind the surface of texts, no depth or multiplicity of meanings for critical inquiry to discover and explicate." While I agree with Kellner's basic argument, there may also be some overstatement of the case. One of the interesting points to be taken from critical theorists such as Jameson is that images cannot be reduced to an interpretation based on one logic or one underlying master narrative, say that of psychoanalysis or classical versions of Marxism; rather a multiplicity of meanings may coexist.

My approach begins with the position that magazine covers are saturated with symbols and icons that relate to cultural narratives and that these images are pervaded with ideology (O'Barr 1994). The symbols and signs found on magazine covers cannot be dismissed as simply the surface phenomena of a consumer-oriented postmodern society (Goldman 1992, 228). Kellner (1992, 147–48) has called this approach a "political hermeneutic," one in which "It is preferable to analyze both form and content, image and narrative, and postmodern surface and ideological problematic in specific exercises which explicate the polysemic nature of images and texts and which endorse the possibility of multiple codings and decodings." This results in two openings, both of which are considered here. First, a particular cover, with its combination of image and text, can have multiple messages, and these messages can be in contradiction to each other, as we shall see in later chapters. Magazine covers can also be read differently by different people.

Magazine covers can be read as texts, but the means of communication, the symbols, icons, metaphors, and references, derive their meaning from their existence in a world of social action (Chilton 1996; Lakoff and Johnson 1980). Reading magazine covers critically means attempting to understand how and why the images "work," and to try and make explicit the "mutual understanding" referred to through visual and textual cues. This implies that a "preferred" reading, or at least "more informed" readings, exist (Hall 1997c, 228). Anyone can read cultural objects but some readings will have more explanatory value than others when trying to understand the social world within which the cultural products were produced. At the same time, positionality is important. The reader is influenced by his or her position in the overall structure of society, and the personal history he or she brings to the reading.

I am offering one informed reading of the magazine covers. While it is not the only reading that can be undertaken, it is one that is informed by a systematic examination of the covers and the articles that accompany them. Through presentation and analysis of this discursive material, I share some of what informs my reading of the cover images, allowing others to agree or disagree with my interpretations. Any authority I have in this informed reading, I derive from undertaking this study, from my training as an anthropologist, and as a member of the society under study, albeit a member from a historically specific position in the overall structure of the society. I would argue that I must make my reading explicit before I can understand the significance of how others read the same images.

CONSTRUCTING A DISCOURSE
ON IMMIGRATION AND THE NATION

Since the thematic focus of the images on the magazine covers concerns the relationship of immigrants to the nation, it is useful to review Benedict Anderson's reflections on the nation. Anderson (1983), in his now classic book *Imagined Communities*, highlights the relationship between the emergence of print media, especially novels and newspapers, and the development of the imagined community of the nation. "These forms provided the technical means for 're-presenting' the *kind* of imagined community that is the nation" (30). The visual images found on magazine covers are merely an extension of this relationship since they too represent the nation. Anderson (15–16) defines the nation as an imagined political community that is imagined as both inherently limited and sovereign. It is imagined because in all but the smallest societies, one cannot know all the members of the society, and yet "in the minds of each lives the image of their communion." The nation is limited because no nation is imagined to consist of all humans alive at the time. Rather, the nation exists in contrast to other nations that lie just beyond its "finite, if elastic, boundaries."

Immigrants are liminal to this definition of nation. They are from outside the borders of the sovereign nation and yet live within the nation (Kearney 1995; Chavez 1991). The extent to which the larger society "imagines" immigrants as part of the nation can vary historically.[8] But even in the contemporary period, the place of immigrants in the nation is subject to laws governing immigration and naturalization, attitudes toward immigrants, the criteria for and benefits of citizenship,[9] and perceptions of what constitutes the nation and its people (Omi and Winant 1994). None of these positions is fixed, immutable, and uniform; each is subject to a process of debate, a debate that has been played out, so to speak, on the covers of the nation's popular magazines.

Images on magazine covers both refer to, and in the process, help to structure and construct, contemporary "American" identity.[10] Immigrants, however, are problematic for the construction of national identity (Coutin and Chock 1995). They are both celebrated in the origin myths of this identity and condemned as a threat to what is increasingly viewed as a fragile identity (Woodward 1997). Representations of immigrants, as found on magazine covers, vacillate between the "we" in America's identity and the "Other," whose very presence is used to construct the "us" (Said 1978; 1997 [1981]). As the morally questionable Other, the immigrant is often perceived as the "alien," "foreigner," "stranger," and "outsider" who is, as Foucault (1970, xxiv) has put it, "at once interior and foreign, therefore to be excluded (so as to exorcise their interior danger)." Although immigrants function as the "Other" in the construction of an American identity, the relationship cannot be reduced to a simple dichotomy between "us" and "them." The "us" were actually "them" in the not-too-distant past. It is perhaps this recognition of the self in the Other/immigrant that underlies the lack of a consistent societal position in regards to immigrants—the love-hate relationship that has been characteristic of much of U.S. history.[11]

In representing both the nation and the immigrant/Other, magazine covers rely on the public's shared meanings and common-sense understandings of the world, and all that is taken for granted about the order of people in the world (Geertz 1983). These ways of implicitly knowing the world, what anthropologists refer to as cultural assumptions, are not outside power relations in a society. In this area, culture theory owes a great deal to Antonio Gramsci. As can be gleaned from his views on hegemony (1971, 12–13) and common sense (1971, 322–26), Gramsci believed that those in power in a society not only controlled the material means of production but the cultural as well, producing hegemony. Civil society is permeated by a system of values, attitudes, morality, and other beliefs that passively or actively support the established order and thus the class interests that dominate it. Common sense, for Gramsci, is the largely unconscious and uncritical way of perceiving the world that is widespread in any given historical epoch. Common sense, then, incorporates within it the prevailing consciousness, or hegemony, that is largely internalized by members of a society.

Gramsci's notions are particularly apt here since popular magazines are part of the "mass culture" of art and entertainment produced by powerful culture industries.[12] Although these industries may seek to speak to the "common" person, Gramsci would argue that the taken-for-granted assumptions that reproduce the existing power structure of a society are often produced, reproduced, and played upon in the popular media of the society (see also Stuart Hall 1973, 179).[13] Michael Parenti (1986, 10) has put it more bluntly: "The Press does many things and serves many functions, but its major role, its irreducible responsibility is to continually recreate a view of reality supportive of existing social and economic class power."[14] Herman and Chomsky (1988), following Gramsci's notion of hegemony, point out that the media does not act in concert, in a kind of "conspiracy." Rather the dictates of the "free market" produce the general context within which members of the media internalize the rules of the game:

> Most biased choices in the media arise from the preselection of right-thinking people, internalized preconceptions, and the adaptation of personnel to the constraints of ownership, organization, market, and political power. Censorship is largely self-censorship, by reports and commentators who adjust to the realities of source and media organizational requirements, and by people at higher levels within the media organizations who are chosen to implement, and have usually internalized, the constraints imposed by proprietary and other market and governmental centers of power. (Herman and Chomsky 1988, xii)

Gramsci's conceptualization of hegemony and the way power relations work to constantly make the class positions viable and sustainable are important for developing a framework for reading magazine covers. Gramsci's views helped move an analysis of cultural products such as magazine covers away from a narrow interpretation in which they might be seen as part of an "ideological machine" that dictates the thoughts of the people (Bennett et al. 1986, xii). It also undermined a strictly culturalist interpretation of cultural products as expressing the authentic interests of "the people" without regard to class and power relationships. Gramsci's theory of hegemony points to the production of the taken-for-granted in society as an ongoing process in which the powerful classes influence the less powerful classes. At the same time, however, the beliefs and positions of the powerful classes must contend with—and are thus influenced by—the beliefs and ideologies of the classes they are trying to persuade.

Magazine covers, following this line of argument, must be seen as a site of cultural production, as a place where political ideas, ideologies, and positions are not fixed but are in a state of negotiation, argumentation, and debate (Bennett 1986, 8). There are, as Pierre Bourdieu (1991, 234–35) might argue, a plurality of points of view that are in "symbolic struggles for the production and imposition of the legitimate vision of the world and, more precisely, to all the cognitive strategies of fulfillment, that produce the meaning of the objects of the social world by going beyond the directly visible attributes by reference to the future or the past." Bourdieu points out that those who publish materials such as magazines have a great deal of social power. They "make public" issues, help define and categorize people, and give form to people's fears and anxieties (Said 1978, 19–20).[15] Through the exercise of such formidable social power, magazine publishers bring groups "into existence . . . by establishing the *common sense,* the explicit consensus, of the whole group" (Bourdieu 1991, 236). Publishing is a continual labor of categorization, of making things explicit and classifying them, but this does not occur without clashes over the meaning of the social world and the meaning of social identity and/or identities. It is in this sense that national magazines are a site of cultural politics, which Glenn Jordon and Chris Weedon (1995, 5) characterize in the following way: "Cultural politics fundamentally determine the meanings of social practices and, moreover, which groups and individuals have the power to define these meanings. Cultural politics are also concerned with subjectivity and identity, since culture plays a central role in constituting our sense of ourselves."

Magazines and their covers are, therefore, a key terrain for examining the struggle over the opinions and attitudes of "the public" concerning immigration and the issues related to it such as race, multiculturalism, sovereignty, and the nation.[16] This explains why manifold contradictions and disagreements may exist within and between various magazines, their targeted audiences, and their editorial stances. It also helps us understand why particular positions on immigration may appear to vary at different times even for the same magazine. The struggle over opinions and attitudes underscores another key point. Magazines acquire referential power among themselves—a magazine will refer to the contents of another magazine—and in the culture at large, what Said (1978, 20) referred to as a "strategic formation." This strategic formation in the national discourse about immigration does not mean that the magazines exhibit consensus on controversial immigration-related issues. Quite the contrary. However, they all, in their own way, draw on culturally embedded narratives to tell their stories.

The images on popular magazine covers attempt to convey, or more precisely, construct, a hegemonic worldview through the integrating stories (narratives) that the images tell about the nation and its people, what Phyllis Chock (1991), following Barthes, has referred to as "myth-making." Magazine covers rely on narratives that are both *of* the nation and easily recognizable by those who constitute the nation. This reliance on easily recognized narratives is especially true when magazines portray immigrants, who are both inside and yet outside Anderson's (1983) "imagined" community of the nation. Some of the narratives weaving in and out of the images portrayed on popular magazine covers include the nation of immigrants narrative, the melting pot narrative, the cultural/racial threat narrative, the "illegal alien" narrative, the multicultural narrative, and the nation and its borders narrative. These narratives often have thematic subplots. For example, the nation and its border narrative is often told using the themes of sovereignty and invasion. Such metaphors suggest a nation experiencing a crisis.

THE IMAGE OF THE NATION IN CRISIS

Contemporary social theory posits that representations of the nation and its people are necessarily ambivalent and liminal (Bhabha 1990). The nation is not in a fixed, immutable state of being. Rather, the nation and its people are constantly in transition, in a state of "becoming." Foucault (1988) captures the modern nation's constant state of transition with the reflexive question "What are we today?"[17] Relevant here are David Harvey's (1989) arguments about the implications of the post-modern condition.

Capitalist production has, according to Harvey, experienced a crisis of overaccumulation that began in the early 1960s and came to a head in the early 1970s. The ensuing "restructuring" moved production away from the style Harvey calls "Fordism" toward greater emphasis on "flexible production and accumulation," in which the production process is broken down into smaller units (see also Sassen 1989). Relatively less-skilled workers who can be trained quickly to perform a small range of repetitive tasks can easily undertake these more flexible units of production. These productive units are particularly amenable to low-cost immigrant labor and to production offshore, in assembly plants in one of an ever-expanding number of foreign countries open to foreign investment, such as Mexico, Singapore, and Malaysia. Participation in, and competition from, a global economic system has lead to fundamental changes in America's capitalist economy, and has, paradoxically, both increased the demand for immigrant labor and exacerbated resentment toward immigrants.

The radical restructuring of production also has implications for the way magazine covers, as cultural artifacts, represent the world. As Harvey (1989, 327) observed: "Aesthetic and cultural practices are peculiarly susceptible to the changing experience of space and time precisely because they entail the construction of spatial representations and artifacts out of the flow of human experience. They always broker between Being and Becoming." The lesson to take from Harvey is that the way magazines, as embodiments of popular culture, represent the issues of immigration, identity, and the nation is necessarily embedded in the economic, social, and political developments of the late-twentieth century, and the tensions related to coming to grips with those changes.

To a certain extent, the changes in society Harvey examines have led to a crisis of representation and identity. Social theorists have emphasized the destabilizing effect of the increasingly rapid flows of capital, technology, culture, and people in the world today (Appadurai 1996; Hannerz 1992; Gupta and Ferguson 1992). As a result, notions previously taken for granted are now in question. Associated with the historical formation of nation-states was the image of nations with clearly demarcated borders within which was a set of people who shared a single, separate, individuated culture. Akhil Gupta and James Ferguson (1997) refer to this as the isomorphism among culture, place, and people that has come to be seen as "natural." Liisa Malkki (1992) views this taken-for-granted relationship between a people and "their" place as "a metaphysics of sedentarism," which is assumed as the "national order of things" in the world. However, the notion that nations embody a singular culture and people is a historical construction that may not actually reflect the reality of the people and cultures found in nations, both past and present (Hall 1996). The contemporary world, in particular, is one in which culture has been "de-territorialized" as people move from one place to another. It is also important to remember, as Renato Ortiz (1996) advises, that people who experience de-territorialization do not stop there but often end up re-territorialized. These theoretical musings have important implications for conceptions of identity. "Rather than following straightforwardly from sharing the 'same' culture, community, or place, identity emerges as a continually contested domain" (Gupta and Ferguson 1997, 14).

Contemporary social theory on "transnational migrants" can, perhaps unintentionally, add to the concern over the future of the "nation." Transnational migrants are said to live in two nations at once, a result of their continued social connections and active participation in decision making and events "back home" (Rodriguez 1996; Basch, Schiller, and Blanc 1994; Rouse 1991).[18] This emphasis on the transnational relations maintained by immigrants is important, and one which I share. However, the concept lacks clarity. Recent theory has done little to clarify who exactly is a transnational migrant or under what conditions a transnational orientation shifts to either greater emphasis toward life in their new country or to returning permanently to life "back home." This processual perspective is missing in the way the concept is currently formulated, which is that one is either a transnational migrant or not. But transnational migrants are human beings, and as such, are subject to changes in orientation due to life experiences. A lack of concern for change becomes particularly problematic when transnational migrants are said to be part of a continuous "migrant circuit," and yet emphasis is still given to what might appear as an essentially unchanging orientation "back home" (Rouse's 1991, 12).[19] An attachment to the home country or community can become reified in academic theory to the point that issues of loyalty come to sound suspiciously similar to nativist concerns. For example, consider Appadurai's (1993, 424) characterization of America's immigrants: "Even as the legitimacy of nation-states in their own territorial contexts is increasingly under threat, the idea of the nation flourishes transnationally. Safe from the depredations of their home states, diasporic communities become doubly loyal to their nations of origin and thus ambivalent about their loyalties to America."[20]

These examples of contemporary academic theory on transnational migrants can easily be read to raise the issue of competing national loyalties ("ambivalent loyalties"), which is central to a nativist view of the threat posed by immigrants. An alleged lack of interest in establishing roots in the United States and their persevering orientation back home underscores the threat to the nation posed by transnational migrants who supposedly insist on linguistic and cultural separateness. It is precisely in these terms that immigrants—transnational migrants—become constructed as immoral Others who threaten what Richard Handler (1988, 7) has called "the nationalist desire for an integrated nation-state" and a uniform national culture. This was clearly part of U.S. Representative Newt Gingrich's intended message when, shortly after passage of California's Proposition 187 in 1994, he promised that as Speaker of the House he would preside over a freewheeling congressional debate about the "cultural meanings of being American" (Healy 1994a, A1).[21]

Also raising the issue of divided loyalties is the increasing number of immigrant-sending nations that allow expatriates to retain some citizenship rights despite becoming citizens of the United States. The Dominican Republic, Colombia, and Mexico currently allow some form of dual citizenship or nationality, and there is pressure in other countries, such as India and South Korea, to follow their example (McDonnell 1998a). In Mexico's case, U.S. citizens of Mexican origin can maintain dual nationality but not dual citizenship, which means that they are not allowed to vote in local or national elections. Dual nationals are, however, able to own land in Mexico and invest in other ways (J. Smith 1998). Allowing dual nationality is a reflection, on Mexico's part, of the increased importance of transnational connections between the two nations, and the needs of Mexicans in the United States to become citizens for a variety of reasons, including protection against anti-immigrant sentiment and policies. For some groups in the United States, however, dual nationality for millions of Mexican immigrants raises concerns about "split loyalties" during periods of war and political conflict.[22]

For Doreen Massey (1994), issues of identity, place, and the past interweave in ways that deserve particular attention. A place is often imbued with notions of identity, belonging, security, and nostalgia for a past that once was, or at least was imagined to have been. For these notions to work, places, such as nations, are often conceptualized as fixed, bounded, and static, as places that can be defended, with the Other conveniently defined as outside. In actuality, Massey (1994, 168) argues that places are unfixed and dynamic and depend on a wide set of social relations that extend well beyond a particular place. And yet, it is often comforting or politically useful to conceptualize the past and the identity of a place in much narrower, bounded terms. For Massey (1994, 5), what is outside is actually part of the inside, and the global is part of what constitutes the local. These terms are not actually in opposition; they are part of relationships that stretch beyond the local and beyond the nation.

Although Massey (1994, 169) asserts that the openness and dynamism of places and identities was as true in the past as it is today, historical reconstructions may often be filtered through nostalgic lenses. In the discourse over immigration, the past—or how history is remembered—is crucial to issues of identity, especially in relation to contested definitions of the nation and the way race and multiculturalism are configured. Walter Benjamin's reflections on history are pertinent here. Benjamin was not concerned with the factuality of history, but with the way images are retrieved from history and then reconfigured in language and script (Seyhan 1996, 237). These reconfigurings are allegories, according to Benjamin, that are actually ideologically inspired versions of history. Representations of history, which are always fragmentary for Benjamin, tend to the allegorical and thus may be separated from historical "facts." For Benjamin, "History decomposes into pictures, not stories" (Seyhan 1996, 238). The power of the past is captured in the present through a pastiche of images about the past that reinforces the position of the allegorist, or the person or group telling the history. For Benjamin, it was the ruling classes that held the power to use history most effectively in this way. As Seyhan (1996, 238) notes about Benjamin's argument:

> The ruling classes, however, always try to project an image of unity, harmony, and continuity. They present a picture of apparent order, like the kaleidoscope in a child's hand, which transforms, by every turn of the hand, one ordered set of images into another one. The order simulated is merely a pastiche of the history of ruling-class styles. Masquerading as a universal rule, this image of truth holds out against the chaos of history. Benjamin declares that the kaleidoscope has to be smashed.

I undertake an attempt to smash the kaleidoscope through the examination of the discourse about immigration. Proponents of conflicting positions use historical images, allegories, to bolster their arguments about the immigrants and their relation to the nation. How the past is imagined becomes central to the stories told of today's immigrants, both in terms of their threat to the nation and their contributions and prospects for integration into the nation.

The following chapter develops the basic elements—what David Spurr (1993) calls "rhetorical strategies"—used by the magazines on their covers to tell stories of immigration and the issues it raises. These basic elements consist of visual and textual metaphors, icons, and images that make up a lexicon for discoursing about immigration and the nation.

CHAPTER 4

A Lexicon of Images, Icons, and Metaphors for a Discourse on Immigration and the Nation

Signs stand for or represent our concepts, ideas and feelings
in such a way as to enable others to "read," decode or
interpret their meaning in roughly the same way that we do.
Stuart Hall, "Work of Representation"

Magazine covers tell stories by combining images and text into an overall message. In telling immigration-related stories, those who compose the covers draw on narrative themes, well-worn tropes and metaphors, cultural elements, social contexts, and stereotypical scenes and characters that are "out there" as part of society's generalized cultural knowledge and social memory (Santa Ana 1999; Santa Ana et al. 1998; Chilton 1996). My intention in this chapter is to contribute to an elementary grammar of the elements—a lexicon[1]—used to build the messages conveyed on magazine covers. In so doing, I intend to show how those who compose the magazine covers choreograph the available elements so that they achieve their end, which is, as Goffman (1976, 27) put it, "the presentation of a scene that is meaningful, whose meaning can be read at a flash." As different as each of these covers is on the surface, a small number of structural forms can be found. In addition, magazine covers rely on a set of recurrent symbols and icons that suggest to the consumer ethnic and racial stereotypes, national interests, social problems, protagonists, and antagonists. These are the ready-made elements of what Barthes calls a "historical grammar of iconographic connotation" (1977, 22).[2]

DIRECTIONALITY OF MOVEMENT

Newsweek's cover for its 25 June 1984 issue is a photograph of a man carrying an older woman in his arms across a shallow body of water. The woman is wearing a headscarf and a long shawl. The man carries her handbag, and she holds a walking cane. The text tells us that this action is being carried out on the Rio Grande, the river separating the United States from Mexico. The phenotype, stereotypical behavior, and text all together suggest that these are Mexicans crossing illegally into the United States (elaborated on in chapter 8). Of particular interest here is the way this cover uses the "directionality of movement" in the image to convey a message. The movement of the people in the image is not lateral, nor away from the eye of the viewer, but is directed toward the observer's eye. The directionality of movement suggests that the people in the image are coming at the reader, metaphorically at us, the consumers. The movement is not random; it is a linear movement that carries the message that people (Mexicans) are crossing water (the border) and moving toward us (the United States).

The technique of directing movement toward the reader to suggest immigration is used in a humorous way on *Atlantic Monthly*'s November 1983 cover, which depicts a drawing of the earth anthropomorphized with a weary and tired face, legs, and arms, and carrying two sets of luggage. At the world's feet is an Asian hat and under his arm is a sleeping mat or rug that appears to be Mexican in design. The world stands on a porch facing and looking at the reader through the frame of a door. The image uses the world as metaphor to suggest that immigrants are coming from countries around the world, while the traveling paraphernalia reminds us that Asia and Latin America are the principal sending regions in the world today. The direction of the world/traveler is directly at the reader; the world is migrating to the United States.

The direction of movement does not have to be at the reader to be meaningful. The cover of *U.S. News and World Report* on 21 June 1993 is a photographic image of Asian men, each wrapped in a blanket, standing, huddled together in a group. A non-Asian, a white man with a jacket that reads "Special Agent, U.S. Immigration," walks in front of the crowd of Asian men. A white man in a suit and three police officers, including one who appears Asian, surround the group of Asian men. The headline reads: "The New Slave Trade: A shocking story of human smuggling/the growing backlash against immigrants." At the bottom of the image is the text, in small print: "Survivors of the Slave Ship *Golden Venture*, New York."

4.1. *Newsweek*, 25 June 1984. "Closing the Door?"

Apart from the text (discussed in chapter 6), the image tells an interesting story. As in the previous image, water is invoked. The image relates the story of undocumented immigrants from China who tried to
sneak into the country by ship. Because the ship foundered, the Chinese
men are now wet, wrapped in blankets to stay warm. The directionality
of movement is again important. The image gives a sense of a group of
people *without* direction. They are huddled together, waiting. They are
not moving anywhere. In fact, their movement is arrested; they are
stopped, rendered immobile. Their bodies have been controlled, in the
Foucauldian (1979) sense, by Immigration and Naturalization Service
(INS) authorities. The only mobile person is an agent of the INS who
walks in front of the huddled group, further emphasizing the arrested

4.2. The *Atlantic,* November 1983. "The New Immigrants."

motion of the Asian men. The image does not resonate well with the text "The New Slave Trade." Although the men are crowded together, their movement no longer under their own control and their bodies wrapped in blankets, the image alone does not necessarily evoke "slaves." The text, while overstated, suggests that the men, as illegal immigrants, often sell their labor cheaply, or worse, work as indentured servants to pay off the price of their voyage to the United States.

NEWS PHOTOGRAPHS

The news photographs that are often found on magazine covers have a particular power. Photographs carry with them the power imparted by

4.3. *U.S. News and World Report,* 21 June 1993. "The New Slave Trade."

their close reproduction of reality. News photographs freeze that specific moment in the stream of time, and thus capture a fleeting moment of reality. As Susan Sontag (1977) has noted, "A photograph is not only an image (as a painting is an image), an interpretation of the real; it is also a trace, something directly stenciled off the real, like a footprint or a death mask."

However, news photographs impart messages that are not purely denotive or "objective." News photographs also experience treatment by their creators, who frame them and include in them signs that position the newsphoto in time and place, and that speak to issues in the "news." Production staff and editors select the specific photo from scores, or even hundreds, of photographs, then crop it to size and add a caption and/or title. The news photo that finally graces the cover of a magazine has a message that is intended and conveyed by the signs and symbols in the image. The news photo, then, is also a connoted message. But it derives its power from its ostensible denotive quality (it "captures" reality). As Barthes (1977, 29) has noted, the reading of a news photograph depends on the cultural knowledge of the reader and "a good press photograph (and they are all good, being selected) makes ready play with the supposed knowledge of its readers, those prints being chosen which comprise the greatest possible quantity of information of this kind in such a way as to render the reading fully satisfying."

In the *Newsweek* and *U.S. News and World Report* covers above, the use of photographs is strategic to conveying the message that "real" events have taken place (Barthes's quality of "having-been-there"—"this is how it was"). The photographs' denotive quality, their supposed capturing of a brief moment of reality, gives the covers the power of an eyewitness testimony, almost in a legal sense. The power of the photographs, however, means that the consumer is likely to ignore or be completely unaware of problems with what Barthes (1982) calls the photograph's "evidential force." The principal problem is that photographs, especially those used on magazine covers, are created and subject to manipulation. As Tagg (1988, 3) has observed, photographs are "not a magical 'emanation' but a material product of a material apparatus set to work in specific contexts, by specific forces, for more or less defined purposes." Moreover, the photographs impart objectivity to the message, which works to minimize any suggestion that a magazine's ideology might be operating to construct the message. This important function of news photographs has been noted by Hall (1973, 188):

> News photographs have a specific way of passing themselves off as aspects of "nature." They repress their ideological dimensions by offering themselves as literal visual-transcriptions of the "real world." . . . News photographs operate under a hidden sign marked, "this really happened, see for yourself.". . . By appearing literally to reproduce the event as it *really* happened, news photographs suppress their selective/interpretive/ideological function. . . . At this level, news photographs not only support the credibility of the newspaper as an accurate medium. They also guarantee and underwrite its *objectivity* (that is, they neutralize its ideological function).

These photographs are intended to give a sense of reality to the "illegal aliens" crossing the border or arriving on boats. News photographs catch the people in action and freeze that action. The photographs become both testimony and evidence for the position that immigration is a problem and that the nation's borders are being tested by people wishing to enter the country illegally.[3] It is unlikely that a drawing or painting could have carried this message with as much authority as these photographs. They also shield, in a sense, the magazines from accusations of ideological bias, since the photographs appear to "tell the story as it was happening."

ASSEMBLAGES OF IMAGES

An iconographic technique used on magazine covers is the assemblage or montage of images. *U.S. News and World Report*'s cover for 21 March 1983 is an example of an assemblage motif. The cover is made up of a number of images of public signs that include or consist entirely of words written in Spanish and Asian languages, many in non-Western lettering. The text reads: "English (Sometimes) Spoken Here" and "Our Big Cities Go Ethnic." The "Sometimes" is written in script, as if it had been written by hand, and inserted into the sentence, as if the text had been edited.

In this example, dissimilar images are jumbled together, pressed against each other, placed one on top of the other, and jutted into each other. The effect of this montage is to convey immigration as a jarring, dis-integrating (the image is dis-united), and conflict-ridden process. The message is that U.S. society and culture is being torn asunder by immigration. The handwritten "Sometimes" inserted into "English Spoken Here" is filled with irony, in the sense that English might sometimes (occasionally? infrequently?) be spoken in America. English is being obliterated, or so the image and text suggest. Linguistic disharmony becomes a metaphor for the breaking up of the nation into its constituent parts, evoking ethnic and racial tribalism. The image taken as a fractured whole suggests a society of separate ethnic and racial groups each pursuing its own (linguistic) interests at the expense of a national, singular, unified society and culture.

The cover of *Time* magazine on the 13 June 1983 also uses an assemblage of images to develop a message about demographic changes being wrought by immigration. The cover is an illustration featuring a twisting mass of freeways in which a capital *L* and *A* are embedded, representing Los Angeles, California. Palm trees and a cityscape in the background are also part of the image. Within the letters are a number of faces with diverse ethnic features. The faces used in the image are a mixed lot. Three are smiling, while the others look concerned. One fellow has

4.4.   *U.S. News and World Report*, 21 March 1983. "English (Sometimes) Spoken Here."

a furrowed brow as his head is squished into the design. The image of the letters, faces, and freeways suggests that distortions (in people's lives? in society?) are sometimes caused by immigrants in Los Angeles. In addition, the range of facial phenotypes is small; all appear to be Asian or Latino. This is surprising given that Los Angeles attracts immigrants from many European countries (e.g., Israel, Switzerland, Russia) and African Caribbean immigrants (e.g., the Garifuna from Belize, Jamaicans). By leaving out these other immigrants, the magazine cover does not include them, as it were, in the "problem." And in case it was not obvious from the image itself, the problem is restated by the text: "Los Angeles: America's uneasy new melting pot." The adjective "uneasy" is echoed by some of the faces contained within the *LA* space (letters) that is itself inter-

4.5. *Time*, 13 June 1983. "Los Angeles."

sected and embedded in a chaotic and confusing mass of freeways. The result is a pastiche of visual elements suggesting disharmony.

The grand narrative of the melting pot is explicitly appealed to in the text. The image and text work together to underscore the alarmist connotation of the text, that the melting pot is not working. The "new" in the text is an explicit reference to an "old," a past time or golden age when the melting pot supposedly worked. This suggests that the immigrants making up the contemporary "stew" in Los Angeles's ethnic "pot," specifically Asians and Latinos, are not melting as easily as past immigrants. Of course, the contrast with the past suffers from the wisdom of hindsight and the difficulty of predicting the future. It is important to remember that at the time of earlier waves of immigration, the public also questioned the ability of immigrants to assimilate American culture. Then, as now, the society was said to have "indigestion" because of the melting pot's inability to transform immigrants into Americans.

The assemblage motif, with its juxtaposition of diverse and seemingly incongruous elements, is well suited to representations of the "postmodern society," which Jameson (1988, 351) has described as the "insertion as individual subjects into a multidimensional set of radically discontinuous realities."[4] The magazine covers using the assemblage motif readily suggest the eclectic mixings of people from various backgrounds and the plurality of very different worlds collapsing upon each other. Space is disrupted, while the coherence of perspective is less important but, in this way, meaningful. As is perhaps obvious, an assemblage motif is a whole image that is created by integrating smaller pieces or images, which makes it particularly useful to communicate a condition of disharmony. Collages of peoples sharing a space can easily suggest that they maintain a difference or distance from each other. Indeed, of the five covers employing an assemblage motif, four are alarmist in tone. The multicultural, postmodern society constructed out of an assemblage of images can be construed as one in which a "strong sense of 'the Other' is replaced with a weak sense of 'the others'" (Chambers 1987, as quoted in Harvey 1989, 301).[5] As Harvey might argue, the message so available to the assemblage motif concerns the representation of identity in a postmodern society, that is, an identity that finds it difficult to maintain a sense of historical continuity in the face of all the flux and ephemerality associated with flexible accumulation (Harvey 1989, 303).

The assemblage taken to the extreme is a hybridized image in which the various pieces no longer exist independently, but are melded together into one overall image. This technique has achieved a level of perfection with the help of computers that can morph or blend together various images of the same general thing (e.g., a face) into one general image (Ritchin 1990). Popular in rock music videos and Arnold Schwarzenegger movies (e.g., *Terminator 2*), a computer-generated image was also used on the cover of *Time* magazine's Fall 1993 special issue to suggest the changing demographic composition of the United States.

Time had a computer morph the "future, multiethnic face of America" based on various ethnic/racial percentages of the total population. The resulting image is of a woman's face that is 15 percent Anglo-Saxon, 17.5 percent Middle Eastern, 17.5 percent African, 7.5 percent Asian, 35 percent southern European, and 7.5 percent Hispanic or Latino. The image can be read in various ways. A first reading is offered in the mag-

SPECIAL ISSUE

Take a good look at this woman. She was created by a computer from a mix of several races. What you see is a remarkable preview of ...

THE NEW FACE OF AMERICA
How Immigrants Are Shaping the World's
First Multicultural Society

4.6.   *Time,* Fall 1993 Special Issue. "The New Face of America."

azine itself. *Time* magazine calls this image "the New Eve." She is the image of the new mother in America. The demographic future is a pretty woman whose skin color is not too dark, not too light. The image is meant to be comforting, soothing. In fact, the magazine notes, "As onlookers watched the image of our New Eve begin to appear on the computer screen, several staff members promptly fell in love. Said one: 'It really breaks my heart that she doesn't exist.'"

Another reading, however, suggests that the New Eve is a retelling of the melting pot narrative. In fact, melting America's ethnic diversity into a singular integrated whole is exactly what the computer has accomplished. The image of the New Eve gains a power from its performance, which fundamentally is an act of erasure of the particular identity of any specific group. The image is comforting because it represents the safe and familiar narrative of America's ability to absorb and transform all difference into a singular American culture. The image is a cool technological meltdown that diffuses the threat posed by multiculturalism. The future is not about difference but about singularity. Any fear of difference is minimized because it is erased, and the resulting singularity is beautiful and comforting, a melding together in which difference is not only meaningless, but lost. The New Eve image is acculturation—the product of the melting pot—at its most visual (discussed further in chapter 6).

THE STATUE OF LIBERTY

The Statue of Liberty is one of the key symbols in immigration because it condenses much of how we think of immigration and its relationship to us as a nation and a people (Perea 1997b). Indeed, 57 percent of Americans (the largest percentage) picked it as their favorite national symbol in a national poll taken in June of 1986, followed by the flag, which was named by 46 percent (McBee 1986). It refracts notions about identity, nationhood, history, values, morality, justice, honor, and all sorts of ideals. Because it condenses so much, its meanings can vary and even be contradictory. Different people can interpret these meanings differently and still be right. This polysemic quality makes the Statue of Liberty the immigration icon par excellence. She is a symbol that can be used to convey various meanings on magazine covers. She can embody the nation and its people. She can be the protector of immigrants, or she can be the defender of the nation's borders against immigration. She can be a symbol of liberty longed for by refugees, and she can represent a nation drowning in immigrants. She can be multicultural, and she can be the guardian against further demographic changes. So important is the Statue of Liberty as an icon for representing the nation, its people and their values in relation to immigration that she is found on 17 percent of the magazine covers.

The Statue of Liberty has been used as an icon in a variety of ways. She can simply be represented alone, the traditional values associated with her suggested in the strength and beauty of her rendering. For example, the U.S. News and World Report cover for 7 July 1986 featured the head of the Statue of Liberty, beautifully rendered as a colorful painting. She exudes the grace, compassion, and wisdom Americans like to associate with the best qualities of the Statue of Liberty. The text on the cover—

TABLE 4.1

MAGAZINE COVERS WITH THE STATUE OF LIBERTY

American Heritage	Feb. 1992	*New Republic*	15 July 1985
American Heritage	Mar. 1994	*Newsweek*	July 1986
Atlantic Monthly	Nov. 1996	*Newsweek*	9 Aug. 1993
Business Week	13 July 1992	*U.S. News and WR*	9 July 1979
Nation	2 Sep. 1978	*U.S. News and WR*	12 Apr. 1982
Nation	17 Oct. 1994	*U.S. News and WR*	7 July 1986
National Review	22 June 1992		

"Only in America"—asserts America's uniqueness, a uniqueness based on the very same values the image suggests. Inside the magazine are success stories of immigrants who came to America from a number of countries around the world. The "Only in America" asserts the grand narrative that the willingness to absorb immigrants into society is fundamental to American values and identity. *Newsweek* provided another example of how an image of the Statue of Liberty alone is enough to evoke powerful sentiments.

Newsweek's July 1986 special issue featured a simple close-up of the Statue of Liberty's head. The text on the cover stated "Sweet Land of Liberty." The power of the Statue of Liberty, also known as "Lady Liberty," is that she easily communicates what are taken for granted as fundamental values in American society. Her presence in an image with immigrants or refugees suggests the basic elements in the grand immigrant narrative: the search and longing for the values and freedoms that America, as embodied by the Statute of Liberty, represents.

Because the Statue of Liberty is imbued with so much meaning about American values and identity, slight changes in her appearance or demeanor can suggest powerful revisions in those values or identity. *Business Week*'s 13 July 1992 cover featured a Statue of Liberty decked out in colorful new clothes. The colors, some hot and tropical, stand in sharp contrast to the staid gray of concrete and green of aged metal of the actual statue. Patterns on scarves and on her skin are varied, not uniform in design, some suggesting Asian prints. Her earring is a stylized version of an Aztec calendar. The multicolored Statue of Liberty in this image symbolizes the nation as a multicultural society. The image is one of strength as a result of this metamorphosis. The Statue of Liberty's arm is raised forcefully, almost in a power gesture, suggesting motive and pur-

4.7. *Business Week,* 13 July 1992. "The Immigrants."

pose. Her face has a determined expression, not a meek or angry look.
She appears ready to get the job done. Her eyes look up and out, into
the future. Above the image is the bold caption: "The Immigrants." To
the right of the image is the text: "How they're helping the U.S. economy." The text and image resonate to form a united message that immigration is both affirmative and a benefit for the United States.

Changing the features of the Statue of Liberty can raise ambiguous
meanings. The *New Republic*'s 15–22 July 1985 cover featured an article on Asian Americans. The text read: "The Triumph of Asian Americans: David A. Bell on our nation's biggest success story." In the upper right-hand section of the cover was the head of the Statute of Liberty
with Asian female facial features. Although the text is ostensibly a positive characterization of Asian Americans, how the image might be read

4.8. The *New Republic*, 15–22 July 1985. "The Triumph of Asian Americans."

is less clear. Any change to the appearance of the Statue of Liberty is suggestive of changes to the nation itself. Does the image mean that America is becoming an Asian nation? That Asian Americans are becoming too powerful and too successful and thus transforming the nation? Are Asian immigrants assimilating American culture, or changing American culture into their own image? These are the types of questions raised by altering the Statue of Liberty's appearance and which are perhaps suggestive enough to raise an interest in the accompanying article.

The Statue of Liberty carries a great deal of meaning simply by being what she is. For example, Boyarin (1992, 15) has called the Statue of Liberty a symbol of redemption "for the primary use of those descended from European immigrants, those who entered through the Golden Door of the Golden Lands." However, the Statue of Liberty can also be presented as an active agent, whose very act of "doing something" about immigration is the message. On the *Nation*'s 2 September 1978 cover, an illustrated Statue of Liberty stands tall and protective as a group of "aliens" huddles behind her in fear. A man stands in front of her with a piece of paper in his hand that has "deportation" written on it. In this image, the Statue of Liberty plays the role of the protector of immigrants, which is a marked contrast to her actions on three other covers, where she stands not merely as a monument but as the arbitrator of the gateway to the "Golden Land." The *U.S. News and World Report*'s 12 April 1982 (fig. 4.9), *National Review*'s 22 June 1992 (fig. 6.5), and *Ameri-*

4.9. *U.S. News and World Report,* 12 April 1982. "Will U.S. Shut the Door on Immigrants?"

can Heritage's March 1994 (see fig. 7.1) covers each featured a Statue of Liberty poised at the edge of the nation, standing tall and firm with an arm out, not up, and with hands motioning immigrants away from the nation. The *U.S. News and World Report*'s image carries a stop sign in place of a torch. These last three images of the Statue of Liberty symbolize a restrictive position concerning immigration. She is an imposing and dominating figure staring out at all who may approach, her arm extended not in greeting but in rejection, as she directs newcomers to either stop and not enter or to go in another direction. The text also affirms this position. *U.S. News and World Report*'s cover states "Will the U.S. Shut the Door on Immigrants?" The *National Review*'s cover has a more pointed message: "Tired? Poor? Huddled? Tempest-Tossed? Try Aus-

tralia. Rethinking Immigration." The magazine features an article by Peter Brimelow about the increasing threat to America posed by continued
immigration, especially of non-Europeans, or more precisely, non-Britons
such as himself. Finally, the text on *American Heritage*'s cover captures
the sentiment expressed by the image: "Go Back Where You Came From:
Since the very beginning, many Americans have wanted this to be our
immigration policy. Is it starting to happen?" The cover text suggests the
historical tension Americans have felt about immigration. The article inside the magazine takes up this theme as it examines immigration in American history during the last two hundred years up to the present. In ironic
juxtaposition to the message of the cover art, the article is a positive interpretation of immigration and its impact on America. These last three
images of the Statue of Liberty and their accompanying text are meant
to capture the public's concern about immigration. The very symbol of
American liberty and welcome stands at the nation's border as a barrier
to those immigrants she once beckoned and whose way her torch once
illuminated. These images question the value of accepting immigrants
and suggest the need to close the nation's borders to them.

IMAGING MULTITUDES AND MASSES

Capturing a sense of large-scale immigration in an image is done in one
of two basic ways. The first I call the "infinityline." This image consists
of a line of immigrants with at least one end emerging or disappearing,
usually at the edge of the cover's border. It is used to give the subtle but
distinct impression that the flow of immigrants does not have a definitive end in sight, it simply goes on to infinity. Ten covers use this image
(table 4.2). The other way of suggesting large numbers of people is an
image comprising a mass of heads or bodies tightly clustered together.
Eleven covers use the mass of heads image. Together, these two types of
images are found on 28 percent of the magazine covers.

The infinityline image is primarily an alarmist image, since it symbolizes an unbounded flow of immigrants. This image can be either illustrated
or captured in a photograph, but in either case the infinityline must be
clearly represented. For example, *U.S. News and World Report*'s 22 June
1981 cover carries the text "The Great American Immigration Nightmare."
The illustration is of several INS filing cabinets from which people are
jumping out, in flight. The line of "aliens" comes from the top file drawer
and the flow appears continuous. Just how many "aliens" will jump out
is anybody's guess, but there is no indication that an end is imminent.

TABLE 4.2

MAGAZINE COVERS WITH INFINITYLINES

American Heritage	Feb. 1992	*U.S. News and WR*	13 Oct. 1980
New Republic	Feb. 1979	*U.S. News and WR*	9 Mar. 1981
New Republic	1 Apr. 1985	*U.S. News and WR*	22 June 1981
New Republic	13 Apr. 1992	*U.S. News and WR*	7 Mar. 1983
U.S. News and WR	4 July 1977	*U.S. News and WR*	19 Aug. 1985

Another example comes from the *New Republic* (see fig. 6.4). Its 13 April 1992 cover features "The INS Mess" and the image is that of a detention camp with men in military uniforms standing about while black men stand in line to enter a small canvas office of sorts. Coiled barbed wire runs parallel to the line of black men. The line of men simply goes off the border of the image. Without a visible end to the line in sight, it implies that the end of the line is somewhere offstage, leaving the question of the line's length unanswered. Thus, the line could go on indefinitely in the reader's imagination. The infinityline is a particularly useful image, therefore, to suggest the unending flow of immigrants. All but one of the ten covers with an infinityline deal explicitly with the flow of immigrants who are crossing, or have crossed, one of the nation's borders. Only one deals explicitly with refugees. For refugees, the more common image is that of the mass of heads or bodies.

Of the eleven covers on which an image of mass figures or heads is found, five are on the subject of refugees. The mass image is used on 39 percent of the covers specifically on the topic of refugees, but on only 10 percent of the covers on immigration more generally. An example of the mass image is found on *Newsweek's* 2 July 1979 cover, which featured Vietnamese men, women, and children huddled together, waiting. *U.S. News and World Report* covers of 9 July 1979 (fig. 2.2) and 6 August 1979 also showed tightly clustered groups of Asian refugees.

Often, the bodies, or simply their heads, are so tightly packed in these mass images of refugees that it is difficult to distinguish individual features. This loss of individuality is particularly true when the image is an illustration, when the mass of heads or bodies is in a tight frame, or when it makes up only a small part of the total cover. The *New Republic's* 1 April 1985 cover is an example of illustrated small circles (symbolic

TABLE 4.3
MAGAZINE COVERS WITH IMAGES OF MASSES

Nation	17 Oct. 1994	*Time*	19 May 1980
New Republic	1 Apr. 1985	*Time*	8 July 1985
Newsweek	2 July 1979	*U.S. News and WR*	9 July 1979
Newsweek	17 Jan. 1983	*U.S. News and WR*	6 Aug. 1979
Time	16 Oct. 1978	*U.S. News and WR*	21 June 1993
Time	9 July 1979		

heads) tightly clumped together to represent masses of people flowing into the United States. This imagery contributes to an overall message of immigrants, particularly refugees, as a flow of anonymous masses. Combine the flow imagery with the mass image implying large numbers of people, and the result is the metaphor of a "sea of humanity" that is on the move (*Time* described a mass image on its 9 July 1979 cover as "A throng of boat people"). The individual as a person with a history and particular lived story becomes lost in such visual representations, creating a certain distance between the reader and the "people" in the image. As Liisa Malkki (1996, 378) has observed, such representations produce a "dehistoricized universalism" in which "Refugees stop being specific persons and become pure victims in general." The image we are left with is simply that of a large-scale movement of homogenous refugees. While such an image may stir sympathies for fellow "humans" in trouble, they can just as equally raise concern over where such a mass of humanity will land.

That the mass image is more likely to be used with refugees is perhaps due to refugee movements occurring in large numbers over a short period of time. Refugee flows are often episodic occurrences that correspond to cataclysmic political and economic events that displace large numbers of people. On the other hand, the infinityline is a more likely visual metaphor for labor migrations and other nonrefugee migrations, which typically occur across an extended period of time. In both cases, the sudden flows of refugees and the relatively continuous movement of transnational labor migrants typically occur within historically constructed relationships between nations as part of an overall political economy. Neither the infinityline nor the mass image is able to historicize these underlying relationships.

4.10.   The *New Republic*, 1 April 1985. "Open the Floodgates?"

WOMAN-CHILD IMAGE

Also related to how refugees are represented is the image of the woman
and child or simply children alone. The combination of at least one
woman and at least one child is featured prominently on four of the
thirteen refugee-related magazine covers (31 percent). This proportion
increases to 46 percent when two covers with children alone are added.
Three of the sixty-three (5 percent) covers dealing with immigration
more generally featured women and children prominently. Two of these
covers, however, featured a Hmong women and her child (*Newsweek*
7 July 1980) and a Vietnamese family (*USN&WR* 20 February 1978),
but the covers and the related articles were about immigration gener-

TABLE 4.4

MAGAZINE COVERS WITH IMAGES OF WOMEN/CHILDREN

Nation	24 May 1975	*Time*	3 July 1989
New Republic	10 Feb. 1979	*U.S. News and WR*	20 Feb. 1978
Newsweek	4 July 1977	*U.S. News and WR*	6 Aug. 1979
Newsweek	2 July 1979	*U.S. News and WR*	23 Oct. 1993
Newsweek	7 July 1980		

ally and did not focus on refugees. If these two images of refugee families were included with the others that would be eight out of fifteen (53 percent) covers with refugees prominently featuring women and children.

Why women and children? By displaying women and children on their covers, magazines elicit sympathy toward refugees. By alluding to the mother-child dyad, these images arouse empathy through recognition of a shared humanity. They suggest that in times of crisis and desperation, we are all the same. Moreover, the peril of the refugees is underscored by the image of women and children in danger or in need of help (as the saying goes, "Save the women and children first"). Images of helplessness and dependency, however, are gendered touchstones in a society still characterized as patriarchal. Mothers and children are generally not considered "dangerous"; they are innocents in a world of danger. That they are such frequent images on refugee-related covers suggests that this vision of helplessness, as people in dire need for protection and assistance, has become a generalization about refugees, who are perceived more as a class of people than as individuals (Malkki 1996, 388). Images of women and children, therefore, are emotional and persuasive symbols that can be used to galvanize public opinion in favor of refugee assistance and international aid.

WATER-FLOOD IMAGERY

Images of lines of people that seem to go on forever and masses of people are visual metaphors for large-scale immigration. Another way to indicate a large volume of immigration is through the use of the metaphor of the "flood," which appeared on 24 percent of the covers. A flood, of course, is a deluge that occurs when too much water flows into an area.

TABLE 4.5

MAGAZINE COVERS WITH WATER IMAGERY

Atlantic Monthly	Feb. 1994	*Progressive*	Oct. 1993
Atlantic Monthly	Aug. 1998	*Time*	23 Nov. 1981
Business Week	23 June 1980	*Time*	24 June 1984
New Republic	10 Feb. 1979	*Time*	5 Sep. 1994
New Republic	1 Apr. 1985	*Time*	3 July 1989
New Republic	27 Dec. 1993	*U.S. News and WR*	3 Feb. 1975
Newsweek	5 May 1980	*U.S. News and WR*	13 Oct. 1980
Newsweek	25 June 1984	*U.S. News and WR*	9 Mar. 1981
Newsweek	9 Aug. 1993	*U.S. News and WR*	7 Mar. 1983

A flood is not a normal occurrence, but an event that is a problem by definition and one for which a solution must be found as quickly as possible. Floods often wreak havoc on an area and the people living there. As a metaphor for immigration, the flood, along with "flow," another water image, has come to stand for the movement of people into the country. But whereas a flow may be of a greater or lesser degree, a flood is conceived of as large in magnitude and uncontrollable.

The flood metaphor can be indicated directly in text, for example, *Time*'s July 1989 cover ("The Refugee Flood") and *Business Week*'s 23 June 1980 cover (The World's Poor Flood the U.S.: The economic consequences of a new wave").

More subtle associations with floods and water, as metaphors for immigration, can be achieved through imagery. Water is depicted in various ways. *Time*'s 5 September 1994 cover provides a direct linkage between text, visual metaphor, and immigration. On the cover, "Castro's flood of refugees" is depicted in the background of the image as a raft carrying several people floating in the middle of the ocean. Although only one raft is depicted, the water imagery connotes a "flow" that complements the "flood" metaphor of the text. The mere presence of water implicitly adds to the overall concern of the covers with immigration, that is, with flows of people to the United States.

Water symbols, infinity lines, and masses of heads or bodies are all metaphors for immigration. They carry the cover's message by tapping into public's concern with increasing numbers of immigrants and refugees. Taken together, these metaphors for immigration are found on thirty-nine (51 percent) of the covers. Their pervasiveness attests to their ability to touch on often unconscious ways of thinking about immigration.

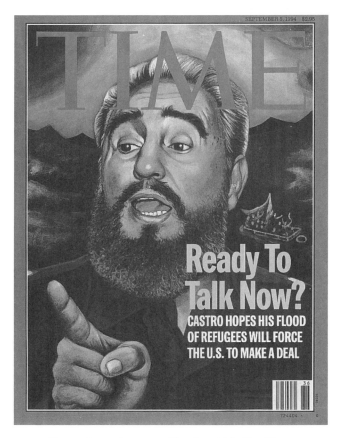

4.11.   *Time*, 5 September 1994. "Ready to Talk Now?"

THE FLAG OF THE UNITED STATES OF AMERICA

The American flag is another important symbol of the nation that is easily associated with immigration. It is, as Orvar Loefgren (1993) has argued, part of the "toolkit" of national symbols, which also includes the
Statue of Liberty, that is essential to nation building. It is, perhaps, less
complex a symbol than the Statue of Liberty. The flag essentially stands
for the nation when it is included in an image, as it was on nine (12 percent) of the covers. Although perhaps evoking a narrower range of meanings and having fewer possibilities to be an active agent, or "doer," than
the Statue of Liberty, the mere presence of the flag establishes that the
nation and its people are an essential part of the image's subject. It can

4.12. *Business Week*, 23 June 1980. "The World's Poor Flood the U.S."

be added to an image to make a linkage between immigrants or refugees in relation to U.S. values, people, or territory.

As a symbol of the nation, scenes in which the flag is changed or acted upon can be a powerful metaphor for changes in the nation itself. For example, *Business Week*'s cover on its 23 June 1980 issue had as its focus the following text: "The World's Poor Flood the U.S.: The economic consequences of a new wave." The image on the cover was that of an American flag with a hole torn in its center, with a man stepping into the hole. In this instance, the image is much more explicit than the text, which is ambiguous as to the consequences of immigration (discussed in chapter 5). The image leaves little doubt that the nation (flag) is being ripped apart by immigration.

TABLE 4.6

MAGAZINE COVERS WITH THE AMERICAN FLAG

American Heritage	Feb. 1992	*Time*	9 Apr. 1990
Business Week	23 June 1980	*U.S. News and WR*	9 Mar. 1981
Nation	17 Oct. 1994	*U.S. News and WR*	21 Mar. 1983
National Review	31 Dec. 1997	*U.S. News and WR*	4 July 1983
Newsweek	17 Jan. 1983		

BORDERS

Because immigrants cross international borders, symbolic representations of the nation's borders are a frequent iconographic theme. So important is the association of immigrants to borders, that borders are referenced on twenty-four (32 percent) of the covers in this sample. Mapping the border is a ready-made imagery that corresponds to the modern age's formation as a world of nations that are, as Malkki (1992) has pointed out, conceptualized "as a discrete spatial partitioning of territory." Borders supposedly establish the territorial boundaries of a nation and people, distinguishing those inside from those outside the nation (Hobsbawm 1992). Immigrants must make a physical, social, and cultural transition across those borders (Chavez 1992). The *Nation*'s 17 October 1994 cover in chapter 1 (fig. 1.2) is an example of the representation of the nation subtly demarcated on a world globe. A man steps across what appears to be the western edge of the North American continent as it is outlined on an image of the globe. The man is a transnationalist, someone who migrates across national boundaries. His transnational character is made explicit by his position just outside the borders of national territory in the image.

Borders, as boundaries, are images that make it clear that immigrants are outsiders who must find a way into the nation. Gates, fences, doors, and walls can suggest borders. The *New Republic*'s 27 December 1993 issue graphically depicted the nation's Pacific coastline with a massive wall running along its entire length. A lone man walks along the beach, outside the wall. Entry to the nation, that is, a way over the wall, looks impossible. Borders can also be suggested very simply. For example, the *Atlantic Monthly*'s November 1983 issue (see fig. 4.2) has the world standing on a porch waiting; the image suggests that the porch, just outside the door, is at the edge of the house (the nation), the border. Water

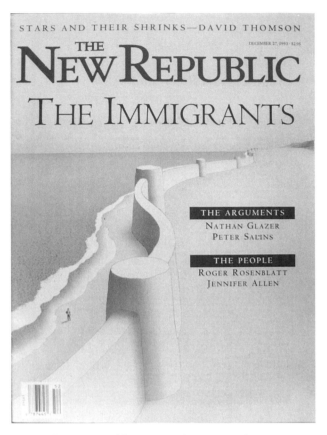

4.13.   The *New Republic,* 27 December 1993. "The Immigrants."

with people in it also help establish a border context. Ocean water with immigrants wading ashore suggests that the coast is a border that is about to be landed upon by people who are either immigrants or refugees. The *New Republic*'s 10 February 1979 cover has a photograph of two large ships in the ocean with Vietnamese men, women, and children leaving the ships and making their way to shore. The text reads "Our Refugee Problem." The refugees in the image are anchorless, to keep on with the image's metaphor, in a world of nations, and are about to cross the border (land on the beach) into a nation where they may seek asylum. In another example, an international border can be suggested by people walking or being carried across a river, which is an image used to signify the Rio Grande river between Mexico and the United States (see figs. 4.1 and 8.6).

A chain-link fence is another border icon. Images of chain-link fences separating territory or used to confine apprehended immigrants evoke the border by suggesting individuals who have yet to cross the border (are on the other side of the fence) or who were caught attempting to cross the border and who now exist in a limbo or liminal state as detainees. *Newsweek*'s 1 February 1982 cover has a photograph of a black man gazing out through a chain-link fence. The text on the cover reads "The Haitians: Refugees or prisoners?" The fence itself becomes the border that separates the man from the United States, and the nation that has failed to determine his immigration status.

Border Patrol agents can evoke the border. As officers whose job it is to maintain vigilance on the nation's borders, they become icons of the border itself. When depicted in the act of doing their job, that is, apprehending border crossers, the action is enough to define the border as the scene of the action. Most of these scenes occur at the U.S.-Mexico border and are discussed in chapter 8. The important point of such images is that immigrants must cross a border to enter the nation, and it is the border that can be guarded, closed, defended, or opened as a way of discoursing about immigration policy.

The Statue of Liberty is another border icon. She is a symbol that can evoke the border because she literally stands on the nation's eastern border and figuratively lights the "golden door" through which immigrants "pass." The images of the Statue of Liberty protecting immigrants or standing in refusal of immigrants, as discussed previously, are images that evoke the border. The actions she is taking in these images are meaningful only as actions at the nation's borders. Her presence symbolizes the border that mark off the nation and across which immigrants may or may not pass.

Ironically, many would argue that the reality of the postmodern world is that borders are less meaningful (Velez-Ibanez 1996; Gupta and Ferguson 1992; Rouse 1991). The world is awash in flows of capital, goods, products, music, and technology that are made all the easier by international commercial treaties such as the 1994 North American Free Trade Agreement (NAFTA) between Mexico and the United States. Millions of people in today's world live outside the nation of their birth. They crossed national borders for economic opportunities or to escape political turmoil and violence. Transnational social and economic networks cross the globe in ever more complex and profound ways. While perhaps not spelling the death of the nation-state, borders are ever more permeable as people form communities that extend across national boundaries.

Representations of the border can also reflect the changing economic and social state of the world. Because of the trend toward ever increasing flexible accumulation, Harvey (1989, 284) has argued, "We have been experiencing, these last two decades, an intense phase of time-space compression that has had disorienting and disruptive impact upon political-economic practices, the balance of class power, as well as upon cultural and social life." The border, in particular, is subject to new understandings of, or preoccupations with, a changing economic and social environment. This can alter how space and time at the border are represented, which, in turn, is a representation of relations between nations and changing demographic realities within the nation itself. The result is that representations of the border are no longer subject to the rationality and order of mapping so defining of the modern world. For example, the images of the border on *U.S. News and World Report*'s 19 August 1985 cover and *Atlantic Monthly*'s May 1992 cover are metaphorical, symbolic, and abstract, and exist in mythical time (see chapter 8 for an extended discussion of the images in their historical context). In the *U.S. News and World Report* cover, letters spelling "U.S." and "Mexico" represent each country by using colors that evoke national meaning. The border is where the two words join. On the *Atlantic Monthly* cover, the border is represented by the word "the border," which is torn in two pieces, seemingly from different fonts of the same words. The colors of each country's flag are used to define which half of the torn words—"the Border"—is the United States and which half is Mexico. In both images, the spatial orientations of "up and down" are metaphors for north and south (Lakoff and Johnson 1980). These abstract border images represent a new (dis)orientation toward the border. The border is represented as the subject of a disruptive impact on American cultural and social life. In the mental or symbolic maps that these representations of the border evoke, there is no concern for a match with current academic research or historical constructions. The message is about a one-way flow of problems north across the U.S.-Mexican border.

CONCLUSION

That magazine covers carry on a discourse about immigration is not in doubt. What I hope to have contributed is an understanding of the some of the basic elements used to communicate meaning in that discourse. The metaphors, icons, and visual allusions found in the covers' imagery and text are not random. They "work," that is, convey meaning to readers, because they tap into shared, but often contradictory, understandings of American history and national narratives about who we are as a people. Magazine covers draw on the often assumed meanings U.S. readers attach to these basic elements in an iconography of immigration discourse. The images play with these elements as the building blocks of their messages, often tossing in multiple symbols or icons to complicate the message.

In this chapter, I have examined some of the basic visual elements in the discourse on immigration found on magazine covers. This exercise, by design, took the images out of their historical context. In the following chapters, the magazine covers are examined in their rightful place in the flow of history, which situates the national debate over immigration. Why certain issues attain sufficient public interest to merit the coveted position of "cover story" can only be understood through a closer reading of the covers in their historical context. What were the issues raised by the stories accompanying the magazine covers? How did these issues change over time? To these questions I now turn.

CHAPTER 5

Immigration Orthodoxies
and Heresies, 1965–85

To articulate the past historically does not mean to recognize
it "as it actually was." It means to wrest a memory as it
flashes up in moments of danger.

Walter Benjamin, Gesammelte Geschriften

The year 1965 was a watershed year in American history. The nation's
immigration laws underwent a radical revision, changing the way
prospective immigrants were allotted visas. Out were the national origins quotas that, by design, favored European immigration. In their place,
the new immigration law established a set of preferences defined by family networks and employment needs. Since 1965, changes have taken
place in both the composition and total numbers of immigrants coming
to the United States. As I discussed in chapter 1, the consequences of these
revisions were perhaps unanticipated and unintended by the framers of
the new immigration law. And not all of these changes, of course, can
be attributed solely to the 1965 immigration law. Other forces have also
been at work. The nation's economy, buffeted by an expanding global
economy, has increasingly turned to flexible production and offshore assembly as a way of meeting world competition. Refugees by the thousands, or even millions, have been set adrift by conflicts in their homelands. And undocumented immigrants, or "illegal aliens," have become
a mainstay of marginal and competitive industries—agricultural, poultry,
meat-cutting, restaurants, etc.—in much of the Southwest, Florida, New
York, Illinois, and an ever expanding number of local communities
throughout the Midwest and South.

This chapter uses magazine covers as a window through which to explore the discourse surrounding these changes and their implications. The
magazine covers serve, in this way, as a finger on the pulse beat of Amer-

ica's concern with immigration, a concern that is often at odds with it-self. Covers of magazines are on the front line in the competition for con-sumer attention. Topics featured on a magazine cover are, in no small way, being highlighted as "timely" and "important" subjects of the day. They are the issues that consumers might find of particular interest at that particular moment in history. What were the issues that warranted such special treatment?

The first cover on immigration in the post-1965 era appeared on the *U.S. News and World Report* on 22 July 1974. That it took almost ten years for immigration to surface as a topic warranting a magazine cover is perhaps explained by fact that demographic changes related to immi-gration did not occur all at once. Changes became more perceptible over time as the total numbers of immigrants increased (see chapter 1).

A DELICATE BALANCE: 1965–79

Although the first cover on immigration appeared in 1974, immigration was the topic of many articles before that time (Fernandez and Pedroza 1982). Beginning in 1965, for example, the new immigration law's im-plications were the source of much speculation. On 25 January 1965, *U.S. News and World Report* included an article that wondered whether immigration reform might lead to an "Open door policy on immigra-tion?" On 21 September 1965, an article in the *National Review* spec-ulated whether there would be "More immigration?" as a result of the new law. These concerns about possible outcomes of immigration reform were accompanied by numerous articles on the growing number of South-east Asian and Cuban refugees desiring asylum in the United States. An-other issue that would receive greater attention in subsequent decades, also appeared shortly after 1965. *U.S. News and World Report*'s 27 No-vember 1967 issue raised the possibility of conflict and competition be-tween immigrants and African Americans in the article "Today's Negroes: Better off than yesterday's immigrants?" Finally, an issue that would also grow in importance, illegal immigration, was the subject of articles such as *Time*'s "Deathtrap for Wetbacks: Trade in illegal immigrants," which appeared on 11 October 1968.

In all, there were twenty covers on immigration issues in the 1970s with both affirmative and alarmist imagery. Some images extol the virtues of immigrants, while other images raise the specter of an immigrant in-vasion. Compassion for refugees is a theme found repeatedly on maga-zine covers during this time. In addition to the themes of undocumented immigration and refugees, the covers appearing in the 1970s contained a lot of imagery that relied on the grand narrative of America as a "nation of immigrants." This narrative intertwines history (past immigrant flows) and the image that the nation absorbs immigrants into its national body (acculturation and assimilation) with a recognition that America's population and culture are changed by immigration.

REFUGEES

Six covers between 1975 and 1979 featured refugees. The first cover appeared on 24 May 1975, also on the *Nation*. The cover, as the text announced, was about "The Camp Pendleton Refugees: Last act in the tragedy." With the last U.S. ground forces leaving Vietnam on 29 March 1973, and South Vietnam's surrender to North Vietnam on 30 April 1975, an exodus began that eventually led to about a million South Vietnamese fleeing their country. Camp Pendleton became the principal resettlement center for Vietnamese refugees in the United States.

As the accompanying article by Alice Marquis indicated, Camp Pendleton, which sits on seventeen miles of coastline between Orange and San Diego counties in California, prepared a "tent village" capable of housing up to eighteen thousand refugees. As allies loyal to the United States, the Vietnamese refugees during these early post-Vietnam war days were received with helping hands. Still early in the decade, compassion for the refugees remained high. Refugees came to symbolize how we thought of ourselves as a nation that helps the world and the uprooted in their times of need. As the author concluded her report:

> But here, too, another face of America appears, from an almost forgotten, naive strain in our history. It is the face of a grizzled Marine sergeant putting a coat around a little girl, a Red Cross woman handing out cocoa. In a larger sense, it is the face of the America that produced the Marshall Plan and the Peace Corps. It is also the corny sentimental face of America that inspired Emma Lazarus' lines on the Statue of Liberty: "Give me your tired, your poor, your huddled masses yearning to breathe free. . . ." From Camp Pendleton, Calif., this May 1975, one can report that, yes, after all that's happened, this America, too, survives.

The Camp Pendleton experience, for the author, offered the opportunity for a retelling of the national narrative of America as a compassionate, immigrant-receiving nation. By generously receiving Vietnamese refugees, America was acting in character, at least the part of our national identity that welcomes immigrants. Two photographs on the *Na-*

tion's cover tell the same story. One is a photograph of Asian men seated at a table across from Anglo or white men. The table is covered with papers. Two Asian women and a young man stand behind the seated Asian men. The impression is that Asian refugees are enmeshed in a time-consuming bureaucratic process of applying for asylum. The other photograph is of a U.S. Marine kneeling in front of two young Asian girls as he hands them a small cup to drink. The Marine's stance, which reduces him in size to that of the children, and his helping gesture neutralizes his otherwise warrior persona. This is a peaceful scene in which the man of war is no longer engaged in warfare. The image underscores the "last act in a tragedy" message, the tragedy of the Vietnam War, is now over, and Marines are now being put to another use, assisting Vietnamese refugees.

Refugees were featured on five magazine covers in 1979 alone. The reason for such sudden and extensive coverage was that the flow of refugees out of Southeast Asia had reached a critical stage. Thousands of Vietnamese, Laotians, and Cambodians were arriving weekly at already overburdened camps throughout Southeast Asia, particularly in Thailand, Hong Kong, and Malaysia. "Boat people" became the epithet for Southeast Asian refugees, many of whom attempted to escape their homelands by taking perilous journeys across dangerous seas in rickety, overcrowded boats. They faced rough seas, pirates, and an increasingly indifferent and even hostile international response (Malaysian authorities at one time threatened to shoot any new refugees attempting to enter its territory). There were even reports of international ships no longer stopping to assist refugees floating in damaged boats on the open seas. At the same time that the numbers of Southeast Asian refugees were increasing, Western nations were becoming reluctant to take any additional asylees. The issue of the boat people became a top item at international summits, including a seven-nation summit conference in Tokyo in early July 1979 and a meeting of the Association of Southeast Asian Nations (ASEAN) also in July. It was at the Tokyo summit that President Jimmy Carter announced that the United States would double the number of refugees (to fourteen thousand) admitted each month as permanent immigrants. The other Western nations responded to President Carter's attempt to prod them to renew their commitment to refugee resettlement at a sixty-five-nation conference sponsored by the United Nations on 20 July in Geneva, Switzerland. They agreed to continue refugee resettlement, or in Japan's case, provide additional funding for such efforts.

Although the coverage of refugees continued to be sympathetic, the debate also focused on a number of concerns. In particular, the growing numbers of refugees became an issue, as were the changing characteristics of the immigrants themselves. In addition, there arose the question of whether or not America was still responsible for the Vietnamese refugees so long after the war. This question was the focus of the *New Republic*'s 10 February 1979 issue. The cover was a photograph of three boats, two of which appeared anchored. The ship just at the top right of image's center was a boat that appeared loaded with people. Asian people were disembarking the ship, stepping into shallow water and walking toward shore. They form a meandering infinityline that crosses from upper right to lower left of the image. The infinityline gives the impression of a continuous stream of people wading to shore. The metaphor of the boat signifies that these are rootless people, refugees, in transition from one nation to another. The text affirms that these are refugees and alerts us to the main point of interest: "Our Refugee Problem."

The article by Michael Walzer (1979), "The Moral Problem of the Refugees," is one side of a debate over what America's responsibility should be to the continuous waves of refugees out of Vietnam. The author argues that America has a moral obligation to take in all the Vietnamese refugees. He is arguing against a position that the refugees leaving Vietnam by the end of 1979 were no longer war-related refugees. The article attributes the position that "'the present wave of refugees' is not connected with the Vietnam War and so is not an American but 'an international problem,'" to undersecretary of state David Newsome (Walzer 1979, 15). The author also acknowledges that the growing numbers of refugees frightens some people, especially when the exclusionary philosophy of "small is beautiful" is so widespread.[1] But, the author argues,

> *These* people in their thousands and tens of thousands are *our* Vietnamese. They are men and women who worked with us, directly as employees in the vast American military establishment, or indirectly as officials and officers in the American-supported government and army of South Vietnam. Or, more generally, they are men and women who shaped their lives to the contours of the American presence—as merchants, journalists, doctors, nurses, smugglers, prostitutes and so on. (Walzer 1979, 15)

The debate over Southeast Asian refugees was carried out on the four covers that appeared in the summer of 1979, three in July and one in August. Each evoked sympathetic sentiments toward refugees. *Newsweek*'s 2 July 1979 cover carried the caption: "Agony of the Boat People." *Time* magazine's 9 July issue featured refugees as a secondary focus of the cover. In the upper right-hand corner was a picture of a mass of bodies tightly packed together with the caption "Refugees: Tragedy of the homeless." *U.S. News and World Report* devoted a full cover to "America: Still the Promised Land" on its 9 July issue (fig. 2.2), which featured a tightly packed boatload of Asian men, women, and children. *U.S. News and World Report* published another cover a month later, on 6 August 1979, that featured a photograph of tightly packed Asian heads and faces behind a wooden fence with barbed wire across the top. The caption reads "A Ray of Hope." Each of these magazine covers evokes sympathy for the plight of Southeast Asian refugees through imagery and text. However, use of the mass of people imagery for refugees also gives the impression of large numbers of people, which raises concerns dealt with explicitly in the corresponding articles.

A primary feature of all the articles was the large number of refugees leaving Southeast Asia. *Newsweek* (2 July 1979, 42) described the 700,000 people who had left Indochina since 1975 as a "flood" that "has now reached staggering proportions. In May, sixty thousand refugees stepped ashore somewhere in Southeast Asia." More than 200,000 ethnic Chinese alone had been forced out of Vietnam, most into camps in China, leading to fears that Vietnam would expel its entire population of 1 million ethnic Chinese. Despite these "staggering" numbers, the magazine generally portrayed the plight of refugees in sympathetic terms, focusing on personal interest stories of individual refugees and the growing unwillingness of Western nations to accept more. Also raised in the issue was the growing concern that each succeeding wave of refugees was less prepared to "assimilate" into Western cultures and societies. As *Newsweek* (52) noted: "Unlike the first wave of refugees—who fled Indochina in the immediate aftermath of the war, and in many cases were well-educated, spoke at least some English and had worked for Americans—the more recent boat people are severely handicapped. Many are poorly educated fisherman or farmers and not a few are illiterate, even in their own language."

Time magazine (9 July 1979) also focused on the large numbers of refugees in the world. The magazine implored Western nations and Japan to increase their quotas quickly to help the Southeast Asian refugees. Failure to do so, as a story on Hong Kong made clear (32), would lead to friction as refugee-receiving nations engage in "Fighting a Refugee Invasion."

U.S. News and World Report's 9 July issue focused in great detail on the increasing numbers of immigrants to the United States, of which refugees from Southeast Asia were but a part. As the magazine noted

5.1.   *U.S. News and World Report,* 6 August 1979. "A Ray of Hope."

(26), 4.4 million immigrants and refugees were taken in by the United States between 1970 and 1979; "Not since the first decade of this century, when a record 8.2 million immigrants entered the United States, have so many arrived in a single decade." In addition to Southeast Asia, the article pointed out that large numbers of immigrants were arriving from Central America and the Caribbean, and that Russia and eastern Europe posed future immigration problems. The number of foreign students had also increased 337 percent between 1960 and 1977. The article pointed out the changing composition of immigrants, fewer of whom were from European countries:

> Through World War I, Europe accounted for the bulk of immigration to the country. Almost 30 million Europeans entered in the century before 1920—

more than 17 million of them from Germany, Austria, Ireland, Sweden and Britain. Asia and South America accounted for fewer than 1 million immigrants each during that period. . . . More than three fourths of America's legal immigrants now come from Asia and Latin America. (27)

The article balances the emphasis given these demographic changes by stating that even though the new immigrants are different, they still come for reasons similar to those that drove earlier waves of immigrants: economic opportunity and political freedom. Although raising the specter of rising immigration and changing demographics, the article ends on the same note as the cover that proclaimed "America: Still the Promised Land": "Yet for immigrants who can reach these shores, the future holds limitless promise" (28). The problems that might be associated with immigration are not the dominant focus. The story being told still holds to the affirmative aspects of the narrative of America as an immigrant nation.

U.S. News and World Report's 6 August 1979 issue reported on the agreement by the nations attending the United Nation's conference in Geneva to dramatically increase their assistance to Southeast Asian refugees. This was the "ray of hope" alluded to on the cover. The magazine also reiterated the large and growing numbers of Southeast Asian refugees. It also compassionately portrayed the harrowing experiences of specific boat people. The magazine drew sympathetic comparisons between the boat people and other refugee flows, such as Russians fleeing the communist revolution in 1917, the Jews attempting to escape persecution in Nazi Germany, refugees displaced in Pakistan and India in 1947, Hungarians fleeing communism in 1956, and Cubans leaving Cuba after the 1961 revolution. Another article positively portrayed Fort Smith, Arkansas, which took in two thousand Vietnamese refugees: "Life has been so good for Vietnamese refugees living in this commercial center at the junction of rivers and railroads that others are flocking to join them" (56). Continuing with this positive picture, the article noted that Vietnamese refugees at the time had a higher employment rate nationwide than native Americans. Finally, the magazine's treatment of refugees ended with an interview with Rev. Emmett Curran, who underlined the moral obligation the world had for Southeast Asian refugees. America in particular, he argued, admitted refugees because:

It confirms a long tradition in this country—a nation of immigrants and refugees from other lands. We pride ourselves on being a nation of nations and the most heterogeneous country in the world. . . . To the extent that we have assimilated originally unwanted groups such as the Irish, the Italians, blacks, Jews, we have incomparably enriched ourselves as a nation. One would like to think that this is a lesson that we have finally learned. Within our limits, there is still so much that we can do—that we ought to do—for any people risking their lives for freedom. (58)

The focus on refugees during the 1970s was overwhelmingly positive. Although a number of troubling issues began to surface, such as the increasing numbers and racial composition of immigrants, the debate remained balanced and tilted toward a sympathetic position. The focus on "our limits," although present, had yet to become the dominant message.

NONREFUGEE IMMIGRATION DURING THE 1970S

The debate over immigration in general was less one-sidedly positive than it was for refugees. The 1970s vacillated between use of affirmative images in the coverage of immigrants and very alarmist images of events at the U.S.-Mexican border. Although positive takes on immigration ranged across a number of magazines, *U.S. News and World Report* appeared to stake out Mexican immigration and the U.S.-Mexican border as its special concern during this period. Although I mention these images here, I will present them in greater detail in chapter 8, which focuses on coverage of Mexican immigration.

U.S. News & World Report published the first cover on the topic of immigration on 22 July 1974. Taking up about one-quarter of the cover, in the middle of the left side, was the headline: "How Millions of Illegal Aliens Sneak into U.S." This initial cover sounded an alarm about immigration through the words "millions" and "sneak." "Millions" underscores the enormity of what is implied as a problem for the United States, while "sneak" characterizes the migration as unfair and surreptitious. Although "sneak" is less inflammatory a word than words used in later years to describe undocumented immigration, especially from Mexico, the tone of the cover suggests that "illegal aliens" are trying to get away with something underhanded.

The problem of illegal immigration is given an implicit boost in severity through its juxtaposition to the other main cover story that week: the possible impeachment of President Richard Nixon. The right half of the cover carried photographs of President Nixon, Chief Justice of the Supreme Court Warren Burger, and Chairman of the House of Representative's Judiciary Committee Peter Rodino, and the headline: "Impeachment Crisis—Key Decisions at Hand." Through its latent association with a national crisis, illegal immigration also assumes the status of a problem of monumental proportions for the nation.

The accompanying article consists of an interview with Leonard F. Chapman Jr., commissioner of the Immigration and Naturalization Service. In the interview, Chapman emphasized the growing number of apprehensions of "illegal aliens" (800,000 in the 1974 fiscal year), the number of undocumented immigrants in the nation ("5, 6, or 7 million") at the time, and the future number of undocumented immigrants (in a "few years," 10 million to 15 million or more). He also clarified how he saw undocumented immigrants taking advantage of the United States: "Many of them do not pay taxes but do benefit from welfare and unemployment compensation. Their children go to our schools" (27). These issues became essential parts of the mantra of the proponents to restrict immigration in the 1980s and 1990s. Chapman's policy recommendations included increased funding for the immigration service, employer sanctions to make it illegal to hire undocumented immigrants, and an amnesty for undocumented immigrants who have been long-term residents of the United States. All of these recommendations became part of later immigration reforms.

The second magazine cover on immigration appeared on the *Nation*'s 25 January 1975 issue, on the heels of an economic recession. It is a cartoon image of a shoeless man with rolled up shirtsleeves floating in the air between two portly men who appear to be kicking the man back and forth like a ball. One of the men doing the kicking appears to be a Mexican with a mustache, wearing sunglasses, cowboy hat and boots, a bandanna, a vest, and a revolver in a holster on his hip. The other man is signified as an American governmental officer of some sort by the stars and stripes on his shirt and the badge on his hat. He is wearing a cleated football shoe. The text accompanying the image is about an article by Christopher Biffle, "Illegal Aliens 'Late on a Moonless Night.'" The words "Illegal Aliens" are right under the shoeless man, identifying him as an "illegal alien" caught in a game between Mexican and American authorities.

Although the image is alarmist in the sense that it portrays an act of violence against a seemingly helpless man, its purpose is to evoke compassion for the man/immigrant. The inside article is a sympathetic, firsthand account of the author's interactions with Mexican farmworkers in Northern California. Biffle outlines the basic contradiction between individual actions taken by the migrants who cross the border illegally and the economic system that promotes and benefits from such behavior. As Biffle (1975, 79) observes:

> The legal position is deceptively simple: these workers have no right to be in the country; they should be ferreted out and sent home. The human problem is however more complex and profound: Mexicans come over because it is to their advantage to do so; that is, it is to their advantage to work like slaves and live like animals, and the border will not restrain them as long as their home conditions remain what they are. The problem is made even more difficult because it is to the convenience of agribusiness to have at its disposal an illegal and easily oppressible labor force.

The image on the cover is meant to convey the position of Mexican labor, caught between two forces, that of the economic conditions in Mexico that propel them to the United States, and those in the United States that attract and yet repel the laborer.

About a week after the *Nation* was published, *U.S. News & World Report* again sounded the alarm about illegal immigration. Its 3 February 1975 cover carried the headline "Rising Flood of Illegal Aliens: How to deal with it." The accompanying article makes a clear connection between the economic recession and concerns over undocumented immigration: "As recession worsens, concern is mounting over foreigners who slip into U.S. undetected and take jobs from citizens" (27). The article recounts the views of INS commissioner Chapman, who was interviewed in the previous *U.S. News & World Report* cover story on illegal immigration. After reviewing INS statistics on the "rising flood" of "illegal aliens," and the need for more funds for the INS and Border Patrol, the article discusses the number of undocumented immigrants and the jobs they take in the nation's major cities, including New York, Detroit, Miami, Chicago, San Francisco, and Houston. Although most undocumented immigrants are said to be from the Caribbean and Latin American, especially Mexico, there were many other countries represented. San Francisco, for example, was said to have a large number of Chinese illegally in the country, Detroit had large proportions of Canadians, Poles, and Asians, and New York had some Chinese, Filipinos, Italians, and Greeks.

The "problems" posed by undocumented immigrants were similar in all the cities. They were characterized as working for low wages, using welfare, taking jobs from U.S. citizens, and not paying taxes. The article concludes by announcing that a new "breed" of immigrants is crossing the United States' borders: "What immigration authorities are dealing with is a bolder and more sophisticated breed of arrival—willing to take his or her chances on finding anonymity and survival in urbanized and welfare-conscious America. And the concerns such people are creating may be around for a long time" (30). As we shall observe, *U.S. News & World Report* helped to ensure that such "concerns" were a featured part of the public discourse on immigration.

America was still "The Promised Land" for immigrants, assured *Time* magazine on the cover of its 5 July 1976 issue (see fig. 1.1). *Time* celebrated the two hundredth birthday of the nation of immigrants with a series of profiles on "America's new immigrants" from various countries, including Italy, Cuba, Lebanon, England, China, and Mexico. The theme underlying the immigrants' stories is the desire for economic opportunities and "a better life" for themselves and their families. A strong immigrant work ethic also permeates the stories. Interestingly, *Time* felt that it was important to let its readers know that immigration was not only part of America's past but also an important part of its present. As the article notes:

> Though many people think of mass immigration as a closed chapter in the nation's history, more than 1,000 newcomers now arrive in the U.S every day. Since American birth rates are declining, that influx from abroad represents about one-fifth of the nation's annual increase in population. . . . All in all, the 400,000 new immigrants arriving every year represent, after decades of discriminatory national quotas, a comparatively enlightened policy that admits more people from poorer countries, particularly more Orientals. (16)

Time uses the face as a metaphor for change, as in "the new immigrants . . . are changing the face of America." The face is used in this context as a symbol that captures how the nation is conceived. Implied in the metaphor is that the national phenotype is changed as immigrant populations mix with existing native populations. But what is the "face" that is being changed? Is there only one face of America? These questions are not raised in the article. Interestingly, the metaphor of the face is one that *Time* returns to with the New Eve computer image in 1992 (see fig. 4.6).

At the end of 1976, *U.S. News and World Report* began what would become a series of covers focusing explicitly on Mexican immigration, the U.S.-Mexico border, and Mexico. Beginning with "Crisis across the Borders: Meaning to U.S." (13 December 1976) and followed shortly thereafter by "Border Crisis: Illegal aliens out of control" (25 April 1977), Mexico and undocumented immigration are characterized as problems for the United States (see figs. 8.1, 8.2). In contrast to the *Nation's* 25 January 1975 coverage, illegal Mexican immigration was not a matter of sympathy for mistreated workers, but as something that posed a dire threat to the nation.

A few months later, however, *Newsweek*'s 4 July 1977 cover (see fig. 2.1) featured a portrait of a family that appears to be from southern or eastern Europe at around the turn of the twentieth century. The caption reads "Everybody's Search for Roots." The photograph takes up about 60 percent of the cover, primarily the lower half. It is set on a field of white and is framed by little blue stars. The text is in red, and the magazine's name is in blue. This image is an affirmative evocation of the nation of immigrants theme. The patriotic colors establish that the family in the photograph is part of an "American story," a common theme for the nation's birthday issue. Inside, the main article describes the growing number of Americans searching out their genealogies, a trend that came on the heels of Alex Haley's Pulitzer prize-winning book *Roots* and extremely successful TV miniseries earlier that year. The "roots" phenomena drew attention to American pluralism, which helped to undermine the myth of the melting pot. In its place, the accompanying article suggests, was a growing recognition of American society as an amalgam of nationalities. Rather than emphasize the possible balkanization effect, *Newsweek* suggests that multiculturalism is a key component of the American identity.

Another read of the "roots" cover is that it emphasizes America's European roots to the exclusion of other roots. The text states "Everybody's Search for Roots," and yet the people in the image do not represent the diversity of the American population even at the time of its publication. The cover's photograph of an Italian family (as we learn inside the magazine) narrows the "Everybody" of the text to Americans of European descent. Perhaps a collage of immigrant families on the cover would have given greater emphasis to the "Everybody." The accompanying article strengthens the image's message by profiling primarily Euro-Americans tracing their genealogies back to their European ancestors. Touching stories of the trip back to ancestral European homelands affirm the connections that continue over generations. Missing was any discussion of the families in New Mexico, Texas, and California that trace their genealogies back to some four hundred years to Spanish explorers who intermarried with American Indian women. American Indians are not mentioned, nor are Japanese and Chinese Americans, who must also have been affected by the "roots" experience. While perhaps not the intention of the magazine, the emphasis on European roots carries an important message at a time when media attention was taking note of increasing Asian and Latin American, especially Mexican, immigration.

The issue (*Newsweek* 4 July 1977) also included an article on illegal immigration, "Amnesty for Aliens?" President Carter was at the time contemplating an amnesty program for undocumented immigrants "who have built new lives in America and are established residents" (16). In addition, Carter favored additional Border Patrol agents along the 1,945-mile Mexican border. Opposition to Carter's proposals included fears that foreign workers would take jobs away from citizens and that once legalized, the immigrants would use social services such as food stamps, medical aid, and welfare, which would put an "intolerable burden" on government budgets. There was also a consideration to fine employers who regularly hired "illegal aliens," but it was dropped as impossible to enforce.

Illegal immigration from Mexico was the theme of *U.S. News and World Report*'s 4 July 1977 cover (see fig. 8.3). This is one of the few covers appearing in July that used alarmist imagery about immigrants. The text on the cover used a war metaphor to underscore the danger of undocumented immigration: "Time Bomb in Mexico: Why there'll be no end to the invasion by 'illegals.'" The image is of Latino men apprehended by a Border Patrol agent. The men are in a meandering infinityline running from left to right across the page. The infinityline image visually emphasizes the "no end to the invasion" message of the caption. The article addresses the difficulty of creating enough jobs for its growing population as the basis for Mexico's unwillingness to find a way to stop Mexicans from migrating to the United States. Mexican emigration serves, from this perspective, as a "safety valve" against possible political instability in Mexico. This was *U.S. News and World Report*'s third cover in about eight months that warns of the dangers posed to the United States by Mexico and Mexican immigration.

Not all of *U.S. News and World Report*'s covers during the 1970s used alarmist imagery in its discourse on immigration. The 20 February 1978 cover featured a photographic portrait of a Vietnamese family. The family members' smiling faces produce an image that is pleasing and appealing. The caption reads "New Faces: How they're changing U.S." The article profiles families from Jamaica, Mexico, Vietnam, the Philippines, and Portugal who are now successfully integrating into American life. A more cautionary tale is presented in the introduction to the profiles. According to the article, the elimination of immigration quotas that discriminated against Third World countries has led to increased immigration from Asia, Latin America, and the Caribbean (from 11 percent of all immigrants in 1951 to 79 percent in 1976). The article also noted that immigrants accounted for more than one third of the nation's annual population growth, and 6 million undocumented immigrants resided in the country at the time. These numbers are top-end estimates. Immigration actually accounted for only 17.9 percent of the nation's population growth during the 1970s. And, as an interview in the same issue with commissioner of the INS Leonel J. Castillo (titled "Why the Tide of Illegal Aliens Keeps Rising") pointed out, experts at the time believed that there were between 3 million and 5 million undocumented immigrants settled in the country. In addition, the new immigrants, readers are told, are more aggressive, have darker skin, and face obstacles to integrating into white, English-speaking America:

> They are a different breed from the "huddled masses" who once thronged to America's shores. Most legal immigrants today are not wide-eyed peasants but aggressive urbanites with considerable sophistication. Darker skins and exotic non-European languages make it harder for some to melt into the predominantly white, English-speaking population. (28)

Although the cover's caption promised to explain "How they're changing U.S.," in the end the reader is left with an odd juxtaposition of sympathetic profiles of immigrant families with provocative statistics and characterizations of immigrants in general. Even within one magazine, the discourse on immigration can reflect the nation's divisions over immigration. Representations of immigrants as a benefit and a reflection of the "nation of immigrants" were countered with concerns over the growing numbers of immigrants and their differences from past immigrants. Although some seemed to "make it," we are left wondering what the changes to American society will be in the long run.

Four other magazine covers appeared in 1978. *Time*'s 24 July 1978 cover featured a sidebar on "Talent: America's hot import," with a photograph of a young, well-dressed man drinking coffee. His successful appearance resonates with the text and the inside article, "Enter the Entrepreneurs: For the talented ambitious, America = Utopia West." The article describes the lure of America's business climate compared to that in nations experiencing economic and political turmoil, or staid bureaucracies that do not reward individual initiative. Immigrants with entrepreneurial and artistic bents come to America and thrive under what they perceive as "an unfettered land in which the newcomer can succeed by applying every Horatian and Algerian virtue from ardor to zeal" (68).

Profiled are immigrant entrepreneurs from Spain, Italy, England, Canada, Portugal, Switzerland, France, and Iran. *Time* leaves little doubt that these new immigrants are enriching the nation, even in intangible ways. "The new immigrants show a certain style wherever they settle. The Europeans, in particular, tend to have a sleek insouciance that immediately sets them apart on the avenue or in a living room" (69–70). The emphasis on European immigrant entrepreneurs leaves one wondering about the entrepreneurial activities of other immigrant groups, especially Koreans, Mexicans, Chinese, Filipinos, and Vietnamese, that by this time are the principal immigrant groups in the nation.

A few months later, the *Nation* (2 September 1978) featured a cover illustration that had the Statue of Liberty with a group of "aliens" huddled behind her in fear. The Statue of Liberty is holding her torch up high, almost as one would a sword; her face has a wide-eyed look of bewilderment. In front of her is a man holding a piece of paper that has "deportation" written on it. The caption reads: "The Chaos of Immigration Policy." Although the word "chaos" does not project an affirmative image, the defensive action of the Statue of Liberty evokes sympathy for the immigrants that she is protecting against deportation. The "chaos" in immigration policy focused on in the article by John S. Rosenberg has to do with the provisions to exclude immigrants on ideological grounds, especially those from socialist countries. The article argues more generally for Congress to approve the establishment of a commission that would completely reexamine the nation's immigration laws (Congress eventually created the Select Commission on Immigration and Refugee Policy).

Time's 16 October 1978 cover alerted America to the growing demographic influence of "Hispanic Americans Soon: The biggest minority." The text appears over a mass of faces of men, women, and children of all ages and races. The diversity of Latinos is well represented in the image. The image evokes an affirmative sentiment with its close-up photographs of smiling faces that look directly at the reader. Two young males in the lower front of the cover represent Latino adolescents. One wears a mustache, longish hair, and a leather jacket, but appears more concerned than threatening. The other, younger male wears short hair, glasses, and a bow tie and is holding a book with the title "Hymns."

The growing Latino population in the United States prompted the cover feature and the article "It's Your Turn in the Sun: Now 19 million, and growing fast, Hispanics are becoming a power" (48). The article is an overview of the various Latino groups in the United States, with

profiles of Mexican Americans in Los Angeles, Cubans in Miami, and
Puerto Ricans in New York. The article points to immigration as one of
the key reasons for the growth of the Latino population. Legal and undocumented Latino immigration was estimated to be 1 million people a
year. That would be a staggering 10 million Latino immigrants alone for
the decade, or more than twice the number of all legal immigrants counted
for the decade (4,493,314) in the 1980 U.S. census. According to that
census, 1.8 million Latinos immigrated to the United States between 1971
and 1980. The possible reason for such high estimates for the Latino population's "real" numbers was that the estimates for illegal immigrants
varied widely. The *Time* article cited 7.4 million undocumented Hispanic
immigrants as a conservative number, citing estimates at the time that
ranged from 2.7 million to 10.8 million undocumented Latinos in the
United States. The problem was that these estimates were not based on
sophisticated methods, which would be developed to a much greater degree in the 1980s (Passel and Woodrow 1987). In addition, little distinction was made between undocumented immigrants who actually
stayed in the United States and added to the population (the stock in demographic terms) and those who crossed the border to work for a short
time and then return to their home country (the flow).[2]

The other fast-growing U.S. population, Asian Americans, was the subject of *American Heritage*'s December 1978 cover (fig. 2.5). The simple
photograph on the cover is of a Chinese man walking down a street in
what could be mistaken as China but is, the caption tells us, "San Francisco, 1900." The photograph is part of a collection of photographs taken
by Arnold Genthe between 1895 and 1906 in San Francisco's old Chinatown. As the magazine points out, the photograph is "a bit of the Far
East set down apparently intact in the middle of an indisputably Caucasian city." The article inside, "San Francisco's Chinatown," is by Max-
ine Hong Kingston, who notes that the artful photographs obscure as
much as they reveal about Chinese Americans in San Francisco. Although
the magazine's objective is to retain America's historical heritage, the image is not totally removed from the then contemporary context of growing Asian immigration and issues of multiculturalism and social integration. The foreignness of the Chinese in America that the image
implies raises questions about the ability and willingness of Asian immigrants to assimilate and acculturate into American culture and society. Are the readers to "imagine" the subject of the photograph as a member of the American community? Or, is he an exotic "bit of the Far East"

that is apart from, and not part of, the larger society? In other words, is the image symbolic of the way "the Asian," as Lisa Lowe (1996, 5) observes, "is always seen as an immigrant, as the 'foreigner-within,' even when born in the United States and the descendent of generations born here before"?

U.S. News and World Report continued with the undocumented immigration theme for its 29 January 1979 cover (fig. 8.4). The image is of three Latino men being detained by an agent of the U.S. Border Patrol. The caption reads "Illegal Aliens: Invasion out of control?" Although framed as a question, the image and accompanying articles leave little doubt that the answer is "yes." The magazine reports on the growing numbers of undocumented immigrants in the country. The estimate of undocumented immigrants is said to be as high as 12 million, although it is noted that experts put the figure at 3 million to 5 million. The 1,058,000 detentions of undocumented border crossers (one crosser, however, could be detained many times before finally making it across) is used to suggest that the number of "illegal aliens" entering the United States each year "is roughly five times the 175,000 Indo-Chinese refugees admitted since the fall of Saigon in 1975." The magazine predicted that at that rate, "assuming all undocumented immigrants stayed and the U.S. birth rate remained the same, illegals would make up 10 percent of the country's population by the year 2025" (40). If, for example, the U.S. population reaches 300 million by that date, this estimate would equal about 30 million undocumented immigrants. But of course, not all undocumented immigrants stay permanently in the United States and those who do often become legal residents. The report ends on the "Mexicanization of Los Angeles: A trend that is spreading" (42).

In sum, the discourse over immigration during the 1970s, as carried out in the magazines under study, vacillated between sympathetic treatments of immigrants, especially refugees, and an emphasis that immigration also carries with it problems. Of growing concern were the increasing number of immigrants, the decreasing numbers of European immigrants, language differences, and undocumented immigration. Embedded in the discourse was the delicate balance in American culture between immigrants as danger and immigrants as central to the nation's identity. Whether immigrants should be welcomed or viewed with suspicion is a question that was being raised, but not definitively answered. The 1980s witnessed a turn toward a decidedly more alarmist discourse, especially in imagery.

IMMIGRATION AS A THREAT TO THE NATION: 1980–85

Twenty-eight covers with immigration-related themes appeared on these ten magazines between 1980 and 1989. However, twenty-five of these covers were published between 1980 and 1986, the year the Immigration Reform and Control Act was passed. The early 1980s witnessed increasing public concern about immigration, eventually culminating in the 1986 immigration law, which was to restrict undocumented immigration. With about 90 percent of the decade's covers appearing in the years before and including IRCA, and few afterwards, it is as if passage of this major legislation on immigration signaled that "something had been done" about immigration and the issue therefore no longer warranted such extensive coverage.

The first two of the five covers in 1980 dealt with Cuban refugees. A third cover featuring Cuban refugees appeared later in the year. The three covers tell a story of an unfolding minidrama in which America wrestled with its position on refugees. *Time*'s 19 May 1980 cover featured a sidebar on the upper right-hand corner in which a photograph of a mass of male heads is framed. The caption reads: "Cuban Refugees: Is there a limit?" Both the image, of a countless number of heads, and the rhetorical question about a limit suggest that the number of Cuban refugees arriving in the United States is high or could possibly be high. The cover's message, of a possible unlimited flow of Cuban refugees, represents a position critical of President Carter's policy on the new refugees, which was the main point of the story. In response to the newest wave of Cubans fleeing, and in some cases being pushed out, of Castro's Cuba, President Jimmy Carter promised to accept them and provide a safe haven: "Ours is a country of refugees. We'll continue to provide an open heart and open arms to refugees seeking freedom from Communist domination and from the economic deprivation brought about by Fidel Castro and his government" (14).

At issue for *Time* were the tens of thousands of Cubans arriving in southern Florida. In response to Castro's sudden agreement to let Cubans leave, a flotilla of private American boats sailed to the Cuban port of Mariel, twenty-seven miles west of Havana. What became known as the "Mariel boat lift" and the "Freedom Flotilla," raised the possibility, according to *Time,* that up to a quarter of a million to 1 million Cubans might eventually seek asylum in the United States. For *Time,* this possibility "raised the difficult question of whether there are practical limits to the number of refugees the U.S. can take in" (14). Adding to the complexity of the problem were reports that Castro was opening his prisons and forcing criminals on the boats (17). Finally, the bottom line on Cuban refugees was their possible cost to taxpayers. *Time* reported on an estimate that each thousand refugees would cost the United States $5 million in welfare and health aid, $2 million in food stamps, and another $2 million for transportation costs.

A week later, *Newsweek*'s 26 May 1980 cover reflected the Carter administration's backtracking on the "open heart and open arms" policy on Cuban refugees. The cover features a photograph of two men and a woman leaning against a boat's rail while at open sea. Their desperate looking faces stare at some point just to the left of the camera. The caption reads: "The Cuban Influx: Can Carter control it?" The issue of control is the key message. Rather than an unlimited flow of Cuban refugees, the Carter administration shifted position to a limited flow controlled by U.S. officials rather than Castro. The image underscores this sense of a controlled flow. Rather than an image suggesting multitudes, the image shows only three people who look as if they are members of a nuclear family: a young man in his late teens or early twenties and an older man and woman who could be his parents.

In a signal that policy had changed, *Newsweek* referred to the Cubans as "illegal refugees." The Carter administration's sudden change in position was a response to criticism such as that in the previously discussed *Time* magazine. The new, more stringent policy was a reaction to the large number of potential refugees desiring to flee Cuba, the inclusion of criminals and other social misfits among the sixty thousand refugees that had already arrived in Florida, and the danger to the refugees fleeing in leaky, overcrowded boats (at least eighteen had died by that time). Public opinion on this issue must also have influenced the Carter administration. *Newsweek* reported on a national poll that found that 59 percent of Americans believed that Cuban immigration was "bad for the United States because it is difficult and expensive to take in so many refugees" (25). *Newsweek* ended by returning to the control theme, but placing it within the America as a nation of immigrants narrative: "America remains to [the Cuban refugees] what it was to previous generations of immigrants, a land of opportunity. The immediate task is to settle them as fast and as painlessly as possible while restoring some order to the immigration process."

Business Week's 23 June 1980 issue took the new wave of Cuban refugees as the starting point for raising the alarm about uncontrolled immigration. The cover immediately establishes the message that immi-

5.2. *Newsweek*, 26 May 1980. "The Cuban Influx."

gration is tearing apart the nation. The Stars and Stripes take up the entire cover (see fig. 4.12). In the middle of the image is a man with brown
skin, black hair, and dark clothes making his way through a huge tear
in the flag. The text reads: "The World's Poor Flood the U.S.: The economic consequences of a new wave." The first paragraph of the accompanying article reinforces the flood metaphor of the cover and the danger of Latin American immigration to the nation. The first sentence begins
"The invasion of southern Florida by Cuban refugees last month . . ."
And continues, "In five weeks some 100,000 Cubans flooded into an unprepared U.S., the confusion of their arrival demonstrating once again
the country's failure to come to grips with the mass migration of peoples from Latin America. Unless the country comes up with a workable
policy, the economic and social strains exerted by these immigrants may

produce conflicts sharp enough to rip an already fragile social fabric" (80). The metaphors of fabric and flag for the nation mesh well, as does the destructive nature of immigration symbolized by the verb "to rip" and the image of the tear in the fabric.

Business Week presents information on what it views as the large number of legal and illegal immigrants entering the country and the shift away from European countries as the primary source of the immigrants. *Business Week* is particularly concerned about the "flood" of poor and low-skilled immigrants competing with citizens for jobs at a time of increasing recession. On the other hand, *Business Week* notes that demographic projections indicate that in the not-too-distant future, the U.S. labor force will grow more slowly, as the baby boom generation ages and as fewer young people enter the labor market. At that time, the United States may need immigrants who are eager to work if the economy is to grow. This leads *Business Week* to advocate a flexible immigration policy, one that can respond to our labor needs and interests. In the meantime, immigration, particularly undocumented immigration, is disruptive to society and reduces the gains made by African Americans, Hispanic citizens, and others. Immigrants also draw resources from state and local budgets for social services. Despite such problems, *Business Week* notes that Mexican migration endows American manufacturing, especially in the Southwest, with a great deal of competitive strength (83). Rather than entirely cutting off immigration from Mexico and other parts of Latin America, *Business Week* ends by stressing the need to reduce and manage the flow, otherwise "the nation is heading for social and economic explosions" (86). Through image and text, immigration from Latin America is associated with destructive tendencies such as ripping, tearing, invading, flooding, displacing, and exploding, which far outweigh its association with any positive productive contributions.

Newsweek's 7 July 1980 cover featured a photograph of a Hmong woman carrying a baby on her back (fig. 2.3). The article provides an overview of recent immigration trends that were beginning to change the "face" of America and the growing public debate over immigration. The article begins with the problem of increased numbers of immigrants: "There is no end in sight. They are coming in numbers that mock the limits written into our laws—coming as fast as they can be admitted, or as fast as they can escape their homelands" (26). Their reasons for coming, we are told, are similar to earlier immigrants: poverty, human misery, and oppression.

Newsweek predicted quite rightly that the national debate over immigration "has barely begun." One of the key issues the article focused on was the number of people in the world who would like to immigrate legally, illegally, or as refugees to the United States. The article underscored the problem of immigration's impact on our population growth with a quote from Roger Conner of the Federation of American Immigration Reform (FAIR): "The overriding issue in immigration policy is not race, not ethnicity, not even job skills. It's sheer numbers." *Newsweek*'s question was, how many immigrants can America take? *Newsweek* anticipated that the debate over immigration would heat up when the Select Commission on Immigration and Refugee Policy submitted their recommendations in the following spring of 1981. Among the commission's expected recommendations were a national identification card proving the person is legally able to work in the United States and a one-time amnesty for undocumented immigrants already in the United States (29). The "new immigrants" wrapped so gloriously in Americana on the cover may symbolize the American tradition of taking in immigrants, but it is not, we are told, without challenges to the future of the nation because of the immigrants' sheer numbers, cultural differences, and hardening attitudes of native Americans.

Three months later, on 13 October 1980, *U.S. News and World Report*'s cover alerted its readers to "Refugees: Stung by a backlash." The cover has a group of mostly male Cubans (fourteen males and three females) on a boat looking confused as they talk to someone just to the left of the camera. Inside we learn that "In a nation of immigrants, some arrivals are finding an increasingly cold reception" (60). The article reports on friction between the large numbers of Southeast Asians, Cubans, and Haitians and the communities where they have suddenly settled. The antirefugee backlash was fanned by a troubled U.S. economy that was showing signs of what would soon develop into a major recession. In addition, media attention had highlighted crimes by Cuban refugees and Vietnamese youth who were unemployed street toughs. Cambodians hunting and eating squirrels, ducks, and stray dogs in San Francisco's Golden Gate Park also added to an alarmist, "un-American" image of refugees. In addition, the report cites public concern regarding increases in legal immigration, large estimates of undocumented immigrants (3.5 million to 12 million), job competition, and costs incurred by local governments for refugees. The backlash against refugees was actually part of a growing backlash against immigration in general. The report cites a Roper poll that showed that 80 percent of Americans favored cutbacks in immigration quotas. Reverend Theodore Hesburgh, president of the

University of Notre Dame and chairman of the Select Commission on Immigration and Refugee Policy, summed up public opinion this way: "People feel the entire immigration system is out of control" (63).

The 9 March 1981 *U.S. News and World Report*'s cover signaled: "Our Troubled Neighbors—Dangers for U.S." The cover was a colorful illustration of North America, with a pristine United States in the image of an American flag (see fig. 8.5 and further discussion in chapter 8). Canada and Mexico were characterized by images of people, places, and flags. The article, "Strains on U.S.-Mexican Ties: Oil, migrants, Castroism," details problems between the United States and Mexico (37). At issue was Mexico's reluctance to sell more of its oil to the United States, illegal Mexican immigration, and Mexico's sympathy with the leftist forces fighting in El Salvador. A specific problem cited for the United States was Mexico's growing population and inability to turn oil wealth into economic opportunities for its population, many of whom remained unemployed or underemployed, which would lay the foundation for continued undocumented immigration. This issue also had an article on the long-awaited recommendations of the Select Commission on Immigration and Refugee Policy, which were submitted on 26 February 1981 (11). Among the commission's major recommendations were an amnesty program for undocumented residents who had established residence in the United States, an increase in annual immigration limits, prosecution of persons who hire undocumented workers (employer sanctions), and more funds for the Border Patrol. The commission decided against recommending a national identification card. Although five years of public debate followed, the commission's recommendations were similar to the provisions established under IRCA in 1986.

U.S. News and World Report followed, on 22 June 1981, with a cover that had the caption: "The Great American Immigration Nightmare." The image was an illustration of old file cabinets with some drawers open, out of which people were jumping and then running away. The caption and the image combine to tell us that these are the files of the Immigration and Naturalization Service, and they are not working properly. The people, or immigrants, jumping out of the file drawers form a humorous example of an infinityline down the right side of the cover and across the bottom from right to left. Just how many immigrants are waiting to jump out of the filing cabinet is anybody's guess. The main point of the inside article is that the INS's outdated system of filing and management of cases is unable to keep up with the large number of immigrants, tourists, students, undocumented immigrants, foreign workers, and refugees entering the country. The article details the problems facing the INS across the nation and some of the horror stories experienced by immigrants whose documents had been lost or misplaced. This focus on the INS's dire need for technological modernization and an increase in the number of agents comes on the heels of the SCIRP's recommendation for increased funds for the Border Patrol. It also supports the agency at a time when the Reagan administration proposed cutting its 1982 budget request and thus eliminating 1,355 positions. The article manages to be sympathetic to both the INS and the immigrants who suffer under its archaic management infrastructure.

The ultimate cost of immigration was highlighted on *Time*'s 23 November 1981 cover. A map of Florida is the backdrop to the caption "Paradise Lost? South Florida." A sun wearing sunglasses and a large frown sits above the words "South Florida," formed by block letters with a different photograph inside each letter. The assemblage creates a chaotic image of life in South Florida. An image of a beautiful beach is followed by problems confronting the area: refugees, drugs, and crime. The inside article reports on the shift in demographic characteristics in South Florida as a result of immigration. Whites, blacks, and Latinos went from 83 percent, 13 percent, and 4 percent of the Dade County population in 1950, to 44 percent, 15 percent, and 39 percent, respectively, in 1980. Adding to the region's Latino population were the 125,000 Cuban "Marielitos" who arrived after the spring of 1980 and about 25,000 Haitian refugees. The Marielitos, reported to be responsible for about half of all violent crime in Miami, provided the clear connection between crime and immigration (23). South Miami's foreignness, as a questionable representative of United States society and culture, was emphasized throughout the report. Beginning with the letter from the publisher, we learn that Miami is *Time*'s only foreign bureau located within the United States. The president of Ecuador, the late Jaime Roldós, is quoted as claiming Miami is the "capital of Latin America" (24). We also read that "The Latins are gradually turning the region into their own colony" (24). Miami's Little Havana, home to many Cuban immigrants, is characterized as "a foreign land" (31). Changes in South Florida have created tensions as local non-Latino Floridians, both white and African American, resent the established Latin immigrants for their economic and demographic success and the newest waves of immigrants who bring with them the likelihood of an increased burden on social services and crime. The South Florida that is being "lost" is clearly one that exists in a cultural and demographic sense. The increasing Latinization of South Florida, the report implies, is the basis for the interethnic tensions, crime, and drug smuggling that is destroying, or at least changing, the way of life in the area. The cover's image underscores these changes through a use of provocative colors. The state of Florida changes from a green in the north, to an orange at about half way down, and then to red in the southern tip. Red as the symbol of blood emphasizes the danger created by the changes. But is red, the color of communism, also meant to symbolize the "invasion" of refugees from communist Cuba?

A few months later, *Newsweek*'s 1 February 1982 cover focused attention on the plight of Haitian immigrants. A young man looks sadly through a chain-link fence, his fingers draped loosely over the wires. He appears caught in a cage, wondering when he will be set free. The caption underscores the plight of the young man and others like him: "The Haitians: Refugees or prisoners?" At issue was the Reagan administration's policy toward Haitians, which was to detain them indefinitely while INS adjudicates their cases. This represented a policy shift from the Carter era, when thousands of Haitians were quickly set free on bond and then just as quickly melted into Haitian communities in the United States, often failing to turn up for their hearings at the INS. The new policy was an attempt to stop such disappearances and to send the message to other Haitians thinking about migrating to the United States that entry was not going be easy. Also under debate was the Haitians' status. Were they refugees escaping oppression and a "well founded fear of persecution," thus deserving asylum in the United States? Or were they economic migrants in search of a better life, like millions of immigrants before them?

Complicating these questions were issues of politics and race. The open door afforded Cubans was based on their "escape" from communism and the regime of one of the United States' longest-running enemies, Fidel Castro. Haitians, on the other hand, were escaping from a country that had long been a friend of the United States. Adding to the complexity of the debate was that the Haitians were primarily of African Caribbean origin and the Cubans more mixed or white in complexion. As this debate continued, thousands of Haitians languished for months in detention camps from New York to Puerto Rico. The image on the cover captures the detained Haitians' resignation at their indeterminate stay in the camps.

A SURGE IN ANTI-IMMIGRANT DISCOURSE

The debate on immigration heated up dramatically in 1982, as the nation was gripped by a major economic recession. The increasing concern

with immigration at that time was suggested by the frequency of magazine covers focusing on the topic to appear shortly thereafter. In the four
years of 1982 to 1985, fifteen immigration-related covers appeared.

U.S. News and World Report's 12 April 1982 cover featured an image of the Statue of Liberty from the chest up (fig. 4.9). Rather than a
torch to guide the incoming immigrants to our shores, she is holding a
large red and white stop sign in her hand that is held high above her head.
The caption reverberates with the image's message: "Will U.S. Shut the
Door on Immigrants?" The accompanying feature article provides a thor-
ough overview of the public's concerns with immigration. "Americans,"
the report tells us, "are increasingly reluctant to welcome newcomers,
no matter where they come from—or why" (47). The concerns stem from
what is presented as massive immigration, "well over 1 million newcomers a year into the U.S.—the highest level since the mass migration
of Europeans at the turn of the century" (47). The report arrives at its
estimate of more than 1 million immigrants a year by combining the average annual number of legal immigrants between 1970 and 1979
(446,518 per year) with an additional 500,000 to 1 million persons believed to enter the United States illegally each year (48). The problem is
that the 500,000 to 1 million figure is difficult to use in such an estimate.
As mentioned, the Border Patrol might catch the same person multiple
times before that person can make it safely into the United States. Also,
most of the undocumented workers at that time were attracted to seasonal employment, especially in agriculture, and typically returned home
after about ten months in the United States. This suggests that the important number to use in such an estimate is the net number of undocumented immigrants who stay and add to the nation's population (Passel and Woodrow 1987, Woodrow and Passel 1990). Regardless of these
subtleties, the public's perception of large numbers of immigrants was
one of the key issues fueling the concern over immigration. Adding to
the public's growing wariness over immigration was a sagging U.S. economy, which in hindsight was a recession of major proportions. Americans, the report states, were concerned with "importing a new poverty
class" that would place additional burden on taxpayers who at the same
time had to compete with immigrants for scarce jobs.

Immigration was also fueling tensions between local and state governments, which bear the burden of providing services to immigrants,
and the federal government, which determines immigration policy. The
National Governors' Association, in February of that year, 1982, de-

manded that the federal government provide additional funds for costs related to refugees. According to the governors, "If the federal government is unwilling to fund the services, then it is incumbent upon the federal government to decrease the flow of refugee admissions" (49). This tension between state and federal governments over funding for immigrants' services continued to smolder throughout the 1980s and 1990s. Immigrant-receiving states such as California and Florida eventually attempted to file lawsuits against the federal government in an attempt to force it to provide additional funds to cover services to immigrants. In 1994, the desire to send a message to the federal government over this issue was also one of the principal reasons for California governor Wilson's support of Proposition 187.

U.S. News and World Report also emphasized that immigrants were no longer primarily from European countries. Europeans, according to the report, accounted for 60.9 percent of immigrants in 1959 but only 13.4 percent in 1979. Moreover, with U.S. fertility relatively low, immigrants, the report states, accounted for up to 50 percent of the annual national population growth (50). These reported trends (50 percent was actually a high estimate—see chapter 1) underscored the issue of how immigration was changing the nation's population. As *U.S. News and World Report* noted, "The changing ethnic character of America is one more cause for worry—an especially troubling one given the issue's obvious racial overtones. Where most foreigners until 20 years ago were easily assimilated Europeans, 81 percent today are readily identifiable Latins or Asians" (50). Accompanying this issue were the related concerns over language and cultural separation that could possibly threaten the unity and political stability of the nation, according to Senator Alan Simpson (R-Wyoming), chairman of the Senate Subcommittee on Immigration. The fear was that the new immigrants would not assimilate into American society.

The report ends with the growing sentiment in the U.S. Congress to pass a law dealing with immigration. Two issues requiring attention, according to the report, were a limit on the total number of legal immigrants annually entering the United States and provisions to curtail illegal or unauthorized immigration. Such efforts in the United States, we are informed, would mirror restrictions on immigration in Britain, West Germany, Sweden, Switzerland, Italy, Japan, and Australia (49). The congressional sentiment identified by *U.S. News and World Report* would finally result in passage of the Immigration Reform and Control Act of

1986. The discourse of a growing public perception of immigration as a threat to the nation was summed up in a statement by then governor of Colorado Richard Lamm, himself the grandson of an immigrant: "Immigration is another of the ideas which served us well in times past, but which hurt us in the decade of the 1980s. It is out of control, and the effects penetrate every layer of society" (50). The image of the Statue of Liberty, stop sign in hand, captures these sentiments quite well.

Newsweek's 17 January 1983 cover was a drawing of the American flag made up of hundreds of human figures standing closely packed to form the red stripes and the blue field where the stars would normally be found. The caption read: "Portrait of America: The hidden revolution at home and on the job." The image represents the people who make up the nation (the flag). The focus of the feature article is the characteristics of the population as described by the 1980 decennial census of the United States. The title of the article alerts the reader to the central role played by immigration in constructing the emerging "portrait of America": "Lands of Our Fathers: New Americans are still pouring in by the millions, and the natives are migrating to the South and West."

The report focuses on the rapid growth of the Asian and Latino populations (22–23). Since the previous decade, Asian and Pacific Island populations grew by 127.6 percent, and Latino numbers increased by 61 percent, both largely because of immigration. The report also emphasizes that since the mid-1960s there were 46.4 percent fewer immigrants from Europe and there were 815.2 percent more Asian immigrants. Koreans, with a 412.8 percent growth, led Asian immigration, followed by Filipinos (up 125.8 percent) and Chinese (up 85.3 percent). Among Latinos, the Mexican-origin population almost doubled in size (up 92.8 percent), which was attributed to immigration and high fertility rates.

Two months later, *U.S. News and World Report* raised the alarm about Mexican immigration. Its cover proclaimed, "Invasion from Mexico: It just keeps growing" (see fig. 8.6). The image is of men carrying people across a river, which, given the caption, is the Rio Grande. More on this image is presented in chapter 8. Suffice it to say here that the discourse on Mexican immigration as presented on this cover again uses a metaphor of war, "invasion," as a way of alerting readers to a threat to the nation's security.

Data on the changing demographic characteristics of the American population, as noted above, raised concerns with how well immigrants and their respective ethnic groups would be integrated into American society. The next two magazine covers are examples of how those concerns become imaged in the visual discourse on immigration. The first cover appeared on *U.S. News and World Report* on 21 March 1983; it is an assemblage of signs in foreign languages and lettering. Across the cover is the caption "English (Sometimes) Spoken Here: Our big cities go ethnic" (see fig. 4.4). The change to the original signaled by the inserted "sometimes" tells us that change has taken place, that English is no longer spoken (only "sometimes") in many of our big cities. An American flag signifies that these signs, despite their languages, are in the United States. The image, with its foreignness on top of familiarity (after all, signs indicating a place of business are common in urban and suburban zones), speaks to changes wrought by immigration. In Benedict Anderson's (1983) terms, the cover challenges the reader to imagine the sum total of these images as representative of the American community. The cover's image suggests a community that is dis-integrated by linguistic separatism.

The accompanying article profiles demographic changes in America's cities by focusing on New York, Dallas, Detroit, and Los Angeles. Each of these urban centers has been "reshaped" by a new wave of immigrants. According to the report, results are: "Some good, some bad." The 6.2 percent of the nation that was foreign born at the time brings with them cultural and linguistic differences with both benefits and costs. Benefits arise because immigrants are often industrious and law-abiding and reinvigorate deteriorating urban centers. But these benefits can cause friction as some low-income natives resent the cost of educating immigrant children in bilingual classes, the success of immigrant entrepreneurs, and rising property values as Asian Americans invest their life savings in homes (50). The new demographic mix can be viewed as the proverbial glass of water, either half full or half empty. In Dallas, for example, African Americans, Anglos, Latinos, and Asians live side by side, a pattern that is described as "a multiethnic jumble" rather than as an example of the melting pot or even as a "rainbow" community.

In keeping with the message of the cover's image, ethnic immigrant communities are separated by their "foreignness." In New York, "a 20–minute subway ride can carry a visitor through a dozen places more foreign than American" (49). Because many Asian Americans (albeit from different countries of origin) live in Flushing, the subway line to Manhattan is "the Orient Express." Los Angeles is an "international city," where the Mexicans' low naturalization rate raises "resentful complaints that [they] do not want to become part of the American mainstream" (53). During the previous ten years, fifty thousand Vietnamese,

Cambodian, and Laotian refugees settled in Los Angeles, creating "entire communities of Southeast Asians who have preserved much of their culture" (53). America's urban centers are, it seems, a conglomeration of separate identities, static and unchanging, with no indication that immigrants might create new "American" ways of being as a result of their varied backgrounds, new experiences, and need to communicate to other members of the society. It also minimizes the power of the larger society and culture to penetrate the seemingly immutable cultures of the immigrants.

Time's 13 June 1983 issue appeared three months later and also used an assemblage motif to image the tensions emerging from immigration-caused demographic changes (see fig. 4.5). The image is of the block letters L and A set in a twisting mass of gray freeways. Palm trees, a few buildings suggesting a skyline, and the mountains surrounding the Los Angeles basin help situate the morass of freeways in the Los Angeles context. Within the block letters are brown faces that appear Asian and Latino. The focus of the image are the L and A letters and faces, with the text confirming what the image already suggests: "Los Angeles: America's uneasy new melting pot." Los Angeles, as the title of the accompanying article informs, is "The New Ellis Island." The metaphor of Ellis Island is used to bestow on Los Angeles the title of the most important port of entry for immigrants coming to the United States from all over the world, including French, British, Armenians, Lebanese, Iranians, Indians, and many others. The report uses various phrases throughout to give a sense that immigration is high. Such phrases include: "Los Angeles is being invaded" (18); "The statistical evidence of the immigrant tide is stark" (19); and "Even before the staggering influx of foreign settlers" (20). The report focuses on how immigration, particularly from Asia and Latin America, is resulting in dramatic changes in the ethnic composition of the city. Between 1960 and 1983, according to the report, Latinos went from one in nine Los Angeles County residents to nearly a third of all residents. Asians went from one in a hundred to one in ten. Immigration is transforming Los Angeles into a place where no single ethnic group maintains a demographic majority. "Today *everyone* in L.A. is a member of a minority group" (19).

Immigration has created diversity within diversity. Latinos in Los Angeles are no longer primarily Mexican. Salvadorans, Nicaraguans, Cubans, Puerto Ricans, Guatemalans, and others also make Los Angeles home. Mexicans, however, are distinctive in that the Southwest was once part of Mexico, and so Mexicans arrive "feeling as much like a migrant as an immigrant, not an illegal alien but a *reconquistador,*" or a re-conqueror (24). Older established Asian Americans, particularly Japanese and Chinese Americans, find themselves inundated by new waves of Chinese, Filipinos, Koreans, and Taiwanese. Even immigrants from various Middle Eastern countries, including Israel, add to Los Angeles's diversity. Immigrants bring with them linguistic diversity, which is perhaps best represented in the schools. The report notes that 117,000 of L.A.'s 550,000 schoolchildren speak one of 104 languages better than they do English (20). This diversity raises concerns about assimilation. The report suggests the possibility that the melting pot metaphor is giving way to other metaphors, such as a salad with separate components that add to the overall flavor, or a rainbow of separate colors making up the whole (although colors in real rainbows melt into each other, they do not have hard borders dividing them). Driving the search for new metaphors are the immigrants: "Many of the new arrivals cling to their ethnic identity, preserving their customs and language . . .Whole neighborhoods seem to rub up against each other without mixing" (20). However, the report also asserts that the children of immigrants are much quicker than their parents to "turn into Americans."

The tensions caused by immigration and Los Angeles's changing demographics, according to the report, are felt more by older, more established ethnic groups (Japanese and Chinese Americans, Mexicans) and African Americans, who in particular "feel besieged, resentful" (19). Interestingly, "Most white locals seem oblivious." Whites are said to live in suburbs and urban zones apart from the areas settled in by immigrants. Whites are connected to Los Angeles's polyglot communities only fleetingly as they race by on freeways. But interethnic "conflict and recrimination," "resentment," and "anger" is created as immigrants settle in and change existing ethnic neighborhoods. The cover's mix of smiling and anxious faces in an unsettled morass of freeways resonates well with the alarmist vision of immigration's effect on Los Angeles as presented in the article.

A related article, "Losing Control of the Borders," reports on undocumented immigration and the U.S. Congress's consideration of a bill to limit it. According to the report, undocumented immigration from Mexico and Central and South America "is turning into a flood" (26). This "new surge" in immigrants is particularly troublesome given that the U.S. unemployment rate was, at the time, the highest it had been at in four decades. Both the House and the Senate considered bills to make comprehensive changes to the nation's immigration laws. Called jointly the Simpson-Mazzoli bill after Republican senator Alan Simpson and Democratic representative Romano Mazzoli, who introduced the bill into their respective chambers of Congress, it would have established employer sanctions and an amnesty program for settled undocumented immigrants and authorized the development of a fraud-resistant worker certification system, but not a national identification card. Although the Simpson-Mazzoli bill did not make it through Congress then, the first two provisions were eventually part of the 1986 immigration law.

A month later, on 4 July 1983, *U.S. News and World Report* reaffirmed that America was "Still the Land of Opportunity," as the caption on its cover queried. This was a time of recession, with a jobless rate of 10.1 percent (15.6 percent for twenty- to twenty-four-year-olds and about 20 percent for African Americans). *U.S. News and World Report* observed that "The nation's economy appears to have grown a swelling underbelly of long-term if not permanently unemployable" (37). Part of what *U.S. News and World Report* was describing was the shift toward a "postindustrial society," as many blue-collar assembly jobs moved overseas or gave way to an information-age economy (see Harvey 1985). But amidst all of these dreary economic statistics, *U.S. News and World Report* notes, are immigrants who retain the view of America as the land of opportunity, as symbolized by the Statue of Liberty. The magazine highlights the life of an immigrant from India who worked as a busboy, obtained a degree in engineering, and managed to build a 1.5 billion-dollar computer-component business. His success was not without risks, but, as he said, "The great thing about America is that you can always do something for survival" (38). Also featured is a Cuban immigrant, part of the Mariel boatlift in 1980. He arrived in the United States with only the clothes he was wearing. He combined skills learned while working for years as a cook in a first-class resort hotel in Cuba with money he saved working in the United States and opened a tiny restaurant of his own. Although his profit margin was extremely small at that point, owning his own business was his definition of success. As he said, "In Cuba you don't ever, ever have a chance of realizing your dreams. In the United States, here everybody can dream those things. If they work hard enough, they can achieve it" (42). At a time of economic uncertainty, the stories of these two immigrants were meant to reaffirm America's self-image. Consequently, the article's message is more about America as a place where opportunities still exist and is less about immigrants and their impact on American society. The cover's image, a beautiful photograph of the U.S. flag waving in the breeze as rays of sunlight erupt from be-

5.3.   *U.S. News and World Report*, 4 July 1983. "Still the Land
of Opportunity?"

hind it and pierce a blue sky, evokes the same response: America continues to be a land of opportunity.

An accompanying article features an interview with John Higham, professor of history at Johns Hopkins University. A well-known historian
of immigration, Professor Higham describes the particular characteristics of immigrants that allow them to perceive opportunities in places
overlooked by natives: "This nation continues to be a place where all
kinds of entrepreneurial possibilities exist for people who see an angle.
And it is a fact that immigrants traditionally are very highly motivated.
They are displaced. They don't have an ongoing set of institutions that
they're working in, so they tend to have their eye out for something" (43).

What we have, then, is a July issue that uses immigrants to retell one of the United States' grandest national narratives, the ability of the disadvantaged to achieve success in America. As symbols of the American dream, immigrants affirm aspects of the national identity and character that Americans would like to believe continue to exist even during economically difficult times. The month of the nation's birthday is the appropriate time to use immigrants to signify these values and beliefs. In a way, they are an essential part of the story about America that is being told. And so the concerns related to immigration, much a part of the times, are left aside for this much needed (given the trying economic times) retelling of the American dream narrative.

The *Atlantic Monthly*'s November 1983 issue featured a cover with an illustration of the world anthropomorphized with a face, arms, and legs with men's pants and shoes (see fig. 4.2). He (the world) is standing on a porch facing the reader as he peers through the frame of a door. He carries suitcases and a rolled-up Mexican blanket, and an Asian reed hat sits at his feet. He is the visitor at the door, the world's immigrants coming to America. The text accompanying the image is "The New Immigrants: How they're affecting us," which is the title of the inside article by James Fallows. The article is an extensive report covering economic, language, and legal issues related to immigration, beginning with the major changes introduced by the 1965 immigration law, the increase in the total number of immigrants since then, and the changing composition of immigrants (i.e., fewer Europeans, more Asians and Latin Americans). At the same time, the world's population is growing, especially in Latin America, which will have difficulty providing enough jobs for all. The public's response is increasing concern about immigrants who compete with working-class Americans for low-wage jobs and whose linguistic and cultural differences may bring too many changes too fast to American culture and society.

Fallows presents both sides of the debate over immigration and finds that the concerns about immigration may be exaggerated. His reasons include the fact that past immigration was proportionately much larger than today's immigration, and the nation weathered it fairly well despite similar fears at the time. As a result of his research, Fallows came to share the view of many economists: "The ingenuity and perseverance that immigrants possess can make an economy richer, because immigrants will adapt and innovate and sacrifice in ways that nonimmigrants are too comfortable to try. They make the pie larger for everyone to share" (49). Immigrants, along these lines, share to some degree an "immigrant personality" that makes them generally more resourceful and determined than nonimmigrants (54). The immigrant's "grit and courage" give to a society productive energy (54).

The report also provides an extensive discussion of the proposed changes to the immigration law in the Simpson-Mazzoli bill. The underlying premise of the bill is that "legal immigration is good for the United States but illegal immigration is bad" (99). In addition to the employer sanctions, amnesty, and increased funding for the Border Patrol included in the Simpson-Mazzoli bill, Fallows suggests some other changes. Principally, he argues that skilled workers wishing to come to American are at a disadvantage because the 1965 immigration law gave a higher value to family reunification. Although he does not recommend scrapping this system entirely, he suggests keeping the preferences for immediate family members of citizens and legal immigrants. But he would reduce the emphasis on extended family members and find a way to give a preference to "the classic immigrant, the independent man or woman who sets out to make a new life" (106). Although Fallows's suggestions did not become part of the Simpson-Mazzoli bill or the final 1986 immigration law, a move to change the preference system was a part of the public debate over immigration during the 1990s.

Returning to the image on the cover of this issue of the *Atlantic,* the weary face of the world traveler waits patiently for some indication of acceptance or rejection. Although he stands at America's door, he has not been invited in. He is motionless, erect and unmoving, arms gripping his belongings in anticipation. The image reflects the unsettled nature of the public debate over immigration during the early 1980s, a debate that is still far from settled.

The three covers that appeared in 1984 all dealt with controlling immigration, particularly illegal immigration. *Time*'s 25 June 1984 cover stated, "Illegal Aliens: Trying to stem the tide" and featured the image of an immigration agent stopping traffic at a checkpoint. *Newsweek*'s 25 June 1984 cover carried the caption "Closing the Door? The angry debate over illegal immigration; crossing the Rio Grande" (fig. 4.1). The cover's image is a photograph of a man carrying an older woman in his arms as he crosses a river on foot. These two covers are discussed extensively in chapter 8. *Time*'s 2 July 1984 issue continued on the theme with the caption "Immigration: Can it be controlled?" in the upper right-hand corner of the cover. The image in the sidebar was a cartoon of a man holding up a stop sign. The figure of the man was labeled "Simpson-Mazzoli." The same man and his stop sign are in a cartoon accompanying the article, only this time the man is standing on the beach as a huge wave of people is about to crash on top of him.

Part of the reason for so much attention to undocumented immigration was that the House of Representatives was at the time debating the Mazzoli part of the Simpson-Mazzoli immigration bill. It was passed by the Senate in the last week of June 1984. The House's version of the Simpson-Mazzoli bill, however, still needed to have its differences with the Senate's version worked out, a process that proved unsuccessful during that session of Congress. The difficulties the bill ran into had to do with opposition to its two main provisions, employer sanctions and amnesty. Together, these two provisions would help regain, in President Reagan's words, "control of our own borders" (*Time* 2 July 1984, 12). According to *Time* 2 July 1984, employers were against the employer sanctions provision, arguing that it would turn them into agents of the INS, since they would become responsible for checking the papers of employees. Employers also feared that checking employees' papers would add time-consuming (and thus costly) paperwork. Advocates for Latino rights organizations feared that employers would discriminate against anyone who "looked foreign" (that is, Latinos) in order to play it safe with employer sanctions. Amnesty raised fears that somewhere around 6 million to perhaps even 12 million undocumented immigrants might qualify, raising the specter of a massive impact on social services for the newly legalized. Amnesty also appeared to some, such as the Federation for American Immigration Reform, as a reward for lawbreakers, which would only encourage more immigration. The House version of the bill also provided for "guestworkers" in agriculture, raising intense opposition from the United Farm Workers union, which called the provision the "rent-a-slave" program (13). The only provision that did not appear to create extensive controversy was more funding for the Border Patrol. *Time*'s image of the little man and his stop sign is meant to be critical of the bill's vagueness as to fiscal costs and its possible success at significantly reducing undocumented immigration.

Almost a year later, on 1 April 1985, the liberal *New Republic* entered the fray with a provocative cover (fig. 4.10). The image is an illustration of two massive doors or gates slightly open in the middle of the frame. Along the top of the doors are what appear to be large urban office buildings. At the bottom of the image is a mass of heads filling the space between the doors, ready to flow through the opening. Colored balloons float upward, which, when combined with the rosy sky and palm tree at the doors' opening, suggest a festive occasion. The text states: "Open the Floodgates? The only honest solution to the immigration mess." The word "floodgates" combined with the mass of heads conjures up an alarmist impression of uncontrolled immigration. The "immigration mess" in the caption adds to the alarmist message. But the "only honest solution" adds irony and thus complexity to the message.

The editors of the *New Republic* stake out a position diametrically opposed to those who would like to restrict immigration (7–8). They see the immigration debate as one over "who deserves the highest distinction in the world—to be an American, with all the rights of American citizenship." The editors side with advocates of an open door for immigrants escaping poverty and oppression. But at the same time they concede that employer sanctions may be necessary and that immigrants would have to commit to learning English, but that "common sense and practical wisdom" was all that was needed for this to occur. They argue that both history and contemporary experience show that "immigration pays off in greater economic and cultural vitality." They question the arguments about illegal immigrants raising overall lawlessness and compromising the nation's sovereignty. But undocumented immigration does raise fundamental problems: "The real problem with illegals is that they may become a permanent servant class, latter-day indentured servants whom we depend on for their labor, but who live as fearful, second-class citizens on the margins of our society. This may not be bad for the economy, but it corrodes the polity."

The accompanying article by Chuck Lane, "Open the Door: Why we should welcome immigration," lays out the magazine's pro-immigration position in greater detail. Lane concedes that there is some truth in the immigration restrictionists' position that America will change as a result of immigration. But he questions the doomsday predictions of such advocates (25). For example, Lane quotes Senator Lawton Chiles of Florida as saying, "I think we would not recognize the United States as we see the United States today within a period of ten years if we do not regain control of our borders." House Majority Leader Jim Wright worried about "a Balkanization of American society into little subcultures." Richard Lamm feared that immigration would result in "a vast cultural separatism" and that the children of Latino immigrants would grow up not as loyal Americans but might lead "secessionist" riots in the Southwest to "express their outrage at this country." To these fears, Lane responds that America has continually changed as a result of immigration. According to him, "The only truly national tradition that defines us as

Americans is our commitment to democratic individualism. . . . The arrival of immigrants can only awake in us a deeper appreciation of, and gratitude for, our Americanness. So why don't we let them in? It becomes us so much better than trying to keep them out" (25). In response to the question posed on the cover, the *New Republic* would open the floodgates to immigrants.

On 8 July 1985, *Time* brought out a special "Immigrants" issue for the nation's birthday (fig. 2.4). Almost the entire issue is devoted to immigration-related issues. The main purpose of the issue is to profile America's newest immigrants, who are, as the cover's caption states, contributing to "The Changing Face of America" (see also Berlant 1997, 191–200). The face metaphor for the changing demographic make-up of the nation is stated visually on the cover by an illustration of a mass of life-like faces, tightly clustered and staring quietly at something to the right of the image. The immigrants' faces are drawn to highlight their phenotypical differences from a stereotypical white, Euro-American face. Of the twenty-six faces on the cover, only one, a woman, is blond. The rest are dark haired with faces various shades of brown. Most look Asian or Latino, with a few African-origin faces scattered about.

Time's special July issue is a celebration of America as a nation of immigrants. It is a very different slant on immigration than *Time*'s earlier "Losing Florida" issue and the tension filled "LA" issue. The contributions of immigrants to making America unique are highlighted from the very beginning of the issue. In "A Letter from the Publisher," *Time* reveals that it has sixty foreign-born staff members who come from twenty-nine countries (3). As one of those staff members, an immigrant from Switzerland when he was six years old, is quoted, "This project has reminded me what makes America unique. No other country has the courage to let its demographic mix change so quickly, and to bet that doing so will continue to enrich it." Another staff member, German-born, comments: "There's nothing quite so invigorating, so refreshing as the mix of people and cultures that is America." Henry Grunwald, Time, Inc.'s editor-in-chief, came to America from Austria at the age of seventeen, and he commented that: "Throughout history, exile has been a calamity; America turned it into a triumph and placed its immigrants in the center of a national epic" (100). Immigrants, then, are symbols of America's identity and character and central to the story we tell about ourselves and our origins.

The profiles of immigrants found throughout the magazine stress their contributions to America and their resemblance to the qualities generally ascribed to immigrants in America's immigrant narrative. Many immigrants are profiled, from everyday working people to famous sports stars, architects, beauty queens, artists, business people, the super wealthy, and the highly educated (who represent a "brain drain" of talent, skills, and knowledge for the countries they left behind). The first article's title states, "Immigrants: Like those who came before them, the newest Americans bring a spirit and energy that preserves the nation's uniqueness." The image of an immigrant that is presented in this narrative is that of a person who is freed from the past and tradition, who is not chained to his or her family's position in society. The immigrant in America is free to *become* something and somebody. America benefits from this as immigrants build new lives with their energy, hope, fresh perspectives, and hard work:

> It was America, really, that got the prize: the enormous energy unleashed by the immigrant dislocations. Being utterly at risk, moving into a new and dangerous land, makes the immigrant alert and quick to learn. It livens reflexes, pumps adrenaline. The immigrant, uprooted, cannot take traditional sustenance form the permanence of home, of place, from an arrangement that existed before he existed and would persist after he died. Everyone is an immigrant in time, voyaging into the future. (25)

Time finds fears about immigrant assimilation unfounded, since it appears to be occurring successfully, especially among the children of immigrants. The metaphor of the melting pot that homogenizes immigrants is not necessarily the best thing for America. A much more pluralistic America has benefits. "Economically, there will be strains, but most evidence indicates that the immigrants create more wealth than they consume. Socially and culturally, the diversity can hardly help benefiting the U.S. by acting as an antidote to everything that is bland and homogenized. The sad fact, indeed, is that uniformity is exactly what the immigrants' children will probably strive for, and their grandchildren achieve" (33).

Articles focus on specific issues. Two groups that receive their own articles are Hispanics and Asians. Both groups are growing rapidly, primarily because of immigration. The article on Latinos stresses their diversity and their movement into regions of the country outside the Southwest. The article on Asians focuses on the skills some immigrants bring to America. The number of Asian immigrants, the report notes, is increasing, but many Asian immigrants do not fit the stereotype of the huddled masses. They are educated and middle class, ready and eager to prosper in America. For example, the report notes that nearly half of Indian immigrants have joined the ranks of managers and professionals,

nearly twice the rate for whites at the time (42). Asians are also represented far beyond their population share at every top-ranking university. Median household income for Asians in 1980 exceeded that of Americans in general and even that of whites. Despite such figures, not all Asian
immigrants do well. The report examines the diversity of backgrounds
among Asian Americans, focusing on Koreans, Chinese, Hmong, and Indians. Entrepreneurship among Asians, especially Koreans, is particularly
strong. But Asians often face resentment in communities in which they
settle, as natives wonder how Asian immigrants managed to open a business, dislike the competition posed by immigrant businesses, or are displaced from changing neighborhoods.

A feature on African Americans stresses the resentment and envy many
low-income African Americans feel toward immigrants. "Many believe
the newcomers' gains come at the expense of blacks and that a 'racist'
system benefits the immigrants" (56). And indeed, immigrants, over time,
often outpace the income of natives, especially native African Americans.
Complicating the picture, however, is the relative success of immigrants
from the Caribbean and Africa. Still unresolved is the place of class and
culture alongside race in determining success or failure in America.

Among the various stories featured in this issue of *Time* is a piece on
the U.S.-Mexico border that stresses cultural "symbiosis" among Mexicans and Americans. The result is that, in the border region, "The mix
of Mexican and American life creates a 'third country'" (54). The report emphasizes the odd juxtaposition of Third World poverty and First
World affluence that characterizes the border region. Out of these differences has come interdependence both economically and culturally.
This merging is given a positive spin in the report: "Increasingly dependent on one another, the 7 million residents on either side of the
boundary have created a cooperative culture that is neither American
nor Mexican. It is a hybrid that has latched on to the strengths of both
national heritages" (54). The author gives examples of how Americans
and Mexicans learn some of the each other's cultures. One Arizona busi-
nessman is quoted as saying, "My kids are not aware of prejudices here
in Nogales. We're probably more Mexicanized than the Mexicans are
Americanized" (54–55). Mexicans on the Mexican side of the border
face greater tensions with Mexico City than with Americans on the other
side of the border, according to the report. Mexicans in the border region, *norteños,* have traditionally seen themselves as distinctive—more
industrious and democratic—than Mexicans in Central Mexico (55).
San Diego is cited as an exception to the harmonious relations along

the border. According to the report, issues such as undocumented immigration and pollution strain relations between San Diego and Tijuana residents.

Female immigrants are featured in one article (82). The reason for the attention is the realization that women made up more than half of the United States' legal immigrants and nearly half of the undocumented immigrants. Long neglected in the academic literature, the presence of female immigrants shatters the long-held stereotype of the single male immigrant. According to the report, women migrate for the same reasons men do: to earn money and build a better life. But women also have some unique reasons, mainly having to do with escaping male-dominated environments. In addition, even in some of the most remote areas, subsistence farming has given way to low-wage jobs, even for young women. Multinational corporations have contributed greatly to this trend by preferring young women to men for work in assembly plants and garment factories. The *maquiladoras* (assembly and manufacturing plants owned by U.S. and other non-Mexican business interests) along the Mexican side of the border are examples of magnets for young women from throughout Mexico. After learning factory work in the maquiladoras, some of the women seek similar work in the United States. Once in the United States, immigrant women often face the burden of the "double day," responsibility for household tasks while also working outside the home. However, men and women often view staying in the United States and returning to their homeland differently. According to *Time,* immigrant men desire to return to their homeland because they had status simply because they are men. Women, on the other hand, often experience a change in their status and a sense of their own autonomy, and thus they desire to root themselves and their families in the United States. As a woman from Sri Lanka is quoted as a saying, "Oh, my God, I'm glad I'm in America! In Sri Lanka you are always subjugated to your husband's whims. I would never go back, not to the servants, not to the beauty. I really appreciate being in this country. It is really a privilege" (83).

Women immigrants, though in some ways having unique motivations for migrating and settling in the United States, are inscripted into the immigrant narrative. Just like male immigrants, female immigrants "yearn to breathe free." In America, they find themselves unshackled from the bonds of a previous status and are able to become something and somebody through their own efforts. The emancipation of self becomes central to their new identities—at least according to the narrative. The narrative, however, glosses over the difficulties of women in America's own cultural system of patriarchy, but such an exploration is not the intent of the narrative. The immigrant narrative is to remind Americans of some of the "essential" features of their national character and identity, as a place where individual freedom and responsibility are central to how we imagine ourselves. The immigrant narrative—in this case that of women—repeats the story of how strangers learn this crucial lesson for becoming American.

In sum, *Time*'s special July issue was an expansive treatment of immigrants in America. In keeping with the cultural tradition that July is the month to speak well of immigrants, and as a time to retell the immigrant narratives that are central to defining our national identity and character, this issue celebrated immigrants. It emphasized positive aspects of immigration for American society, culture, arts, entertainment, sports, education, and the economy.

The *New Republic* chose to focus on Asian Americans for its 15–22 July 1985 issue. The cover has a sidebar illustration of the head of the Statue of Liberty, her facial features changed to that of an Asian American woman (see fig. 4.8). The caption reads: "The Triumph of Asian-Americans: David A. Bell on our nation's biggest success story." Although the caption is affirmative, the image raises the specter of Asian Americans transforming America into their own image rather than assimilating the national culture. Ironically, this is exactly the imagery that Asian Americans dislike, a point that the inside article begins with in its discussion of the images of Asians in Los Angeles presented in the opening sequences of the film *Blade Runner*. The image, then, apart from the affirmative message of the text, evokes mixed messages, depending on the reader's attitude toward Asian Americans and on perceived changes to American society and culture.

Bell's article is an overview of the growing demographic presence of Asian Americans, primarily as a result of immigration. By 1980, Asian Americans grew to 4.1 million persons (or 1.8 percent of all Americans), a 125 percent change from the previous decade (24). With immigration has come increased diversity. Previously, Chinese Americans were mainly from one small area of mainland China and the other principal group of Asian Americans was of Japanese origin. Now, Chinese Americans trace their origins to many places in China and Taiwan, and there are large numbers of Filipinos, Koreans, Vietnamese, Hmong, and others. The article reviews the difficulties of some of these groups, particularly the rural Hmong, to adapt to American society. But overall, the article finds, Asian Americans are doing very well in terms of income, work, and education. The main problem is, perhaps, too much success. One of the biggest problems confronting Asian Americans at the time were the unofficial quotas on the number of Asian Americans allowed into some universities. Being a July issue, the success of Asian immigrants and Asian Americans in general is presented as a triumph for the American way:

> For Americans in general, however, the success of Asian-Americans poses no problems at all. On the contrary, their triumph has done nothing but enrich the United States. Asian-Americans improve every field they enter, for the simple reason that in a free society, a group succeeds by doing something better than it had been done before: Korean grocery stores provide fresher vegetables; Filipino doctors provide better rural health care; Asian science students raise the quality of science in the universities, and go on to provide better medicine, engineering, computer technology, and so on. And by a peculiarly American miracle, the Asian-Americans' success has not been balanced by anyone else's failure. Indeed, as successive waves of immigrants have shown, each new ethnic and racial group adds more to American society than it takes away. This Fourth of July, that is cause for hope and celebration.

In keeping with the July theme, Asian Americans are a symbol of America's ability to incorporate different immigrant and ethnic groups. The emphasis on their success, though not without problems for some Asian Americans and perhaps a source of concern to some non-Asian Americans, offers a chance to retell this grand, even "miraculous" American narrative. An ambivalence toward the Asian American "success story" is implicitly suggested by the cover's image of the Statue of Liberty. Her Asian features could be read as an exaltation of Asian American success or as a beacon of caution and concern. The *New Republic*'s provocative tampering with this symbol of the nation could simply be a way to lure potential readers who might find the changed features of the Statue of Liberty shocking and thus want to find out what it means, but such is the power of the Statue of Liberty icon that any change to her image raises a multitude of responses, especially when those changes evoke a history of often negative ethnic and racial relations and a current concern over demographic changes.

With August, we see a return to a more threatening view of immigration. *U.S. News and World Report*'s 19 August 1985 issue featured a cover with the caption: "The Disappearing Border: Will the Mexican migration create a new nation?" The image is an illustration of the letters "US" in white above "Mexico" in red, with the border between the letters gone and the red spilling into the white of the "US" (see fig. 8.7). Small male figures with Mexican hats and females with full skirts and braided hair are moving to the top (north) of the picture, into the "US" side (this image is discussed in greater detail in chapter 8). Suffice it to say here that the topic of the cover and inside articles is on the implications of increasing Mexican immigration. Mexicans are portrayed as the "new conquistadors in the American southwest. The heirs of Cortés and Coronado are rising again in the land their forebears took from the Indians and lost to the Americans" (30). As a result of the "invasion," Latinos are presented as changing the politics, language, and economy of the states that border Mexico. The events taking place on the U.S. side of the border appear more ominous than the "symbiosis" of cultures that characterized *Time*'s treatment of a similar issue just a month earlier.

FROM DISCOURSE TO PUBLIC POLICY

Since 1965, the public debate over immigration, as viewed through the window afforded by covers on national magazines, showed an evolution of interests and concerns. Early in this period, covers frequently affirmed immigrants as central to the nation's identity, as a "nation of immigrants." The story told about immigration was more often than not a story about America itself as a land of opportunity for the world's downtrodden or as a place of compassion for those seeking refuge. Interspersed among these affirmative images, however, are covers focusing less charitably on Mexican immigration and the beginnings of an interest in the nation's changing demographic characteristics. The frequency of magazine covers with images of the negative implications of immigration dramatically increased during the early 1980s. The national discourse that emerged underscored a series of concerns with immigration: changes to the demographic composition of America as Americans of European descent decreased in relative proportions; immigration's growing contribution to population growth; the impact of immigrants on fiscal resources (e.g., welfare); economic competition between immigrants and natives and citizens; the foreignness, separateness, and unwillingness of immigrants to assimilate into U.S. society; and the "reconquest" of the Southwest by Mexicans. America's compassion for the plight of refugees was also in question. However, even during the years of high-decibel rhetoric over immigration, we can still observe the tendency to also consider immigrants as symbols of America. The month of July, in particular, continued to serve as the culturally appropriate time to extol the virtues of immigrants. The magazines often took this opportunity to remind the nation of the values and benefits accrued to America because of its immigrant history and identity.

The post-1965 debate over immigration culminated in the 1986 Immigration Reform and Control Act, the purpose of which was to reduce undocumented immigration. The following chapter examines the magazines' discourse surrounding immigration reform and its aftermath. What can be observed here is that while it is difficult to measure the effect of public discourse on the formation of public policy, it is evident that alarmist covers increased in intensity in the years preceding passage of the 1986 immigration reform law. This crescendo of concern over immigration must have resonated loudly in the corridors of power in the nation's capital. Passage of IRCA was one way for policy makers to show the public they were listening. Whether IRCA would prove an effective deterrent to undocumented immigration would remain to be seen; at the very least, IRCA responded to public opinion at the time by "doing something" about immigration.

CHAPTER 6

Discourses on Immigration and the Nation, 1986–93

We increasingly face a racism which avoids being recognized
as such because it is able to line up "race" with nationhood,
patriotism and nationalism. A racism which has taken a
necessary distance from crude ideas of biological inferiority
and superiority now seeks to represent an imaginary definition of the nation as a unified cultural community.

Paul Gilroy, "The End of Anti-Racism"

Two magazine covers featuring the Statue of Liberty appeared in July of
1986, the only relevant covers to appear that year. This year marked the
one-hundredth birthday of the Statue of Liberty, and both magazines took
the opportunity to devote a great deal of space to celebrating America
as a nation that provides opportunities to immigrants. This is also the
summer (in August) that both houses of the U.S. Congress finally passed
immigration bills that would be signed into law and become known as
the Immigration Reform and Control Act (IRCA) of 1986.

Although often raising distress signals concerning immigration for
most of the early 1980s (see chapter 5), *U.S. News and World Report*'s
7 July 1986 was a beautiful and colorful painting of the Statue of Liberty's head. The caption reads: "Only in America." Inside is an essay by
William Broyles Jr., "Promise of America," which is a sympathetic rendering of America as an immigrant nation. As we might expect from a
July issue, retelling America's immigrant narrative is a reaffirmation of
America: "Violence, repression, persecution and poverty may encircle
their lives, but they dream of something better—of freedom. Almost five
hundred years old, the dream still works on the imagination like a magnet. The dream has a magic name: "America" (25). The article places
current immigration in a historical context, showing that immigration

today is proportionately less significant than in the past. Annual immigration was only about 0.2 percent of the total population at the time, compared to before 1924, when it was often more than 1 percent. The foreign-born percentage in 1980 was less than half of what it was in 1910. And in 1885, almost 70 percent of Boston's residents were foreign born, compared to almost a third of Los Angeles's population in 1980 (26). However, immigration is still an important factor in the nation, especially in New York, California, Florida, and Texas. Texas, in particular, "is being reclaimed by Mexico" as a result of immigration (27). But despite the fears, the report claims that the process of immigration and immigrant adaptation is about the same as in the past. As a result, Broyles concludes that "Despite the costs—and even the pain—that may be caused by immigration, the benefits are incalculable. Our neighborhoods, our schools, our workplaces are being renewed and invigorated. Each immigrant re-creates the American dream" (29).

A separate article reports on a *U.S. News and World Report*–CNN poll conducted that June (31).[1] Its findings are both at odds with Broyles's positive interpretation of immigration yet not as negative toward immigrants as might be expected. Fifty-one percent of respondents said legal immigration (then running at about 500,000 a year) should be decreased, 8 percent said it should be increased, and 35 percent thought that it was about right. Although a majority thought that immigration should be decreased, it was a very slim majority that could easily shift downward because of the survey's margin of error. Surprisingly, given the high level of anti-immigrant sentiment in the public debate during the proceeding few years, over 40 percent of the Americans surveyed thought that immigration levels were okay. *U.S. News and World Report* interpreted these findings as reflecting an "unease" over legal immigration, which it attributed to the national concern over "illegal aliens": "For years, the public has been barraged with reports of overrun borders, and Congress has grappled since 1982—so far unsuccessfully—with measures to halt the surge of illegal immigrants."

Interestingly, the same poll found that only a minority of respondents (28 percent) thought immigrants "take away good jobs" from Americans. Many more (42 percent) thought that immigrants "take only jobs Americans don't want anyway," and another 17 percent believed that immigrants "create new jobs." These are not the views that correlate well with the larger percentages of respondents who believed immigration should be decreased. Perhaps influencing such "close the border" views is that 44 percent of the respondents cited Europe "as the area of the world from which they would like to see the bulk of future immigrants come." Only a small percentage wanted future immigration to come from Latin America, Asia, and Africa.

The final article in the issue is about the members of the four-generation American family of a seventy-seven-year-old Italian immigrant woman. Her and her family's story represent the saga of immigrant integration into American society. For this woman, the Statue of Liberty on the cover symbolizes her life as an immigrant, and the country that offered her, her children, and her grandchildren opportunities.

Newsweek's July 1986 issue was given the distinction of "Collector's Edition." The image is a photograph of the Statue of Liberty cropped to show only the head and crown. Beginning with the exuberant heading, "Sweet Land of Liberty," to a listing of the article titles to be found inside, the cover text tells the reader that positive aspects of America and immigration are the focus of this issue. The titles listed on the cover are: "Home of the Brave: A hundred heroes for our time"; "Miss Liberty at 100: A birthday salute to a great lady"; "The Immigrant Adventure"; "Making It in a New World: The many faces of America"; and "The Torch Still Glows." There is no indication on this July cover of any preoccupation with immigration.

The Statue of Liberty's importance as a national symbol serves as the focus point for articles on patriotism and immigrant experiences. As the "Mother of Exiles," so named by Emma Lazarus's poem that was affixed to the statue in 1903, the Statue of Liberty has stood as an icon of the nation of immigrants. As the poem states:

> Give me your tired, your poor,
> Your huddled masses yearning to breathe free,
> The wretched refuse of your teeming shore.
> Send these, the homeless, tempest-tost to me,
> I lift my lamp beside the Golden Door!

The article, "The Immigrant Adventure" is a moving, personal tale by Edmund Morris, an immigrant from Kenya, and the official biographer of Ronald Reagan. Morris tries to explain the emotional appreciation of America held by immigrants seeking a different, and better, way of life. Morris finds examples of the immigrant narrative among Koreans, Vietnamese, Europeans, and others. In each case, they, the immigrants, give up a past life for the dream of America. "I think I speak for all pieces of wretched refuse when I say that we love the United States for its tolerance, its welcome even of misfits. Immigrants are by definition abnormal, and by nature we feel more normal here than anywhere else. America is a refuge from homogeneity, a haven for the eccentric. It encourages a profligate exchange of genes, the more different the better" (28).

An article features photographs and short quotations from European immigrants who sailed to American and passed through Ellis Island during the late 1800s and early 1900s. The title of the article defines them as "Miss Liberty's Children: Voices from the melting pot." The reference to the melting pot suggests that the immigrants profiled in image and voice eventually blended into the American society and culture.

"The New Faces" article focuses on seven recent immigrants, whose stories attest to the enduring power of the American dream and to the diversity of contemporary immigration. The immigrants include a Russian, a Tongan, a Cuban, a Cambodian, a black South African, a Yugoslavian, and an undocumented Mexican. Their lives, work, and aspirations for themselves and their children are variations on the immigrant narrative. Interestingly, even undocumented immigration is presented as having benefits for the economy and the social security system that receives windfall contributions from immigrants who will not collect benefits. By keeping the focus on individuals and families, *Newsweek* presents immigration in human terms that evoke sympathy for the immigrants and underscores the "Americanness" of their immigrant experiences.

IRCA AND ITS DISCONTENTS

IRCA (Immigration Reform and Control Act) emerged from a joint conference committee to work out differences between the House's and the Senate's versions in the fall of 1986 and was promptly signed into law by President Reagan on 4 November (U.S. House of Representatives 1986). IRCA established provisions that would (a) fine employers for hiring undocumented immigrants and possibly jail repeat offenders; (b) legalize some undocumented immigrants already living and working in the United States; (c) bolster the enforcement capabilities of the Border Patrol and Immigration and Naturalization Service; and (c) expand the temporary labor program for agricultural workers, if and when it was needed. Congress believed that the provisions to fine and possibly jail employers who hired undocumented workers (employer sanctions) would attack the problem of illegal immigration at its root cause: jobs. By making it illegal to hire undocumented workers, undocumented immigrants would go back to their country of origin and others would consider it futile to even consider migrating to the United States (Chavez, Flores, and Lopez-Garza 1990).

Perhaps because Congress and President Reagan finally took definitive action by making IRCA the law of the land, interest in immigration, at least as represented by publication of magazine covers on this theme, took a downturn. Only three immigration-related magazine covers appeared between 1987 and 1989. The one in 1987 focused on the new 1986 immigration law, and the two in 1989 both dealt with refugees. Moreover, the first two of these magazine covers, both on *Time*, devoted only a corner section to the topic rather than a full cover. The sudden lack of interest in immigration is noteworthy. After all, twenty-five covers appeared between 1980 and 1986. It is possible that interest waned because the new immigration law symbolically capped the debate by promising "to do something" about undocumented immigration and because the new law required time to implement its provisions. In addition, the severe economic recession of the early 1980s had given way to a moderate recovery.

Time's 4 May 1987 cover relegated the issue of the legalization program established under IRCA to sidebar treatment. In the upper right-hand corner was a partial photograph of Latino men sitting at a table in front of a woman who appears to be going over papers, pen in hand, mouth open, talking to the men. The image suggests something bureaucratic is taking place, a message confirmed by the caption: "Making the Illegals Legal." Inside is an article examining the legalization and employer sanctions provisions established under IRCA. The profound possibilities of the new law are summed up on the magazine's contents page: "A new immigration law could change the texture of American life" (3). IRCA was the culmination of five years of congressional effort to pass immigration reform, specifically to staunch the flow of undocumented immigration. The unauthorized flow of people across the borders raised issues of sovereignty and danger to the nation. As Representative Romano Mazzoli was quoted, "Any nation that doesn't have control over its borders is a nation whose central core might be threatened" (15).

IRCA was inaugurated on 5 May 1987, a date with a symbolic message for Latinos, especially of Mexican origin, who celebrate *Cinco de Mayo*. The article reports on the tremendous efforts involved as the Immigration and Naturalization Service geared up to implement the amnesty program and employer sanctions. About half of the 3 million to 5 million undocumented immigrants estimated to be in the country at the time

were expected to come forward. The law actually provided for two legalization programs. One for undocumented immigrants who arrived in
the United States before 1 January 1982, and another for seasonal farmworkers who had worked in U.S. agriculture for at least ninety days in
each of the past three years.[2] Not only would the legalization of possibly millions of undocumented immigrants likely lead to profound changes
in American life, according to the article, but employer sanctions also
promised major changes for most Americans. Now immigrants and citizens alike must show an employer documents (e.g., birth certificate, U.S.
passport) proving their eligibility to work in the United States. They must
then sign the I-9 verification form swearing to the authenticity of the documents. The employer, however, is not subject to penalties once the em-
ployee has signed the form, nor does the employer have to guarantee the
authenticity of the documents. A good faith effort when looking at the
documents is sufficient. IRCA did not authorize a counterfeit-proof national identification card.

The article also discussed the concerns of civil rights groups, particularly those representing Latinos, who feared that employer sanctions
would increase discrimination against Latinos and other "foreign-look-
ing" workers who would be singled out by employers fearing employer
sanctions. *Time* itself expressed reservations over the ability of IRCA to
actually control undocumented immigration. As the article noted: "U.S.
businesses may be so hooked on the supply of cheap foreign workers that
the new immigration controls are doomed to fail, no matter how tough
the penalties for violations" (17). *Time*'s observation was prescient in
that the inability of IRCA to significantly curtail undocumented immigration was one of the underlying factors in the rise in anti-immigrant
rhetoric of the early 1990s.

Time published the next cover on 3 July 1989. In the upper left-hand
corner of the cover was a photograph of an Asian woman holding a baby,
with the caption: "The Refugee Flood." The article concerned the increasing numbers of refugees worldwide: growing from 4.6 million to
almost 14.5 million over the past decade. At the same time, the world's
affluent countries were increasingly closing their doors to refugees. *Time*
attributed this to "compassion fatigue" in the face of the sheer numbers
of refugees seeking asylum. At issue was whether the refugees were escaping political repression or economic hardship. Refugees who failed
to pass the stringent test of political repression found themselves un-
welcomed and often returned to their countries of origin. The report
noted that for the United States, refugees from Southeast Asia, Haiti, and

Central America found asylum difficult to obtain. The look in the woman's eyes on the cover's image was meant to represent the refugee's appeal for compassion, an appeal that was increasingly ignored because of the large numbers ("the flood") of refugees involved.

U.S. News and World Report's 23 October 1989 cover was a full-page photograph of a white woman wearing a dark scarf on her head and holding a girl about ten years old in her arms. The woman stares at the camera/reader with a beseeching look in her eye while the little girl, her blond, disheveled hair about her head, stares upward. The caption reads, "The New Refugees: Should America take them in?" The article discusses the contradictions of a U.S. refugee policy that allows large numbers of eastern European (Russian, Polish, Ukrainian) refugees escaping communism while at the same time intercepting Haitians at sea and refusing to consider Salvadorans and Guatemalans to be anything but undocumented immigrants seeking economic advancement. U.S. News and World Report also notes that the United States and other Western countries are suffering from "compassion fatigue." In the United States, the federal government that year reduced by half its aid to state and local governments for refugee support (37).

The "new refugees" referred to on the cover, and represented by the woman and her daughter, are white Europeans, who stand in marked contrast to the Asian and Cuban refugees that have hitherto made up most of the refugee flow. The question, "Should America take them in?" is not really a question because, as the article indicates, Russians, Poles, Ukrainians, and others escaping communism at the time were receiving large numbers of refugee visas to the United States. At the same time, U.S. News and World Report is critical of U.S. refugee policy because it does not allow more refugees into the country. An article by James Fallows, "America Helps Itself By Helping Others," continues this argument. It asserts that America should take in even more refugees. "Our view of refugees shouldn't turn solely on calculations of self-interest. We are supposed to stand for human liberty, and we must sometimes defend our principles at cost to ourselves. But we should be glad for any chance to defend our ideals and our interests at the same time. Welcoming more of today's refugees lets us do both" (47).

MULTICULTURALISM AND RACE: THE EARLY 1990S

As the post-IRCA 1980s gave way to the 1990s, immigration reignited as an issue of public debate. Two factors contributed to this resurgence

6.1.   *U.S. News and World Report,* 23 October 1989. "The New Refugees."

of immigration as a hot-button political issue: concern about continued undocumented immigration and economic recession. The general conclusion among researchers is that employer sanctions have not been effective in controlling undocumented immigration (Bean, Edmonston, and Passel 1990). Employers and workers have managed to find ways—especially the use of fraudulent documents—to circumvent the law. With little disruption, other than increased paperwork, most businesses that used undocumented labor before IRCA continue to do so. Despite IRCA, it's "business as usual" (Chavez 1992, 19).[3]

In addition, beginning in 1990, the United States was gripped by a major economic recession that held the nation at bay for the next few years. California, where recession was exacerbated by withdrawal of federal funds for military bases and related programs, took longer to recover from the recession than the rest of the country, but by 1996 the state was also considered to be in full economic recovery. But the depth of the recession in the early 1990s, especially in California, fanned the flames of a growing public discontent with immigration, which was registered by the frequency of magazine covers devoted to the topic. In just three years, 1992 to 1994, eighteen covers appeared, accounting for the lion's share of the twenty-eight covers that appeared on the ten magazines in the sample between 1990 and 1999.

As the nation entered the 1990s, two issues—multiculturalism and race—dominated public discourse about the implications of immigration for the nation. *Time*'s 9 April 1990 cover seemed to correspond with a point made in the magazine in 1987, that the "New immigration law could change the texture of American life." The "texture of American life" that could be changed was the racial composition of American society, an issue confronted directly, yet metaphorically, by the image on *Time*'s 9 April 1990 cover, which featured an illustration of the American flag. The colors of the flag were not the traditional red, white, and blue. Black, brown, and yellow stripes almost completely filled the three previously white stripes, which still retain a small amount of white along the edges. The blue field, where white stars traditionally are found, had no white stars. In essence, the color white has been squeezed out of the stripes and obliterated from the field of stars. What has happened to the flag? The flag stands for the nation and the colors represent race in America's racial thinking. White, black, brown, and yellow represent white Americans, African Americans, Latinos, and Asian Americans, respectively. The image conveys the message that white Americans are becoming less demographically important as minorities increase demographically, a message reinforced by the text: "America's Changing Colors: What will the U.S. be like when whites are no longer the majority?"

What is particularly interesting is not just the image's suggestion that whites are on the verge of disappearing (there is very little white left in the flag) but the proportional weight given the colors. Black is allocated to the smallest stripe. Brown is the next largest stripe. Yellow is the largest, most dominating of the previously white stripes. This is interesting in that Asian Americans, though growing fast, are still a small proportion of the nation's population. Latinos, as a group, are the ones that will surpass African Americans as the nation's largest minority group. Why, then, is such prominence accorded Asian Americans in the new demographic makeup of the nation? Is the image suggesting that the

6.2. *Time,* 9 April 1990. "America's Changing Colors."

growth of the Asian American population is driving demographic change? While it is contributing to it, it is hardly the driving force. What we are left to conclude from the cover's imagery is that Asian Americans have a power beyond their numbers and, therefore, they are the dominant threat to white Americans.

There are two articles related to the cover. The first, "Beyond the Melting Pot," discusses the demographic trends that will result in racial and ethnic groups outnumbering whites in the nation sometime in the twenty-first century. As *Time* put it, "The 'browning of America' will alter everything in society, from politics and education to industry, values and culture." This change represents a fundamental shift from a "traditional" or "real" America that is envisioned by some as a white, European-origin society. The "browning of America" poses opportunities and risks. The risks are a multiracial society that is harder to govern as Hispanics "maintain that the Spanish language is inseparable from their ethnic and cultural identity, and seek to remain bilingual, if not primarily Spanish-speaking, for life"; and as racial and ethnic conflict increases, particularly as African Americans "feel their needs are getting a lower priority" (28–30). Multiculturalism, in particular, poses a threat to those who believe that every society needs a universally accepted set of values (31).[4] But apart from multiculturalism, the article predicts that becoming a multiracial society will also cause serious adjustment among whites, who believe the nation reflects their own image.

> While know-nothingism is generally confined to the more dismal corners of the American psyche, it seems all too predictable that during the next decades many more mainstream white Americans will begin to speak openly about the nation they feel they are losing. There are not, after all, many non-white faces depicted in Norman Rockwell's paintings. White Americans are accustomed to thinking of themselves as the very picture of their nation. (31)

It is an interesting idea that a nation can be lost through demographic change. The association of race with nation has been around as long as nations themselves. Thus, it was common in the past to refer to the French race, the American race, and the Japanese race. Such phrasing is no longer in vogue. It appears, however, that in the minds of some there continues to exist a collapsing of culture, which as humans we construct, with differences inherent to what Americans call "races." According to this logic, differences in beliefs and behaviors attributed to races are not constructed; they come with the racial package of the person. Race, with the inherent beliefs attached to it, becomes equated with the nation. It is not, therefore, American culture, values, and ethics that define the nation, but the color of skin, the texture of hair, the shape of a face that characterizes the nation. What *Time* is pointing out is the belief that follows from such assumptions, that the nation can be lost should these physical traits change.

But what of American culture? The article notes that "The deeper significance of America becoming a majority nonwhite society is what it means to the national psyche, to individuals' sense of themselves and the nation—their idea of what it is to be American" (30). Is "being American" a fixed, immutable idea and therefore "lost" as well if it changes as a result of new influences, ideas, and behaviors? Or is American culture constantly reinventing itself by incorporating novelty, whether home grown or brought by immigrants? The article suggests that while history may hold lessons indicating that America manages to sustain itself through change, only the future will tell if these lessons still hold true.

The second article in this issue focuses on Asian Americans. The title, "Strangers in Paradise," is meant to distinguish Asian immigration from the more dominant European immigration into the Pacific Coast region. Although Asians began immigrating into the region shortly after it came under U.S. control, recent immigration has increased their numbers dramatically and led to a diverse Asian American population. The article examines this diversity. Although Asian Americans in general have been relatively successful economically and educationally, some groups, especially the Cambodians, and some individuals in all the groups have not been able to "make it." In addition, Asian Americans continue to face discrimination, racism, and ethnic jealousies.

The article emphasizes the transnational connections of recent Asian immigrants that bind them culturally and financially to Asia. Because of these connections and the diversity among Asian Americans, *Time* notes that they have brought profound changes to the region. "The Pacific coastland is a twentieth-century Asia Minor, a continent in miniature, with a diversity of mores and languages not matched anywhere else" (33). Moreover, *Time* argues that Asian American influence offers a "case study" of the changes that the nation will experience as a result of demographic changes. "As Asians bring vitality and a renewed sense of purpose to the region, is history repeating itself with a twist? Just as Europeans took the region from Native Americans, is the West being won all over again by Korean entrepreneurs, Japanese financiers, Indian doctors, Filipino nurses, Vietnamese restaurateurs and Chinese engineers?" (32).

The "strangers in paradise" are characterized here in military terms, as engaged in a struggle over territory. Asian Americans are characterized as seeking to "win" the sovereign territory of those who "took" it from Native Americans. The article places Asian Americans in the same category as Mexicans, who have also been characterized as engaged in a "reconquest" of this same territory. The image on the cover is a not-so-subtle message that this conquest is taking place. The demographic erasure of whites suggested by the colors in the image, therefore, is not the entire message. The flag as a symbol of the nation's territory that is being "won" is also part of the message. Race and nation, race and sovereignty over land become intertwined in the image and the accompanying article. In this equation, perhaps the greater threat is that posed not by demographic strength, but by economic strength. At least, that would help to explain the yellow stripe's dominance in the cover's image of the American flag. By emphasizing the yellow, or Asian threat, over the other colors, the image subtly evokes the "yellow peril" metaphor central to the anti-Asian narrative of a not-too-distant past.

Racial discord was also the topic of the *New Republic*'s 10 June 1991 issue. The cover is an illustration of two young men, one African American and one Latino, standing with their backs to each other, arms folded across their chest. Their folded arms and serious facial expressions suggest that they are not engaged in a dialogue. They stand in front of a wall that is deteriorating so that the underlying bricks show through in two places, suggesting that these two men are in a low-income area. The text underscores the gulf between the two: "Racial Rifts: Hispanics, blacks, and the Washington riot."

The ostensible reason for the cover and the article was the riot that occurred on 5 May of that year in Washington, D.C., after a rookie female African American police officer shot a Salvadoran immigrant who had been drinking in a neighborhood park. Drunk, the Salvadoran had brandished a knife at the officer. Believing that her life was in danger, she fired, wounding him fatally. The officer was acquitted and tensions arose between Latinos, particularly recent immigrants, and African Americans. As African Americans find their communities changing as immigrants move in, a number of issues arise. Some of the problems are traditional tensions that surface between natives and immigrants. Latinos pressure for more political representation, social services, and government jobs in the largely African American city. An African American member of Washington, D.C.'s City Council was quoted as saying of Latinos: "If they don't appreciate our country, [they should] get out" (16). According to the article, large numbers of African Americans view Latinos as competitors for jobs and public assistance. The presence of stores owned by Asian immigrants in African American communities was also a source of tension. The fault lines between African Americans and immigrant Latinos and others were exacerbated by the economic recession that gripped the country in the early 1990s. The *New Republic* noted that "With urban economies in decline and immigrant levels at historic highs, some even saw the D.C. riots as a harbinger of future intra-minority battles over urban turf" (16). Thus the *New Republic* anticipated the Los Angeles riots of 1992, which followed the acquittal of the two white officers for the beating of a black suspect but in many ways reflected tensions between African Americans and Latino immigrants and Korean immigrant entrepreneurs.

The rift between immigrants and African Americans has surfaced in the magazines before (see chapter 5). The difference here is that the cover

6.3.   The *New Republic*, 10 June 1991. "Racial Rifts."

treatment shines the spotlight on the issue. Latin American immigrants
are characterized as detrimental to African Americans in the workplace
and dilute reforms aimed at providing social justice to African Americans for past discrimination. "Will not solutions, whether social programs
or racial gerrymanders, necessarily be at the expense of black Americans,
whose claims antedate the arrival of the vast majority of Hispanics?"
(19). Missing from the discussion, however, is an evaluation of these assertions against empirical evidence derived from economic studies or political science and a balanced discussion of the pros and cons of immigration for African Americans. The impression we are left with is that
immigration has a totally negative effect on the African American community, and that this is the source of escalating tensions between the
groups.

The contrast between the multiculturalism supposedly pursued by to-day's immigrants and by yesterday's "melting pot" immigrants is the sub-ject of the *American Heritage* March 1992 issue. The cover has a pho-tograph taken of immigrants in the late 1800s or early 1900s. The immigrants, dressed in dark clothing, gaze at a figure of the Statue of Liberty with a statue of President Abraham Lincoln standing next to her. Behind the group of people is an American flag. A sign at the foot of the Statue of Liberty states, "The Wanderer Finds Liberty in America." This romantic vision of past (white European) immigrants longing to become Americans is contrasted with contemporary immigration by the text: "What Should We Teach Our Children about History? Arthur Schlesinger Jr. on the multiculturalism furor." Multiculturalism is not the message of the image. In fact, the "melting pot" image of the photograph is pre-sented as a binary opposite of multiculturalism. Schlesinger's message in the accompanying article elaborates on the historical significance of these two concepts for the future of the nation. The article is an interview with Schlesinger, focusing on the views he presented in his recently pub-lished book, *The Disuniting of America: Reflections on a Multicultural Society.*

Professor Schlesinger points out that America has always been a mul-tiethnic society. Since its inception, the nation has attempted to forge a national identity out of many ethnic strands, and thus the national motto *E pluribus unum* (making one out of many). Newcomers became Amer-icans but at the same time they changed American society and culture. "American culture was transformed by the immigrants while they adapted and adjusted to it" (49). He also notes that the "cult of ethnicity" started up after World War II mainly among whites whose origins were in east-ern and southern Europe, and who resented the Anglo-Saxon establish-ment (47). The civil rights movements of the 1960s and immigration since then have altered the ethnic landscape. In addition, the old "unmeltable" European ethnics overstated the durability of their distinctiveness, and multiculturalism is now mainly, according to Schlesinger, part of an African American and Latino political agenda.

A comparison between the early 1900s and today shows improvement in America's tolerance for social integration and difference. As Schlesinger notes: "In the past there was a high degree of ethnic diversity, but the nation was mostly white and mostly European. At the turn of the cen-tury the Indians were on reservations, the blacks were segregated, and the Asians kept to themselves. White Americans face a new situation to-day, with the new visibility of black Americans and the new influx of

Latinos and Asians" (46). Schlesinger also notes that while the immigrant generation retains much of its native culture, the children of immigrants continue to feel the immense attraction of American culture. Although these unifying forces still operate, Schlesinger is concerned about the power of multiculturalism to disunite the nation. "The radical multiculturalists make the preservation of alien cultures their objective. They think that the public school, which has been a great mechanism for the creation of a new American identity and nationality, should now devote itself to the reinforcement, celebration, and perpetuation of ancient ethnic identities" (52). In addition to the efforts of the "radical multiculturalists" on the ideological front are the immigrants who isolate themselves in ethnic neighborhoods, where their native cultures only slowly give way to becoming American. "But in the meantime these efforts to re-create separate ethnic and racial communities increase conflict, and now it's not just whites versus nonwhites. It's blacks versus Hispanics in Miami, Hispanics versus Cambodians in Long Beach, California, and so on. The reason we avoided much of this in the past is in large part that there was a massive shared commitment to the ideal of becoming American. I think that ideal remains essential in a multiethnic society like ours" (50).

Two related issues remain unresolved in Schlesinger's characterization of the recent immigrant experience. First, the "efforts to re-create separate ethnic and racial communities" leaves out the subject of the sentence. Who is conducting these efforts? Are immigrants actively recreating enclaves by isolating themselves? Or does residential segregation in America's urban and suburban areas result from availability, or lack thereof, of low-cost housing for immigrants and others earning relatively low incomes. In other words, do immigrant neighborhoods arise because of limited available housing? To what extent do immigrants and their children, over time and with increased incomes, move to better housing? The second unresolved issue concerns the "massive shared commitment to the ideal of becoming American." Imagining oneself as part of a community is often not enough. The larger society must also imagine members of ethnic, racial, or immigrant groups as part of the society (Chavez 1991). Schlesinger acknowledges this crucial point later in the interview. He notes that integration is a "two-way street." Society cannot simply expect immigrants to join. "The responsibility of assimilation rests at least as much on the smug majority as it does on the sullen minority. The majority has until very recently excluded and rejected racial minorities to a degree that makes any wish to assimilate irrelevant" (50).

The image of the immigrants on the cover, American flag in the background, the Statue of Liberty in the foreground, is even more subtle and meaningful after reflecting on Schlesinger's comments. At first reading, President Lincoln's presence seemed inconsequential to the melting pot narrative of the image. He is an important American icon, but not necessarily a symbol associated with immigrants or the "nation of immigrants" narrative. Indeed, this is the only cover on which he appears. But Lincoln's greatness comes in large part from his efforts to keep the nation from disuniting. If ever there was a greater challenge to the unity of the nation, it was the Civil War. Lincoln's presence, therefore, underscores the threat of multiculturalism and immigration to the unity of the nation. The suggestion of a nation under stress implied by Lincoln's presence adds weight and a sense of gravity to the image's use of the melting pot narrative as a historic lesson for contemporary society. By so doing, the image sends the same message as Schlesinger; that is, America must return to the historical commitment to making immigrants into Americans, and immigrants must express attitudes that welcome "becoming American."

The difficulties, caused by bureaucratic inefficiencies and negligence at the Immigration and Naturalization Service, of actually immigrating to the United States are the subject of the *New Republic*'s 13 April 1992 issue. The cover is an image of mostly men, all black, lined up to enter a makeshift office. Guards in military uniforms are also present. The infinityline of men forms an *S* across the page, and a line of coiled barbed wire parallels it. The text reads "The INS Mess," leading the reader to believe that the people in line are receiving some type of official processing in the office.

The article by Weston Dosova focuses on problems at the Immigration and Naturalization Service. Based on a 1990 report by the General Accounting Office and other information, the article details problems with redundant forms that immigrants must pay for in advance. It also notes the INS's focus on police work rather than processing immigration requests. Another major problem is the lack of consistency about rules, which vary by regional office and are sometimes capriciously applied by officers within the same office. The article suggests splitting the INS into two agencies: one concentrating on police activities and one for immigration and naturalization. It also recommends reducing the number of required forms and simplifying the nation's immigration laws.

The cover's image resonates with the article. The image suggests an interminable wait experienced by those in line. Not only is the line long,

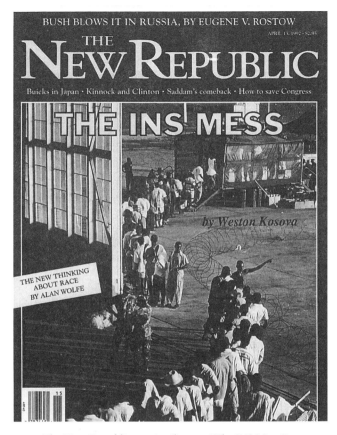

BUSH BLOWS IT IN RUSSIA, BY EUGENE V. ROSTOW

APRIL 13, 1992 · $2.95

THE
NEW REPUBLIC

Buicks in Japan · Kinnock and Clinton · Saddam's comeback · How to save Congress

THE INS MESS

by Weston Kosova

THE NEW THINKING
ABOUT RACE
BY ALAN WOLFE

6.4.   The *New Republic,* 13 April 1992. "The INS Mess."

extending off the page, but there is no exit line. Men enter the building but none are seen leaving it. In addition, race is a factor here as well, since all the people waiting to be processed by the INS are black. The cover underscores the issue of race by the way it includes a sidebar about another article inside the magazine. In a yellow box, reminiscent of yellow stick-on note sheets, is the text: "The New Thinking about Race by Alan Wolfe." Although the "note" refers to a separate article, it implies a connection with the black immigrants waiting in line. Is the INS mess related to the new thinking about race? Although not discussed in the article on the INS, the question lingers.

The following month, in May of 1992, the *Atlantic Monthly* published a cover with the text "The Border: In the tense, hybrid world along the U.S.-Mexico border, Mexico's problems are becoming America's prob-

6.5.   The *National Review*, 22 June 1992. "Tired? Poor?
Huddled? Tempest-Tossed? Try Australia."

lems." The image is discussed in detail in chapter 8. Suffice it to say here
that immigration is viewed as one of many problems flowing north across
the border.

The *National Review* entered the debate over immigration and the nation's changing racial composition on 22 June 1992. The cover featured
an illustration of the Statue of Liberty standing with a very serious expression on her face and her arm straight out with palm out in a halting
gesture. She has been transformed into a traffic cop, stopping the flow of
immigrant traffic into the nation. The text informs us that she is actually
redirecting the flow of immigrants to another country: "Tired? Poor?
Huddled? Tempest-Tossed? Try Australia."

The feature article, "Rethinking Immigration," begins with an image of an INS waiting room, which the author, Peter Brimelow, suggests would have become a tenth Circle of Hell had Dante ever visited one. In the article, Brimelow presents his views on immigration, which he later expanded upon in his controversial book, *Alien Nation: Common Sense about America's Immigration Disaster* (Brimelow 1995). Brimelow, an immigrant from Britain, favors restricting immigration from Third World countries. He also advocates developing a policy that would reverse demographic trends so that Americans of European racial/national backgrounds would equal pre-1965 proportions.[5]

There is much about immigration and today's immigrants that Brimelow does not like, but underlying all his reasons seems to be race. His view of race appears to include both biological differences and difficult-to-lose beliefs and behaviors. Early in his article he uses the New York subway as a metaphor for immigration. "Just as when you leave Park Avenue and descend into the subway, on entering the INS waiting rooms you find yourself in an underworld that is almost entirely colored" (30). Later, he returns to the subway metaphor for America's racial diversity when he compares his own views with those of the economist Julian Simon, who enjoyed the diversity of faces on the subway: "This is obviously somewhat different from my own reaction to the New York subway, although presumably we are both also studying those faces to see if their owners plan to mug us" (45).

Brimelow generously cites the Federation for American Immigration Reform as support for his own anxieties about immigration. He is concerned about the increasing numbers of immigrants, the declining birthrate of Anglo Americans that increases the proportional impact of immigration on the nation's population growth rate, the decline of "whites" in the population, from 88.6 percent in 1960 to 75.6 percent in 1990, and the possibility that minorities may become the majority (31–32). He blames the 1965 immigration act, which he claims "actively discriminated against Europeans," for these disastrous demographic trends. "A change in public policy opened the Third World floodgates after 1965. A further change in public policy could shut them. Public policy could even restore the status quo ante 1965, which would slowly shift the ethnic balance back" (32).

Brimelow holds in disdain America's self-image as a "nation of immigrants." He calls this refrain something that children are taught in schools nowadays, "a sort of multicultural Pledge of Allegiance" (33). That this key aspect of America's identity predates current debates over multiculturalism is immaterial. He seems to place little faith in America's ability to continue as a nation in the face of demographic change. There are two problems with multiculturalism for Brimelow. First, assimilation is unilinear in that all immigrants should lose their old culture and acquire the dominant U.S. culture, which, his discussion suggests, is fixed and immutable to a large degree. Second, multiculturalism means fewer Americans of northwestern European descent, especially British. More immigrants from northwestern Europe would mean greater assimilation since they come genetically pre-programmed, as it were, to fully learn American culture.

Brimelow bases his argument, in part, on the word "nation," which is derived from the Latin root *nascere,* to be born. He takes from this that the word *nation* "intrinsically implies a link by blood" (34). This biological linkage, which he interprets as a shared ethnic background, is crucial for Brimelow in order to avoid conflicts over language, ethnic strife, and dual loyalties, all of which could cause a nation to collapse like the "Tower of Babel" (34). Only by maintaining a majority of Americans who share "blood"—European Americans—will the nation survive. He does not even mention that an alternative interpretation of the Latin root, "to be born," is possible. The word *nation* could also intrinsically imply a link by *birth* on common soil, and the shared cultural understanding of the world derived from a common experience. In a geographically and demographically large and heterogeneous nation, such common experiences may vary greatly and yet exist in more generalizable terms at a broader level influenced by education, the media, and easy mobility.

Thus, Brimelow also disagrees with the argument that America is defined by its core values and beliefs, especially the fundamental spirit of individualized democracy, rather than by a particular race or ethnic group. Such a conceptualization of the nation raises the question, If America is an idea, why is it only people of white European descent who can hold that idea? For Brimelow, this position for a nation is not tenable. Promoting America as an "idea," as the idealization of democratic principles, is tantamount to urging Americans "to abandon the bonds of common ethnicity and instead to trust entirely to ideology to hold together the state (polity)" (35).[6] He goes on to argue against such a position through another metaphor: "This is an extraordinary experiment, like suddenly replacing all the blood in a patient's body" (35). For Brimelow, taking out the "blood" of America is taking out the European Americans and replacing them with nonwhite minorities. Will it still be America if the ideas, values, and ideologies remain but the "blood" is different? At the base is the primacy of race, not ideas or culture. White

Americans of European descent are the best bearers of the true American culture. This line of argument leads Brimelow to extol the virtue of the national-origins quotas and President Calvin Coolidge's remark that "America must be kept American," by which he meant, Brimelow suggests, of white European background (35).

Brimelow presents assimilation as a process of "swallowing and digesting" immigrant groups. It is a one-way process of change. Immigrants lose their cultural baggage and become Americans. "Slowly, over generations, America changed the Irish—and they changed themselves." That the Irish may also have changed America is not even discussed. American culture is fixed, and any change presents a danger to its perpetuation. The American nation (i.e., culture) is formed; it is not presented as being in a constant state of change as new peoples, new ideas, and new technologies for communication add to the mix. Quite to the contrary, the impression one derives from Brimelow is that American culture is essentially English culture formed on American soil, and any change to that essential state is a threat. But, one must ask, did the harsh Puritanism of the early colonists really persist unchanged from colonial times? Or is America a different, yet similar, place because of changes introduced by European and non-European immigrants?

Brimelow is particularly critical of conservative Americans who view immigration positively and who are afraid to acknowledge the link between race/ethnicity and immigration (38). Non-European immigrants (the ethnicity and race factor) are equated with underdeveloped countries. Particularly telling is Brimelow's response to Paul Gigot's comment in the *Wall Street Journal,* in which he expressed his distaste for Patrick Buchanan's comment during the 1992 presidential campaign about whether a million Englishmen or a million Zulus would assimilate more easily into Virginia.[7] Gigot's comment was that "The Zulus . . . would probably work harder than the English," about which Brimelow said,

> The comment reveals an utter innocence about the reality of ethnic and cultural differences, let alone about little things like tradition and history—in short, the greater part of the conservative vision. Even in its own pureblind terms, it is totally false. All the empirical evidence is that immigrants from developed countries assimilate better than those from underdeveloped countries. It is developed countries that teach the skills required for success in the United States. (3)

By focusing on the Zulus, Brimelow is able to ignore the experiences of many of America's immigrants who originally came from underdeveloped nations and who have been successful, and whose children and grandchildren have been successful. What did these immigrants have in addition to "the skills that were lacking for success"? What opportunities did America offer for success that were not available in their birth country? What about the tradition and history that America imparts, especially to the children of immigrants? Once again, the image of culture, the immigrants' culture, that Brimelow imparts is one that is fixed and immutable, leaving little room for change. As Brimelow tells us, agreeing with Thomas Sowell, certain groups have cultural values toward education and work that are "intrinsically related" to economic success. "Germans, Japanese, and Jews are successful wherever they are in the world" (42). Then, following on the work of the economist George Borjas, Brimelow argues that national origin is a good proxy for culture and an excellent predictor of economic failure or the propensity to go on welfare. These cultural traits persist, according to Brimelow, for generations. The cultural traits related to crime also persist among ethnic groups. "That certain ethnic cultures are more crime-prone than others, however, must be considered a possibility" (42). The connection between race and beliefs and behaviors is suggested when Brimelow discusses the claim that West Indians are different because they have been more economically successful than American blacks. He dismisses any positive aspects of the West Indians' economic success by stating that "it must be said that nowadays part of their enterprise goes into drug 'posses' and car-theft rings" (44). Brimelow could have taken this opportunity to suggest that perhaps West Indians bring with them a strong work ethic or some set of values that are seemingly common to immigrants that helps them to rise above the race issue in America. Instead, Brimelow tarnishes all West Indians by implying that their success in America is due to inalienable cultural traits making them prone to crime.

Brimelow argues that Republicans should basically write off all minorities and persist as the party of the American majority. In a rather revealing section, he dismisses the "visible minorities" (the post-1965 immigrants) as not really Republican material. "It may reflect the more divergent [nonwhite] minorities' different values, and their more radical feeling of alienation from white American society" (42). Even Cuban Americans and Asian Americans are suspect as to whether they will really become true Republicans, and so even they may not be "good for" Republicans. Why? The logic here is somewhat hard to follow but goes something like this: because some Cuban-Americans vote Democratic, and Hawaii, which has lots of Asian Americans, is a Democratic stronghold, there may be something intrinsic (genetic?) about these groups that may lead them to turn Democratic, even if they are Republicans now.

Among the problems facing America's assimilation of immigrants are multiculturalism and affirmative action. Brimelow finds that Hispanics are particularly troublesome, going so far as to claim they are "symptomatic of the American Anti-Idea," which is neither defined nor clarified. But Brimelow leaves no doubt what he means:

> Symptomatic of the American Anti-Idea is the emergence of a strange anti-nation inside the U.S.—the so-called "Hispanics." The various groups of Spanish-speaking immigrants are now much less encouraged to assimilate to American culture. Instead, as a result of ethnic lobbying in Washington, they are treated by U.S. government agencies as a homogenous "protected class," even though many of them have little in common with one another . . . In effect, Spanish-speakers are still being encouraged to assimilate. But not to America. (45)

The "anti-nation" Brimelow refers to is not located geographically, nor are its contours figured in any descriptive sense. But that it is out there somewhere is clear, at least in Brimelow's mind. How these characterizations of Latinos squares with the data on the use of the English language among immigrants and their children and the climb into the middle class by U.S.-born, English-speaking Latinos presented in chapter 1 is not at all clear. But from this basis, Brimelow moves to deplore bilingualism, multiculturalism, multilingual ballots, citizenship for children of illegal immigrants, the abandonment of English as a prerequisite for citizenship, the erosion of citizenship as the sole qualification for voting, welfare and education for illegal immigrants and their children, and congressional and state legislative apportionment based on populations that include illegal immigrants (45).

Brimelow ends with a call to stop immigration to the United States. "It may be time to close the second period of American history with the announcement that the U.S. is no longer an 'immigrant country'" (46). He adds a final postscript to his article concerning the riots that erupted in Los Angeles in April of 1992 following the acquittal of white police officers accused of beating a black suspect. The postscript notes that nearly a third of the first six thousand riot suspects arrested during the riot were "illegal aliens." Although no comment was included in the postscript, it serves as a symbolic exclamation point to Brimelow's concerns regarding immigration.

The cover's image captures quite well Brimelow's anti-immigrant message. The Statue of Liberty standing against the flow of immigrants states

emphatically Brimelow's suggestion that America cease to be an immigrant country. The words, however, are ironic and humorous. Can America now erase from American consciousness the Statue of Liberty's association with immigrants? Even though Lazarus's poem was added later
to the statue, it resonated well with her original meaning, as "Liberty
Lighting the World," and she is now universally known as "The Mother
of Immigrants." The humor of the cover arises from adding the question
marks to what has been taken for granted, that she would welcome the
tired, poor, huddled masses. "Try Australia" capitalizes further on the
irony-induced humor. Perhaps at the very basis of the humor lies the
uniquely American view of immigration as part of the nation's identity
and yet something to fear. Even though trying to sound tough on immigration (the "halting" gesture of the statue), the humor softens the message and undercuts its intentions. The humor makes one think, is stopping immigration really possible? Even desirable? Or is it the bluster of
political rhetoric? The ambiguity of the message may ultimately reflect
America's ambiguous relationship to the topic.

THE ECONOMIC CONTRIBUTIONS OF IMMIGRANTS

A month later, on 13 July 1992, *Business Week*'s cover used an affirmative image to convey its message about immigration. Although it stands
out among the other mostly alarmist images during this period, it underscores the contradictory views colliding in America's discourse on immigration. Indeed, the message of this cover is the exact opposite of *Business Week*'s own message twelve years earlier, in June of 1980, that the
nation was being torn apart by immigration (chapter 5). However, it is
important to note that *Business Week* chose July, the nation's birthday
month, to make its statement: "The Immigrants: How they're helping
the U.S. economy" (see fig 4.7). The image is an illustration of the Statue
of Liberty rendered in multicolored clothes and flamboyant jewelry. Her
new appearance combines a mixture of influences, which, because she
symbolizes the nation and its people, represents a multicultural America. The pink (white-flesh colored) nose sits amid the other colors symbolizing that whites are only one among many influences (groups) in the
nation.

In contrast to Brimelow's sentiments, *Business Week* extols the symbolism of the Statue of Liberty for what it says about America's vision
of itself: "We were, and still are, a nation of immigrants" (114). *Business Week* acknowledges the American public's concerns over immigra-

tion during a period of economic recession, high unemployment, and strained social services. In a *Business Week*/Harris poll reported on this issue, 68 percent of all respondents said that today's immigration is bad for the country. However, *Business Week* examines recent census data and research findings and concludes that immigrants have both costs and benefits: "But on balance, the economic benefits of being an open-door society far outweigh the costs" (114). The magazine offers this positive assessment of immigration despite the large proportion of immigrants from Asia and Latin America.

Business Week provides information on the current immigrants' education, taxes, use of social services, entrepreneurial activity, and contribution to urban renewal. In terms of education, recent (in the United States, five years or less) immigrants (26.6 percent) are slightly more likely to be college educated than natives (25.1 percent). At the same time, recent immigrants (66.9 percent) are less likely to be high school graduates than natives (86.8 percent). *Business Week* attributes this to the demands of the U.S. labor market, in which highly educated immigrants are sought after in high-tech industries such as computers and biotechnology, while unskilled, less-educated immigrants find their way into service jobs such as hotels, restaurants, and household services. In both cases, the magazine finds that immigrants are making a major contribution to the economy. At the highly educated end, immigrants help to make our industries competitive, and they use their links to their old countries to boost U.S. exports. Less-educated immigrants contribute as workers, consumers, business owners, and taxpayers. "Some 11 million immigrants are working, and they earn at least $240 billion a year, paying more than $90 billion in taxes. That's a lot more than the estimated $5 billion immigrants receive in welfare" (114).

Business Week finds that immigrants do not use welfare in significant proportions. Undocumented immigrants are not eligible for welfare, and "even many legal immigrants shun it, fearing that it will make it harder to become a citizen in the future" (120). Citing George Borjas (the same scholar cited by Brimelow above), *Business Week* points out that in 1980, only 8.8 percent of immigrant households received welfare compared to 7.9 percent of all U.S.-born Americans. In the 1980s in Los Angeles County, immigrants accounted for 16 percent of the people on Aid to Families with Dependent Children, yet immigrants accounted for more than 30 percent of the county's population (120).

Immigrant entrepreneurs start businesses and create jobs for immigrants and citizens alike. And not just Asians, but immigrants "from Poles

to Mexicans" develop businesses that contribute to the economy (117).
Business Week also credits immigrants with invigorating America's urban centers. They have kept urban populations steady or growing and
their businesses have revitalized decaying neighborhoods. They also provide the labor force for the many low-paid service jobs in America's cities
(118). The people hurt worst by immigrant labor are native-born high
school dropouts. But, according to *Business Week*, Americans who have
at least a high school education have not been negatively impacted by
immigration. A drop in their real wages during the 1980s can be attributed primarily to import competition and the rising skill requirements
of many jobs (118).

Business Week notes that the 1990 Immigration Act actually increased
legal immigration by 40 percent. The law doubled the slots available for
skilled workers. In addition it opened up immigration to citizens of countries with relatively few immigrants in recent years, such as Argentina
and Ireland. Although *Business Week* did not elaborate on this policy to
increase legal immigration, it occurred with little controversy.

Business Week also reported additional findings from the national
Business Week/Harris poll conducted for this issue. What is particularly
interesting about the poll are the differences between African Americans
and non-African Americans (119). In response to the question, "Right
now, do you think immigration is good or bad for this country?" 40 percent of African Americans said "good," compared to only 26 percent of
non-African Americans. African Americans were also more likely to believe that a lot of immigrants start new businesses, which helps the U.S.
economy grow (67 percent compared to 55 percent of non-African Americans), that immigrants bring needed skills (60% compared to 49%), and
that immigrants should receive bilingual education (77 percent compared
to 43 percent). They were also more likely, however, to believe that employers prefer to hire immigrants over African Americans (73 percent
compared to 49 percent). These findings counter the conventional wisdom that African Americans generally resented immigrants. However,
Business Week points out that in some urban areas there is tension between African American- and Korean-owned businesses. Immigrants,
Business Week concludes, are a net positive gain for America: "In today's white-hot international competition, the U.S. profits from the ideas
and innovations of immigrants. And by any economic calculus, their hard
work adds far more to the nation's wealth than the resources they drain.
It is still those 'huddled masses yearning to breathe free' who will keep
the American Dream burning bright for most of us."

Business Week's contribution to the national discourse on immigration focuses almost entirely on economic characteristics. And yet, the grand narrative of immigration fuels the arguments and descriptions of immigrant successes and contributions to America. The symbolism of the Statue of Liberty, both on the cover and in the article, refers us directly to the "nation of immigrants" narrative. Only this time the multicultural character of the immigrants is foremost in the image and in the information in the article. But by narrowly focusing on the economic aspects of immigration, *Business Week* avoids an in-depth discussion of the thornier issues of culture, race, and the nation that were central to Brimelow's article in the *National Review*. By simplifying the debate in this way, the article and the image send the same message: an increasingly multicultural Statue of Liberty/nation stands strong and eager to face the (economic) challenges of the future.

The *Atlantic*'s October 1992 cover revisits the theme of conflict between Latin American immigrants and African Africans. The cover's image juxtaposes two stylized heads, one black and one brown, with their faces posed inches apart, facing each other. The conflict suggested by the "in your face" stance of the heads is enhanced by the faces themselves. They are similarly drawn masks or cut-outs with large, rounded jaws and flattened noses, suggesting the broken noses of boxers. The text situates the conflict more specifically: "Blacks vs. Browns: Immigration and the new American dilemma."

Although the two faces are drawn as equals, of similar size, the text establishes the source of the conflict by linking "immigration" with the "new American dilemma." Even though many immigrants are black: Haitians, Jamaicans, Dominicans, Garifuna from Belize and Honduras, and Ethiopian and Nigerian refugees, these immigrants are not linked, at least in my reading, to the problem. The brown face—Mexicans and other Latin Americans—represents the immigrants linked to the "dilemma," and the black face represents African Americans or natives. The message of the image and text is that the dilemma, and the conflict, is between these two groups; that is, the problem for African American natives are Latino immigrants.[8]

The accompanying article by Jack Miles takes off from the postscript at the end of Brimelow's article in the *National Review*. The focus of the article is the civil unrest in Los Angeles that followed the culmination of the trial of the officers accused of beating a black suspect. Miles's main argument is that African Americans are the most oppressed group in Los Angeles, and that the L.A. riots symbolized the role of Latino immigrants

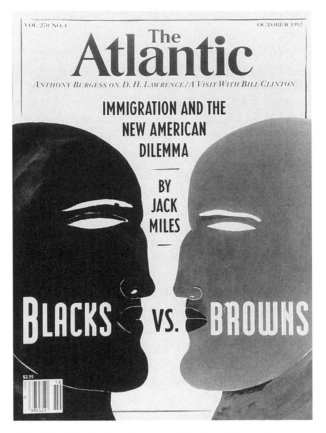

6.6.   The *Atlantic,* October 1992. "Blacks vs. Browns."

in fostering African Americans' depressed economic and social position.
Latin American immigrants compete with under-educated African Americans for low-wage jobs, depress wages for such jobs so that African
American youth are unwilling to take them, and are viewed as less threatening than African Americans by white employers and people generally.
As Miles put it: "The immigration story becomes the riot story by becoming a part of the labor story. And by an irony that I find particularly
cruel, unskilled Latino immigration may be doing to American blacks at
the end of the twentieth century what the European immigration that
brought my own ancestors here did to them at the end of the nineteenth"
(69–60).

For Miles, the situation for African Americans in Los Angeles would be much better if Latinos were not there. "If there were no Latinos—and no other immigrants—around to do all the work that is to be done in Los Angeles, would blacks not be hired to do it? I think they would be. Wages might have to be raised. Friction might be acute for a while. But in the end the work would go looking for available workers" (58). Lowering the number of immigrants coming into the nation is the solution to the problems facing African Americans. This solution, Miles believes, would place immigration policy on the side of natives rather than immigrants. As Miles sees it, "desperately poor, fifteenth-generation African-Americans might be within their rights to resent sudden, strong, officially tolerated competition from first generation Latin Americans and Asian-Americans" (51).

Although written persuasively, the article presents little historical or social science research to support its claims (the views of the Federation for American Immigration Reform are, however, prominently cited). A Los Angeles without Latinos may seem like wishful thinking on Miles's part, but ignores the history of the region. While Latinos have been present since the founding of the city, African Americans migrated to Los Angeles in large numbers after World War II. Even the Watts area included Mexican immigrants, who worked building the "blue line" of light rail trains that crossed the L.A. basin, among its original settlers in the early part of the twentieth century (Romo 1983). And the question of whether African Americans are hurt or helped by immigration is not so easily answered. A study by the Urban Institute found that African Americans did economically better in cities with immigrants than in cities without them (Muller and Espenshade 1985). As a consequence, Miles's article, though provocative, raises as many questions as it attempts to answer. Did not discrimination toward African Americans, both past and present, take place, and does it not continue to take place, in areas of the country without an appreciable Latino population? Are economic problems encountered by African Americans in Detroit or elsewhere really attributable to immigration rather than global competition? Or to decisions on where to invest capital? Or to the state of public schools in poor urban areas?

Perhaps because such questions are exceedingly difficult to answer, Miles seems willing to focus on Latino immigrants as the "bad guys" in the contemporary American story of race relations between whites and blacks. While this may make intuitive sense, especially in the midst of an economic recession and in the wake of a devastating riot, separating out the effect of recent immigration from a history of discrimination toward African Americans is difficult to do. The image on the cover thrusts these two antagonists together, as if they are the only combatants in the "new American dilemma." However, the faces are but masks, cutouts, and one has to wonder whose hands are also there, hidden, supporting the masks, bringing them together. Of course, this suggests that the new American dilemma is not new at all, only now it is much more complex than a black-white paradigm for understanding social differences.

THE DEBATE ON UNDOCUMENTED IMMIGRATION HEATS UP

The six magazine covers in 1992 were followed by six more in 1993, beginning with *Time*'s 1 February 1993 cover on the travails of Zoë Baird, President Clinton's nominee for attorney general. The image is a photographic portrait of Zoë Baird in a pose of thoughtful reflection. Only the left half of her face is visible on the cover. The text reads: "Clinton's First Blunder: How a popular outcry caught the Washington elite by surprise. Zoë Baird."

Baird's nomination for attorney general faced stiff opposition after she admitted to hiring undocumented Peruvians to work in her home as a nanny and a driver. The accompanying articles emphasized a number of contradictions in American life exemplified by the case. As a family with a net worth of more than $2 million, it was difficult for the public to understand her "cheating" the system by not paying Social Security and worker's compensation for domestic help. In addition, she was being nominated for the nation's top law-enforcement job and yet appeared to be willing to flout the law when it benefited her personally. Feminists found it ironic that the first woman nominated for the attorney general position was forced to resign over child-care problems. Finally, Baird's revelation came at a time of rising concern with immigration, especially undocumented immigration. But despite such concern, Baird's case underscored the dependence on immigrant labor in some sectors of the nation's economy, which lies at the root of the difficulties encountered in attempting to stop immigration, especially undocumented immigration.

The half-face of the cover's image reflects the nation's split personality toward immigration. Despite benefiting from immigration in many ways (as Baird illustrates), we are still concerned about the implications of immigration. On the cover is the nation's repentant face. Not shown is the face that welcomed the work and benefits of immigrant labor. One can ask, Does the somber image of Baird on *Time*'s cover represent the fallen hero in a morality play about the nation ultimately having to pay the price of benefiting from immigration while turning a deaf ear to the problems raised by immigration? Or, does she symbolize the sacrificial lamb to a system that decries the use of undocumented labor while failing to find the will to end a system of immoral benefits? Baird's image and story seem to evoke these grander, almost mythical connotations about the nation and immigration.

Undocumented immigration from China was the theme of *U.S. News and World Report*'s 21 June 1993 cover (see fig. 4.3). The image is a photograph of Asian men huddled together in a group. The headline reads: "The New Slave Trade: A shocking story of human smuggling/the growing backlash against immigrants." At the bottom of the image is the text: "Survivors of the Slave Ship *Golden Venture*, New York."

As the text suggests, the overall message concerns the illegal smuggling of Asians (in this case, Chinese) into the United States. Although the text suggests that the men in the photograph are victims, since they are the subject of "a shocking story of human smuggling" that can be equated with the dehumanization that occurs in a "slave trade," the consumer is also told of the growing backlash against immigrants. The message balances compassion with hardening attitudes against immigrants.

The articles follow the same pattern. The first article, "Coming to America," describes the hardships endured by Chinese from Fujian province in southern China who left home at tremendous cost to themselves and their families and placed their fate in the hands of organized smugglers they call "snake heads." The subheading for the article, "An endless tide of illegal aliens leaves many living as virtual slaves in the promised land," suggests that there are problems both because of "the endless tide" and the conditions under which the immigrants are forced to work to pay off their debt to the smugglers. The cost of traveling to the United States illegally is high, but more so given the relatively low wages of both urban and rural Chinese. For example, one man, a rice farmer, made a down payment of six thousand dollars to his smugglers, which is equal to 34.7 years of work based on his average yearly income of $173. He still owed the smugglers another fourteen thousand dollars, to be paid with his earnings in the United States. Even urban workers in Fujian province earn only an average of $367 a year. With the cost of passage running between fifteen thousand dollars and thirty-five thousand dollars, undocumented Chinese immigrants are forced to become indentured servants or worse for many years to pay off their debts.

Interestingly, the risk of deportation back to China was low, according to the article. Chinese were able to claim political asylum if they said they were escaping China's strict family-planning policies, the so-called one-child rule. At the time, four out of five of those claims were approved (29). As a result, some fifty thousand to eighty thousand Chinese were successfully smuggled into the United States each year. Despite the high costs and hard work experienced by undocumented Chinese immigrants, the possibility of eventual economic gain continues to act as a magnet.

Two other articles are less sympathetic to the plight of immigrants. An article entitled "Return to Sender—Please" reports on the ways "illegal aliens" take advantage of the nation's deportation system. The article focuses on crimes committed by aliens in the midst of deportation hearings, the lack of facilities to keep deportable immigrants locked up, the number of undocumented immigrants in jails, and the loopholes in the immigration laws that make it easy for illegal immigrants to stall their deportation. The image of immigrants ready and eager to take advantage of America is summed up in the article's last sentence: "But when immigration once again slips off the evening news, prospective immigrants will still be calling their relatives in America, finding new ways to beat the system" (32).

The final article focuses on the growing backlash against immigrants. Titled "Immigration Crackdown: Anxious Americans want new restrictions and tougher enforcement," the article notes that a recent Roper poll found that 54 percent of Americans said they think too many immigrants are allowed to enter the country (34). The report finds that the refugee and asylum systems need reworking and that the total number of refugees allowed into the United States should be lowered. The article claims that "many experts" want the Clinton administration to rescind the regulation that allows Chinese to claim asylum because of their objections to China's one-child policy. Undocumented immigration should also be brought under control, perhaps with tamper-proof worker ID cards (35).

The article notes the growing anti-immigrant sentiments in the country and cites the articles by Brimelow and Miles discussed above as evidence of this trend. It also notes that a report by the National Bureau of Economic Research found that native-born high school dropouts experienced a decline in relative earnings because of competition from low-skilled immigrants. However, the article balances this with the report's other finding, that the rest of Americans benefit by immigration. According to Richard Freeman, a Harvard economist and author of the report, "The net effect of immigration is still that it raises the GNP" (39).

The article also discusses the concern over the cost of immigration to local and state governments, particularly Los Angeles and California. Denying citizenship to children of illegal immigrants, as Simi Valley, California, Republican representative Elton Gallegly suggests, is one way to "reduce the incentive for illegals to cross the border" (39). The fear that more immigration will lead to balkanization of "the culture" is flamed, according to the article, by Hispanic students in California universities protesting for Chicano studies departments. The article ends by noting that a case for a generous immigration policy is compelling, but before the American people will believe that argument they must first perceive that America has control of immigration.

The articles, like the cover, contain information that elicits both sympathy for immigrants and concern about immigration. Compassion for the "shocking story" of hardships endured by immigrants wishing to come to America exists in a state of dynamic tension with the "backlash against immigrants" once they are here. This tension exists on the cover, in the articles, and, finally, in the nation.

DEATH OF THE NATION?

Two months later, on 9 August 1993, *Newsweek*'s cover was an alarmist image of immigration's impact on the nation. The Statue of Liberty is pictured drowning. She is barely visible above a flood of water. Only the top half of her head and her arm holding the torch remain above water. Dark-skinned people circle her in boats, unwilling to leave her alone in her torment. Her eyes are downcast, as if in shock and bewilderment, as she watches the coming peril but is powerless to act.

The meaning of the image is not difficult to read. The nation, in the guise of the Statue of Liberty, is in danger. The flood is a common metaphor for the flow of immigrants to the United States. And with floods comes danger as the raging waters overwhelm people, land, and nations. The people in the boats represent the immigrants themselves, who are characterized as relentless in their pursuit of America and who ultimately destroy that which they so eagerly seek. The image speaks clearly that the nation is at risk because of the uncontrolled movement of large numbers (floods) of immigrants. The text underscores the image's message: "Immigration Backlash: A Newsweek poll: 60% of Americans say immigration is 'bad for the country.'"

In the image, the Statue of Liberty, the nation, is on the verge of death by drowning. The cause of death is immigration. The image draws us to

6.7.   *Newsweek*, 9 August 1993. "Immigration Backlash."

conclude that changes wrought by immigration spell the death of the nation. The theory of culture embedded in this message is that culture is
static and nonresilient. There is nothing about change being transformative or of the ability of American culture to absorb that which is new
and then to turn the newness into something quintessentially American.
Many examples of this process exist in American history. American culture is neither static nor immutable; it has constantly recreated itself. And
yet, the message conveyed by this image is that of the impending death
of the American nation and culture because of immigration.

Other readings are possible, however. Emphasizing another of the set
of related meanings signified by the Statue of Liberty suggests that America is no longer willing to offer the opportunities and liberties that are

America's ("Lady Liberty's") promise to immigrants. Her inaction in response to the rising tide of immigrants, therefore, could also serve as a comment—perhaps even critique—on the anti-immigrant attitudes indicated by the public opinion poll. In this reading, the alarm that is being raised by the Statue of Liberty's predicament concerns America's unwillingness to act according to the principles inscribed on the Statue of Liberty—the nation of immigrants no longer opening her doors to immigrants or providing safe haven to refugees.

The main article accompanying the cover raises a fundamental question in its title: "America: Still a melting pot?" The public's answer to that question, as reflected in a *Newsweek* poll, was "No." Only 20 percent of respondents in the poll said that "the U.S. is still a melting pot," while 66 percent indicated that "immigrants today maintain their national identity more strongly" than in the past (19). *Newsweek* provides an overview of the public's fears and concerns over immigration. Those concerns include competition for jobs, the increasing numbers of immigrants coming to the United States, the predominance of Asians and Latin Americans in the immigrant flow, and the failure of IRCA to control undocumented immigration. Undocumented immigration, in particular, raises related issues of sovereignty and the image of "losing our borders." As President Bill Clinton is quoted as saying, "We must not—we will not—surrender our borders to those who wish to exploit our history of compassion and justice." A related article, titled "Why Our Borders Are out of Control," examines the need to once again reform the nation's immigration laws, focusing on such problems as visa abuse, fraudulent documents, lax deportation controls, and a lack of formal departure controls.

In contrast to public opinion, *Newsweek* concludes that America can absorb many people with different languages and cultures, but that it is not always an easy process. It generally takes two or three generations to assimilate immigrants and their offspring (22–23). As *Newsweek* observes, with a rousing rendition of the immigrant narrative, "Much as Americans tend to regard the new immigrants as poor, uneducated and less skilled, the vast majority are surely enterprising. What they seek is opportunity—the opportunity to hold two jobs that no Americans want, to buy a television set and a beat-up car, to start a family and invest in the next generation" (21).

Newsweek also touched on two topics that have since grown into major political issues. When discussing the economic cost of immigration, *Newsweek* noted that immigrants, according to traditional economic theory, increase the supply of goods and services through their labor and increase the demand for goods and services when they spend their money. But during a recession, the short-term costs may be higher; in the long term, immigration is still a plus for the economy (18). However, public opinion runs counter to this traditional theory. *Newsweek*'s poll finds that most Americans (59 percent) believe that "Many immigrants wind up on welfare and raise taxes for Americans" (23). *Newsweek* points out that in California, in 1990, 7.7 percent of native Californians received public assistance vs. 10.4 percent of "new" immigrants.[9] This is not much of a difference, given that new immigrants tend to work in low-paying jobs and are more likely to have young children than generally older and better off natives. *Newsweek,* however, interprets this difference in the use of social services as a problem because it reduces the benefit of immigration to the nation. In other words, by supporting low-income immigrants with social services, it reduces the general "profits" society reaps from immigrant labor. As *Newsweek* put it: "The rise of the U.S. welfare state has placed a cushion under the immigrant experience—and diminished the benefits of immigration to the country at large" (19). Eliminating immigrants' eligibility for welfare and other social services became a central issue of California's Proposition 187 campaign in 1994 and a key feature of the 1996 welfare law.

Another issue highlighted by *Newsweek* is benefits for minorities generally, especially affirmative action and minority-voting rights. These "benefits," according to *Newsweek,* undermine America's unique civic culture. Citing Lawrence Fuchs, acting chair of the U.S. Commission on Immigration Reform, a central belief in the Constitution and U.S. political tradition is the emphasis on individual rights rather than group rights. Affirmative action and minority-voting rights raise the specter of group rights, and as Fuchs states, "The whole concept of group rights is tribalism—the road to Bosnia, not East L.A." (23). Fuch's use of East L.A., a predominantly Latino community, underscores the implicit association of "tribalism" with Latinos. Not surprisingly, therefore, affirmative action has become a politically "hot" issue in California, where, in 1996, voters passed Proposition 209, which eliminates affirmative action in state schools and employment.

In sum, the alarmist image on the cover is challenged somewhat by the accompanying articles, which present a mixed review of immigration. There is cause for alarm, but there are also positive aspects of immigration that the public may overlook during periods of economic downturns. In the long run, *Newsweek* asserts, immigration is a benefit for the nation. The problem that surfaces from the articles is how to increase the benefit from immigrants while ensuring minimum change. The strategy for achieving that end is to reduce the cost of immigration by cutting social services provided to immigrant families, on the one hand, and eliminating affirmative action and voting-rights policies on the other hand. The image on the cover argues that immigration is bad for the nation. The accompanying articles clarify the remedy: a return to an earlier period in which immigrants received less governmental support (i.e., social services) and other benefits (i.e., affirmative action and voting rights).

ANTITHETICAL VIEWS OF IMMIGRATION

The *Progressive* also uses alarmist imagery on the cover of its October 1993 issue. A montage of photographs forms an image at the center of which is a person standing in the ocean up to his/her hips in water. The person is dressed in Asian looking clothing: high-waisted pants with a belt of the same material wrapped around the pants many times and tied on the hip, a black sweater or sweatshirt, a band across the shoulder and chest with U.S.A. printed on it, a binocular case strapped across the shoulder and hanging on a hip, a dark scarf wrapped around the head. The clothing and visible facial features suggest that the person is Asian. The person looks at the coast through binoculars as six small male figures carrying luggage on their head or shoulders wade ashore. Two World War II vintage airplanes fly over head, away from shore, as if they just discarded the men in the water. The war motif of the image is a play on, and critique of, the allusions to war and metaphors of war in the discourse on immigration at the time. The cover text affirms this reading: "The War on Aliens: The right calls the shots."

The accompanying article by Ruth Conniff examines the groups and individuals promoting restrictions on immigration. As the summary on the context page points out, "White supremacists, environmentalists, population-control groups, and disgruntled citizens have forged an alliance in the anti-immigration movement." The main point of the article is that once-marginal, right-wing views on immigration have suddenly become mainstream. It is part of the accepted wisdom of the times, according to the article, that "the United States is being 'invaded' by the Third World, that immigrants pose a threat to the American economy and way of life, and that the borders need military fortification" (22).

Conniff focuses on the many anti-immigration groups that have sprung up across the nation, most of which maintain a direct or indirect connection to the Federation for American Immigration Reform, or FAIR. John Tanton, an ophthalmologist from Michigan, who was once president of Zero Population Growth, founded FAIR in 1978. He is personally responsible for building a network of organizations promoting conservation, population control, restricting immigration, and making English the official language of the United States (22). Tanton was at the center of a controversy in 1988 when Linda Chavez, then-director of U.S. English, which Tanton helped found, quit over a memorandum he wrote on "the Latin onslaught." In the memo he asked: "Will Latin American immigrants bring with them the tradition of the *mordida* (bribe), the lack of involvement in public affairs, etc.? Will the present majority peaceably hand over its political power to a group that is simply more fertile? . . . On the demographic point: Perhaps this is the first instance in which those with their pants up are going to get caught by those with their pants down!" (24).

The article presents a number of examples of the war metaphors and allusions to war in the current discourse on immigration promoted by the groups under examination. A prevalent theme is ethnic warfare, a la Bosnia. As Robert Goldsborough, founder and president of Americans for Immigration Control in Virginia is quoted as saying, "The melting pot is melting down. The ethnic strife is tearing the country apart." Another leader, Bette Hammond of Stop the Out-of-control Problems of Immigration Today (STOP-IT), is quoted as saying, "We're against illegal aliens. They don't belong in our country. Just by being here they are criminals. We believe we're being invaded and we're out to stop it. . . . American citizens don't like some of the neighborhoods in Southern California being taken over by illegals. . . . I have to stop our members from taking up weapons. We're out to *stop* the bloodshed. But I'll tell you, I have a feeling the reason there haven't been any more riots in L.A. is because so many people lined up to buy guns. White American citizens got guns to fight back against the illegal aliens and the criminals" (26). A member of the Light Up the Border campaign in San Diego (a group of people who would drive to the border at night and shine their headlights across the border in a symbolic effort to dissuade illegal border crossings) is quoted as saying, "The inevitable result is its going to be a border war. We're very serious about our sovereignty here and our families. If our government don't do something, by God we will" (29).

The *Progressive,* a liberal magazine, finds these apocalyptic associations with immigration to be based more on fears than facts. The article asserts that immigrants have always been a part of the nation and their legacy has been positive, a position similar to that of the more conservative *Business Week* discussed above. Rather, it is the rhetoric of the anti-immigrant groups that may be contributing to the problem by laying the groundwork for a self-fulfilling prophecy. As Conniff concludes, "With its divisive rhetoric and undercurrent of racial hate, the anti-immigration movement promotes the very ethnic divisions its members warn about" (29). The article and the image on the cover combine to present a critique of anti-immigrant discourse. The cover's "war on aliens" inverts the metaphors of invasion by immigrants. By turning the discourse into a war on immigrants, the *Progressive* makes the immigrants the victims of the discourse. In this way, the image on the magazine's cover mocks the anti-immigrant discourse that the *Progressive* finds so pervasive in the nation at this time.

IMAGING ASSIMILATION

Time magazine's second cover with an immigration-related theme in 1993 was a special fall issue (fig. 4.6). The cover's text exclaimed: "Take a good look at this woman. She was created by a computer from a mix of several races [see also Berlant 1997, 208]. What you see is a remarkable preview of . . . The New Face of America: How immigrants are shaping the world's first multicultural society." The face referred to is that of a young woman with short brown hair and light brown eyes. The woman's face was created by a computer program that combined, or morphed, a number of faces into one consisting of 15 percent Anglo-Saxon, 17.5 percent Middle Eastern, 17.5 percent African, 7.5 percent Asian, 35 percent southern European, and 7.5 percent Latino. For *Time,* the face of the "New Eve" gracing its cover was a metaphor for a multicultural America and as such was meant to focus the reader's attention on the dramatic demographic changes that have occurred in America during the final decades of the twentieth century. "America's face is not just about physiognomy, or even color, although endless varieties of each can be seen throughout the land. It is about the very complexion of the country, the endless and fascinating profusion of peoples, cultures, languages and attitudes that make up the great national pool" (3).[10] Immigration has produced this new multicultural society of unparalleled diversity. *Time* celebrates America as a nation of immigrants in the exuberant terms and sympathetic profiles usually found in the July issues of magazines. As the editors tell us: "This issue of *Time* is devoted to American diversity, and thus by definition to the differences among Americans. Those differences gain their impact, however, from the bonds that unite them in one vast and variegated country. They are differences that should not divide or weaken America, but distinguish and strengthen it. They are the reason to keep the welcome mat, however worn and tattered at times, always ready at the door" (9).

Time begins with an overview of current immigration trends, public opinion toward immigration, and America's immigrant history. *Time* attributes the roots of the growing diversity in American life to a shift in national policy in the 1960s, particularly the 1965 immigration law, from one that favored European immigration to one that favored the rest of the world, particularly Asia and Latin America. The results of this shift became apparent only slowly, but are now fully recognizable. Demographic predictions are that descendants of white Europeans will slip into minority status sometime in the second half of the twenty-first century. These changing realities are forcing Americans to confront their implications. *Time* finds that liberals and conservatives differ in their views even within their own ranks. Some liberals argue for an open door, while others worry about the impact of immigration on labor and minorities. Some conservatives support immigration as a source of low-wage labor, while others worry about the "cultural transmogrification" of American society. Transmogrification means, according to Webster's 1997 College Dictionary, the changing in appearance or form, especially strangely or grotesquely. Among those with this concern, *Time* includes the influential group FAIR, whose executive director Daniel Stein worries that immigration will result in an irrevocable altering of the American character (12). Toni Morrison, an African American writer and a staunch defender of civil rights, argues that immigrants succeed in America by displacing African Americans, or, as she puts it, "On the backs of blacks," whose views on the issue are often overlooked (57).

Demographic trends have moved the general public toward a restrictionist stance on immigration, or, as *Time* stated, "the public mood over immigration is turning sour again" (10). Based on a *Time* public opinion poll, almost three-quarters (73 percent) of Americans favored strictly limiting immigration. Another 64 percent believed that most immigrants come to the United States illegally (when only about 24 percent did so in 1992). On the other hand, a majority of Americans polled believed recent immigrants were hardworking (67 percent), productive citizens (65 percent), and basically honest people (58 percent), but that they take jobs from Americans (64 percent) and add to the crime problem (59 percent). A majority (65 percent) of those polled favored spending more federal tax money to tighten security at the U.S.-Mexico border, but only 29 percent favored the building of a fence along the entire border. Americans were evenly split on the issue of providing government health benefits and public education to immigrants and their children (47 percent for stopping such aid, 48 percent for not stopping it). They also split on the issue of a constitutional amendment to prevent children born here from becoming U.S. citizens unless their parents were also U.S. citizens (49 percent favor such an amendment, 47 percent oppose it) (12). Even though *Time* may be correct that the public's mood is decidedly less welcoming toward immigrants, the public still retained some favorable attitudes toward immigrants and was not fully convinced that extreme measures against immigrants were warranted.

In its overview of the history of immigration, *Time* continues with its multiculturalism theme. *Time* points out that all Americans migrated from somewhere else originally and that America has always been multicultural or multiethnic. In 1789, one-fifth of the new nation's population was African American and thousands of Indians from various cultures were also present. Even those of European descent came from different cultural backgrounds. In 1643 in New Amsterdam (today New York), eighteen languages were spoken. It took quite a while for all of these multicultural influences to "melt" into a broader cultural pattern. In many cases, communities such as the Dutch and others held on to their own ways for quite some time (29).

Throughout America's history, the "face" of America has changed as a result of intermarriage, which occurred frequently among Americans of European descent. On the other hand, beliefs and laws against miscegenation made intermarriage among whites and nonwhites less frequent. However, there is less inhibition toward intermarriage in today's multicultural America. "Intermarriage, of course, is as old as the Bible. But during the past two decades, America has produced the greatest variety of hybrid households in the history of the world" (64). *Time* finds that this trend is increasing despite the rhetoric of cultural separatism and resurgent ethnic pride. In the previous two decades, the early 1970s to the early 1990s, interracial marriages in the United States rose from 310,000 to more than 1.1 million. The birth of mixed-race babies multiplied twenty-six times faster than that of any other group. As a consequence, *Time* argues that "Americans are being forced to rethink and redefine themselves" (64).

To a certain extent, the image of the New Eve on *Time*'s cover is an attempt to assist in this rethinking of the American face or society. But in doing so, *Time* returns to an older explanatory model. The image of the New Eve is really just a graphic way of restating the melting pot metaphor. In its own way, the New Eve says what J. Hector St. John Crèvecoeur wrote about America in 1782, in his famous *Letters from an American Farmer:* "Here individuals of all nations are melted into a new race of men, whose labors and posterity will one day cause great changes in the world" (30). Two hundred plus years later, *Time* uses computer technology to represent exactly what such a melting might look like.

The new face of America, the New Eve, is a pleasing one, and in this sense *Time* is making an ideological statement. America's future, the image tells us, is not the transmogrification that some fear. The New Eve is not strange or grotesque in appearance. Rather, she is a quite appealing symbol of the new American society. But the New Eve image succeeds in this representation of the nation under change because, in fact, the image resonates quite well with the high level of anti-immigrant, antimulticultural, and anti-affirmative action mood of the country that *Time* identifies. The New Eve image is meant to mollify those who believe that multiculturalism means divisiveness, entrenched differences, and adherence to primordial affiliations. Or, put more simply, the New Eve is a reassuring counterpoint to the explicit notion that today's immigrants, ethnic groups, and racial groups do not want to become "Americans" anymore. The image of the New Eve melts away the problems of difference, forging them into a new American singularity. Any suggestion of difference, of multiculturalism, is erased in the image. Uniculturalism wins the day.

The discourse on race, American culture, and immigration is continued in the *New Republic*'s 27 December 1993 issue (fig. 4.13). The cover's image is an illustration of a beach, with the ocean on the left. Running up and down the image is a massive wall, paralleling the coastline. A lone male walks along the beach, a bundle of clothes under his arm. Since the ocean is left, or to the west, in spatial metaphorical terms, the image depicts the western edge of the nation. The water symbolizes the tide of immigrants that the border wall is keeping from flowing across the nation. The wall and the man (immigrant) contemplating the wall's (border's) impenetrable enormity represent hardening public opinion on immigration. The text confirms that the image is about immigration: "The Immigrants: The arguments, Nathan Glazer, Peter Salins, the people, Roger Rosenblatt, Jennifer Allen."

The two main articles on the arguments over immigration by Peter

Salins and Nathan Glazer stake out somewhat opposing positions on the implications of current trends in immigration and possible future policies. To a great extent, these articles are in an explicit dialogue with the discourse discussed in this chapter, but most specifically with the issues raised by Peter Brimelow (the *National Review* 22 June 1992) and to a certain extent Jack Miles (the *Atlantic Monthly* November 1992). Salins begins his article by claiming that "The trouble with the immigration debate of the past year or so is that much of it is simply unreal." Intellectuals, in his opinion, have focused mainly on abstractions, while ordinary Americans "have been inflamed by prejudice and misinformation" (13). The reality of immigration politics, in Salins's view, is that Congress would find it impossible to drastically reduce legal immigration. Any such efforts would face a combination of liberals who see liberal immigration as central to their "universalist American idea" and conservatives who view immigrants as an element of a free market whose long-term benefits outweigh their short-term costs.

Salins presents facts and figures on the relative numbers of immigrants (proportionately less than in previous decades) and their benefits to once depleted cities and on how unemployment rates of African Americans living in or near immigrant enclaves actually fell while the wages of young African Americans fell by 4 percent or less because of immigration (14). As for the "nightmare scenarios" promoted by those who believe, America will become—God help us—*a nonwhite nation,* Salins replies "So what?" He argues that Hispanics are not a racial category and many do not look very different from southern Europeans. The real problem, he argues, is not about how many immigrants come, but who comes and how they should be let in the country. As it is currently structured, the system of family preferences allows too many immigrants from too few countries, which also results in their concentration in a few regions and states. Salins argues that this system is actually similar to the previous quota system in that, once established, recent nationalities have preference over possible immigrants from many other nations. Salins notes that Mexicans, who account for 30 percent of all legal immigrants since 1981, have been the primary beneficiaries of the family reunification system. Salins advocates retaining some numerical quota for reuniting families, but that the vast number of immigrant slots should be opened up to the world on a "first-come, first-served" basis (15).

Nathan Glazer focuses on the issue of policies that would increase the flow of European immigrants. He finds that the arguments of those who would restrict immigration as a way of keeping the nation's population more like what it once was, and a preference for a less populated country, to be "not ignoble" (18). He puts himself in the camp of American public opinion that he believes is now modestly restrictionist. This camp believes America should not become a country of mass migration again, and they ask "why the stream of immigration should be so unrepresentative of the nation that already exists" (18). They also believe that immigrants should improve the country, that is, more valedictorians and science-award winners.

As for fears that the country cannot assimilate today's immigrants, Glazer asks if those holding these fears have adopted earlier nativist views. His answer is that America may not be able to absorb new immigrants as it once did, "But it *is* a different country: less self-confident, less willing to impose English and American customs and loyalty as simply the best in the world" (18). Rather than their desire to learn English, which he believes does not occur at a slower rate than among past immigrant groups, Glazer points to the low rate of acquiring citizenship as evidence of a weakening power to assimilate immigrants. Immigrants, he believes, have fewer reasons to become citizens since civil rights laws have spread protections to immigrants, thus reducing the advantages of citizenship. Glazer, here, raises an issue that surfaced after the 1996 welfare and immigration laws reduced those protections and underscored the advantages of citizenship, especially for social services. As a result, the number of citizenship applications surged among immigrants.

The cover's image of the massive border wall along America's coast combines well with the Salins and Glazer articles. Neither article advocates increased immigration or open borders. Salins would redirect the opportunities for admission, but would retain a system of limitations on immigration. Glazer finds current immigration to be "insensible" mass migration that should be slowed down. Moreover, Glazer finds no ethical or moral problem with tailoring immigration to keep America a nation that is predominately of white European descent. One final point about the cover's image that relates to Glazer's arguments. The border wall in the image faces west, not east toward Europe, symbolizing the discourse that laments the low numbers of European immigrants and the need to increase that flow in order to preserve America's population of European descent.

FINAL THOUGHTS

The debate over immigration and its impact on the nation during the early 1990s reflected the public's growing dissatisfaction with the government's policies, specifically IRCA, to curb undocumented immigration. But the discourse found on the magazine covers and their accompanying articles was more than about undocumented immigration and discontent with IRCA. Central to the discourse was the way demographic trends were changing America. Images of whites being squeezed out of the nation by growing numbers of Latinos and Asians were featured prominently on magazine covers. Culture change attributed to immigration, and especially the specter of "multiculturalism," raised concerns over the ability of the nation to withstand such change. American culture, once perceived as resilient and capable of integrating the new with the old, is now presented in images that spell the possible death of the nation. Even the Statue of Liberty no longer greets immigrants with a lighted torch showing the way through the Golden Door. She is now a border guard, deflecting immigrants seeking entrance to a land not of economic opportunities but of opportunities for ill-gotten social services, medical care, education, and other "handouts." Concerns over demographic shifts and the threat of culture change resulted in a longing for increased immigration from northwestern Europe as a way to maintain America's ethnic/racial proportions. Despite counter discourses to these images of immigrants and their impact on the nation, the weight of the discourse was decidedly unfriendly toward immigration during the early 1990s. The culmination of this discourse can be found in the heated debate over immigration that emerged in 1994 over Proposition 187 in California then swept across the nation in the debate over federal welfare and immigration reform.

CHAPTER 7

Immigrants outside the Imagined Community of the Nation, 1994–99

Identity only becomes an issue when it is in crisis, when something assumed to be fixed, coherent and stable is displaced by the experience of doubt and uncertainty.

K. Mercer, *"Welcome to the Jungle"*

A watershed moment in the public debate over immigration was the 1994 election in California. On 8 November of that year the voters of California overwhelmingly passed Proposition 187, which was to, in the words of its supporters, "Save Our State" by denying "illegal aliens health care, education, and other publicly-funded benefits" (California Ballot Pamphlet 1994; P. Martin 1995).[1] The Proposition 187 campaign signaled what Kitty Calavita (1996) has called a "new politics" of immigration, one based on "balanced-budget conservatism." Most of these provisions were brought to a halt by the court on the grounds that regulation of immigration was a matter for the federal, not state, government.

Six magazine covers appeared in 1994, beginning with *American Heritage*'s March issue. The cover featured a photograph of the Statue of Liberty, her entire body visible above her pedestal, the buildings of the city discernible through a hazy sky. Noticeably different is that the statue's arm is not holding a torch. Instead, the photograph has been altered so that her right arm is held horizontally, finger pointing away. The unwelcome gesture is underscored by the text: "Go Back Where You Came From: Since the very beginning, many Americans have wanted this to be our immigration policy. Is it starting to happen?" Importantly, the Statue of Liberty is facing east; her right arm, therefore, points south, indicating that the place to "go back" to for the immigrants she is addressing is to the south. She is not pointing straight ahead, that is not back to the east.

7.1. *American Heritage*, March 1994. "Go Back Where You Came From."

The text—"since the beginning"—suggests the historical tension Americans have felt over immigration. The article takes up this theme as it examines immigration in American history, beginning with the colonial period and continuing to the present time. In ironic juxtaposition to the image on the cover, the article, by Bernard A. Weisberger, is a positive interpretation of immigration. Although the cover uses alarmist imagery about immigration, it is perhaps but a lure to attract an immigration-wary public to buy the magazine. Once "caught," the reader will find that many of the concerns over immigration expressed so widely at this time have their antecedents in American history. As the article points out, issues of language and cultural differences, assimilation, economic competition, and even political participation were raised about previous waves of immigrants, including those from Europe.

The author stakes out his position quickly:

> So let us begin at the beginning, with the statement that offends the new exclusionist. "We are a nation of immigrants." It's a politician's generality at an ethnic picnic, a textbook bromide swallowed and soon forgotten. It is also, as it happens, a profound truth, defining us and explaining a good part of what is extraordinary in the short history of the United States of America. There is no American ancient soil, no founding race, but there is a common ancestral experience of moving from "there" to "here." (76–77)

Weisberger finds that today's immigrants come to America for the same reasons as past immigrants: the promise of a better life, economically, and a chance to experience political freedom. Moreover, immigrants have contributed to what was already here, making changes to American society and culture beginning in the seventeenth century. And, the historical record shows, melting into a larger society was not always an easy process, or a quick one. Immigrants, more so than their children, often held onto old ways, and natives could be standoffish or, worse, build barriers based on discriminatory attitudes that made it difficult for immigrants to integrate into society. But as the article shows, this is the immigrant story writ large.

In contrast to the alarmist imagery of the cover, the article reaffirms the power of America to absorb immigrants and change itself into something different and yet still American. As the author concludes: "It seems safe to say that, like the English, Scots, Irish, Germans, Swedes and Finns, Greeks, Poles, Italians, Hungarians, and Russians before them, they [today's immigrants] will neither 'melt' into some undistinctive alloy nor, on the other hand, remain aloof and distinct from one another. Some kind of functional American mosaic will emerge. It is the historic way" (91). Although perhaps unintentional, the assertion that immigrants will not "melt into some undistinctive alloy" serves as a critique of, or at least a cautionary note about, the assimilation motif of the New Eve image on *Time* magazine's earlier cover.

THE DEATH OF THE NATION-STATE?

Reasons similar to those presented for the possible demise of the American nation—rapid population growth, environmental degradation, international migration, and ethnic rather than national loyalties—are also leading to a breakdown of the world system of nation-states. As the February 1994 cover of the *Atlantic Monthly* made clear, the result will be cataclysmic. As the almost full page of cover text states, in bold, upper-case letters:

> The Coming Anarchy: Nations break up under the tidal flow of refugees from environmental and social disaster. As borders crumble, another type of boundary is erected—a wall of disease. Wars are fought over scarce resources, especially water, and war itself becomes continuous with crime, as armed bands of stateless marauders clash with the private security forces of the elites. A preview of the first decades of the twenty-first century. By Robert D. Kaplan.

The "anarchy" predicted by the text is caused by "refugees," "stateless marauders," "crumbling borders," "disease," "crime," and class warfare. These terms are all negative, except perhaps for the term "refugees," which takes on a negative connotation by association. The text sits above an image of a paper globe that has been squeezed out of shape and sits on an oak floor. The upper left part of the globe is on fire, yellow flames extending up into the text. The map of the North American continent is located just left of center of the globe's surface facing the reader so that it is the continent commanding the greatest focus. It is also the continent that is burning. Both the text and the image of the world tell the same story: the world as we know it is coming to an end.

Robert D. Kaplan's article by the same title, "The Coming Anarchy," elaborates on his rather pessimistic vision of the near future of the world, and more specifically, the United States. Kaplan's "symbol" for the way things will become is West Africa, where government forces have only a tenuous control over criminal activity, and even that is primarily only during daylight hours in urban centers. Control has given way to "Disease, overpopulation, unprovoked crime, scarcity of resources, refugee migrations, the increasing erosion of nation-states and international borders, and the empowerment of private armies, security firms, and international drug cartels" (46). The lessons for the United States are many, according to Kaplan. Foremost is a danger less from ideological conflicts than from cultural conflict: "As refugee flows increase and as peasants continue migrating to cities around the world—turning them into sprawling villages—national borders will mean less, even as more power will fall into the hands of less educated, less sophisticated groups. In the eyes of these uneducated but newly empowered millions, the real borders are the most tangible and intractable ones: those of culture and tribe" (60).

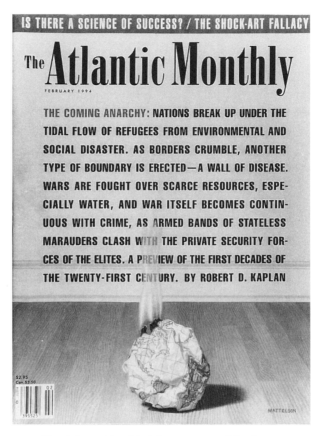

7.2.   The *Atlantic Monthly,* February 1994. "The Coming Anarchy."

As an example of these new border conflicts, the author notes that in the United States, African Americans are "besieged" by an influx of Latinos who compete with them (62). Latinos also figure in a "new cartography" in which political borders as fixed and abrupt lines are replaced by "buffer entities." The Latino buffer entity replaces the precise U.S.-Mexico border (75). This new map is "an ever-mutating representation of chaos" that changes in response to migrations of people, explosions of birth rates, and disease (75). Loyalties will increasingly be regional, even in the United States. As an example of the new loyalties that will emerge, Kaplan cites Spanish speakers in the Southwest who will have less in common with Washington, D.C., than they do with Mexico City.

Kaplan questions whether the United States will survive into the next century, at least in its present form. He questions America's ability to survive as a multi-ethnic society, which he asserts has meant that America, as a nation-state, has always been more "fragile" than more homogenous nations such as Germany and Japan. In what way America has been more fragile in practice is not clear. But Kaplan argues that homogenous nations have a mass-conscription army and standardized public school system that promote nationalism and patriotism. The United States was closest to this vision of a strong nation-state during World War II. "Multicultural regimes," on the other hand, have all-volunteer armies and influential international media and entertainment industries that do not promote a national political class or a common national culture (76). According to Kaplan, during the 1960s the United States began a transformation toward this latter form of nation-state: "The signs hardly need belaboring: racial polarity, educational dysfunction, social fragmentation of many and various kinds" (76).

As horrifying as the future Kaplan paints is, it is difficult, as least for this reader, to be convinced by the appropriateness of stretching the West African metaphor to the United States. Different regions have different histories. Kaplan does not distinguish the U.S.-Mexican relationship, which has consisted of an asymmetrical interdependence involving the flow of people, culture, capital, and technology between the two nations (part of this flow was formalized under the North American Free Trade Agreement), from relationships among the nations he uses as examples in other parts of the world. For instance, the demand for Mexican labor in the United States, which has existed for most of this century, is not exactly the same as the flow of refugees in the West African region. Kaplan also does not elaborate on the importance of his other assertions. For example, it is unclear what it means for Spanish speakers in the Southwest to have something in common with Mexico City. Language in common? Clearly. But surely we cannot assume they have a loyalty to the federal government in Mexico City. Policies that helped to produce a lack of jobs and continued social inequality in Mexico led Mexican Spanish speakers in the Southwest to leave Mexico and thus such policies are as likely as not to create animosity toward politicians in Mexico City. And what about the many Spanish speakers in the Southwest from nations other than Mexico? What, other than language, would they have in common with Mexico City? Perhaps even more alarming, the author appears to include the children of immigrants, U.S. citizens, when he questions the loyalty of Spanish-speaking Americans. Moreover, there is little attempt by the author to place current issues in a historical context. Questions of loyalty, patriotism, and tribalism directed toward immigrants are not new. Such questions were raised about earlier waves of immigrants in America's history, with equally fervent questions about America's ability to survive.

The article and the cover's image work well together to raise fears over globalization. The globe in the image is a metaphor for globalization, the increasing linkages of all parts of the world and also the increasing vulnerability of each of the parts to events occurring in other parts. The article underscores the possible apocalyptic consequences of globalization for the United States, which the image also highlights by having North America go up in flames first. The isolationism and wariness of globalization inherent in Pat Buchanan's "America First" rhetoric during his 1992 presidential bid would find ample support in both the image and article, both of which make us painfully aware of world events. But as the world burns, no possible solutions are offered as a way of avoiding the coming anarchy. What is evoked, therefore, is a defensive posture toward the world, refugees, and immigrants. Some readers' reactions (as intended) will be to pull back from the fire before it burns the hardwood floors and brings down the house, and to consider sealing off the rest of the world before it brings down our way of life.

CONSERVATIVE RIFTS OVER
IMMIGRATION AND MULTICULTURALISM

The threat to the American nation posed by immigration-led multiculturalism is the subject of the *National Review*'s 21 February 1994 issue. The cover is a clear rebuke of *Time* magazine's New Eve cover and any positive connotation of multiculturalism intended by that cover (see also Berlant 1997, 207). The *National Review*'s cover reproduces *Time*'s cover in its entirety, but reduced in size, and places it on a brick wall, as if it were a broadside on a building in some urban center. At the bottom left of the cover is the fleeing figure of a white teenager. He is fleeing apparently after placing the graffiti that now graces the image of the New Eve. A black mustache, curled flamboyantly at both ends, and a pointed goatee have been penned onto Eve's face. Across the bottom of *Time*'s cover and on the brick wall are scrawled the words "demystifying multiculturalism." The act of vandalism by the white youth suggests that "The New Face of America" heralded by *Time* magazine is not a pleasing sight to all who encounter it.

As a symbol of multiculturalism, the adulterated New Eve serves as

7.3.   The *National Review,* 21 February 1994. "Demystifying
Multiculturalism."

the catalyst for a series of articles on immigration, the nation, multiculturalism, and even a critique of conservatives who fail to see the implications of their own views on immigration. Linda Chavez, director of
the Center for the New American Community, begins with a critique of
multiculturalists who treat race and ethnicity as if they were synonymous
with culture. "They [multiculturalists] presume that skin color and national origin, which are immutable traits, determine values, mores, language, and other cultural attributes, which, of course, are learned" (26).
Chavez finds that multiculturalists believe that culture is transmitted
through a person's genetic material rather than learned through experience, and thus they claim that ethnic or racialized Americans have more
in common with people in different countries who share their genetic

background than they do with other Americans. She is particularly concerned that this is the view of the promoters of the Afrocentric education movement. She argues against the notion that because Americans have heritages that can be traced to different places, no common American culture can exist. Immigration brings people of different cultural backgrounds to America, but that does not mean that America must be multicultural. Indeed, she argues that immigrant children and the children of immigrants are unable to resist American culture; they are "seduced" by it. Only groups that maintain strict rules of intermarriage with persons outside their group and seal themselves off geographically or religiously—the Amish or ultra-Orthodox Jews, for example—and thus avert all but the most superficial contact with the larger society are able to maintain separate cultures. Hispanic immigrants, she finds, though often cited as not learning English and failing to assimilate actually do learn English over time, especially in succeeding generations, and about one-third of Hispanics marry non-Hispanic whites.

For Chavez, then, the problem is not that immigrants lack a desire to assimilate into American society. Even if immigrants retain some attachment to their ancestral roots, that is to be expected and part of a process of give and take that enriches American culture. The problem for Chavez is an ideology of multiculturalism that privileges difference. She finds that this ideology is especially problematic in the schools, which in the past saw it as a duty to teach immigrants English, instill in them a respect for American institutions and individual liberties, and introduce them to American heroes whom they can admire as their own. As Chavez states, "Lately, we have nearly reversed course, treating each group, new and old, as if what is most important is to preserve its separate identity and space" (32).

Chavez's critique of multiculturalism is, interestingly, one that places her squarely behind the assimilation premises of the *Time*'s New Eve image. Chavez finds that America continues to have the capacity to absorb immigrants and that immigrants and their children have the capacity to learn and contribute to American culture. Her brand of conservatism privileges culture over race. She does not engage the issue of America's changing ethnic and racial composition, focusing instead on the divisive impact of programs such as bilingual education and multiculturalism that, in her view, enhance separatism and an ideology of victimology. Reducing or eliminating these programs would allow immigrants of whatever background to proceed along the path that they most often desire, that of becoming American. The issue of America's changing racial and ethnic composition is dealt with more directly in two long articles by John O'Sullivan and Lawrence Auster.

John O'Sullivan, editor of the *National Review,* develops an extended critique of multiculturalism in his article "Nationhood: An American Activity." He begins by agreeing with Peter Brimelow (see chapter 6) and Lawrence Auster (see below), that America's language, laws, institutions, political ideas, customs, prayers, etc., essentially derived from Britain (38). Even though it has been "modified and enriched" by the "adhesion" of different immigrant groups, the British legacy has remained, according to O'Sullivan, the central tradition of American "civilization." This unifying tradition is now challenged by a "radical multiculturalism" that views America as an idea rather than as a nation with a common national character:

> [Multiculturalism] accepts the central tenet of the dominant *liberal* theory of American nationality—namely, that America is a set of political, constitutional, and legal principles. But where the liberal theory sees these principles as protecting and uniting individuals and individual rights, multiculturalist theory sees them as protecting groups and group rights—in particular ethnic groups and ethnic identities. Protecting yes; uniting no. Multiculturalism regards assimilation as a form of oppression; its vision is of America as a permanent conversation among different tribes. (38)

The "new" post-1965 immigration has given added impetus to a "more aggressive" multiculturalism. O'Sullivan notes that since the 1965 immigration law "abandoned" quotas for the system of family reunification, most immigrants now come from Asia and Latin America. In addition, the total numbers of immigrants, both legal and illegal, have increased, which adds to the multicultural argument that American identity must be redefined along multicultural lines. But for O'Sullivan the more problematic argument of the "ideologues of multiculturalism" is that Asian and Latin American immigrants have less of a capacity to assimilate into American society than earlier waves of immigrants from Europe—that today's immigrants can't identify with America's heroes and myths.

The problem with assimilation, according to O'Sullivan, is the failure to restrict immigration so that the large number of new immigrants can be absorbed into the national culture through education, intermarriage, and other forces of assimilation. "Today, however, we are pursuing exactly the opposite policies—namely, keeping the level of immigration high and keeping the immigrants insulated from the rest of us through bilingual and multicultural programs" (38). Americans, O'Sullivan argues, are willing to accept immigration only as long as they view it as a benefit. They would not accept immigration if they believed it meant "the wholesale remaking of American culture" (39). And yet, O'Sullivan also argues that as America absorbs the new immigrants it will develop a national culture or ethnicity that is not purely a WASP identity. "When people combine, they produce something new. That something may have cultural characteristics that are predominantly from one of its ethnic constituents, but a predominance is not a totality. People from all ethnic groups inherit this enriched cultural heritage; they all look to the same cultural ancestors. And these will be increasingly multi-ethnic over time. The latest American hero, after all, is Colin Powell" (44).

It is here that we can see the main logic of O'Sullivan's argument for the need to draw a distinction between a "multi-ethnic" society and a "multicultural" society. In O'Sullivan's view, for America to persist as a multi-ethnic nation it must develop a broad "mono-cultural" tradition that all ethnic/racial groups share to some degree. What is shared (a common history and language) and therefore unifies must outweigh that which is different and therefore disunites. This leads O'Sullivan to stand firm against bilingualism and affirmative action quotas and to support restraints on immigration in order to allow "the continuing evolution of an American ethnicity encompassing all other ethnicities" (45).

O'Sullivan and Chavez share a basic position on multiculturalism and immigration. A radical multiculturalism is bad for the nation because it emphasizes differences among people. Given time and opportunity, America can absorb immigrants who will contribute to a grand American culture that all Americans will, to some degree, share. Although acknowledging the British legacy to American culture, O'Sullivan does not advocate a return to quotas favoring European immigration to restore or ensure the racial composition of the nation along early nineteenth-century lines. Instead, he stresses the processes that will form a broad national culture or ethnicity. In this sense, there is little here to contradict the essential message of the New Eve image. Indeed, the New Eve is a blending of America's ethnic and racial difference into a single whole, which is a metaphorical restatement of O'Sullivan's argument. Although O'Sullivan may "demystify" multiculturalism by drawing out its implications from his perspective, he does not propose a line of racial argumentation like Peter Brimelow or Lawrence Auster, who follows, that would be antithetical to the racial blending inherent in the New Eve imagery.

Lawrence Auster's position on immigration in his article "Avoiding the Issue" is more strident than that of Linda Chavez or John O'Sullivan. This is perhaps to be expected given that Auster is the author of *The Path to National Suicide: An Essay on Immigration and Multiculturalism,* which was published by the American Immigration Control Foundation, the publishing arm of the Federation of American Immigration Reform or FAIR. Auster begins with the position that America is already suffering "profound social disarray" due largely to the increasing number of immigrants from "Third World" countries (48). The possibly "incurable" cultural ills Auster blames on immigration include the loss of a common language, literature, and national identity. A common American citizenship is being dismantled in favor of group rights and quotas based on race, thus adding to the growth of "victimology." White men are demonized as oppressors of minorities and women. America's schools and law enforcement are overwhelmed, especially in California and Florida. "U.S. sovereignty" has been lost to foreign-based criminal gangs in parts of New York City. Murderous interracial conflict is occurring in the nation's major cities, as exemplified by the L.A. riots. Contributing to these problems, for Auster, is demographic change. "Underlying all these problems is the steady decline of Americans of European descent from majority toward minority status, with the concomitant redefinition of America as a 'multicultural' nation—an oxymoron if there ever was one" (49). At stake, according to Auster, is that the "submergence" of America's white majority might also lead to a submergence of America's Western cultural traditions.

Auster is highly critical of conservatives whose "defining ideology" on immigration blinds them to the dangers of immigration and the changing racial composition of the nation. Conservatives, according to Auster, adhere to the following "myth": "America was built on universal principles of human rights, equality, and open borders; therefore America, by definition, must have a virtual infinite capacity for absorbing racially and culturally diverse peoples into its national fabric; and therefore any *serious* concerns about what immigration is actually doing to the country are un-American and must be automatically dismissed" (49). He is particularly critical of the nation of immigrants and melting pot tropes, which he labels "incantatory bromides."

To a certain extent, the criticism Auster applies to conservatives generally applies specifically to Linda Chavez and John O'Sullivan, both of whom emphasized the absorption of racially and culturally diverse peoples into a national fabric or culture. In contrast, Auster finds that Americans should be worried about "Third World" immigration because it is leading to "an unprecedented transformation of this country in social, political, cultural, and racial terms" (51). Auster attacks Chavez for not calling for a halt to "massive" Hispanic immigration. In arriving at this critique, he miscasts her argument as it appears in her book *Out of the Barrio* and in the article discussed above. She argues against the position that Latinos are permanently disadvantaged and discriminated against in this country. As she sees it, the status of recent immigrants, who make up a large proportion of the Latino population, obscures the advances in education, income, the use of English, and many other factors among Latinos who have been in the country for many years and for generations. Auster translates Chavez's position as one that argues against the "darkening prospects for Hispanic assimilation and economic advancement" (51). In addition, he recasts her findings as "massive Hispanic immigration is retarding or reversing the assimilation of the Hispanic community as a whole, and thus exacerbating the economic and cultural divisions in the country," which, in his view, should have led Chavez to conclude that Hispanic immigration should be reduced for the sake of "Hispanic assimilation and national unity" (51). The problem, from this reader's perspective, is that Chavez's position is not the same as saying immigration is "retarding or reversing" the assimilation of Latinos generally. Chavez is arguing that Latinos are assimilating, only that such change is obscured by the weight given to the readily apparent characteristics of recent immigrants. To say that she finds Latinos generally do not change or become less integrated into American society, at least on the indicators of income, education, language use, etc., is to flip her argument on its head. Chavez argues for the assimilative powers of the nation, a process Auster has little faith in. But even if Third World immigrants did become American in thought and behavior, the real danger, for Auster, is the "unimaginable changes in this country's ethnic and racial composition" that conservatives such as Chavez apparently fail to consider. As Auster argues:

> Once our notions of political order are completely abstracted from the ethnic and cultural matrix that gave them birth, the notions themselves begin to dissolve under the onslaught of rival particularisms, which rush in to fill the cultural vacuum. Thus our universalist immigration policy, by bringing in cultures and people too diverse to be incorporated within a single national and civilizational identity, has inadvertently helped release the very forces of cultural separatism and groups rights that the conservatives dread. The attempt to reconstitute the American identity solely in terms of a *civic* bond defined by universal ideas is therefore doomed; as America's current fragmentation

indicates, a civic bond cannot long endure the absence of an experienced *cultural* bond. (54)

Auster's argument about the inability of diverse peoples from different cultural backgrounds to become incorporated into a national or "civilizational" identity begins to take on dimensions that make it vulnerable to Chavez's criticism of multiculturalists. Is Auster not blurring together the independent processes of cultural learning and biological/racial inheritance? For example, Auster argues that even though some immigrants may have values such as that promoting a strong family structure, it does not mean they have a "national and civilizational identity" amenable to American culture and society. "Mexican or Cambodian immigrants might have the most stable families in the world and still not be *American* in any meaningful sense of the word" (54). Those who argue for the assimilability of such immigrants (Weisberger above, for example) are criticized by Auster for their misguided vision of America as "an economic or philosophical abstraction capable of absorbing the entire human race" (54). Auster, in turn, is favorable toward a concept of the civic nation that is undergirded by a distinct cultural and ethnic experience that could be typecast as "a Christian Anglo-Saxon nation." At one point Auster appears to step back from the implications of his arguments: "To recognize the ethnic and cultural dimension of nationhood does not imply . . . that cultural values cannot, in individual cases and under the right circumstances, be transmitted across ethnic and racial lines. Nor does it preclude spontaneous cultural change from within the society itself" (54). It is, according to Auster, the introduction of large numbers of "ethnoculturally distinct" populations that challenges the ability of the nation to assimilate them.

Auster's argument that America is no longer able to absorb "ethnoculturally distinct" immigrants has its antecedents in arguments against southern and eastern European immigrants in the late nineteenth and early twentieth centuries (Simon and Alexander 1993; R. Simon 1985; Steinberg 1981; Steinfeld 1970). Nor is the linkage of American "culture" to a narrowly constructed set of original ethnic origins—primarily British— new. Auster attacks a conservative image of America as an idea or set of civic beliefs that are capable of being learned by all peoples regardless of their ethnic or racial background. By doing so, Auster is attempting to redefine America's identity in much narrower terms. Rather than the "nation of immigrants" metaphor that is so often evoked by conservatives and liberals alike when speaking of the nation's identity and uniqueness,

Auster characterizes this self-identification as the source of the nation's problems: multiculturalism, incoherence, and social conflict.

Of the three conservative authors featured in this issue of the *National Review,* the image on the cover resonates most completely with Auster's position. For Auster, the New Eve is antithetical to his position that America is letting into the nation "cultures and people too diverse to be incorporated within a single national and civilizational identity." The New Eve symbolizes the loss of European-American preeminence in the composition of the nation's population, which is exactly the road to national suicide that Auster warns against. In this light, the white teenager's graffiti strikes out against multiculturalism and racial hybridity represented by the New Eve image. Parenthetically, Auster argues that one of the key cultural features that has historically constituted America as a distinct nation and is now on the verge of being lost is marriage customs. The vandalized image of the New Eve signifies not simply a desire to "de-mythify" multiculturalism, it is an act of resistance to a changing America. The intentionally beguiling and benign face of the young woman is transmogrified by this act into the threatening face of a male—the New Adam—whose facial markings, the mustache and more specifically the stylized beard, identify him as "foreign."

Five months later, on 11 July 1994, the *National Review* again criticized conservatives for an alleged lack of attention to the problems associated with immigration. The cover featured an illustration of three elephants sitting, one with hands over its eyes, one with hands over its ears, and one with hands over its mouth, in the classic pose of "see no evil, hear no evil, and speak no evil." The text read "Republicans on Immigration." The cover story, "Right of Silence," was by Roy Beck, the Washington editor of the quarterly the *Social Contract.* In the article, Beck criticizes the majority of Republican leaders for not having a position on legal immigration and thereby supporting the status quo, or large-scale immigration. Focusing on ten national Republican leaders who were possible presidential contenders, Beck finds that only two, Bob Dole and Pat Buchanan, actually advocated lowering the number of legal immigrants allowed into the nation each year. Two others, Phil Gramm and Jack Kemp, were explicitly against tough restrictions on legal immigration. The remaining six—William Bennett, Dick Cheney, Dan Quayle, Pat Robertson, Bill Weld, and Pete Wilson—did not have explicit positions on legal immigration at the time, although they were all against illegal immigration. Leaving aside the middle position, or those without a formal position, Beck argues that what is left are two radical positions

on immigration among conservatives and that these radical positions lead
to two different demographic futures for America.

The first position is that of the "traditionalists" who would like to cut
yearly immigration levels to an average of about 297,000 per year, which
was the average annual rate between 1820 and 1965. This would slow
population growth but ethnic minorities would still grow in proportion
to the larger population, only at a slower rate than under higher immigration levels. The advantage of restricting immigration for the traditionalists is that "the country would retain its European-descended
majority and its traditional cultural identity in which an American
nationhood—encompassing different ethnicities but based on a British/
European culture—would continue to evolve" (28).

The counter position—the "government version"—is enthusiastic
about immigration and would maintain the status quo. Beck argues that
the result of this position is rapid demographic change leading to a country "made up primarily of minority groups, with no majority ethnic/cul-
tural group" (28). Phil Gramm is presented as holding this position while
failing to recognize the disastrous course on which it will lead the nation. According to Gramm: "Not only is America a nation of immigrants,
but new immigrants continue to build America and to expand its prosperity and freedom. We don't have room for people who want to live off
the work of others. But I don't believe for a moment that new legal immigrants have been a burden to the economy. They have been a great
boon" (32).

Beck argues that public opinion polls favor the traditionalist position
and that conservatives who support the status quo, either explicitly or
though their lack of a position, are out of touch with the mood of the
nation. The article reviews no fewer than five bills in Congress at the
time seeking to lower the annual rate of legal immigration. The bills range
from one that would leave legal immigration at current levels but reduce
total immigration by reducing illegal immigration to one that would cut
legal immigration to 235,000 per year. This latter bill is the one favored
by Beck, who describes it as the most popular immigration bill in Congress at the time. This low level of immigration would, according to the
article, allow the nation time to develop the infrastructure for a slowly
growing population. As Beck argues: "This also would be an America
in which the sense of common American nationhood would be advanced
by the assimilation of earlier and new immigrants, by the evolution of
an enriched common culture, and by ethnic, racial, and religious intermarriage" (34).

The *National Review* both pokes fun at Republicans—the dim-witted, childish elephants on the cover—and chastises conservatives for failing to recognize the dangers presented by large-scale legal immigration. Beginning with Peter Brimelow's article in 1992 and continuing with these later two issues, the *National Review* has consistently offered the most restrictionist perspectives on immigration of the ten magazines examined. At the same time, the articles in the *National Review* have revealed the complexity of the issues surrounding immigration and the contradictions over how the nation is imagined, even among conservatives. The rhetoric emanating from Brimelow, Auster, and Beck places the nation on a precipice and is meant to act as a clarion call to conservatives who fail to see the enormous dangers of immigration: multiculturalism and racial/ethnic change (or, proportionately fewer Americans of European descent). The "evil," then, which is left unsaid on the cover, and which is allegedly neither seen, heard, nor spoken by many conservatives, is the demographic change that is altering irrevocably the "face" of America. Interestingly, none of the reductions in legal immigration mentioned here became part of the Republican-led Congress's 1996 Immigration Law, which actually slightly increased legal immigration.

The issue of refugees turned up again in 1994. *Time*'s 5 September cover featured an illustration of Cuba's Fidel Castro, mouth open and finger pointing, as if delivering a lecture (fig. 4.11). In the background was a turbulent ocean on which floated a makeshift raft filled with people. The image of the raft people and water to symbolize a flood of refugees is restated by the cover's text: "Ready to Talk Now? Castro hopes his flood of refugees will force the U.S. to make a deal." The cover story, "Cubans, Go Home," discusses President Clinton's new (17 August) policy toward Cuban refugees, one that refused their entry to the United States. Clinton's policy reversed thirty-five years of policy that welcomed Cuban refugees, as Jimmy Carter said in 1980, with "open heart and open arms" (see chapter 5). According to the article, President Clinton did not want a repeat of the 1980 Mariel boatlift. American soldiers at Guantanamo Bay were preparing tent shelters to house up to sixty-five thousand refugees indefinitely. *Time* viewed President Clinton's tough stance on Cuban refugees as a capitulation to Cuban-American hardliners on Castro and because he feared the political fallout should he be viewed as "cozying up to the communist devil." *Time* also believed the president feared appearing "soft" on immigration at a time of heightened sentiments against illegal immigration, especially in California and Texas (33).

THE LEFT'S RESPONSE

The last magazine cover dealing with immigration in 1994 appeared on the *Nation* (see fig. 1.2). The image is a collage that includes the upper portion of the Statue of Liberty, a vicious-looking dog, an upside-down American flag, a mass of people posed just to the left of the coastline of the North American continent, and a man dressed in black and wearing a sombrero, with a suitcase strapped over one shoulder. The man is walking north along the border of the North American continent as flames form the background to the image. The text reads: "The Immigration Wars."

The feature article, "The New Know-Nothingism: Five Myths about Immigration" by David Cole, leaves no doubt that the "war" referred to on the cover is one being waged over the public's views of immigration. Cole's article is an attempt to refute some of the common negative arguments about immigration found in the public debate. He finds that immigrants are not overrunning the nation. In contrast to the average 15 percent of the population that the foreign born accounted for between 1870 and 1920, they were only 8 percent of the population in 1990. Even undocumented immigrants, he finds, account for only 13 percent of all immigrants and 1 percent of the American population (410). Cole discovered that data supporting the belief that immigrants take jobs away from U.S. citizens is difficult to find. He argues that immigrants create more jobs than they take. He also finds that the pressure to conform in America society is tremendous. Cultural separatism rarely enjoys much support beyond the immigrant generation, despite claims that immigrants and their children refuse to assimilate and are therefore a threat to the nation's cultural and political unity. He also finds it disturbing that noncitizen immigrants are treated as if they are not entitled to constitutional rights. Even the Clinton administration has argued in court that permanent resident aliens lawfully living in the United States should not enjoy full First Amendment rights.

Rather than being a drain on society, Cole finds that immigrants pay more than their share of taxes. The problem is that the majority of those taxes wind up in the federal treasury rather than at the local and state levels where the costs associated with immigration occur. This issue was particularly salient during 1994, the year California had the Save Our State (Proposition 187) initiative on the November ballot. Proposition 187 would have denied undocumented immigrants access to public services as a way of saving the state money and as a way of reducing incentives to immigrate illegally and to stay in California. Cole, however, finds that undocumented immigrants were already ineligible for most social services. They did, however, receive public school education for their children, emergency medical care, and nutritional assistance offered to poor women, infants, and children.

An accompanying article—" 'Save Our State' Initiative: Bashing Illegals in California"—by Elizabeth Kadetsky examines Proposition 187 in greater detail. After reviewing opinion polls and comments by some of the proposition's supporters, Kadetsky concludes: "If S.O.S.'s visible advocates personify either fringe populism or cynical manipulation of public sentiment for political gain, their movement has crossed over to the mainstream" (420). In the final analysis, the popularity of Proposition 187, especially among white voters, has pushed consensus on the immigration debate toward the restrictionist perspective.[2] According to the author, "the shrillness of the anti-immigrant rhetoric" has cowed even immigrant advocacy groups, who have had to concede ground on the negative impacts of immigration. Despite the volatile and often meanspirited rhetoric of some of the promoters of Proposition 187, the author finds that they fail to address the underlying causes of immigration, particularly the increasing economic interdependence of Mexico and the United States.

Returning to the image on the cover, the fear that immigration is about to overwhelm the nation is signified by the mass of people posed just off the western coast of the nation. The unwelcoming tenor of the immigration discourse examined in the magazine is suggested by the barking dog. Although the "mother of all exiles" is found in the image, the upside-down American flag sticking out of her head suggests that her values have also been turned upside down. America no longer welcomes immigrants to its shores. Through all the incendiary rhetoric (the flames in the image), the lone male immigrant serves as a constant; he still moves serenely north, his clothes on his back, drawn by an economy hungry for the labor he provides.

POST–PROPOSITION 187

Although the proponents of Proposition 187 may have lost the battle in California, they were more successful at the national level. Following the assumption central to Proposition 187, that social services—not jobs—are the magnet drawing undocumented immigrants to the United States, national immigration and welfare reform proposals began to target aid to immigrants, both documented and undocumented (Johnson 1995). On 22 August 1996, President Clinton signed into law the Personal Responsibility and Work Opportunity Reconciliation Act of 1996, ending the federal government's sixty-one-year commitment to provide cash assistance to every eligible poor family with children (Shogren 1996). The law was expected to save the government $54 billion over the following six years, with about half of those savings, or $24 billion, to come from restricting legal immigrants' use of food stamps, Supplemental Security Income, and aid for low-income elderly, the blind, and the disabled. Undocumented immigrants, who already were denied virtually all federal assistance, continued to be barred from assistance except for short-term disaster relief and emergency medical care.[3]

In addition to welfare reform, the U.S. Congress also passed the Illegal Immigration Reform and Immigrant Responsibility Act of 1996, which made dramatic changes to the nation's immigration laws (Bunis and Garcia 1997). Apprehended undocumented immigrants can no longer demand a hearing and stay in the country until their case is adjudicated; they can now be sent home immediately. A federal appeals court, however, ruled in May of 1998 that immigrants could not be barred from appealing a deportation order (Stout 1998). In addition, a hearing before an immigration judge is no longer automatic for asylum petitioners. People seeking political asylum must now petition for it within one year of entering the country. An INS agent will interview them within forty-eight hours, and the agent will determine if the refugee is to be deported or held for a hearing. Other changes mean that undocumented immigrants must now have been in the United States ten years rather than seven years before they can appeal a deportation decision, and they must prove good moral character, and show that deportation would cause extreme hardship to a family member who is a U.S. citizen. Waivers of deportation for aggravated felonies are no longer possible, and this class of felonies has been greatly expanded. The new law also places a nationwide cap of four thousand on the number of deportation reversals that can be granted annually. Moreover, an individual sponsor for an immigrant must now sign an affidavit and prove that his or her income (not her household's income) is at least 125 percent above the nation's poverty level, or about twenty thousand dollars for a family of four. An estimated one-third of immigrants who had sponsored relatives in 1994 would not meet the new income test (Bunis and Garcia 1997, 6). The new law, however, did not strengthen the employer sanctions laws. A pilot program in which employers could verify the documents of new workers was created, but participation by employers was voluntary.

There were no covers dealing with immigration or related topics during 1995. After a frenzy of public discourse on immigration began in 1990, it almost seemed as if there was little left to be said. The struggle for the "hearts and minds" of the American public had been waged. Various positions were put forward and conservatives and liberals attacked each other and themselves, as the battle over whose vision of America would gain hegemony. As this review suggests, hegemony, or a totalizing vision shared by all or imposed on all, did not emerge. The discourse was varied and continued to fluctuate between a fear of immigrants and a resolute view of immigrants as central to America's identity, both in the past and for the future. Although a totalizing vision of immigrants and the nation may not have emerged, the outcome—the vote on Proposition 187 and the denial to immigrants, even legal immigrants, of most social services in the 1996 welfare reform law—suggests that the characterization of immigrants as dangerous and undeserving members of society carried the day, if only for this moment in history. I say only for this moment in history because this analysis suggests that attitudes toward immigrants are not fixed; they follow an underlying rhythm that ebbs and flows according to the public's feelings about its own security. Anti-immigrant sentiments, while perhaps never completely disappearing from American consciousness, are not maintained at peak levels indefinitely. How the economy is doing appears to influence attitudes toward immigrants. For example, in Orange County, California, where Proposition 187 found a great deal of support in 1994 (Chavez 1997), only a minority of residents (36 percent) in 1997 believed that immigrants "are a burden on our country," compared to 54 percent nationwide who held that belief (Sforza 1997). This low level of anti-immigrant sentiments correlates with record low levels of unemployment (4.7 percent) nationwide at the time (Rosenblatt 1997).

In 1996, three magazines published covers focused on immigration. Although none of these covers used affirmative imagery, there were important differences in how the magazines presented "the problems" associated with immigration. Two magazines—the *Progressive* and *U.S. News and World Report*—published covers that did not target immigration as "the problem." Rather, these covers focused on the economic system that attracts, relies, and to a certain extent, exploits immigrants. For example, the cover on the *Progressive*'s September 1996 issue featured an illustration of fieldworkers bent over rows of lettuce. They hold

7.4.   The *Progressive*, September 1996. "Baiting Immigrants."

knives in their hands as they move along the crops. The style of the artwork is reminiscent of a van Gogh painting of peasants in the French
countryside. Above the straining workers is a large, white sun radiating
heat. But more significantly, hovering prominently in the sky above the
workers is a helicopter with "INS" written on it. The INS helicopter, in
the role of overseer, gazes down on the workers, policing their work rather
than keeping them out of the country. The text reads: "Baiting Immigrants." Although the workers on the cover are nondescript and could
be on any nationality, the accompanying articles are about Latin American immigrants.

Inside the magazine are two articles, the first of which is "Heartbreak
for Latinos" by Mercedes Lynn de Uriarte. This article discusses the anti-
Mexican and other Latin American immigration rhetoric prevalent dur-

ing and after California's Proposition 187 campaign. The article notes that both Republicans and Democrats used anti-immigrant rhetoric during this period. Presidential candidate Bob Dole proposed barring the children of undocumented immigrants from attending school (a proposal already ruled unconstitutional by the U.S. Supreme Court in 1982). President Clinton was also not above using immigration for political purposes. At a rally in San Diego, Clinton spoke of the special efforts his administration was making in regard to immigration in "our border communities," which he described as "under siege." Both the Republican and Democratic National Committees put negative ads on television that featured brown-skinned undocumented immigrants. A great deal of media attention was also paid to major deployments of resources at the border, known as Operation Gatekeeper in San Diego and Hold the Line in El Paso, which resulted in large increases in the number of illegal border crossers caught by the Border Patrol. Although the INS touted these operations as a success, the article notes that most undocumented immigrants arrive on commercial carriers and then overstay their visas, or they cross the U.S.-Canadian border (20). In addition, concentrations of Border Patrol agents has had the effect of pushing would-be border crossers to less guarded but more dangerous areas (Eschbach et al., 1999).[4]

The heightened attention to undocumented immigration across the southern border, according to the article, spilled over into treatment of Latinos who are legal immigrants and U.S. citizens. For example, the article noted that U.S.-born students with Mexican immigrant parents found that their requests for passports were delayed until they could provide substantial evidence that their parents resided in the United States at the time the students were born. Students who were legal immigrants also found it increasingly difficult to get federally subsidized loans and grants. Undocumented college students who had lived in California most of their lives had to pay out-of-state tuition as if they were foreign students (4). In one poignant example noted by the editor, Luis Gutierrez, a member of the House of Representatives, took his daughter to visit his office in the Capitol. Because they were Puerto Rican Americans, his daughter carried a small Puerto Rican flag, which caught the attention of the Capitol police security guard. The guard told them that they could not unfurl the flag in the Capitol and then asked Representative Gutierrez who he was. After telling him, the guard responded, "I don't think so," and he demanded identification. According to the *Progressive,* the guard then said, "It must be fake. Why don't you and your people just go back to the country you came from?" (3). For the *Progressive,* these examples are evidence of the type of behavior that becomes acceptable when politicians and the media scapegoat immigrants. As the author notes: "Today the nation faces major changes as technology retools the workplace, as demographics reconfigure the population, and as trade becomes globalized. These changes require discussion of public policies, including immigration. But instead of looking for solutions, our leaders are carting out the old scapegoats" (20).

The second article, by Julie Light, titled "Women Bear the Brunt," focuses on a number of first-hand accounts by immigrant Latin American women who have alleged physical and sexual abuse during their attempts to illegally cross the U.S.-Mexico border. These experiences came at the hands of smugglers, *coyotes,* and agents of the U.S. Border Patrol. The testimonies of these women point to abuses after being detained by the Border Patrol that include being placed in crowded cells, removal of underwear, and denial of sanitary napkins for menstruating women. A woman seven months pregnant was kept overnight despite policies to the contrary. Women also claimed to being fondled repeatedly by Border Patrol agents, even in the presence of a supervisor. The article notes that women are increasingly subject to such treatment because of changes in immigration policies. In July of 1995, the U.S. Justice Department began a policy of tough enforcement against those who attempt to enter the country with false documents (21). Up until this time, women preferred using false documents to enter the United States because it was safer than the dangerous trek across the border on foot (Chavez 1998). But the new enforcement policy has pushed some women to take more dangerous routes across the border, thus increasing their reliance on unscrupulous smugglers and increasing their likelihood of apprehension by the Border Patrol.

Returning to the cover's image in light of the articles, the helicopter takes on additional meaning. It implies more than the INS performing an act of surveillance, although this is a powerful act. The workers cannot escape the INS's gaze. It is a totalizing surveillance that works in a way that Foucault (1977) would appreciate as similar to a panopticon.[5] The workers face the ground as they work; they do not need to see the helicopter to know its power to observe. However, the helicopter also signifies a bird of prey, its hunter's eye watchful for the weak and vulnerable below. Immigrants as victims, even as subjects of Border Patrol abuses, places them in the position of prey. Indeed, if they are undocumented, they are "chickens" *(pollos)* in local terminology, which metaphorically suggests their vulnerability.

U.S. News and World Report's 23 September 1996 cover is a photograph of a man with dark hair wearing a white coat and white hat pushing a side of beef in a cold storage area lined with many sides of beef hanging from hooks (see fig. 8.9). The text identifies the man as an undocumented Mexican worker: "Illegal in Iowa: American firms recruit thousands of Mexicans to do the nation's dirtiest, most dangerous work." The image reinforces the characterization of the undocumented Mexican as a worker, someone engaged in productive activity. He is at the center of the picture, his body straining as he pushes the side of beef. His activity is not called into question in the image. Rather, the text targets American businesses that "recruit" Mexican labor and exploit that labor "to do the nation's dirtiest, most dangerous work." The immigrant is characterized as both productive and victim, lured by an economic system that benefits by his (and her) labor. The accompanying article details the system that emerged to ensure that the nation's meatpacking industry gets a ready supply of undocumented labor, which is examined in greater detail in chapter 8.

The third magazine published in 1996 was the *Atlantic Monthly*'s November issue. Its cover did not fit the system-as-villain/immigrant-as-victim theme of the previous two covers. The cover is an illustration of the Statue of Liberty's head, with one hand holding a pen with which she is marking a tablet with one to four lines and crossing them with a fifth line. She wears glasses and looks very serious as she goes about her work. The image is green, the color of weathered copper and the color of money. The text reinforces this image of a stern accountant summing up costs: "The Price of Immigration. Can we still afford to be a nation of immigrants? A view from the perspectives of history and economics."

Inside the magazine are articles by David M. Kennedy, a historian, and George J. Borjas, an economist. Although the cover suggests a cost-benefit analysis of immigration that does not align itself with the immigrant-as-victim pattern, the editors, in their introduction to the two featured articles, leave little doubt that they interpret the articles as positive and reasonable treatments of immigration in contrast to more strident anti-immigrant rhetoric. Kennedy's comparison of past and present immigration patterns, in which he finds unprecedented and worrisome patterns in the Southwest, arrives at conclusions that nevertheless "should shame nativism" (51). Borjas's analysis of labor and wage data finds that undereducated and low-income Americans' wages are lowered as a result of competition with immigrants, for which he argues for changes in the nation's immigration laws. The *Atlantic Monthly*'s spin on Borjas's

7.5.   The *Atlantic Monthly*, November 1996. "The Price of Immigration."

arguments is that he calls for "rational change in the name of justice to the least-advantaged among us, not a xenophobic, demagogue-led retreat from decency, compassion, and memory" (51). Although it does not mention specific authors or magazines, the *Atlantic Monthly* is clearly establishing its position in the discourse over immigration as one that is more centered than the positions it implies are nativistic and xenophobic and which lack a sense of America's immigration history.

Kennedy finds that in the nineteenth and early twentieth centuries, many Europeans left their homes because of population growth and the industrial revolution, with an accompanying increase in agricultural productivity. Workers displaced from farmwork and unable to find jobs in the expanding cities emigrated to foreign lands, including the United States, in search of opportunities. Quite often, these migrants never intended to stay permanently away from their home country and family; return migration averaged nearly 40 percent (58). Current immigrants, according to Kennedy, move for more or less the same reasons. Latin America and Asia are experiencing similar population displacements as Europe did in earlier times as their economies industrialize, agricultural production becomes more efficient, health care delivery improves, populations increase, and despite relatively rapid economic growth, job creation, cannot keep pace with the workers flocking to their cities.

Kennedy argues that historically, America was able to successfully integrate immigrants for three reasons. First, the foreign born have been few relative to the general population. In 1910, the foreign born accounted for only 14.7 percent of the nation's population. Second, America's economy was expanding and thus creating enough jobs for natives and immigrants. And finally, European immigration was characterized by "pluralism," by which he means they were "remarkably variegated in cultural, religious, national, and linguistic origins" (61). Moreover, European immigrants were distributed over a large geographic area.

Today's immigration has some of these same characteristics, but also, for Kennedy, some troubling differences. Even though the total number of foreign born is higher today than in 1910, they still accounted for only 8.7 percent of the population in 1994 (in Canada and Australia, for comparison, the foreign born account for 16 percent and 22 percent). This suggests that the relative impact of today's immigration is "relatively modest" and that the nation should be able to incorporate today's immigrants at least as well as in the past. As for economic integration, Kennedy concludes: "But on balance, though today's low-skill immigrants may not contribute as weightily to the economy as did their European counterparts a hundred years ago, and though some do indeed end up dependent on public assistance, as a group they make a positive economic contribution nevertheless" (67). As for Mexican immigration, Kennedy finds that the United States will create more jobs than can be supplied by domestic sources, while Mexico will produce more workers than it does jobs. Consequently, "Mexico and the United States need each other" (67).

Despite the seeming interdependence between Mexico and the United States, it is precisely the characteristics of Mexican immigration that Kennedy finds troubling. In a section titled "The Reconquista" (the reconquest), Kennedy argues that Mexican immigration does not follow the pattern of pluralism supposedly exhibited by European immigrants. Mexicans are from a single cultural, linguistic, religious, and national source, and they concentrate in one geographical region, the Southwest. The United States, according to Kennedy, has had no experience comparable to this regional concentration of Mexican Americans. The possibilities of this trend are that Mexican Americans can, if they choose,

> Preserve their distinctive culture indefinitely. They can challenge the existing cultural, political, legal, commercial, and educational systems to change fundamentally not only the language but also the very institutions in which they do business. . . . In the process, Americans could be pitched into a soul-searching redefinition of fundamental ideas such as the meaning of citizenship and national identity. . . . If we seek historical guidance, the closest example we have to hand is in the diagonally opposite corner of the North American continent, in Quebec. The possibility looms, that in the next generation or so we will see a kind of Chicano Quebec take shape in the American Southwest, as a group emerges with strong cultural cohesiveness and sufficient economic and political strength to insist on changes in the overall society's ways of organizing itself and conducting its affairs. (68)

To combat this challenge, Kennedy calls on Americans to be "less confrontational, more generous, and more welcoming than our current anxieties sometimes incline us to be" (68).

Kennedy's characterization of Mexican immigration and its possible consequences is curiously absent a sense of history, or at least "Chicano history." Mexican immigration to the Southwest, let alone the presence of Mexican Americans in the region, is not new. It would appear that the historical experiences of these earlier waves of immigrants and their descendants would provide some lessons for today's immigration. For example, a large proportion of the millions of Mexican immigrants arriving between 1900 and 1929 also settled in California and Texas, adding to the already existing Mexican-origin populations. Is it really alarming or historically novel, as Kennedy seems to find, that California is today home to more than half of all Latinos in the nation and more than half of the Mexican-origin population? Moreover, these earlier immigrants and their second- and third-generation offspring have yet to establish a separate society even though exclusionary attitudes toward Mexicans prevalent in the Southwest in the nineteenth and twentieth centuries might have led them to do exactly that. Rather these Mexican Americans engaged in a struggle to gain their civil rights in U.S. society and participated in the economic and social affairs of the nation (Romo 1996). Along these lines, Mexican Americans made significant contributions to the economy of the region, providing much of the labor power for economic growth in areas such as agriculture, manufacturing, and construction. At the same time, they and their children fought in America's wars (from the Civil War to Desert Storm) with valor, exhibiting the kind of loyalty

Kennedy notes that General Patton assumed for the soldiers whose parents were European immigrants (Carrasco 1997). And English is the language of each postimmigrant generation among Latinos during this century with little evidence of a reversal of this trend (Espinosa and Massey 1997; Portes and Shauffler 1996).

More curious than not looking to Chicano history for precedents and patterns, Kennedy characterizes the American response to previous immigration in a way that is historically inaccurate. The unprecedented presence of a particular ethnic group, Mexican Americans, in a region is not really so unprecedented. For example, the 8 million Americans who were German born or of German descent in 1900 often lived in concentrated areas, with half of the German immigrants at the time living in four states (Sowell 1981, 57). German Americans in the nineteenth and early twentieth centuries often lived in social isolation from other groups, with whom they interacted very little. As Sowell (1981, 57) notes, "Whether in a rural or an urban setting, concentrations of Germans perpetuated the German language and German culture for generations."

Kennedy also argues that contemporary efforts to make English the official language for conducting civil business is unprecedented action undertaken because of a fear that immigrants would not acculturate: "In previous eras no such legislative muscle was thought necessary to expedite the process of immigrant acculturation, because alternatives to eventual acculturation were simply unimaginable" (68). This, too, is overstatement. By the early 1900s, there were forty-nine monthly publications, 433 weekly publications, and seventy daily publications in the German language (Sowell 1981, 58). There was great concern in the nineteenth century about the prevalence of the German language, with some Americans advocating making English the official language as a way of thwarting its advance. These fears led Nebraska, in 1920, to pass a constitutional amendment to affirm English against German speakers (Tatalovich 1997, 78). Not just concerns with German language eclipsing English, but America's concern with acculturation earlier in this century led to other forms of legislative "muscle." The 1924 immigration law, which instituted origins quotas with a preference for immigrants from northern European countries, was itself legislation that came about largely because of the fears that southern and eastern Europeans were genetically inferior to U.S. natives and thus were incapable of acculturation (Reimers 1985). In addition, concerns with acculturation led to the establishment of "Americanization" schools and classes for Mexican and Asian immigrants and their citizen children, as well as

American Indians (Gonzalez 1990). What these schools and classes lacked in the three Rs, they made up for in drilling the children in manners and homemaking, at least for the girls. The court battles over these "separate but equal" Americanization schools and classes for Mexican-American children in Lemon Grove (in 1931) and Santa Ana (in 1947), California, led to some of the first successful desegregation cases, which eventually culminated in the historic *Brown v. Board of Education* case that struck down separate but equal schools. Many other examples could be examined, but the point is clear. Contrary to Kennedy's characterization, previous generations of Americans who were concerned about immigrant acculturation readily applied the necessary muscle to insure it occurred.

George J. Borjas's article focused on the narrower economic question of who gains and who loses by immigration. Borjas is troubled by what he perceives as immigration's link to increased income inequality in the nation and to increased costs for maintaining welfare programs (73). He advocates a formula for admission to the United States that relies less on family connections and more on the skills and socioeconomic characteristics of the immigrants. His views are based on his findings that immigration raises the per capita income of Americans generally, but that some Americans, those with low education and skills, may see their incomes lowered as a result of immigration. Even though immigration is, in his calculation, a net economic gain, it is not enough of a gain to outweigh its shortcomings, especially the differential impact on those who compete most directly with immigrants.

Borjas's policy recommendation centers on admitting immigrants based primarily on their skills.[6] Businesses would gain more from skilled workers, who would also earn more and therefore pay more taxes than their low-skilled counterparts. Borjas is less clear on the possible competition and lowering of wages resulting from the importation of skilled workers. For example, in a case made famous by the television show *60 Minutes,* a Texas computer company hired skilled computer programmers from India at wages lower than the native programmers whom they replaced, raising a great deal of public furor. Would such examples increase under Borjas's recommendations? Would increased funding be required to monitor for such hiring violations? Unfortunately, Borjas is less clear on the cost-benefit analysis of his recommendations, but his economic accounting matches well with the image of the Statue of Liberty on the cover. Rather than holding the lighted torch above the Golden Door to those yearning to breath free, she is assessing gains and losses before opening that door, metaphorically suggesting that perhaps the door need not be as open as before.

Three covers also appeared in 1997. The *Nation*'s 3 February 1997 cover focused on the meatpacking industry. It featured a color photograph of a man visible from his shoulders to his shoes. He is wearing a white apron that extends almost to the floor. A long knife hangs from a belt around his apron, which is almost completely red from the blood of the meat he has been cutting. He has gloves on both hands and a shirt with sleeves rolled up to his armpits. Blood covers his gloves, arms, and shoes. Bloody footprints are also visible across the bottom of the cover. The text reads: "The Heartland's Raw Deal: How meatpacking is creating a new immigrant underclass." The ethnicity of the meatcutter featured on the cover is not decipherable nor is it mentioned in the cover's text. However, the feature article is primarily about Mexican immigrant labor in the meatpacking industry and it also uses the town of Storm Lake as a case study to cover much of the same ground as the *U.S. News and World Report* article above (see also chapter 8). Marc Cooper, the author, connects the dependence of the meatpacking industry on immigrants willing to accept low wages and dangerous working conditions to the cutbacks in social services for immigrants in the 1996 immigration law and to the reduction in the channels of due process open to detained undocumented immigrants in the 1996 immigration law. The outcome of these factors is that immigrant workers are ever more vulnerable, with fewer opportunities for upward economic and social mobility. "Taken together, these economic and political factors have converged in the heartland to lay the foundation for a new rural underclass. Welcome to Mexico on the Missouri" (12).

The image of the headless body reinforces the message that it is the immigrant's body that is desired by the American economy. Indeed, a term used for Mexican immigrant laborers, who make up an overwhelming majority of the new poultry workers, is *bracero*, which was also the name given to the labor contract program that brought Mexicans to work in the United States between 1942 and 1964. Bracero means "arms" in Spanish, which serves as a metaphor for the immigrant laborer whose body is sought after for production but who is not necessarily desired as a person (head/personality) who might settle and raise a family. In this image it is once again the U.S. economic system that is exploiting (the "raw deal") immigrants with jobs that offer little opportunity for economic mobility (the "new underclass").

The *National Review* followed with two articles in 1997. The first ap-

FEBRUARY 3, 1997

$2.50 U.S. $X.50 CANADA

The Nation.

THE HEARTLAND'S RAW DEAL

HOW MEATPACKING
IS CREATING
A NEW IMMIGRANT
UNDERCLASS
BY MARC COOPER

WILLIAM DALEY'S
'HONEST GRAFT'
Doug Ireland
LARRY FLYNT ON SCREEN
Katha Pollitt
ADRIAN PIPER IN CONCEPT
Grant Kester

7.6.   The *Nation*, 3 February 1997. "The Heartland's Raw Deal."

peared on 16 June 1997 and featured a photograph of Ronald Reagan with huge tears flowing from his right eye filling the lower right quadrant of the cover. In the upper left quadrant was the smiling face of Hillary Clinton. Separating the two faces is a step scale that runs diagonally from the lower left to the upper right of the cover, with dates beginning at the year 2000 and ending at the year 2052 next to each step at four year intervals. The lower left of the step scale is shaded to just above the year 2000. The shading corresponds to an upright scale of percentages that runs along the right side of the cover, beginning at 48 percent at the bottom of the page and going up to 55 percent at the top of the page. The shaded area aligns with 49 percent on the scale. The text at the top of the cover states: "Special Issue: Immigration and politics." To the left of

Hillary Clinton is the text: "The Emerging Democratic Majority." To the left of Ronald Reagan is the text: "Increasing Democratic Vote Share as a Result of Immigration," with a line pointing to the top of the shaded area. Reagan stands as a symbol for the Republican party, and the message appears to be that Republicans should be despondent over an increase in Democratic voters caused by immigration.

A number of short articles reinforce the cover's message that immigration is a problem and that Republicans and other conservatives should heed the National Review's "wake up call." (This call was also made in the National Review's 21 February 1994 and 11 July 1994 issues discussed above.) As the editorial comment introducing the articles noted, "Mass immigration is transforming America in ways most Americans dislike; yet the political parties refuse to discuss it in front of the voters. Welfare/multiculturalism/illegal immigration is the problem, run the mantras, not legal immigration" (32). Rejecting this "mantra," each article emphasizes a specific argument as to why dramatically reducing legal immigration is the work left unfinished by the 1996 welfare and immigration reform acts. Should the Republican party fail to grasp the importance of restricting immigration, then "it will make itself irrelevant even before the impact of immigration on America's demography does so" (32).

The first argument for dramatically restricting legal immigration is demographic and is put forward by Peter Brimelow, a senior editor at the National Review and Forbes, and Ed Rubenstein, National Review's economics editor. They argue that "Demography is destiny in American politics," and that the Republican party is being "drowned" as a result of changes introduced by the 1965 Immigration Act. The overwhelming majority ("nine-tenths") of post-1965 immigrants, they argue, have "Democratic propensities" (32). They project that the percentage of the Republican vote in presidential election years will decline from 50.7 percent in the year 2000 to 45.3 percent in 2052, a direct result of white voters' declining proportion of the voting-age population and black, Latino, and Asian increases. Not discussed are ways the Republican party can change itself to include a wider diversity among its party membership. Rather, the authors' solution for reversing this trend is for Republicans to push for severe restrictions on the number of legal immigrants (i.e., future Democrats) allowed into the nation.

The next argument is economic. The economist George Borjas examines the link between immigration and welfare. His research finds that immigrants use welfare at higher rates than natives. Borjas uses his research to criticize the 1996 welfare reform act and to set forth his reasons for a future policy agenda that would restrict legal immigration. He argues that the political, social, and economic costs of removing immigrants already in the United States from the welfare rolls may be costs too high for society to bear. Borjas recommends changing the preference system so that less weight is given to a prospective immigrant's family networks and more weight given to a person's education, age, occupation, and future job prospects. Such "point-of-entry restrictions" would, in Borjas's opinion, reduce the likelihood that immigrants would use welfare. It is not clear, however, how refugees play into Borjas's argument and data. Refugees have had greater access to welfare and other income-transfer social programs than other immigrants, and thus are the most likely immigrants to use welfare. And yet, refugees are not admitted based on a system of preferences but on humanitarian grounds.

Immigration should be reduced because immigrants are becoming America's new underclass, argues Linda Thom, a retired budget analyst for the Santa Barbara County administrator. She finds that the foreign-born in 1996 had lower average incomes than natives ($14,772 to $17,835), to have higher poverty rates, and to have not graduated from high school. She believes that these differences are caused by illegal immigration and a family reunification policy that admits immigrants without regard to their education levels. Exacerbating the problem, according to Thom, is that the immigrants' underclass status is now being passed on to second and third generations. As a consequence, she concludes that "Common sense says that millions of uneducated immigrants do not benefit America and that their hard work will not necessarily bring financial success to them" (38).

Glynn Custred, a professor of anthropology and one of the writers of the anti-affirmative action Proposition 209 in California, makes a social and cultural argument for cutting immigration. He argues that immigration does not just bring new laborers but also new "clients for the 'diversity' industry" (40). Immigration, according to Custred, fosters ethnic enclaves and a balkanized society, increases social instability, ethnic tensions, and class turmoil, ultimately undermining the nation's sovereignty and culture.

Legal immigration should be cut because it leads to illegal immigration, according to Mark Krikorian, executive director of the Center for Immigration Studies. He argues that legal and illegal immigration are two parts of the same process (39). Legal immigrants provide assistance to undocumented immigrants, who are usually their relatives and who are waiting for their immigration papers to be processed, which could take decades in some cases. Cutting legal immigration, in this logic, is necessary to control illegal immigration because it would reduce the number of people who help undocumented immigrants with lodging, finding jobs, and learning about American culture and society.

Next is the environmental argument. John A. Baden, chairman of the Foundation for Research on Economics and the Environment and Douglas S. Noonan, research assistant at FREE and the Gallatin Institute, argue that "reducing immigration is a necessary part of population stabilization and the drive toward sustainability" (40).

Drastically reducing immigration is the will of the people, argues Roy Beck, Washington editor of the *Social Contract*. He bases his argument on reviews of public opinion polls and concludes that even though most Americans want to reduce immigration levels, their political leaders and lobbies in Washington misrepresent them by not advocating for such reductions.

Finally, Peter Brimelow argues that continued legal immigration not only changes America, but also "destroys" and "ends" America as it was before 1965. He asks, somewhat tongue-in-cheek, "If immigration destroys America, does that make the people who favor it un-American?" (44). He concludes by stating that immigration enthusiasts are not really guilty of treason because they are largely unaware of the implications of their position (the "ending" of pre-1965 America). He restates the demographic argument that almost one-third of the U.S. population in 2050 will be post-1970 immigrants and their descendants, most from "non-traditional" sources of immigration. By "non-traditional" he means Latin America and Asia, and yet immigration from those parts of the world has occurred at least since 1850. It is clear that "traditional" carries more meaning than simply a history of immigration; it refers to European immigrants. For Brimelow, the descendents of non-European ("non-traditional") immigrants do not seem to become Americans in beliefs or behavior. "There is an obvious and undeniable risk that a country which in 2050 will be, for example, one-quarter Latino, must also be, in some degree, Latin American in its politics and culture. Will it then be tranquil domestically? Will the blessings of liberty be secured?" (45). The answer to these questions must be "No" because the next single sentence paragraph asks the question: "And do the supporters of current immigration policy know and intend that it will 'weaken' the United States?"

In sum, the *National Review* marshals these arguments in an attempt to keep immigration a "hot" topic in national discourse and to influence the nation's political agenda. In its view, the 1996 welfare and immigration reform acts did not go far enough since neither restricted the number of legal immigrants into the country. The cover is an alarmist appeal to the magazine's readers, most of whom are conservatives, that immigration is undermining the party of Ronald Reagan, and in the process, so we are told, destroying the "traditional" America that Ronald Reagan symbolizes.

The *National Review*'s second cover story of 1997 relating to immigration appeared on 31 December (see fig. 8.10). An illustration of Uncle Sam standing in a radiant but empty desert fills the cover. Uncle Sam's red, white, and blue hat sits on the arm of a cactus just behind him to his right. His right hand holds a beige Mexican sombrero as he stares at the reader with an odd, slightly bemused look. The relevant cover text states: "De-Assimilation, California Style." The heading and subheadings of the accompanying feature article by Scott McConnell emphasize the cover's message: "North of the Border, Down Mexico Way: Americans No More? Can assimilation operate today as it did a century ago? Or is it going into reverse?" The answer to that question is yes, it is going into reverse, as we learn in the accompanying article, which is examined in the following chapter.

The *Atlantic Monthly* published the two covers appearing in 1998, both for a two-part series by Robert D. Kaplan. The first appeared in July and again featured a desert scene to represent the Southwest and also examined the issue of assimilation of Mexican immigrants. This issue of the *Atlantic Monthly* is examined in detail in the following chapter. Suffice it to say here that the author does not find Mexico's influence in the U.S. Southwest to be one of uniform alarm, deassimilation, or re-Mexicanization. Rather, Kaplan finds people of Mexican descent in places such as Nogales, Arizona, where Spanish is commonly heard in the streets and places of business, behave in ways that are easily recognizable as "American." He bases his observations by contrasting life in Nogales, Arizona, with life just across the border in Nogales, Mexico.

Kaplan's travelogue continues in the August 1998 issue. The cover is an illustration of a map of the southwest United States. Emerging out of the map are five enormous brown heads, sculptures in sharp, angular form, bringing to mind the statues on Easter Island. Two heads face west and three east. Although the heads suggest traditional culture, symbols of modernity complicate the image. On two heads stand men in business suits, a radar dish sits atop a third, and a fourth wears spectacles.

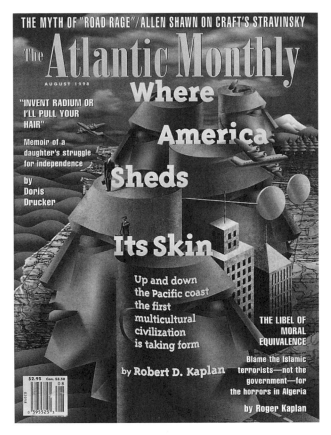

THE MYTH OF "ROAD RAGE"/ALLEN SHAWN ON CRAFT'S STRAVINSKY

The **Atlantic Monthly**

AUGUST 1998

"INVENT RADIUM OR I'LL PULL YOUR HAIR"

Memoir of a daughter's struggle for independence by Doris Drucker

Where America Sheds Its Skin

Up and down the Pacific coast the first multicultural civilization is taking form

by **Robert D. Kaplan**

THE LIBEL OF MORAL EQUIVALENCE

Blame the Islamic terrorists—not the government—for the horrors in Algeria

by Roger Kaplan

$2.95   Can. $3.50

7.7.   The *Atlantic Monthly,* August 1998. "Where America Sheds Its Skin."

Two jet airplanes fly up and away from the heads, one heading west and the other east. Enmeshed between two of the heads facing east are two skyscrapers representing the modern that has now become supplanted— or rather engulfed—by this postmodern world. The text reaffirms this image of transformation: "Where America Sheds Its Skin: Up and down the Pacific Coast the first multicultural civilization is taking form, by Robert D. Kaplan."

Kaplan's travels takes him to Los Angeles and Orange Counties, the heart of the new multicultural civilization, as he sees it. He observes and engages in conversations with many immigrants to explore the lives they are creating, and he finds the process much the same as that experienced by immigrants a hundred years ago. There are differences because today's immigrants have different historical and cultural experiences and because America is a different place today, more of a high-technology-based society. The immigrants he encounters are both attracted to and contribute to a pervasive cultural force in Southern California that places a primal emphasis on economics.

Rather than discuss assimilation or deassimilation per se, Kaplan emphasizes America's ability to absorb immigrants while at the same time, immigrants are transforming Southern California. Latinos are increasingly becoming middle class and opening their own businesses in Los Angeles and Orange Counties. Asians are mixing in ways that were unheard of before coming to the United States because of old national antagonisms. As a result of their efforts, Asian and Latino immigrants are further reducing "the distance between America and the rest of the world" (39). As for the economic threat posed by emerging Asian nations, Kaplan finds that America's Asian immigrants will provide a dynamic counterbalance: "Why, I asked myself, worry about 'the Asian threat'? The best way to contain Asian dynamism is to absorb it—which is exactly what the United States is doing" (41).

Returning to the cover's image, the sculptured heads are monuments of a new culture being erected in Southern California. The image is alarming in that only the vestiges of a "modern" American society remain, overshadowed and supplanted by the colossal heads representing the new "multicultural civilization" that has taken its place. And yet, the image also has a certain appeal, with the wry smiles on the faces of the statues and the pleasing sense of continuity presented by the businessmen, radar dish, and airplanes. The new "civilization" does not appear threatening; indeed, the glasses and smiles offset the bulk of the heads themselves. For some, the fact alone that the image suggests that American culture is changed is enough to render it alarming. But a closer look suggests that American culture is not so much destroyed as built upon. While the skyscrapers may no longer dominate the skyline, do not the businessmen, radar dish, glasses, and airplanes suggest that much of America's way of living persists, carried to new heights by the towering heads?

THE IMMIGRANT AS SUBJECT
IN THE NATIONAL IMAGINATION

If the magazine covers and articles examined here can serve as a guide, it seems clear that immigrants serve, to a great extent, as a national Rorschach test. Immigrants, as the object of discourse, are characterized in ways that reflect the anxieties (or lack thereof) over change and the visions of the nation held by the authors and the magazines they represent. This is not to say that immigrants are not engaged in observable material (economic) activities, social relationships, community formation, and use of social services. Immigrants do all of these things and more. What varies significantly is the interpretation of the effect of immigrants on the future of the nation.

The discourse over immigration during the last decades of the twentieth century has vacillated between affirmative and alarmist characterizations, just as it has done over the last two hundred-plus years of U.S. history. Immigration, as both the movement of people and as a symbol of something larger, at times the nation itself, at other times as a threat to the nation, continues to play a central role in the national imagination, what the French refer to as the *imaginaire* and anthropologists following Émile Durkheim refer to as the *collective consciousness* (Appadurai 1996, 31). The grand narrative that constitutes America's core identity is that of a nation of immigrants, and this narrative continues to wield a fierce influence on the national imagination as reflected in the discourse found on and in these national magazines.

Both those advocating a positive stance toward immigrants and those who view immigrants as a threat to the nation use history as allegory for the present. This use of history bears remembering Walter Benjamin's observation: "To articulate the past historically does not mean to recognize it 'as it actually was.' It means to wrest a memory as it flashes up in moments of danger" (Seyhan 1996, 236). The discourse that presents current immigrants in a positive light draws on history in essentially two ways. First, it represents past and future immigrants as economic contributors because of their willingness to work hard for low pay, their consumption of goods and services, and their entrepreneurial spirit. In addition, history is used to tell a story of immigrants as contributors to a continuously changing national culture and character. Even when it is acknowledged that they do not simply "become Americans" but add new ways of thinking and acting that change forever American life, the eventual integration of immigrants into the American fold is taken as a given. The focus is on the long-term adjustments by both immigrants and the larger society.

The discourse against immigration tells a different story, one in which the long term is irrelevant since immigration is leading to the death of the nation today. To enable this death metaphor, the discourse against immigration has constructed a complex image of the immigrant as the immoral Other whose power for destroying the nation is great. History is invoked as a way of comparing today's immigrants with the alleged beliefs and behaviors of past immigrants. The message imparted by this discourse is that the "new" immigrants from Latin America and Asia are qualitatively different from the "old" immigration from Europe, especially northwestern Europe. In contrast to past immigrants, who in the grand immigrant narrative rapidly embraced the singular cultural heritage America offered them, the new immigrants scoff at such acculturation. In addition, this discourse is laden with nostalgia for a past time when America was imagined to be singular in ethnic/racial composition and cultural formation. Changing demographics and the introduction of new cultural beliefs and behaviors threaten this imagined past of the nation, which is presented as essentially fixed and immutable. The new immigrants are harbingers of a nonwhite majority, multiculturalism, and an end of English-language dominance. Discourse, both visual and textual, depicts immigrants as a threat to an imagined "national culture." They are characterized as undermining a singular American identity, which is also imagined to have existed in pristine form at some time in the not-too-distant past. The appeal to a singular cultural heritage and identity in this discourse relies upon a taken-for-granted image of the nation as united, harmonious, and continuous. And it is this fundamental image that gives the anti-immigrant discourse its power, since these qualities of the modern nation are presented as under attack by the forces—the "new" immigrants—of a postmodern, multicultural world.

At ground zero in the political struggle carried out in the discourse examined here is the nation of immigrants trope. Some advocates of restricting immigration would like to supplant the nation of immigrants idea with a reimagined place for immigrants. Rather than being nascent "us," immigrants are recast as undeserving members of society. Thus, the "immigrant" encapsulates a number of potential dangers. As the "enemy," immigrants "invade" and threaten U.S. sovereign territory. Their sheer numbers, both coming across our borders and reproducing once here, threaten the stability of the nation by adding to social discord, increasing the cost of social services, displacing citizens from jobs and lowering wages, and maintaining cultural and linguistic differences. The benefits that immigrants may have historically brought to the nation no longer hold true as the cost of immigration has come to the forefront of the anti-immigrant discourse. To be immigrant today is tantamount to being a "cost" to society, a cost that must be reduced if the nation is to get its house in order and its budget in balance.

The "immigrant as us" position is questioned in another way in the discourse examined here. Today's immigrants, mostly Asians and Latin Americans, threaten the ethnic/racial make up of America, which is envisioned as essentially a British/northwestern European nation. Thus, race, in the guise of the "face of America," has emerged as a central issue in the anti-immigration discourse (see Balibar 1991). Rather than speaking of immigrants as biologically and genetically inferior or directly in terms of social evolution as was prevalent in the late nineteenth and early twentieth centuries, today's discourse cloaks race talk under the guise of acculturation, language acquisition, conquest, and sovereignty, and concerns with a nonwhite majority. At other times, the cloak is off, as in the direct appeals for maintaining America's English and northern European racial heritage through restrictive immigration laws.

In addition to racial composition, multiculturalism and assimilation emerged as central issues related to immigration's impact on society. Would the social and cultural changes introduced by immigrants benefit society or render it incapable of maintaining cohesiveness, civility, and order? Must immigrants shed their cultural heritages if they are to gain acceptance into American society? Are immigrants even capable of assimilating? As the magazines spin out their takes on these questions, contradictory images of America's future emerge: a grim place filled with dangerous Others or a dynamic place that endures while it is transformed by immigrants.

Emerging from the discursive analysis presented here are the particular concerns raised by Mexican immigration. Even among liberals, or at least authors who write relatively positively about immigration, such as David Kennedy or Jack Miles, Mexicans are singled out as raising troubling issues. Their numbers, their sociodemographic characteristics, their presence in a limited geographic region, their use of Spanish, and their willingness to work for low wages combine to pose a threat to the nation and particular groups within the collectivity, particularly African Americans and other low-skilled, undereducated Americans. Even when Mexican immigrants are recognized as having such valued characteristics as a strong sense of family, they are dismissed, as by Auster, as not really exhibiting "American" values. The special case of Mexican immigration is so pervasive a subtext in the immigration discourse that it warrants special attention, and is, therefore, the subject of the following chapter.

CHAPTER 8

Manufacturing Consensus on an Anti-Mexican Immigration Discourse

Leaders of the media claim that their news choices rest on
unbiased professional and objective criteria. . . . If, however,
the powerful are able to fix the premises of discourse, to
decide what the general population is allowed to see, hear,
and think about, and to "manage" public opinion by regular
propaganda campaigns, the standard view of how the system
works is at serious odds with reality.

Edward S. Herman and Noam Chomsky,
Manufacturing Consent

The U.S.-Mexico border has become theater, and border
theater has become social violence. Actual violence has
become inseparable from symbolic ritual on the border—
crossings, invasions, lines of defense, high-tech surveillance,
and more. . . . [T]he violence and high-tech weaponry of
border theater is at once symbolic and material. Social
analysts need to recognize the centrality of actual violence
and the symbolics that shape that violence.

Renato Rosaldo, "Cultural Citizenship,
Inequality, and Multiculturalism"

Discourse on Mexican immigration does not follow the overall pattern
found for immigration generally. Since 1965, the ten national magazines
examined here have used both affirmative and alarmist imagery in their
discourse on immigration. In contrast, the striking pattern that emerges
from an examination of the magazine covers that reference Mexican immigration is that the imagery has been overwhelmingly alarmist. The
magazine covers on Mexican immigration begin with alarmist images

and maintain that perspective during the entire thirty-five-year period. Of the sixteen covers referencing Mexican immigration, fifteen have alarmist images and one is neutral. Alarm is conveyed through images and text that directly or metaphorically invoke crisis, time bomb, loss of control, invasion, danger, floods, and war. Of all the magazines examined here, *U.S. News and World Report* was the one to focus on Mexican immigration most frequently, with eight of the sixteen covers (50 percent). Six of the first seven covers on Mexican immigration, beginning in 1976 and continuing up to 1983, are all from *U.S. News and World Report*. Five other magazines then followed with their own covers referencing Mexican immigration. But it is clearly the case that *U.S. News and World Report* moved early and consistently toward influencing a discourse on Mexican immigration, contributing to both defining the issues and setting the general tone of the discourse.

The *Nation*'s 25 January 1975 issue was the first cover on one of these ten national magazines that focused on Mexican immigration. The simple cartoon image of an "illegal alien" being kicked back and forth between Mexican and American authorities was alarming and yet evoked sympathy for the person caught in such a predicament. The accompanying article by Christopher Biffle documented the living and working conditions of Mexican farmworkers in Northern California (79). Despite their having come to the country illegally, Biffle is sympathetic to the conditions that push the farmworkers to the United States, and he is critical of agribusiness, which greatly benefits by a ready source of immigrant labor.

The following year, *U.S. News and World Report* began what would become a series of alarmist covers and less sympathetic reports on Mexican immigration (see also Fernandez and Pedroza 1982). *U.S. News and World Report*'s 13 December 1976 issue appeared on the heels of an economic recession that the United States experienced from about November 1973 to about March 1975. The text alerts the magazine's readers to "Crisis across the Borders: Meaning to U.S." The image is a map of North America with two arrows, both beginning in the United States, one pointing to Mexico and one pointing to Canada. Although simple in design, the telling words are "crisis across the borders." The discourse on Mexican immigration begins by associating transnational flows (the arrows) with problems for the United States. The problem in Canada was Quebec, where many French-speaking residents were pushing for greater sovereignty and even separation from the English-speaking provinces. The crisis in Mexico was multifaceted: "inflation, hunger, and

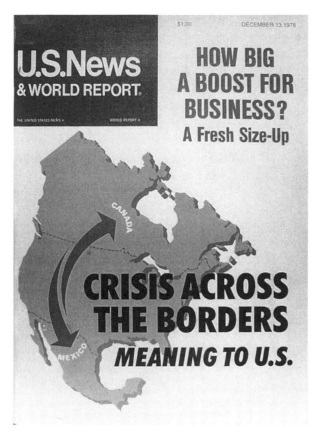

8.1. *U.S. News and World Report,* 13 December 1976.
"Crisis across the Borders."

violence," all of which spelled problems for U.S. investment in Mexico and increased undocumented migration to the United States (52–54).

The ostensible reason for focusing on Mexico at this time was that José López Portillo had assumed the presidency of Mexico two weeks earlier, on 1 December. As *U.S. News and World Report* shows, he inherited a host of problems from his predecessor, Luis Echeverría, who had confiscated fertile farm land to give it to landless peasants, developed an atmosphere of distrust toward Mexico's industrialists, increased the foreign debt from 3.5 to 20 billion dollars, and overseen a devaluation of the peso, which lost half of its value. Mexico's population was also growing at a 3.5 percent yearly rate. For *U.S. News and World Report,* Mexico's problems had immediate implications. "If López Portillo

fails to get his country back on track in the next few months, Americans
can count on a swift rise in the number of Mexicans illegally going north
across the border to find jobs in the United States. Most of the estimated
8 million to 11 million illegal aliens already in America are Mexicans."
The estimate for undocumented immigrants was extreme from today's
viewpoint. As the article also noted, about 1.5 million immigrants—
mainly from Mexico—entered the United States illegally each year (54).
Since it was obviously assumed that these 1.5 million stayed, rather than
returned home after a brief stay, it was easy to arrive at high estimates
of undocumented immigrants in the country.

U.S. News and World Report points out that a major problem for Mexico at this time was the possibility that the United States would limit Mexican immigration, both legal and illegal. The magazine reports on upcoming changes to the nation's immigration laws (effective 1 January
1977) that would reduce the number of legal entries from Mexico from
forty thousand to twenty thousand, excluding minor children, spouses,
and parents of American citizens. The expected outcome of this policy
was to put more pressure on families to reunite illegally rather than wait
years for their visas to move up the queue. The meaning of "crisis" in
Mexico for the United States, the question implicitly posed on the magazine's cover, is increased immigration. Over the next two decades, the
rather abstract nature of this cover's image of "crisis" will become increasingly clarified.

THE U.S.-MEXICO BORDER AS A "WAR ZONE"

Four months later, on 25 April 1977, U.S. News and World Report published another cover on the "crisis." This time, however, the publication
was more explicit as to the nature of the crisis: "Border Crisis: Illegal
aliens out of control?" The image is a photograph of two Border Patrol
agents standing on either side of their vehicle, which sits next to a long
chain-link fence topped by barbed wire. A single-engine plane flies low
overhead, paralleling the fence. The whole scene sends a message of vigilance. The officers stand facing south, toward Mexico, both keeping a
sharp eye ahead, one with binoculars. Their vehicle's searchlights are on,
shining brightly. The airplane faces the same direction as the officers and
their vehicle. All the elements of surveillance are seeking the same target. One officer's gun and long black flashlight are clearly visible, which,
along with the airplane, give the image the look of a pseudo-military op-

eration. Since the Border Patrol situates the place, the fence becomes the U.S.-Mexico border. Taken all together, the image sends a message of a border under surveillance and hints at what would become a common way of describing the border—as militarized—in the discourse under study (Andreas 1998). This time, the crisis wasn't far off somewhere in Mexico's interior; the crisis was right at America's doorstep.

Interestingly, the image and text are somewhat out of synchronization. The text raises the question, are "illegal aliens out of control?" Although posed as a question, the vigilance captured by the image leaves little doubt that the forces of control, the Border Patrol, are needed. But the paradox in the image is that there are no "illegal aliens" to be seen. The reader does not get to see the immigrants acting out of control. Notice that the text does not say illegal immigration is out of control. It is the immigrants themselves who are out of control. Their behavior, the statement suggests, is the problem. The image thus leaves one wondering, what exactly is out of control?

The accompanying article focuses on undocumented immigrants and the question of their "out of control" behavior. At issue is whether these "invaders" abuse the welfare system, displace citizens from jobs, and turn to crime (33). The article provides viewpoints from the Immigration and Naturalization Service supporting these characterizations of immigrants and their behavior as well as the views of a number of academic researchers that challenge the assumption that immigrants, particularly undocumented Mexican immigrants, engage disproportionately in these behaviors. One key point presented in the article is that most of the undocumented Mexicans, and possibly other undocumented immigrants, come to the United States to work for a short time, earn some money, and then return home to develop a business or live more comfortably. Moreover, the academics argue that the undocumented immigrants' fear of deportation limits their use of social services, especially welfare. Concluding its survey of informed opinions on undocumented immigration, *U.S. News and World Report* notes that "Despite disagreements over the nature and the seriousness of illegal immigration, there is general agreement that it is a problem—and that it is going to get worse" (38). No evidence of that "general agreement," however, was provided.

U.S. News and World Report summarizes some of the suggestions for reforming the nation's immigration laws that were under consideration by the Carter administration (33–34). These suggestions include an amnesty program for undocumented immigrants, a national identification

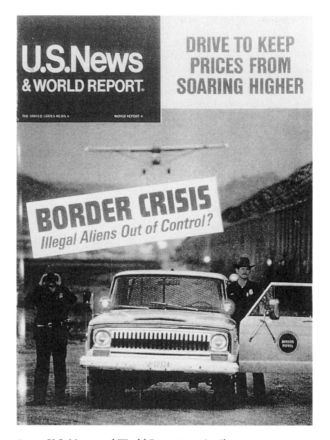

8.2.   *U.S. News and World Report,* 25 April 1977.
"Border Crisis."

card, and employer sanctions. These recommendations were key elements
of the immigration debate that eventually resulted in the 1986 immigration law, which included amnesty for undocumented immigrants and
employer sanctions.

The military-like surveillance of the cover's image is reinforced in the
article. Undocumented immigrants are referred to as "invaders." Invaders
are, of course, unwelcome intruders, often hostile in their intentions. A
nation that is invaded suffers an incursion into its sovereign territory,
which could be interpreted as a hostile act, even an act of war. The
metaphor of invasion leads easily to the next level of severity for a nation, which is to succumb to the invasion. "On one point there seems
little argument: The U.S. has lost control of its borders" (33). The siege

mentality is further emphasized by the following statement: "In some communities along the Mexican-U.S. border, residents are so angry about crime committed by border crossers that they are arming themselves and fortifying their homes" (33). The "fort" image is one that resonates well with the overall "at war" image that is developed. Finally, the U.S.-Mexican border is likened to the Maginot Line the French built between themselves and the Germans before World War II. According to Representative Lester L. Wolff, a Democrat from New York who toured the border, "We really have a Maginot Line. It is outflanked, overflown, and infiltrated. And you know what happened to the French" (33). The discourse that characterizes the U.S.-Mexico border as a war zone that is under siege, "invaded," "defended," and "lost" slips easily between war as a metaphor and practice.

Ironically, the Border Patrol officers and the airplane in the image on the cover appear to be in control, standing firm and vigilant. No one appears to be getting by the officers in the image. Is the image a false image? Is the reader duped by their "in-charge" appearance? Is the invasion and loss of the very border the officers are standing on so insidious that we, the readers, do not even notice it? Is it possible to have lost control and be in control at the same time? The image and the accompanying article suggest that the Border Patrol stands strong in a futile battle, one that they have already lost, but are unaware of, since so many undocumented immigrants manage to get past them and the border.

Three months later, on 4 July 1977, U.S. News and World Report's cover again focused attention on Mexican immigration. Although a July issue, the cover carries an alarmist image of immigration. The cover's text reads: "Time Bomb in Mexico: Why there'll be no end to the invasion by 'illegals.'" The image is of a group of men standing, most with their hands in the air or behind their heads. The scene is taking place at night, a strong light making the men visible. The men all have dark hair and appear Latino. A lone Border Patrol agent, barely visible in the background, helps to establish the scene's location: the U.S.-Mexico border. The men's stance, the officer, and the word "illegals" tell us that this is an apprehension scene. The image uses the visual technique of the infinityline—detained border crossers are strewn haphazardly across the cover from left to right—to suggest that the line of men continues on in one or both directions beyond the cover's physical border. The use of the infinityline image in this way reiterates visually the message of the text, that the invasion of illegal immigrants has "no end" in sight.

This is the first instance of the word "invasion" to be used on one of

8.3. *U.S. News and World Report,* 4 July 1977. "Time Bomb in Mexico."

the magazine covers under examination. This is a noteworthy escalation in the alarmist discourse on Mexican immigration. "Invasion" is a word that carries with it many connotations, few of them friendly or indicating mutual benefit. When coupled with the geopolitical context of the nation's borders, it suggests that enemies, not friends, are invading. The invasion metaphor on this cover builds upon the visual imagery of *U.S. News and World Report*'s last cover, which gave a subtle impression of the U.S.-Mexico border under military-like surveillance by the Border Patrol. Escalating the rhetoric, the invasion metaphor evokes a sense of crisis related to an attack on the sovereign territory of the nation. Invasion is an act of war, and puts the nation and its people at great risk. Exactly what the nation risks by this invasion is not articulated in the image's message. The vagueness of the risk implied by "invasion" leaves it up to the reader to imagine the risk in much the same way that a horror movie might rely on the technique of letting the audience's imagination conjure up a terror rather than showing the menace directly. The war metaphor is enhanced by the prominence of the words "time bomb." The text conjures an image of Mexico as a bomb which, when it explodes, will damage the United States. The damage, the message makes clear, will be the unstoppable flow of illegal immigrants to the United States. Although in hindsight, the time bomb has had a rather long fuse, its image is very disconcerting. It suggests that the bomb will go unnoticed and unprepared for, which adds to its destructive force.

The accompanying article clarifies that the "time bomb" is Mexico's population (27). The article cites predictions that Mexico's population, then at about 64 million, could grow to as many as 132 million by 1997 or so. The yearly population increase at the time was somewhere between 3.2 and 3.5 percent. In addition to population pressures, Mexico had to confront high levels of unemployment and underemployment (then affecting about 40 percent of the working-age population), rapid urbanization that further strained a limited infrastructure, a level of agricultural production that failed to meet the needs of the country, growing inequality between the rich and poor, and political corruption at all levels of government. Added to these problems was the political consideration of America's interest in maintaining political stability in Mexico. In this sense, immigration is an escape hatch for Mexicans who might otherwise stay and foment political unrest. Finally, from Mexico's viewpoint, the emigration of some of its population was not a problem but a natural response to limited economic opportunities at home and available jobs in the United States. As President José López Portillo is quoted as saying, "Forget about police measures. They do not help—and never will help. These people aren't criminals. They are ordinary people looking for jobs. . . . Our two countries have a mutual economic relationship that requires people to move from one side of the border to the other. The fact that part of this movement is not properly documented does not mean that we should end the healthy relationship. Closing the border would only cause harm" (28).

In short, all of these problems in the Mexican economy and society, combined with Mexico's attitude toward emigration, mean, according to *U.S. News and World Report,* that controlling the flow of migrant workers across the border will be difficult. The "invasion by illegals" is being propelled by forces in Mexico that are, the information suggests, getting worse. The article does acknowledge, however, that the Mexican government had taken steps to reduce its fertility levels and rate of yearly population growth. For example, radio stations regularly broadcast messages about the advantages of a small family—"the small family lives better"—and that women should control their own fertility—"Señora, you decide if you want to become pregnant" (28). Parenthetically, these efforts have had the effect of reducing annual population growth in Mexico to 2.2 percent per year, resulting in a total population of 94 million in 1995, well below dire predictions (Martin and Widgren 1996, 12). Whether the United States has the means or desire to stop undocumented immigration is not examined in the article. Importantly, however, this magazine and its cover draw our attention to the external threat posed by the reproductive capacity of Mexican women, a threat that is also internal since Latinas' fertility levels are implicated in the nation's changing demographic profile.

Eighteen months later, on 29 January 1979, *U.S. News and World Report* published another cover on undocumented immigration. The cover's text read, "Illegal Aliens: Invasion out of control?" The image is a photograph of three Latino men being arrested by a Border Patrol agent. The setting is dry, hilly land. The article, with the same title as the cover text, examines illegal immigration and the difficulties involved in reducing it. "The guardians of America's borders, handcuffed by policy disputes at home and diplomatic hazards abroad, are falling steadily behind in their struggle to close the door to thousands of illegal aliens sneaking into the U.S. every day" (38). The article notes that "up to 12 million" undocumented immigrants may have been in the United States at the time and that they could account for 10 percent of the population by the year 2025. But controlling immigration, according to *U.S. News and World Report,* is hampered by a lack of funding for the INS and the unwillingness of politicians to upset Mexico, whose sudden oil wealth raised the possibility of Mexico's supplying the United States with 30 percent of its oil needs. In addition, Mexico's population is once again cited as a problem, as is the wage differential between the two countries (menial jobs are said to pay ten times as much in the United States as in Mexico). Another problem was complaints by unnamed sources that commissioner of the INS, Leonel Castillo, was "soft on enforcement."

The article also discusses the negative implications of undocumented immigration. Issues raised include displacing U.S. citizens from jobs, use of welfare, and crime. Labor Secretary Ray Marshall was worried that illegal immigration "sows the seeds of a bitter civil-rights struggle in the

8.4. *U.S. News and World Report*, 29 January 1979.
"Illegal Aliens."

1990s by the children of today's illegal aliens" (41). Solutions to these problems are few, but include immigration reform as suggested by President Carter and discussed above. Although it sounds humorous today, Mexico's possible oil wealth is presented as raising the possibility of economic development in Mexico so that by the mid-1980s few Mexicans would have to migrate north for work. None of the experts mentioned in the article foresaw the cycle of severe currency devaluations and economic recessions experienced by Mexico beginning in 1982.

The invasion metaphor is underscored in an article titled "Mexicanization of Los Angeles: A trend that is spreading." As the article asserts through a quotation attributed to an unnamed official: "For all intents and purposes parts of Los Angeles are colonies of Mexico" (42). Claiming that parts of Los Angeles are "colonies" of Mexico suggests that Mexico has not only invaded California but has managed to establish political control over territory. How did this come about? Los Angeles's growing Latino population, "swollen" by undocumented immigration, has "inherited" portions of the downtown area. The article goes on to argue that the influence of Latinos is magnified because "the traditions of Mexican Americans remain undiluted, refreshed daily by an influx of illegal immigrants from the mother country" (42). "Undiluted traditions" is another way of saying that Mexican Americans do not assimilate into American society and culture. They remain separate and apart. So separate and apart, in fact, that there is no mixture, no dilution. Are we to interpret from this that Mexican Americans speak only Spanish no matter how long or for how many generations they have lived in Los Angeles? Are Mexican Americans really so impervious to influences other than that of "illegal immigrants," such as the behavior and beliefs of the many other people in Los Angeles, the school system, the media, that their "traditions" remain undiluted? Although the answers to these questions may seem so obvious as to make one wonder why *U.S. News and World Report* would write about "undiluted traditions," the metaphor of dilution/purity of culture is one that fits well with the invasion motif. Characterizing Mexican Americans as foreigners who remain foreign (undiluted) gives added urgency to the invasion metaphor of the article and the cover.

To return to the cover, it provides us with an example of how text referring to seemingly unrelated articles can imply linkages. Above the photograph of the men being arrested by the Border Patrol agent are bullets for two other articles: "Carter Budget: Where a half-trillion dollars goes" and "How Bosses Get People to Work Harder." It is the second one that sits right above the text "Illegal Aliens: Invasion out of control." How do bosses get people to work harder? By employing "illegal aliens" seems to be the answer. This connection may be unintended, and yet it speaks to one of the concerns about immigrant labor, that is, that immigrant workers are used to discipline native laborers by suggesting that they can be replaced should they complain about working conditions or wages. Connections can also be made with the text for the first article and the image. If more of Carter's half-trillion-dollar budget were going to the Border Patrol, would the invasion of "illegal aliens" be "out of control"?

The cover's image also provides a good look at the invaders themselves. The caption notifies the reader of an "invasion" and the photograph captures the invading force, or the three men being detained by the Border Patrol officer. The claim for an invasion is somewhat undermined by the image of the invaders, who do not exude the persona associated with an invading army. They are relatively thin, physically unimposing young men. They are not dressed in military fatigues or carrying weapons of any kind. One young man is wearing a shirt with a flower design. They appear to be subdued and docile and are relatively nonthreatening in their demeanor and appearance. Moreover, the Border Patrol agent is rather nonchalant. His gun is holstered and he is not looking at two of the migrants. The invading illegal aliens appear to be young men looking for work rather than combatants in a foreign army.

On this cover and one of the previous covers, the invasion metaphor is coupled with the idea of control, which is a concept with profound meaning in U.S. society. Emily Martin (1987) has discussed at length the importance of "control" in American culture, which places a great deal of emphasis on order. In this context, "control" and its implied opposite "disorder" connote a set of meanings apart from the invasion metaphor. The often implicit value on control found in American culture means that any suggestion of a loss of control is particularly troubling, even terrifying. The fear of disorder—crime, riots, social upheavals—leads to ample support for the institutions of control—policing, surveillance, and information-gathering—that permeate American society. Linking invasion with a loss of control plays to these underlying cultural values and fears, thus making the "invasion" alluded to on the cover that much more of a problem. In other words, what is worse than an invasion that is out of control? As if there really is any other kind of invasion. Would a controlled invasion be an invasion or a regulated flow? The seeming redundancy of a lack of control coupled with invasion is understandable when we consider that including a loss of control conjures up its own set of underlying fears.

The next cover, again from U.S. News and World Report, appeared on 9 March 1981 and featured an illustrated map of the North American continent, including Mexico. The United States is the focal point of the map and the stars and stripes of the U.S. flag cover it. To the north is Canada, with symbols of the nation and its people (e.g., Inuit, Mounties, a man holding a flag of French-speaking Quebec), animals (e.g., polar bears), and economic strengths (e.g., cattle, farming, fishing, oil wells, factories). Tension is created in the image between the Mountie who holds the Canadian flag and the French-Canadian who holds the Quebec flag

8.5. *U.S. News and World Report,* 9 March 1981. "Our
Troubled Neighbors."

in one hand and raises his other hand in a defiant, closed-fisted gesture
toward the Mountie. To the south is Mexico, also with symbols of the
nation and its people, animals, and economic strengths. There is the colonial cathedral representing the nation and its religious and colonial history. A modern tourist hotel on the Pacific Coast, oil wells and an oil
worker on the east coast, and cattle on the Yucatan peninsula represent
Mexico's economic strengths. Fishing, agriculture, manufacturing, all of
which Mexico engages in, are not symbolized on the map. Mexico's
people are, however, represented. There is a man wearing white peasant
clothes sitting in a stereotypical resting pose—usually he is found under
a cactus—with legs bent at the knee, arms on knees, head resting on one
hand. The sleepy peasant sits in the southern mountain area, and he is

perhaps meant to represent Mexico's Indian populations in the southern states of Oaxaca and Chiapas. An infinityline of men (all the humans appear to be male in the image) emerge from the mountains and walk in a single file toward California. The man in front actually has his left foot ready to step on the red and white of California, at about San Diego. Five men emerge from the mountains, but how many are in line waiting their turn to move forward? The text tells us that the image is about "our troubled neighbors—dangers for U.S."

Inside the magazine, we learn about the problems posed for the United States by its neighbors. To the north is the possible political turmoil resulting from the French-speaking Canadians' movement for political independence from English-speaking Canadians. Western provinces also pose a separatist threat should the federal government usurp power at the expense of the provinces. For the United States, economic stability under such political pressures is a concern (38). On the Mexican side, a familiar litany of problems includes poverty, lagging farm production, an "explosive" birth rate, and illegal immigration. Added to these problems are two additional concerns. First is Mexico's support for leftist forces that were seeking to overthrow El Salvador's government, which the United States supported, and Mexico's public friendship with Cuba's Fidel Castro, who is anathema to the United States. Another problem for the United States was Mexico's desire to lessen its dependence on the United States as the principal purchaser of Mexican oil. The United States purchased 70 percent of Mexican oil at the time, which was a proportion Mexico indicated it wished to lower. This would mean the United States would have to increase its reliance on oil from the Middle East.

Both the cover's image and the information provided in the accompanying article present events in Canada and Mexico as if they were occurring with little U.S. influence. In the cover's image, the United States is presented as a pristine, unadulterated element.[1] There are no symbols of the nation's people or its economic strengths. It sits passively, as if it is not an active agent in the events pictured. The United States simply waits to be impacted by events across its borders. I'll return below to this image of the United States as a place that receives, rather than propels, problems from across its borders.

THE THREAT OF REPRODUCTION

Two years later, on 7 March 1983, *U.S. News and World Report* returned to the invasion theme. The cover's text announces: "Invasion from Mexico: It just keeps growing." The image on the cover is a photograph of men and women being carried by men across a canal of water. The people in the picture are phenotypically Latino or Mexican. The line of people "invading" the United States disappears at the upper border of the image, leaving the impression that the (infinity) line continues on indefinitely, in this way visually restating the message of the text: "It just keeps growing." The overall message of the cover is assured through redundancy in both text and the visual elements of the image. We learn more inside the magazine about the events depicted on the cover: "As dawn breaks over El Paso, professional porters carry aliens across the Rio Grande, collecting their fees on the U.S. side." I will put aside further commentary on the cover's image until I have introduced the following *Newsweek* cover since the two share many of the same visual elements.

In the accompanying *U.S. News and World Report* articles, we learn about the "flood of illegal aliens in unparalleled volume," which is no match for the understaffed and beleaguered U.S. Border Patrol (37). The reason for the increase in undocumented immigration was the economic crisis that began in Mexico in 1982 (42). Flush with oil money, Mexico overborrowed, accumulating a large foreign debt, and overheated its economy. Unable to withstand high inflation and a drop in oil prices, Mexico devalued its overvalued peso, throwing its economy into turmoil. Austerity measures reduced government investment in jobs, exacerbating the push of Mexicans toward the United States. The "invaders," we learn, are desperate job seekers, willing to "risk all" to cross the border (38). With an increase in the clandestine flow across the border came a rise in the number of deaths due to exposure to the elements in rugged hill country and open deserts. Deaths also occurred from accidents as migrants frantically crossed busy streets or attempted to jump freight trains moving north.

The story of Mexican immigration that is told here places the United States in the role of powerless victim and the U.S. Border Patrol as the hapless but well-meaning defender of the victim's honor and the stalwart but ineffective guard against an insidious enemy with powerful friends. The U.S. Border Patrol is hampered in its efforts to halt illegal immigration by many factors. First of all, "The border itself is hardly more than a line on a map" (38). Border fences, where they exist, are full of holes. The Rio Grande at El Paso is shallow, often only a foot deep. Thus, the long border, guarded by relatively few officers, offers many opportunities for entry. The Border Patrol, therefore, is unable to stop or even significantly reduce the flow of undocumented immigrants,

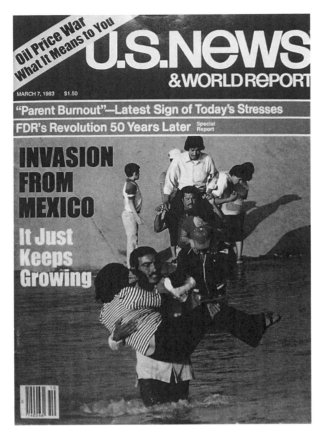

8.6. *U.S. News and World Report,* 7 March 1983. "Invasion
from Mexico."

who then use social services and compete for scarce jobs. This is particularly controversial given that it "occurs at a time of the highest American unemployment in four decades, and as governments at all levels are
hard pressed to provide even for citizens" (37). Unnamed sources in Los
Angeles and New York City provide estimates of the cost of providing
social services to undocumented immigrants in those cities. Not spoken
of here are any positive benefits of immigration, except as an "escape
valve" for Mexico, nor even a nod toward the tax contributions of undocumented immigrants as a way of balancing the presentation. Moreover, Mexico is characterized as culpable in the flow of undocumented
immigrants by its refusal to take action. "Mexico, consequently, has no
intention of policing its side of the border" (42). *U.S. News and World*

Report ends by recommending that the U.S. Congress provide funds for more border guards and laws that would fine employers for hiring undocumented workers who make it across the border. Both of these recommendations were part of the Immigration Reform and Control Act of 1986.

Newsweek's 25 June 1984 cover relies on many of the same basic visual elements to tell its story as *U.S. News and World Report*'s cover (see fig. 4.1). Once again we have a photograph of a man carrying a woman across a shallow body of water. The woman is wearing a headscarf and a long shawl. The man carries the woman's large woven bag, and she holds a walking cane. The text states: "Closing the Door? The angry debate over illegal immigration. Crossing the Rio Grande." This is *Newsweek*'s first cover to explicitly reference Mexican immigration.

Leaving aside the text on this and the previous cover for a moment, the images themselves do a lot to establish the theme and location of the events taking place. They do so through the use of stereotypical phenotypes, clothing, and "common sense" understandings of how Mexicans cross the border. In short, the images hit upon a number of touchstones related to undocumented Mexican immigration. For example, the water in the image could be anywhere, even a little pond somewhere, but the phenotypes, complexion (the color photographs clearly show their brown skin and black hair), and clothing suggest the people are Mexicans. In addition, the people—Mexicans—in conjunction with the activity they are engaged in—crossing water—situates otherwise nondescript water as "border water." This message derives from the American public's cultural understanding of the history of Mexican immigration to the United States. As Claire F. Fox (1996, 60) has observed, "Generally speaking, the Rio Grande/Rio Bravo and the fence are the two primary contemporary icons used to establish the location of a narrative in the border region." The cultural stereotype is that Mexican immigration occurs over water (water is also a basic metaphor for immigration). Mexicans in this immigration narrative arrive "wet" after having crossed the Rio Grande to illegally enter the United States. The derogatory label "wetback," commonly applied to undocumented immigrants from Mexico, derives from this migration narrative. The image relies on this commonly held understanding of Mexican immigration to develop its narrative and to quickly engage the consumer's attention.

It is also important to examine the "directionality of movement" in the images. The movement of the people in the images is directly toward the reader's eye. The directionality of movement suggests that the people in the images are coming at the reader, metaphorically, at us, the consumers. The movement is not random; it is a linear movement that carries the message that people (Mexicans) are crossing water (the border) and moving toward us (the United States). The images, therefore, capture place (the U.S.-Mexico border), activity (illegal immigration), actors (Mexicans), and directionality (to the United States). The text on the covers, which refers to "invasion from Mexico," "illegal immigration," and "crossing the Rio Grande," are redundant but essential to ensuring there is no mistaking the message.

There is also an important reference to women on the two covers. In both cases, it is a woman who is prominently featured as being carried across the water and into the United States. Since we are also warned that an "invasion" is occurring, the prominence of females in the images must be read as conveying an important message about the "invaders." Rather than an invading army, or even the stereotypical male migrant worker, the images suggest a more insidious invasion, one that includes the capacity of the invaders to reproduce themselves. The women being carried into U.S. territory carry with them the seeds of future generations. The images signal not simply a concern over undocumented workers, but a concern with immigrants who stay and form families and, by extension, communities in the United States. The image of the Mexican women being offered up, as it were, to American society brings to mind another image, that of the Trojan Horse. Indeed, a prominent feature of anti-immigrant discourse has been the fears of political unrest by the children of Mexican immigrants and a reconquest of U.S. territory by reproduction. Moreover, reproduction of immigrant families not only raises issues of population growth, but of their use of prenatal care and children's health services, education, and other social services. Importantly, the woman on *Newsweek*'s cover also carries a walking stick, which subliminally raises the possibility that she is infirm and may require medical services in the United States. These reproduction-related concerns, as we shall observe below, were a central part of California's Proposition 187 and the 1996 federal welfare law.

Focusing on *Newsweek*'s cover, the headline—"Closing the Door?"—is immediately jarring given the image with which the text is meant to interact. The movement of people occurs in open space, which undercuts the "closing the door" statement, making it seem futile and even Don Quixote-esque in its very utterance. There is no door to close against the incoming flow of undocumented immigrants in the image. This contradiction or irony adds an ominous and foreboding note to the overall message about undocumented immigration. The inability to actually close the door on undocumented immigration suggests a reason that the debate over "illegal" immigration is characterized as "angry" on the cover.

The issues surrounding undocumented immigration to the United States were the subject of *Newsweek*'s feature story. The timing coincided with the House of Representative's upcoming debate on its version of the Simpson-Mazzoli immigration bill, which targeted undocumented immigration. *Newsweek* characterized the public as deeply concerned with undocumented immigration and yet conflicted in their attitudes and views as far as what to do about it. *Newsweek* alerts us to the "fact" that "America has 'lost control' of its borders" (18). The report cites President Reagan, who envisioned the nation in grave peril because of this loss of control: "The simple truth is that we've lost control of our own borders, and no nation can do that and survive" (18). *Newsweek* viewed Reagan's comment as overstatement, but it did find that increasingly negative attitudes toward immigrants might jeopardize America's tradition of receiving immigrants. Although Congress failed to pass immigration reform legislation during this session, employer sanctions and an amnesty program were key components of the 1986 immigration law.

Newsweek provided evidence from its own poll that showed that the American public was "ambivalent" about legal immigration and "disturbed" by a "historic new wave of immigration" (20). The poll indicates that among those surveyed, 53 percent and 49 percent believed there were too many immigrants from Latin American and Asian countries, respectively. Only 26 percent thought there were too many immigrants from European countries. Those polled agreed on a number of seemingly conflicting characterizations of immigrants: a majority agreed that immigrants take jobs from U.S. workers (61 percent); that immigrants work hard, often taking jobs that Americans don't want (80 percent); that many immigrants wind up on welfare and raise taxes for Americans (59 percent); and that immigrants help improve our culture with their different cultures and talents (61 percent). As for the two key components of the Simpson-Mazzoli immigration bill, employer sanctions and amnesty, a majority (61 percent) favored penalizing companies that hired undocumented workers but only a minority (34 percent) favored amnesty for undocumented immigrants.

As for the costs and benefits of immigration, *Newsweek* presented information on both sides of the equation. Undocumented immigrants put a downward pressure on wages and displace some workers, but their presence also results in the creation of jobs, and they keep low-skilled manufacturing jobs from moving to other countries. Although they compete for low-skilled jobs with minorities and native youth, the jobs created to supervise undocumented labor often go to minorities, even African Americans, who are "pushed up" the economic ladder. Undocumented immigrants require outlays by local and state governments for social services, which may be more than the immigrants themselves pay in taxes at those levels of government. The federal government, however, reaps a substantial windfall in taxes paid by undocumented immigrants, as much as $80 billion annually to the Social Security Administration alone. The report provides insight into the tensions between state governments and the federal government over the cost of immigration. The overall impression left by *Newsweek,* and which appears as an attempt to prod Congress "to do something" about undocumented immigration, is that "The U.S. government, in short, has an enforcement crisis—immigration policies that cannot be enforced and whose widespread evasion erodes the intent of Congress" (23). *Newsweek*'s cover and accompanying report challenge Congress to find a way to "close the door" on undocumented immigration.

Time jumped in on the immigration issue the same week, on 25 June 1984, but devoted only a sidebar of the cover to the issue. On the upper right corner of the cover was a box cut diagonally from upper left to bottom right. The upper right side was a photograph of a U.S. Border Patrol agent standing with arm up, waving. He is standing in front of a stop sign, with the "p" visible. Behind him is a sign above the road that reads "Stop Here, U.S. Officers." This is a scene that quickly conjures up the surveillance undertaken by the Border Patrol at one of its internal checkpoints, the "second line of defense" to catch illegal immigrants who manage to cross the U.S.-Mexico border. The officer is scanning vehicles and waving innocent-looking cars through the checkpoint. Below the photograph is the text: "Illegal Aliens: Trying to stem the tide."

Time's focus on undocumented immigration also corresponds to the House of Representative's debate on the Simpson-Mazzoli immigration reform bill. Once again, the U.S. Border Patrol is portrayed as beleaguered. The title of the accompanying story is a quotation from a Border Patrol officer: "We Are Overwhelmed." The article finds that the debate over immigration expresses a legitimate concern about the United States' ability "to absorb immigrants at the rate they are now flooding in" (17). The report notes that the Simpson-Mazzoli bill has provisions for more Border Patrol agents and a guest-worker program that would allow up to 500,000 migrants to work up to eleven months in agriculture. The article goes on to discuss employer sanctions and the amnesty provisions, both of which have their critics. Concerns about employer sanctions include the availability of forged identity documents and the possible willingness of some employers to risk fines in order to continue using undocumented workers. Moreover, eleven states, including California, already had employer sanctions laws that were ineffective in curbing undocumented immigration (Calavita 1982). Critics of an amnesty program worried that this would act as a magnet, luring even more undocumented immigrants who would come in hopes of benefiting from a future amnesty program. Despite the possible problems with the immigration bill, *Time* noted that there was a "growing consensus" in the country that "something has to be done [about undocumented immigration], and nobody can think of anything better" (17).

MAPPING THE BORDER

U.S. News and World Report's 19 August 1985 cover escalated the invasion theme to a new level by suggesting that the United States is losing cultural and political control over its territory. The text announces: "The Disappearing Border: Will the Mexican migration create a new nation?" But it is the image that artfully and colorfully tells the story of Mexicans taking over the United States. *Colorful* here refers to more than simply an aesthetically pleasing palette of colors. The cover's image renders the two nations, the United States and Mexico, through the strategic use of colors. Central to the image are large block letters *U* and *S*; their color is white. The "US" letters sit in a field of green and rest atop the smaller letters forming the word *Mexico*. These letters are in red and sit on a field of yellow. All of these colors carry symbolic messages. The white of the "US" letters connotes the United States since white is a key color in the American flag. But white also suggests purity and at the same time subtly marks the "US" as a white—racially—nation. White, however, is also one of the three primary colors of the Mexican flag, which also includes red and green. Is the white of the "US" letters the white of the Mexican flag or the U.S. flag? Placing the white "US" letters on a field of green suggests that the question of to which flag the color belongs is irrelevant, since the "US" is embedded in—surrounded by—the green of Mexico. The "US" is already absorbed into Mexico's field.

The red in the image is not the red of Old Glory (and blue figures only in the sky, not in the abstract rendition of the two nations). This red signifies Mexico, which is bleeding into the pure white of the "US" let-

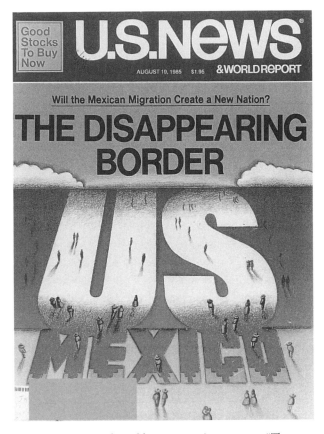

8.7. *U.S. News and World Report*, 19 August 1985. "The Disappearing Border."

ters. The transfusion of red Mexico to white "US" is made possible by the disappearance of the lines (borders) between the letters. Without the barriers, a one-way flow moves up (north) in the image. Lest this is still not clear enough, the image has little people drawn in stereotypical fashion to suggest Mexicans (Rodriguez 1997). The males have sombreros and the loose shirts and pants of peasants, and the women have full skirts and their hair falls in a single braid from the back of their heads, once again suggesting peasant or rural women. All the Mexicans are oriented north, toward the "US," both in their stance and in the directionality of their suggested movement. Finally, the blood metaphors used above to describe the red's flow north into the white of the "US" are suggested by the image itself. A step pattern found on pre-Hispanic Indian pyramids in Mexico runs along the bottom of the letters that make up the word Mexico. The design is more than simply a folkloric addition. Rather, the design connotes a premodern Mexico, a backwardness, and Third Worldness that corresponds to the "traditional" dress of the figures. But even more subtle is that the allusion to Mexico's Aztec heritage conjures up blood imagery, because some Americans associate the Aztecs (based on history books, novels, and movies) with their human sacrifices and blood-drenched temples. In essence, the cover relies on a number of accepted narratives about Mexico's history and perceived contemporary backwardness to tell its story.

But the colors connote still more in this not-so-simple image. Why is Mexico on a field of yellow? Yellow is not found on the Mexican flag, or on the American flag for that matter. Is yellow added merely for its decorative qualities? It would appear not. Yellow and red are the colors of the flag of Spain. So here we have yet another layer of meaning added to the mix. The image subtly references Spain and its legacy to Mexico, the Spanish language. The takeover of the "US" and its territories is at one and the same time a movement of people and culture. The image tells the reader about a disappearing border between the United States and Mexico and the movement north of a culturally distinct people. Text and image mutually reinforce each other, once again using redundancy to ensure that the message is transmitted effectively if not economically.

Immigration-related issues are covered in no less than six of the magazine's articles. The first of these is titled "The Disappearing Border," and it sets up the magnitude of the changes wrought by Mexican immigration and profiles the immigrants' socioeconomic characteristics. The article begins by telling a story, a narrative of contemporary Mexican immigration that establishes a "reconquest" theme:

> Now sounds the march of new conquistadors in the American Southwest. The heirs of Cortés and Coronado are rising again in the land their forebears took from the Indians and lost to the Americans. By might of numbers and strength of culture, Hispanics are changing the politics, economy and language in the U.S. states that border Mexico.
>
> Their movement is, despite its quiet and largely peaceful nature, both an invasion and a revolt. At the vanguard are those born here, whose roots are generations deep, who long endured Anglo dominance and rule and who are ascending within the U.S. system to take power they consider their birthright. Behind them comes an unstoppable mass—their kin from below the border who also claim ancestral homelands in the Southwest, which was the northern half of Mexico until the United States took it away in the mid-1800s. Like conquistadors of centuries past, they come in quest of fabled cities of gold.

America's riches are pulling people all along the continent's Hispanic horn
on a great migration to the place they call *El Norte*. (30)

What is occurring in the American Southwest is a "reconquest" by
Mexicans of land they lost during the Mexican American War. It is occurring because of the "unstoppable mass" of Mexicans migrating to the
United States. The narrative makes it clear that the outcome of Mexican
immigration is a transformation of the region's politics, economy, and
language. As more Latinos become citizens and vote, they will increasingly influence politics, especially since they are concentrated in nine states
that control 71 percent of the electoral votes to elect a president. *U.S.
News and World Report* suggests that influence was already being felt,
claiming that the bills in Congress to toughen enforcement of immigration laws never seemed to go anywhere because of the "Hispanic voting
bloc" (31). In addition to straining social services, the growth of the
Latino population "signals that American folkways are endangered," a
fear that is linked, by the article, to eleven states considering laws to de-
clare English their official language (31). In the meantime, the merging
of English and Spanish is resulting in "Spanglish," and both business and
government are increasingly bilingual in the borderlands.

The title of the next article reveals the implications of these changes:
"On El Main Street, U.S.A., the Birth of a New Nation." The subtitle
expands on the story: "Part Hispanic, part Anglo, the Southwest meshes
customs and peoples to create a unique way of life. Its prime engine of
change: A new wave of immigrants" (32). The narrative of this merging
of cultures and behaviors along the border is not simply a retelling of
the melting pot metaphor. The conditions under which the new immigrants work and live, often crowded together surrounded by disease and
squalor, make problematic such a metaphor. "In still other places, such
as the teeming Los Angeles barrios that house an army of Mexican factory workers, the life and language belie any notion of a melting pot"
(32). The U.S. border, as presented in the vignettes of the article, appears
as a place of dynamic interactions as a wide variety of Latinos, Anglos,
and others intermarry, do business together, and engage in politics. While
blending and hybridization appeared to be occurring along a number of
dimensions in the Southwest, the article did not present any evidence that
this was advancing a movement for political separation. And it is here
that a certain contradiction is apparent in the narrative of the Mexicans'
takeover of the Southwest. The new immigrants, for all their "problems"
and poverty, change with their experiences and as they develop helpful

social networks. In time, they may become similar to other Latinos profiled in the article, who, while actively participating in the larger society are perhaps changing it in some ways, giving it distinctive local cultures and flavors, but who did not appear to advocate separating the region from the larger nation. Indeed, the lives of the Latinos and non-Latinos profiled in the article appeared to suggest the opposite: the Southwest as a site of everyday struggle as individuals live their lives in a heterogeneous society. While the struggle to survive and compete in a diverse society was filled with friction, it was also characterized as containing communication and social relationships that cut across social groups. It must be noted here that in addition to Mexicans, the Southwest, especially California, is home to people of many different ethnic and national backgrounds, which the article had to ignore to develop its "new nation created by Mexican immigration" theme.

POST-IRCA IMAGES

Passage of the Immigration Reform and Control Act of 1986 ushered in a series of measures to reduce undocumented immigration (see discussion in chapter 6). After IRCA was passed, magazine covers on immigration-related themes in general, and those referencing Mexicans in particular, experienced a hiatus. One cover appeared on *Time* on 4 May 1987, but it devoted only a sidebar to the topic of the legalization program, which was to begin the following day. The image in the upper right-hand corner of the cover was of two Latino men sitting at a table covered with papers, across from an officially dressed woman. The image plays on the metaphor of "papers" (*papeles*) that Spanish-speaking, undocumented immigrants use when discussing legalizing their immigration status. The text explains what is occurring: "Making the illegals legal." The accompanying article discusses the legalization program and the employer sanctions regulations, noting that it would impact all Americans who will have to show identification when seeking employment. In a somewhat pessimistic appraisal, that has turned out to be rather prophetic, *Time* notes: "U.S. businesses may be so hooked on the supply of cheap foreign workers that the new immigration controls are doomed to fail, no matter how tough the penalties for violations" (17).

It was not until 1992 that another cover referencing Mexican immigration appeared. By this time, it was clear that IRCA was not effective in curbing undocumented immigration (Woodrow and Passel 1990). In addition, beginning in 1991, the nation was rocked by another major re-

8.8.   The *Atlantic*, May 1992. "The Border."

cession. The timing of the *Atlantic*'s May 1992 cover must be viewed in
this context. The cover's image was an abstract representation of the U.S.-
Mexico border. The image consists of the words "The Border" placed
in the center of the cover. The upper (northern) half of the words "The
Border" are in blue on a white field with a band of red across the top.
The lower (southern) half of "The Border" has letters in yellow on a field
of green, a central color in the Mexican flag. Thus, the image uses color
to define national territories. But the image signals that something is
amiss. The words "The Border" are not of one piece. Rather, they are in
two parts, as if the words had been torn lengthwise across their middle,
from left to right. Moreover, the upper and lower portions of "The Border" look as if they came from two separate places; they are of different
colors and slightly different dimensions. The two halves of the words are

joined together in a clearly mismatched union; they are out of sync. The torn edges of the words, combined with their lack of congruence, posit the uneasy pairing of the two realities that the words are meant to signify: the two sides of the U.S.-Mexico border.

The text tells us that "In the tense, hybrid world along the U.S.-Mexican border, Mexico's problems are becoming America's problems." The image itself suggests the movement of problems from south to north. Little green bubbles are breaking off the green field of the lower half of "The Border" and floating upward (northward). The unsystematic and uncontrolled flow north of the green bubbles suggest the chaotic penetration of things Mexican into the United States. What specifically the bubbles are meant to represent is not exactly clear. They could, and do, however, abstractly represent a whole host of "problems" moving north from Mexico into the United States. Incidentally, one of the negative images of the times is that of a virus (e.g., AIDS, Ebola) that floats from one body to another, infecting its unsuspecting host. Such associations underscore the negative charge of the bubbles, which might otherwise be associated with fun and frolic. At the very least, the image suggests an uneasy, permeable, and violated border. The flow of bubbles—the "problems"—originate in the south and then move north, mirroring the public's perception of the political geography of U.S.-Mexican relations. We learn of this association between the flow of problems and geography in the accompanying article.

The *Atlantic* suggests that the timing of this cover and the feature article is influenced by what it perceives as an important area of interest, the U.S.-Mexico border, that "must loom large among the concerns of a United States freed from preoccupation with the Cold War" (2). The article is a first-hand account of the author's, William Langewiesche's, travels on the U.S. side of the border. Through his interviews and observations, we learn about the problems of immigration, poverty, and drug smuggling, all of which flow north across the border. As a place, the border region is not pleasant:

> It is also grimy, hot, and hostile. In most places it is ugly. The U.S. side is depressed by the filth and poverty in Mexico. On the Mexican side the towns have become ungovernable cities, overrun by destitute peasants, roiled by American values. The border is transient. The border is dangerous. The border is crass. The food is bad, the prices are high, and there are no good bookstores. It is not the place to visit on your next vacation. (56)

The irony is that despite these general impressions of the border region, it attracts newcomers from both nations. Mexicans, just like their

American counterparts who move to U.S. border cities, come to the booming border towns in search of jobs; unemployment is actually low in Mexican border cities. But it is precisely this population growth that has resulted in the border being incapable of serving as a "buffer against our chaotic southern neighbor. Quite the opposite: growth on both sides of the border has physically bound the countries. Mexico's problems inevitably become ours" (56).

Those problems are primarily undocumented immigration and the illegal traffic in drugs. We learn about these problems through interviews with a disparate group of border "types," which include the head of the U.S. section of the International Boundary and Water Commission (himself an immigrant from India); a Chicano activist; a Border Patrol agent (the son of an immigrant); an American Indian whose tribe spans the border; and various drug enforcement officers. The author is also the son of an immigrant. Not lost on the author is the irony of so many immigrants and children of immigrants telling the story of controlling of the border. Adding to the irony is that it is the Chicano activist who is a fifth generation American and the Native American who, for all intents and purposes, does not recognize the border's political significance.

The issue of undocumented immigration has heated up, the author notes, because of IRCA's failure to solve the problem. Even during a recession, undocumented immigrants are drawn to economic opportunities. As a result, "California beckons, and the immigrants feel neither reformed nor controlled," a veiled criticism of the 1986 immigration reform law (60). The author notes that there is a growing resentment in America over the inability to control the border. Calls to seal the border, however, would require enormous manpower, including perhaps deployment of the U.S. armed forces. As will be discussed below, such deployment would not occur without risks for both immigrants and American citizens alike.

Images of a militarized border and metaphors of war are strewn subtly throughout the article. For instance, the Chicano activist keeps a photographic catalogue of alleged abuses by Border Patrol agents and police officers against immigrants and Latino U.S. citizens. He also notes the Orwellian doublespeak that has evolved to mask police actions. The raids INS agents make on workplaces or even on private homes in search of undocumented immigrants have changed to "sweeps" and then again to "surveys." The use of "survey," a term to indicate one of many "objective" social science techniques to collect information, is an attempt to mask and sanitize the police function of the activity. The barrio near the

Chicano activist's home is decried as "the other war zone" because of poverty and gangs. The futility of the officers' nightly vigilance against illegal border crossers is compared to Vietnam: "We didn't win there either" (74). Although most border crossers are peaceful, the possibility of running into a violent person or drug smuggler keeps the Border Patrol agents at a high level of concern. It is the pursuit of illicit drugs that elevates the "war" on the border. The author describes the high level of technology used along the border to "fight" smuggling, and the various contributions of U.S. military personnel to the antidrug smuggling effort.[2] In remote deserts, the author finds that the Army carries out training exercises designated in part to intimidate would-be drug smugglers. In southern Arizona, National Guardsmen, the reserve army, search vehicles. A frustrated Customs agent also compares his work trying to stop the entry of drugs to his Vietnam experience: "It's a civilian version of Vietnam. That makes it the second losing war I've fought" (84). The recurring Vietnam metaphor not only helps to characterize the U.S.-Mexico border region as a war zone, but it heightens the level of frustration and anxiety over problems associated with the region. Raising the Vietnam analogy challenges us not to lose again.

What the author missed in his travels along the U.S.-Border is any indication that problems also flow south. While the "Tijuana river is an open sewer" (61) that pollutes U.S. beaches, the flow of salinated and chemical-rich water into Mexico along the All American canal was a problem for Mexican agriculture at the time. In addition, farmworkers often pick up diseases (including AIDS from prostitutes working migrant camps) and injuries while working in the United States and then return home with those problems. To a certain extent, the problem of youth gangs and an urban street culture has flowed south with youth who have returned (sometimes deported) to their country of origin. While many examples could be presented, the point is that although the cover's image and the accompanying article paint a picture of a one-way flow of problems north, the border actually is permeable to problems flowing in both directions. Although such balanced imagery is missing, the mappings of the border coincide with what we might expect given the historical moment in which they occurred and the role of maps as political statements.

These abstract mappings of the U.S.-Mexico border matter (Jackson 1989). They represent the state of discourse and struggle over an interpretation of the changing conditions between the two nations and the place of immigration in those changing conditions (Saldívar 1997; Vélez-Ibánez 1996; Alvarez 1995; Kearney 1991). In his discussion of maps, J. Harley (1988) insists that they be read as an exercise in the deployment of power and knowledge, à la Foucault. Maps are value-laden images. They are not inert records or passive reflections of the world; rather they are "refracted images" that contribute to a discourse about a socially constructed world. As Harley (1988) puts it:

> Both in the selectivity of their content and in their signs and styles of representation maps are a way of conceiving, articulating, and structuring the human world which is biased towards, promoted by, and exerts influence upon particular sets of social relations. By accepting such premises it becomes easier to see how appropriate they are to manipulation by the powerful in society. (278)

The maps of the United States and Mexico found on the *Atlantic* and *U.S. News and World Report* covers articulate a particular view of the world. Mexico is the source of problems. The flow of problems is one-way from south to north. This arrangement forecloses a discussion of a wide array of more positive social relations between the two nations and among people from each nation living on either side of the border. It is a perspective that is defined from a singular place, one that does not include Mexican immigrants or Mexican Americans in its fold. In this sense, these imagined landscapes, with all their explicit implications, can be said to serve a disciplinary function, that is, to discipline these groups by making them the object of scrutiny as "the problem."

David Harvey's notions about time-space compression in the *Postmodern Condition* also have implications for these representations of the United States and Mexico: "How we represent space and time in theory matters, because it affects how we and others interpret and then act with respect to the world" (1989, 205). These maps reflect the manner in which U.S. society is reacting to recent social and economic changes that have altered how we represent space and time to ourselves. As Harvey (1989, 284) notes: "I want to suggest that we have been experiencing, these last two decades, an intense phase of time-space compression that has had disorienting and disruptive impact upon political-economic practices, the balance of class power, as well as upon cultural and social life." In these two images of the U.S.-Mexico border, the two nations are not represented in a rational way, as a modernist object of delineation and order. These images are metaphorical and symbolic and exist in mythical time. They represent a new (dis)orientation toward the border. The border is repre-

sented as the subject of disruptive impact on American cultural and social life. In the mental or symbolic maps that these representations of
the border both represent and evoke, there is not a concern for a match
with current realities or historical constructions; the message reduces
reality to a one-way flow of problems north across the U.S.-Mexican
border.

These mappings occur at a time of intensified flexible production symbolized by U.S. investment in manufacturing plants that extend across
northern Mexico, and even deep into central Mexico, as well as an increasingly interdependent economic relationship that would eventually
become formalized as the North American Free Trade Agreement between
Mexico and the United States. Has this increased binational integration
led to a change in mental maps of how the two nations relate to each
other? If these magazine covers are a guide, then the change has been
one toward a focus on the disruptive impacts of increased integration.
These examples of border maps suggest a strong assertion of nationalism and a protection of place in response to fears, real or imagined, associated with immigration and perhaps the advances in flexible production and accumulation signified by increased binational integration. This
would support Harvey's (1989, 306) point that "Indeed, there are abun-
dant signs that localism and nationalism have become stronger precisely
because of the quest for the security that place always offers in the midst
of all the shifting that flexible accumulation implies."

REAL-WORLD POLITICS AND
THE DISCOURSE ON MEXICAN IMMIGRATION

During the 1994 to 1996 period, three major political events signaled
that the pendulum had swung in the direction of less favorable attitudes
toward immigrants. In 1994, California's Proposition 187 sought to es-
calate the war on illegal immigration not only by denying them social
services but also by making social service providers and educators into
instruments of surveillance whose duties would include informing on undocumented immigrants to the INS. Although passed by voters, a federal judge declared the proposition unconstitutional on the grounds that
it trespassed on the federal government's mandate to construct immigration policy (McDonnell 1997). The Proposition 187 campaign did,
however, succeed in drawing national attention to immigration, and it
influenced passage of the 1996 welfare law, which denied immigrants,
both legal and undocumented, many social services. That same year, Con-

gress also passed adjustments to the nation's immigration laws, but only after a rancorous debate over the worthiness of immigrants.

What is interesting is the extent to which the rhetoric among supporters of Proposition 187 and, later, welfare reform, echoed the same themes found on the covers of the magazines over the preceding twenty years (Mehan 1997). The narratives that get repeated include those of invasion, war, reconquest, cultural and linguistic chauvinism, the magnet of social services as the cause of Mexican immigration, and Latin American immigration's negative impact on African Americans. The *Nation*'s 17 October 1994 issue presented some of the views of the proponents of Proposition 187 in the article " 'Save Our State' Initiative: Bashing illegals in California," by Elizabeth Kadetsky. This is the issue of the *Nation* with the cover announcing "The Immigration Wars," a war it characterized as being waged over the hearts and minds of the American public (see fig. 1.2).

Kadetsky notes that SOS core supporters were a diverse group with little in common "but their rhetoric of invasion" (418). Bette Hammond, one of the organizers of SOS, characterized immigrants in her hometown in a way that emphasized the threat of reproduction: "They come here, they have their babies, and after that they become citizens and all those children use social services" (418). The supporters of SOS also included members less vitriolically inclined, such as Alan Nelson, a former INS director, who helped write the initiative and who defined the proposition's purpose of cutting off social services for undocumented immigrants because "We want to demagnetize the draw for illegal aliens" (418).

The article also cites an African American volunteer representative for the SOS campaign. A former Black Panther from New York City who moved to California in 1980, he worked as a union computer technician for the telephone company. His speeches focused on a "fight over jobs" in the Los Angeles South Central district. As he said, "These people want you to be like them, poor and mumbling in half-Spanish and half-English. I thought California was supposed to be palm trees and beautiful girls on the beach. Instead we got gang war. You almost have the enemy presence in your midst" (420). He also noted his belief that all Mexican immigrants knowingly participate in a "conspiracy" to "take over all this territory that was theirs back in the 1800s" (420–21).

Governor Wilson also capitalized on the invasion metaphor in television ads supporting his campaign for governor that year. His ads, in wobbly black and white, show a chaotic scene at the Tijuana/San Diego checkpoint. The image captures some fifty people running through the customs gates, in a mass attempt to get into the United States illegally (421). United States representative Dana Rohrabacher (a Republican from Huntington Beach, California), arguing for passage of Proposition 187 shortly before the election, carried the war metaphor even further when he said, "Unlawful immigrants represent the liberal/left foot soldiers in the next decade" (Martinez and McDonnell 1994).

In addition to the rhetoric cited in the *Nation,* leaders of the plethora of grassroots organizations supporting Proposition 187 were vocal in many forums during the 1994 campaign. Ruth Coffey, the director of Stop Immigration Now and a proponent of Proposition 187, frequently raised the specter of "multiculturalism," commenting that "I have no intention of being the object of 'conquest,' peaceful or otherwise, by Latinos, Asians, blacks, Arabs or any other groups of individuals who have claimed my country" (Martinez and McDonnell 1994). Ronald Prince, one of the cofounders of the SOS initiative, speaking to a gathering in Orange County, explained how Proposition 187 would stop undocumented immigration by using a metaphor that harkened back to images of frontier justice, when Mexicans were routinely hanged by vigilante mobs: "You are the posse and SOS is the rope" (McDonnell 1994).

Glenn Spencer, founder of the Voice of Citizens Together, a San Fernando Valley–based group that was a principal grassroots backer of Proposition 187, also put his views into a war metaphor framework. Before the November elections in California, he argued for passage of Proposition 187 because illegal immigration is "part of a reconquest of the American Southwest by foreign Hispanics. Someone is going to be leaving the state. It will either be them or us" (Martinez and McDonnell 1994). After passage of Proposition 187, Spencer spoke at a rally to deny public education to illegal immigrants and the Clinton Administration's proposed $40–billion aid package to Mexico, at which he said, "It boils down to this: Do we want to retain control of the Southwest more than the Mexicans want to take it from us?" Spencer went on to compare "the conflict" to the Vietnam War: "It's a struggle between two groups of people for territory" (McDonnell 1995). Even when confronted with academic research that suggested immigrants generally assimilate and improve their economic well being, Spencer commented that "What we have in Southern California is not assimilation—it's annexation by Mexico" (McDonnell 1995).

Central to the war metaphors applied to immigration, especially from Mexico, is the characterization of transnational migrants as people who do not respect traditional borders and the sovereignty of nation states;

thus they pose a threat to the national security, sovereignty, and control
of U.S. territory. As Hammond put it: "We've got to take back our country" (McDonnell 1994). Newt Gingrich, speaking about immigration reform, also raised the sovereignty issue: "If they're illegal, why aren't they
gone? Whatever law we have to pass to be able to protect American sovereignty and to be able to say we're not going to have illegal people in
the United States, we should pass" (Healy 1994b). According to Linda
B. Hayes, the Proposition 187 media director for Southern California,
the loss of U.S. territory can occur as a result of the rapid demographic
shifts caused by Mexican immigration and, implicitly, the threat of reproduction in the growth of the Mexican-origin population. As she wrote
in a letter to the *New York Times* in 1994:

> By flooding the state with 2 million illegal aliens to date, and increasing that
> figure each of the following 10 years, Mexicans in California would number
> 15 million to 20 million by 2004. During those 10 years about 5 million to
> 8 million Californians would have emigrated to other states. If these trends
> continued, a Mexico-controlled California could vote to establish Spanish as
> the sole language of California, 10 million more English-speaking Californi-
> ans could flee, and there could be a statewide vote to leave the Union and an-
> nex California to Mexico.

Hayes does not explain why people who left a country in search of
economic opportunity and a better life would vote to return California
to the country they left. Nor is it clear why, in the year 2004, the children and grandchildren of immigrants—all U.S. citizens who did not grow
up in Mexico and who will not have the same nostalgia for Mexico as
their parents or grandparents—would vote to annex California to Mexico. Importantly, the rhetoric of Proposition 187's proponents cannot be
comfortably dismissed as the sole currency of a fringe element in American society. It is precisely the same discourse that is found over the previous two decades on the covers and in the articles of mainstream national magazines.

REPRODUCTION VERSUS PRODUCTION

Another observation on the relationship between the themes featured on
the magazine covers and real world politics has to do with reproduction,
an issue that surfaced in the images of women being carried into the
United States. Reproduction must not be viewed as a separate category,
but as embedded in a larger narrative about immigration as an invasion,
as an attack on the nation's sovereign territory, as a war, and as spelling

the death of the nation through cultural and demographic changes. Reproduction is referenced in three interrelated ways in this discourse. First, there is the actual biological state of pregnancy and then birth. Cutting off prenatal care to undocumented mothers directly targets this aspect of reproduction. Reproduction of the immigrant family is also a focus of immigration discourse and policy. Many of the social services denied to immigrant families as part of Proposition 187 and national welfare reform target services that assist in the maintenance and reproduction of the family, that is, AFDC, education, health care, even SSI for the elderly. Finally, reproduction is referenced in a third way, as the formation and reproduction of a community. Reducing social services, medical care, and education—and even citizenship—to immigrants is an explicit attempt to inhibit the ability and interest among immigrants to stay in the United States. Governor Wilson emphasized this point when, shortly after President Clinton's signing welfare reform into law, he ordered state agencies to stop providing prenatal care services to undocumented women. Prenatal services are, according to Wilson, a "magnetic lure" that causes women to come to the United States illegally (Lesher and McDonnell 1996). Since immigrant women and children are more likely than immigrant men to use health care, educational services, and other social services, denying immigrants these social services would, supposedly, reduce the incentives for family formation (i.e., reproduction), and thus fewer spouses and children of immigrant workers would decide to come to the United States (Chavez et al. 1997). Immigrants, especially women and children, already in the United States would decide to go "back home."

Women as symbols are harbingers of immigrant families and communities that are capable of reproducing themselves, highlighting the distinction between the concepts of reproduction and production (Chavez 1997; Hondagneu-Sotelo 1995; Meillassioux 1975). Proposition 187 and welfare and immigration reform did not develop or implement new techniques that would target production or the immigrant worker. For example, Proposition 187 did not advocate more funds for ensuring fair labor standards and practices, and thus reducing the incentive for hiring immigrant, especially undocumented, labor. Nor did the proposition propose increased enforcement of employer sanctions. The 1996 immigration law included pilot-testing systems of verification of worker's status, but employers' participation is voluntary (Lacey 1996). The implicit message in these reforms is that we are going after the reproduction of the undocumented worker's family but not the laborer or the employer.

This is not to suggest that some proposals do not advocate increased funding for the Border Patrol and that the Justice Department does not occasionally "get tough" on employers, because both statements are true (Bornemeier 1995; Hook 1995). Rather, the point is that denying immigrants social services would clearly make immigrant families' lives more difficult. But if the families of immigrant workers decide to return to Mexico or other family members back home stay put, then we will have reduced the costs associated with immigrant labor while maintaining, and even increasing, the profits of that labor.

It is certainly true that immigrant families have reproductive costs, some of which are subsidized by society, such as education and health care. Immigrant workers, on the other hand, have many benefits for production. They cost society little to produce (the costs of raising and educating them were borne by their families and home societies), are often willing to perform low-wage work, are typically young and relatively healthy, and are often afraid to pursue, or are unaware of, their rights as workers. But policies that target reproduction do very little to undermine the lucrative and highly profitable relationship between employers and workers.

This relationship between production (positive) and reproduction (negative) is revealed most clearly in the proposals for a guest-worker program. At the same time that proponents of immigration reform appear to be clamoring for an end or reduction in immigration, there are serious proposals to bring foreign workers to the United States on a temporary basis to work in agriculture and highly competitive high-technology companies. Shortly after Proposition 187 was passed in the November 1994 elections, Governor Wilson was in Washington promoting just such a new guest-worker program (Brownstein 1994). An advocate of providing California agribusiness low-cost seasonal labor (guest workers) when he was a U.S. senator, Wilson again made his plea for a guest-worker program on 18 November 1994, in an address to the Heritage Foundation. Wilson justified a guest-worker program as a way "to alleviate the pressure for illegal immigration created by Mexico's inability to produce enough jobs for its people." Wilson clearly stated his vision of a return to a use of primarily Mexican male labor that would exclude the workers' families: "It makes sense—it has in the past, it may well continue to do so in the future—to have some sort of guest-worker program. But not the kind of thing we have been seeing where there has been massive illegal immigration, where whole families have come and where

they are . . . requiring services that are paid for by state taxpayers"
(Brownstein 1994, A28). Following Wilson's lead, Dan Lungren, California's attorney general, made a new guest-worker program a central
issue in his campaign for the 1998 race for governor (Capps 1997). A
guest-worker program institutionalizes the perfect cost-benefit ratio for
immigrant labor: bring the foreign workers produced at no cost to the
American public. Since they would be forbidden to bring their families,
there would be minimal reproductive costs (i.e., health care and education). In essence, production without reproduction, workers without families, sojourners not settlers.

THE BORDER AS WAR ZONE: FROM METAPHOR TO PRACTICE

Finally, the theme of the border as war zone is one that has had important, and even tragic, consequences. It was not long after the "invasion"
metaphors started appearing on national magazines that calls began for
involving military personnel in vigilance activities at the U.S.-Mexico border. In 1986, San Diego's sheriff publicly advocated for Marines to be
stationed every fifteen to twenty feet, day and night, along the border
(Meyer 1986). Senator Pete Wilson also publicly supported this idea,
should immigration reform not work to reduce the flow of undocumented
immigrants across the border (Gandelman 1986). Duncan Hunter, a
member of the House of Representatives from San Diego, suggested
rather than the Marines, the National Guard should be stationed on the
border (McDonnell 1986). As discussed above, the military's involvement has steadily increased since this initial controversy, with National
Guard and U.S. Marines regularly deployed along the U.S.-Mexico border (Reza 1997; Dunn 1996).

The problem of moving from the metaphor of the border as a war zone
to acting as if this were actually the case became painfully obvious on 20
May 1997. On that day, a Marine Corporal shot to death eighteen-year-
old Esequiel Hernandez Jr., an American citizen, who had been herding
his family's sheep on a hilltop near his family's home on the U.S. side of
the border near Redford, Texas. The corporal (a Latino himself) and three
privates were stationed along the border to help the Border Patrol detect
drug smugglers under an agreement with a federal agency called the Joint
Task Force Six, which was established in 1989. The Marines were to observe and report to the Border Patrol. However, Hernandez carried a
.22–caliber rifle and was shooting at rocks as he passed the time guarding

his sheep. Believing themselves under attack, the Marines, who were hidden from view, observed the young man for twenty-three minutes, determined that he was tending his flock, but then shot Hernandez when he looked as if he was going to fire his .22 again. Controversy developed over the length of time the Marines watched Hernandez, and the fact that Hernandez was shot in the side, not in the chest, indicating he was not facing the Marines as he shot his rifle. In addition, the Marines never identified themselves nor did they render first aid to the dying Hernandez. Medical assistance was not called until the Border Patrol arrived twenty minutes later, but by then it was too late for intervention (Prodis 1997).

The harsh reality between the metaphor of a war zone and the actual practice of increased militarization of the border region raises a number of issues, including those of human rights (Dunn 1999). At the very least is the incongruence between military personnel trained for war and the job of the Border Patrol, which more often than not involves servicing unarmed civilians seeking work or to reunite with their family. The relationship between the magazine covers and the increased militarization of the border region that must be underscored here is not that the magazine covers *caused* this to occur. However, the discourse on invasion, loss of U.S. sovereignty, and Mexican immigrants as the "enemy," surely contributed to an atmosphere that helped to justify increased militarization of the border as a way of "doing something" about these threats to the American way of life.

POST-1996 WELFARE AND IMMIGRATION REFORM

One cover appeared in 1996 that focused on Mexican immigrants. *U.S. News and World Report*'s 23 September 1996 cover featured a photograph of a cold-storage area where sides of beef hung from hooks. A man with dark hair wearing a white coat and white hat pushes a side of beef. The text identifies the man as an undocumented Mexican immigrant: "Illegal in Iowa: American firms recruit thousands of Mexicans to do the nation's dirtiest, most dangerous work." Rather than depicting Mexicans as "invaders" or a drain on society, the image characterizes undocumented Mexicans as workers whose productivity is not questioned. Rather, *U.S. News and World Report* targets American businesses that "recruit" Mexican labor and exploit that labor "to do the nation's dirtiest, most dangerous work." Lured by an economic system that benefits by their labor, undocumented Mexican immigrants are both productive and victims at the same time.

8.9. *U.S. News and World Report,* 23 September 1996.
"Illegal in Iowa."

The accompanying article, "The New Jungle," details the system that
has emerged to ensure that the nation's meatpacking industry receives a
ready supply of undocumented labor. Meatpacking is a $94 billion-a-
year business with low profit margins of about 2 or 3 percent. Compe-
tition-led restructuring has resulted in a decrease in wages as the union-
ized workforce gave way to nonunion workers earning an average of
seven dollars to ten dollars an hour. The constant pressure to increase
production levels correlates with a high percentage of job-related accidents, affecting about 36 percent of workers, and high turnover in employees, as high as 83 percent in one plant. For the meatpacking industry, the problem is finding a steady supply of labor. The solution has been
active recruitment of labor along both sides of the U.S.-Mexican border.

Recruitment of Mexican labor extends deep into Mexico, with some re-cruiters receiving as much as $300 a head for workers. Employees re-ceive bonuses up to $150 to bring new employees north.

The article focuses on one plant, owned by Iowa Beef Processors (IBP), in the town of Storm Lake, Iowa, to show the implications of the de-pendence on Mexican labor for the company and the town. At the same time that the meatpacking plant relies on Mexican immigrant labor, much of it undocumented, the IBP plant works to maintain satisfactory rela-tions with the INS. Their cooperation ensures that they are not subject to fines under employer sanctions laws. The loophole in the law that guar-antees such an outcome is that employers do not have to verify the au-thenticity of identification shown by prospective employees, who may use false documents. Meatpacking plants can, in good conscience, claim they do not knowingly hire undocumented workers. As a result, the INS estimates that about 25 percent of the workers are undocumented in the 220 packing plants in Iowa and Nebraska alone (38).

Residents of Storm Lake resent the meatpacking plant for its lack of financial assistance to offset the costs associated with the immigrant workers and their families. They cite additional costs to the town's treas-ury for bilingual education, crime, medical services, and other social serv-ices, for which the plant provides only minimal assistance. Residents also complain about Spanish spoken in the checkout lines at the local Wal-Mart, the run-down look of the apartments and houses where immigrants live, and the crowding that occurs on Friday afternoons in the post office where plant workers buy money orders to send to relatives back in Mex-ico. According to the *U.S. News and World Report,* however, the town's residents "harbor a deeper resentment, not for the immigrant workers so much as for the plant and company that have brought them to the town" (43). Rather than the immigrants being cited as scapegoats for the town's problems, the plant and its interests were put forward in the article as the focus of the residents' wrath.

U.S. News and World Report portrays immigration as a problem that welfare and immigration reforms will not solve. Reducing immigrants' eligibility for social services does not get at the root cause of the prob-lem, U.S. business's use of immigrant labor. And yet, the message that also comes through loud and clear is that the dependence on immigrant labor in some sectors of the economy such as meatpacking, but also con-struction, agriculture, nurseries, and now computer programmers, is such that attempts to restrict immigration may ultimately prove as futile as they have in the past.[3]

8.10.   The *National Review,* 31 December 1997. "De-Assimilation, California Style."

The *National Review*'s 31 December 1997 cover subtly referenced Mexican immigration. Uncle Sam stands in a radiant but empty desert. His red, white, and blue hat sits on the arm of a cactus just behind him to his right. His right hand holds a beige Mexican sombrero as he stares at the reader with an odd, slightly bemused look. The relevant cover text states: "De-Assimilation, California Style." The heading and subheadings of the accompanying feature article by Scott McConnell emphasize the cover's message: "North of the Border, Down Mexico Way: Americans no more? Can assimilation operate today as it did a century ago? Or is it going into reverse?"

The author is identified as a writer based in New York City. The ar-

ticle begins as a classic American road trip, with the author driving south
on a California freeway, describing the geographic sights and lines of
Mexican fieldworkers as he enters the greater Los Angeles area. But curiously, the road trip ends. The author does not recount his adventures
and there are no discussions with local people, no colorful characters,
no human interest stories, and no sense of personal growth as a result
of having taken the trip. Instead, the author pulls back from the lessons
one might gain from experience to provide an overview of writings, some
academic and some ideological, about attitudes toward assimilation
among Mexicans and Mexican Americans. Many of writers cited do not
even live in Southern California.

Assimilation, according to McConnell, is the new "magic word" used
to placate those who worry about the deterioration of national cohesion
because of large numbers of immigrants from "not always compatible
cultures" (30). The author begins with the assumption that "traditional"
assimilation processes are not working in California and therefore must
be "revived" primarily because 38 percent of the foreign born are from
Latin America, and well over half of those are from Mexico. "If assimilation can be revived it has to be revived among Latinos," the author
states, but he suggests that the "obstacles are daunting" (32). The problems, according to McConnell, are both economic and attitudinal. Economically, he believes that Latinos face blocked upward mobility because
of their high dropout rate and high poverty rates that will continue for
generations, although virtually no academic research to support these
assumptions is presented.[4] More problematic is the history of the
Southwest, which was once part of Mexico. The author notes that "The
Latino sense of the United States has always been different" (33), and to
prove this point he focuses on the terms *Aztlan*, *Reconquista*, and *Chi-
canismo* (Chicano nationalism). The author explains that Mexican
American writers, especially during the 1960s and early 1970s, expressed
the attitudes of contemporary Latinos who have not forgotten that the
Southwest was once part of Mexico (their mythical "Aztlan" homeland)
and who believe that they do not have to assimilate into American culture but instead are reconquering the land they lost through immigration. Assimilation, the author concludes, is reversing itself in Los Angeles, where neighborhoods are being "re-Mexicanized," a phrase the
author attributes to another writer but does not really describe the process
other than to say people speak Spanish in public and Mexican music is
played in the streets. The author concludes that assimilation requires that
immigrants and their children use English as their primary language, are

politically loyal to the United States, and embrace the ideals of the Founding Fathers as their own. Importantly, no evidence or studies are provided on the use of English by Mexican immigrants and their children or to examine issues of loyalty to the United States (e.g., military service, acts of espionage) or on what they think about the ideals of American democracy and its economic systems. Without such information, we are left wondering what everyday Mexican immigrants and U.S.-born Latinos actually believe and how they behave (there is a difference; the two are not always the same) and how they might differ from what intellectuals write and politicians say. The author ends with the assertion that earlier waves of immigrants from Europe assimilated "brilliantly" and that the Mexican American experience is not an updated version of the Ellis Island experience.

In the end, Southern California remains as enigmatic as Uncle Sam's expression on the cover. What insights into America would de Tocqueville have found had he followed a similar method of consulting the "experts" (but not really research-based informants) rather than exploring America as it was being lived? The article is as empty of human experiences as the cover's desert scene. And as for Uncle Sam, the slight smile on his face suggests he knows something the author does not; perhaps it is that he has been through this before.

The *Atlantic Monthly*'s July 1998 cover also featured a desert scene to represent the Southwest. A lonesome road cuts through tumbleweeds and cacti with purple mountains in the distance. Near the mountains is a small cluster of buildings. The text states: "Travels into America's Future by Robert D. Kaplan. Mexico and the Southwest. The drug trade as a bulwark against uncontrolled immigration." The accompanying article is also about a road trip taken by the author, who travels from Mexico City to the American Southwest, ending up (in the next issue) on the Pacific Coast. Unlike McConnell's piece in the *National Review,* Kaplan fills his article with his experiences, impressions, and dialogues with many of the people he met on the road. The cover's image of a desert without physical borders impeding movement is reinforced by the editor's preface to the article, which emphasizes that the author's "excursions expose the borderless forces that are pushing America into its next life" (47).

Kaplan pauses in Mexico City, Guadalajara, Culiacan, and Nogales, on the Mexican side of the border. He is impressed with Mexico's growing and modern middle class, but finds that the influence of the United States, especially its demand for drugs, is having a deleterious effect on

Mexico's economic, political, and social systems. There is also a "catch-22" for the United States. Were the United States able to end the economic opportunities provided by the drug trade (by drastically reducing its appetite for marijuana and cocaine), it would, in the author's opinion, run the risk of further destabilizing the Mexican political system, thus exacerbating migration to the United States. Mexicans migrate to the United States for other reasons as well, especially for economic opportunities to be had simply by crossing the border. But such economic migration is nothing, the author warns, like the threat posed by the mass refugee flow that would follow the collapse of the Mexican political system.

The contrast Kaplan draws between life on opposite sides of the border speaks directly to concerns over assimilation. Nogales, Sonora, and Nogales, Arizona, represent, to the author, different physical worlds, or cultures. In American Nogales, everything from billboards to telephone cables were constructed along straight lines, curves and angles are uniform, and people carried out their work efficiently. Even though it was a "cold and alienating landscape" compared to that of Mexico, it was also a comforting, American landscape, a place where air-conditioners did not rattle and even old buildings were painted and generally in good repair. The author notes that the way of doing things in Nogales, Arizona, could not be reduced to Anglo culture since 95 percent of the population is Spanish speaking and of Mexican descent.

> Rather, it was a matter of the national culture of the United States, which that day in Nogales, seemed to me sufficiently robust to absorb other races, ethnicities, and languages without losing its distinctiveness. The people I saw on the street were in most instances speaking Spanish, but they might as well have been speaking English. Whether it was the quality of their clothes, the purposeful stride that indicated they were going somewhere rather than just hanging out, the absence of hand movements when they talked, or the impersonal and mechanical friendliness of their voices when I asked directions, they seemed to me thoroughly modern compared with the Spanish-speakers over in Sonora. The sterility, dullness, and predictability I observed on the American side of the border—every building in its place—were signs of economic efficiency. (55)

For Kaplan, Nogales symbolizes how immigration works. Immigrants, in search of opportunity, "erase the past" and replace old technology with new, more efficient technologies, jobs, and social patterns. It is, for the author, the immigrant story of "liberation: the chance to succeed or fail, and to be judged purely on their talents and energy and good fortune" (56). Assimilation, as Kaplan encounters it, is not a simple process of change in one direction, but multidirectional. Kaplan's image of life in Nogales, Arizona, contrasts sharply with McConnell's more abstract portrayal of noncompatible cultures, a difference that underscores just how Rashomon-like are the competing discourses on immigration.

FINAL THOUGHTS

Unlike the national discourse on immigration generally, Mexican immigration has been represented almost entirely in alarmist imagery. At no point in the three and a half decades examined here has there appeared an image that constructs Mexican immigration or its influence as an affirmative story about the nation. Rather, since the mid-1970s, the border has consistently been characterized as permeable and therefore an inadequate barrier to transnational flows of people and other "problems" into the United States. Moreover, the transnational flow of problems is primarily imaged as a one-way flow, moving from south to north, never the reverse. Metaphors of conflict and impending disaster—crisis, bombs, invasions—have consistently filled the visual discourse of the magazine covers. When Mexican immigrants are visually represented, they appear in ways that stress their backwardness, peasantness, and lack of modern sophistication. They appear as a metaphor for the "Third World," which stands in contrast to the United States as the reigning symbol of the "First World." A subtle threat posed by these premodern images is one of social devolution, that is, the danger that they will reduce the United States to a "Third World" nation. Finally, what we are left with is that the U.S.-Mexico border—the place where Latin America comes into direct contact with the United States—is a place of danger in American imagery.

It must be emphasized that the visual metaphors and images used to characterize Mexican immigrants and Mexican immigration are not natural. They are used because they resonate with taken-for-granted assumptions and narratives about Mexicans and Mexico prevalent in American society. That is what gives the images their power to communicate. They are also images and visual tropes that are particularly related to the issues of immigration. A good way of showing this point is to shift the topic to see how images can change. How are Mexicans characterized when the topic is not immigration but the issue of NAFTA?

When the subject is immigration, Mexicans are imaged as low-income, low-skilled people whose threat of "invasion" derives from their numbers,

8.11.   *Business Week,* 19 April 1993. "The Mexican Worker."

reproductive capacities, and competition for jobs with low-educated, low-skilled U.S. citizens. NAFTA, however, raised competition to another level. In this discourse, it is not a Mexico of peasants and poorly educated, working-class people that is to be feared. On the contrary, it is the quality of the Mexican workforce that raises the specter of competition.

Business Week's 19 April 1993 cover boldly states "The Mexican Worker: Low wages, high quality. How Mexico does it—and the impact on world trade." The image is of four Mexicans, poised and dressed as assured members of a modern workforce. A man and a woman wear white technicians' coats and a third person is covered from head to foot in white overalls, faced masked with only his eyes showing, clothing common in computer-chip production. A computer terminal sits prominently in front of the workers and one man has goggles and an electronic device in his hand. A fourth man, though not dressed in the white technician's coat, is neatly dressed and appears as an integral part of the team, although perhaps on the less-technical end of the production line. All are relatively young, they appear to be twenty-something, with a pleasant and confident demeanor. Nothing even remotely close to the way these workers are characterized appeared on a magazine cover depicting Mexican immigrants. This is a different type of threat, a different level of competition for the U.S. worker, with whom the implicit comparison is suggested. As *Business Week* notes: "How did Mexico become a new economic powerhouse? . . . It now has a work force that's trained, motivated, young— able to turn out world-class products at a fraction of what U.S. workers earn." Images characterizing Mexicans are embedded in broader narratives. The desperation of poor Mexicans invading the nation and Mexico exporting its problems (and people) to the United States is a grand and potent narrative (Klahn 1996). It stands, however, in stark contrast to the narrative of a capable and skilled labor force in Mexico ready to steal U.S. industries. It's not so much that the two narratives are contradictory and therefore cancel each other out; rather, they serve different interests, and can therefore coexist. Ultimately, both narratives speak about anxieties in a changing economic and social environment in which transnational flows of capital and people are commonplace.

CHAPTER 9

Alternative Readings
from America's Future

Cultural products have complex production sites; they often
code ambiguity; they are rarely accepted at face value but are
read in complicated and often unanticipated ways.

Catherine A. Lutz and Jane L. Collins,
Reading *National Geographic*

Every interpreter is a reader, and there is no such thing as a
neutral or value-free reader. Every reader, in other words, is
both a private ego and a member of a society, with affiliations of every sort linking him or her to that society.

Edward Said, Covering Islam

California is America, only more so.

Wallace Stegner, in Peter H. King,
A Welcome Wagon

Images on magazine covers are produced with a purpose: to capture the
public's interest and increase magazine sales. To accomplish these goals,
the images evoke touchstones in American culture. The signs or symbols
on magazine covers convey the beliefs, values, and assumptions of the
society for which their consumption is explicitly intended. This is not to
say that an image has a single meaning; symbols can, and if they are important symbols in a society often do, have multiple referents (Turner
1967). At the same time, images on magazine covers are not opaque or
indecipherable. They are there to be read, perhaps many times. In this
chapter, I examine how students at the University of California, Irvine,
read a sample of magazine covers, which involved a process of reap-
propriation and negotiation. Negotiation refers to the way the students
actively engaged with the magazine covers to produce meanings that are
informed by their lived experiences (Traube 1996, 135). This process of

reading can result in unanticipated outcomes, as Lutz and Collins note in one of the quotations that begin this chapter. As we shall observe, young people, especially those close to the immigrant experience themselves, do not simply take what the makers of images might have desired to communicate. Their readings of the images reflect their own experiences and, in some cases, their resistance to what they perceive as widespread alarmist portrayals of "the immigrant."

Before proceeding to their readings, it is useful to first know something about the students. They were all at the University of California, Irvine, enrolled in Introduction to Sociocultural Anthropology. I went to each discussion section's first meeting and asked students if they would respond to a series of slides of magazine covers.[1] Participation was purely voluntary.[2] Students were shown eleven photographic slides of magazine covers, both alarmist and affirmative images, which were presented in random order. For each cover, students were asked to look at the image and text and to write down what they perceived was the magazine cover's message about immigration. They were also asked if the magazine cover left them with a positive, negative, or neutral impression of immigrants or issues related to immigration. Neutral was defined as a cover that seemed, in their opinion, balanced toward the issue of immigration or did not appear either negative or positive toward the subject. A total of 298 students responded.

Students at UC Irvine reflect the demographic changes that are anticipated, and by some feared, for the nation. The student body during the 1996–97 academic year consisted of whites (Anglos in local parlance) (22.6 percent), Asian Americans (56.8 percent), Latinos (12.7 percent), African Americans (2.4 percent), and others (5.6 percent). The students who volunteered to read the magazine covers (the "respondents") followed about the same proportions as the general UC Irvine student body.[3] Student readers were white (19.5 percent), Asian American (52.4 percent), Latinos (18.1 percent), African American (1.3 percent), and other (8.7 percent).[4] Students noted many combinations when describing their ethnic identity, including Latino-African Americans; students of various Asian backgrounds combined with Latinos, African Americans, and whites; Middle Eastern combined with European or white American; and African Americans combined with whites. The broad categories of Asian American, Latino, and white also showed variation. Asian Americans included those of Japanese, Korean, Filipino, Indian, Bangladesh, Vietnamese, and Chinese origins. Chinese included Chinese from Mainland China, Hong Kong, Taiwan, Vietnam, Myanmar, and the United States.

Latinos were of Mexican origin, as well as from various Latin American countries, including Cuba and Puerto Rico. Even whites often listed complex genealogies, such as "Euro-mutt/American Indian," "Irish-Native American-Italian-German-French," "English, German, Scottish," and "Jewish/European/Mediterranean/half Polish." I have included the student's self-definitions with their quotations as witness to their diversity.

Forty-one percent of the students were foreign born, but this varies considerably by group. Asian Americans (60 percent) were the most likely to be foreign born, with 30 percent of both Latinos and others foreign born.[5] Few whites (3 percent) were foreign born. The proportions rise, however, when the students' parents are considered. Most of the Asian American (88 percent), Latino (89 percent), and other (60 percent) respondents had at least one parent who was foreign born. Even one out of five white students had at least one foreign-born parent. In short, most student respondents have direct knowledge of the immigrant experience since they themselves are immigrants or they are the children of immigrants.

STUDENT READINGS OF AFFIRMATIVE COVERS

Students responded to four covers with images that I had categorized as affirmative: *Newsweek* 4 July 1977; *U.S. News and World Report* 9 July 1979; *Newsweek* 7 July 1980; *Business Week* 13 July 1992. More students read the images on these covers as positive rather than negative messages about immigrants, except in one case (*Newsweek* 4 July 1977) where students were about evenly split. Negative aspects of the images, even if unintentional on the part of the magazine, did not go unnoticed by many of the students. They were often cautious and critical of the representations of immigrants put forward by the magazines. The students often resisted such tactics as singling out a particular ethnic or racial group. They were sensitive to portrayals of immigrants that suggested class differences. They even noted that the very act of marking some members of society as "immigrants" sets them apart, suggesting their difference and making them the object of special scrutiny. Through such readings, students undermined the essentialism the magazine covers relied on in their portrayal of "the immigrant." It could be said that these students resisted what is essentially the hegemonic representation of immigrants. As a consequence of their heightened sensitivity to the portrayal of immigrants, the students often read the images as negative or in many cases as neutral or balanced, that is, containing both positive and negative messages. The cover with the largest proportion (63 percent) of students clas-

sifying it as positive appeared on *Business Week* 13 July 1992, which did
not feature a photograph of an immigrant. As we will see below, students were more likely to agree about the negative messages found on
covers I classified as alarmist, with few students classifying them as positive or even neutral/balanced.

NEWSWEEK, 4 JULY 1977

Newsweek's 4 July 1977 cover features a portrait of what appears to be
an extended family of European immigrants from around the turn of the
twentieth century (see fig. 2.1). The text reads: "Everybody's Search for
Roots." The photograph is framed by patriotic colors, blue stars, red text,
and a blue magazine title, all on a field of white. I read this image as an
affirmation of America's identity as a "nation of immigrants." The family's portrait harkened back to an earlier period of large-scale immigration from southern and eastern Europe, evoking nostalgia and romanticized memories of the "old" immigrants. This cover illustrates the
multidimensional complexity of reading such images. The photograph
of people living in the late 1800s or early 1900s is used as part of a message intended for consumers in 1978 being reread again at the end of
millennium.

Students were evenly split between reading the cover as sending a positive (36 percent) or negative (37 percent) message about immigration,
with many also claiming the image presented a neutral or balanced message. There were no significant differences by gender, age, years at the
university, ethnicity/race, or foreign born/U.S. born, in how the students
classified the cover's message.[6]

Students who read the image positively did so for a number of reasons, which were similar to my reading. The "roots" metaphor was an
obvious touchstone. One-quarter of the students who indicated that this
was a positive image read it as an affirmation of recognizing one's heritage as an important aspect of one's identity. Examples of the students'
comments included:[7]

> It seems to say that knowing where you are from is important because it
> defines who you are.
>> Mexican American female, foreign-born student

> It's saying that immigration is responsible, in part, for most people's sense
> of self. Everyone needs to know where they came from.
>> Caucasian female, U.S.-born student

Students also focused on the facial expressions of the people in the photograph, especially the smiling face of the central woman in the photograph. From this they interpreted that the immigrants were "happy" with their migration to the United States. The sense of happiness was often combined with a reading of the image as a retelling of the immigrant narrative of coming to America to start a new life or to search for opportunities.

> Immigration seems to be glorified by the happy faces of the characters and their search for what is hoped to be a Promised Land.
>
> Jewish/white female, U.S.-born student

> Families immigrate to find better lives, to escape the harsh lives of their native country. Immigration is saving people.
>
> Vietnamese female, foreign-born student

The image's immigration theme touched off responses that alluded to immigration uniting Americans in a common experience (18 percent of the positive readings mentioned this). The "all Americans were once immigrants" trope establishes a commonality that underlies an imagined national community. A sampling of the students' comments:

> Most people have roots that extend from outside the United States and that all have the "Pilgrim"-like stories of arrival to the United States.
>
> East Indian male, U.S.-born student

> Immigration is an "American" thing, like baseball, apple pie, and Mom. Nice stars around the border.
>
> Scottish/Irish/English female, U.S.-born student

Students who read the image negatively were not grabbed by the image's historical significance nor its retelling of the nation of immigrants narrative. Rather, these students focused on what they perceived were negative characterizations of immigrants implied by the people in the photograph. Students (59 percent of those classifying the cover as negative) paid particular attention to aspects of the image that related to class. They read the image as characterizing immigrants as poor and lacking in hygiene ("dirty" and "unclean"). In addition, students noted that the number of children in the picture suggests that immigrants have high fertility levels, which added to the image's negative impression. Comments on the "large family" were often included in observations about the image's emphasis on poverty and hygiene.[8]

> It seems as though immigrants are viewed as filthy and poor, as though immigrants are seen to be inferior.
>
> Korean male, foreign-born student

It seems to say that immigrants are dirty, unhappy people with a lot of children.

Mexican American/African American female,
U.S.-born student

Some students (15 percent of those classifying the cover as negative) focused on the race of the immigrants. For these students, the white European family in the photograph raised issues about the exclusion of other ethnic and racial groups. The image suffers by its lack of representation of America's ethnic and racial diversity.

I am surprised that there were no Asian Americans up there. Asians did immigrate at that time and even before, looks like it's from the 1920s.

Vietnamese female, foreign-born student

It says people are beginning to acquire pride for their roots. However, the picture is biased. There are some ethnicities not represented. It seems racist to me. It says America would probably be lost without whites.

Latino male, U.S.-born student

Finally, some students (10 percent of the students who viewed the image as negative read the faces of the people on the cover as "unhappy," "scared," or "hopeless."

The faces on the mother and children of the picture are faces of fear and anything but happiness. The father seems tired, serious about the situation.

Mexican female, U.S.-born student

Both the positive and negative readings of the cover's image are instructive and provide insights into how this multicultural group of young people approached the topic of immigration. The students picked up on the cover's use of common narratives to communicate a message about America's identity. They read narratives about "a nation of immigrants," "all Americans have immigrant roots," "all Americans were once immigrants," and "America as a land of opportunity." The students interpreted these narratives as suggesting America's willingness to include immigrants in the imagined nation, as forming a discourse of inclusiveness by casting a wide net around the "we, the people." Such affirmative messages were appealing to the students.

On the other hand, the students showed themselves to be wary, and even somewhat cynical, when reading images about immigrants. They were quick to react to what they perceived was a contradiction between the "Everybody" of the text and the lack of diversity in the image. They focused on negative messages about the character of immigrants, espe-

cially suggestions that immigrants are lower class, which implies igno-
rance, a lack of education, and a lack of self-control (e.g., high fertility).
These perceived negative characterizations of immigrants washed out (the
photographic metaphor seems particularly apt here) any positive, but
more abstract, historical theme or message about immigration.

U.S. NEWS AND WORLD REPORT, 9 JULY 1979

Refugees were the subject of *U.S. News and World Report*'s 9 July 1979
cover (see fig. 2.2). The cover's text—"America: Still the Promised
Land"—and its image of Asian refugees looking longingly at the Statue
of Liberty was, in my reading, an affirmation of America's grand narrative as the "Land of Liberty," especially for exiles "yearning to breathe
free." A majority of all students (56 percent) also read the image as saying something positive about immigration, but almost one out of five (18
percent) read it negatively. While there was no significant difference between foreign- and U.S.-born students, white students (72 percent) were
significantly more likely than Asian Americans (55 percent), Latinos (44
percent), or other students (50 percent) to view the cover's image as conveying a positive message about immigration.[9]

Students who read the cover as a positive message about immigration
made comments that consistently reiterated aspects of a single theme:
the narrative of "America as the land of opportunity for immigrants."
Their readings raised similar themes as the positive readings of the last
cover. Many focused on the cover's text, which they interpreted as affirming America's self-image as a place that welcomes immigrants, holds out
the American Dream to them, and integrates them into the nation's melting pot. The students noted that the overall message is that the United
States is not only the "land of opportunity" but "the savior of people,"
"the land of hope," "the best place to immigrate to," "hospitable," "welcoming," "land of refuge," and "a place of hope and promise." A sampling of their comments on the cover's message:

> It shows that no matter what state America may be in today that it's still
> the best place to live. It shows liberty and patriotism and suggests that the
> country can handle immigration.
>
> French/Russian/Scottish male, U.S.-born student

> Immigration is still considered positive—the immigrants continue to see
> America as positive for their futures and Americans continue to make the
> country strong as a melting pot.
>
> Jewish/white female, U.S.-born student

It is making out that the United States still takes in immigrants. It shows how our Liberty Lady is standing strong and allowing all the "poor, suffering" immigrants in.

Chinese/Mandarin female, foreign-born student

Students who read the cover as conveying a negative message about immigration again focused on class issues, characterizing the immigrants as "low class," "inferior," and "bringing problems" to the United States. Students pointed to the way the image is composed for constructing these negative messages. The crowding or mass of people, the rope keeping the people penned in, and even the contrast of the people in black and white to the color of the rest of the image are elements read as contributing to a negative overall message. Quite often, the students' responses combined issues of race (only Asians depicted on the cover), class, inferiority, and immigrants as the bearers of problems. One or more of these issues were found in 55 percent of the negative responses.

Immigrants are trying to seek opportunities but the picture of immigrants in the boat gives out the message of them being underclass and inferior.

Korean American female, foreign-born student

America in color. Immigrants in black and white. They're older, less modernized, less fit and adapted. They try to come into color, into "the Promised Land."

White American female, U.S.-born student

Everyone is still trying to get into the United States. The picture seems to focus on Asians in particular, like Vietnamese. It looks like they're bringing problems.

Chinese/Cantonese male, U.S.-born student

This cover, like the last one, speaks to the students using easily recognizable narratives affirming America's openness to immigrants. In both cases, many students were wary of how immigrants are represented.

NEWSWEEK, 7 JULY 1980

Newsweek's 7 July 1980 cover, with the photograph of a Hmong woman carrying a baby on her back, is another one that, in my reading, used affirmative imagery to send a message about the United States as a nation that accepts immigrants into its social fold (see fig. 2.3). I read this image as affirming the United States to be a nation of immigrants and as a country that continues to take in immigrants. More students (42 percent) viewed this cover positively than negatively (16 percent). U.S.-born students (48 percent) were more likely than foreign-born students (33 percent) to classify the cover as positive toward immigration.[10]

Students who read the image positively believed the message it conveyed was that immigrants are welcomed and accepted into American society. They pointed to a number of elements in the image as contributing to this message. They interpreted the woman's smile and the baby's facial expression as indicating that immigrants are "happy" and content to be in America. This state of happiness suggested a number of positive associations between immigrants and the nation. The "happy" aspect of the image was often combined with explicit references to the colors, ribbon, stars, or eagle that frame the photograph of the woman and her child in "American" symbols. These symbols contributed to the welcoming message and the message that the United States is accepting of these immigrants. Some examples:

> Makes immigration seem like a very nice thing. Smiles, a baby and all the fancy patriotic framing—immigration is great!
>
>   Filipino male, U.S.-born student

> The stars, the American eagle, and the happy, clean people in the picture present immigrants in a positive light. Also "new" immigrants (hard workers, happy, clean) vs. old immigrants (lazy, sick, dirty).
>
>   Russian/Japanese female, U.S.-born student

Race was an issue raised by students who read the cover positively. The Asian woman and child, combined with the symbols of Americana, signaled that Asian immigrants were the "new" immigrants referred to on the cover. Students noted that this meant that Asians were now welcomed, that immigrants were no longer predominantly from Europe. Even when reading the cover's message as positive, some students noted the implied insidious comparison between Asian immigrants and other immigrant groups, especially from Latin America. A sampling of their comments:

> Immigrants aren't white anymore, but they are still part of American society.
>
>   Filipino/English female, U.S.-born student

> The immigrants of today are not the same as the immigrants of yesterday to the New World (from Europe). Instead, immigrants of today now come from all over the world to America, the melting pot of the world.
>
>   White European American female, U.S.-born student

> There are new immigrants coming to the United States. Positive, although I am quite mad because Mexican immigrants seem more like a nuisance and Asian immigrants are welcomed.
>
>   Mexican American female, foreign-born student

Negative readings of the cover's message focused prominently on race issues. Over half (61 percent) of the students reading the cover negatively focused on race, especially Latino students (77 percent of those who read the message negatively). In some cases, students interpreted the image of the Asian woman and her baby as singling out Asians, and thus associating Asian immigration with increasing numbers of immigrants and problems associated with immigration. Class was also an issue with a few students (12 percent of all negative readings) who focused on aspects of the image that implied, in their opinion, that immigrants are "poor," "lower class," "inferior" people bringing problems to the United States. For example, some students believed that the image of the woman carrying the baby on her back depicted immigrants as "poor" and "uncivilized." Taken together, issues of race and class were present in 74 percent of the negative readings. A sample of negative readings:

> Shows Asians as the new threat to America.
>
> > White male, U.S.-born student

> Now instead of Mexican immigrants, Asian immigrants seem to be the ones coming into America in great numbers.
>
> > Filipino female, U.S.-born student

> I'm not sure. The way the picture is shown—the banners and eagle—it looks as if the people at *Newsweek* are happy with Asian immigrants, but setting them apart is still not good. (They are totally set apart from everyone else.)
>
> > German female, U.S.-born student

> It shows how the United States has to prepare to accept another new race of immigrants. It implies, "Great, there's more. We're not done yet."
>
> > Vietnamese female, foreign-born student

> It's biased, racist, because it targets one race. This is Asian-bashing!
>
> > Filipino male, foreign-born student

In sum, in both their positive and negative readings students were critical of one particular immigrant group being singled out. Singling out one immigrant group, in this case Asians, creates tensions not only by suggesting the singled out group is "special," and therefore in need of heightened scrutiny (surveillance?), but also because of the invidious comparison it promotes with other, unnamed, immigrant groups. Since the comparisons are "unsaid," the reader simply fills in the blanks. Students were wary of the implications of this visual discourse, preferring more generic representations, such as that found on the following magazine cover.

BUSINESS WEEK, 13 JULY 1992

Business Week's 13 July 1992 cover prominently featured the headline "The Immigrants" above the head of a multicolored and eclectically dressed Statue of Liberty, a portion of her upraised arm visible (see fig. 4.7). The subheading reads "how they're helping the U.S. economy." I read this cover as an affirmation of America's strength through diversity narrative and an example of a prominent conservative position that immigration is economically beneficial. This cover had the highest level of consensus among students (63 percent) that the message was positive about immigration among all the ostensibly affirmative covers. Still, some students (19 percent) read the cover's message as negative. Although white students (74 percent) were the most likely to classify the cover as positive (compared to 63 percent of Asian Americans, 59 percent of Latinos, and 47 percent of Others), the difference was not statistically significant. Many (54 percent) of the students who read the cover as conveying a positive message about immigration explicitly made comments related to the economic theme of the cover's text, which they interpreted as meaning immigrants make a positive economic contribution to society.

> Immigrants from all over bring in different skills and ideas and take advantage of the opportunities the United States offers. And, in turn, immigrants help the economy tremendously.
> > Punjabi (India) female, foreign-born student

> They [immigrants] are improving the economy. Would you go out in the fields at 12 noon and bend your back for 12 hours for $1 an hour?
> > Korean/white male, U.S.-born student

Other students (24 percent of those classifying the cover as positive) focused on America's ethnic and racial diversity, a message that they drew from the changed image of the Statue of Liberty, especially the many colors in her new image. Some students mentioned both economic contributions and the diversity theme. For these students, the cover conveyed a positive message about America as a multicultural and multiethnic society.

> It says that the unification of all the different immigrants is beneficial for the economy. It shows how people should accept the concept of the melting pot.
> > Vietnamese female, foreign-born student

> This [cover] is great. The Statue of Liberty is shown not in danger. Rather it is shown as a conglomeration of different racial identities. This is what makes America great. Very positive.
> > English/German/Scottish male, U.S.-born student

> This [cover] seems to be objective and looks at the different people in the
> United States as being important and able to contribute productively to the
> society.
>
> African American female, U.S.-born student

Still other students (28 percent) made more general comments, often
playing off of the "help" in the text, translating that into a message that
immigrants are generally "helpful," "beneficial," or "positive" for society. As the comments make clear, many believed that this cover sent a
positive message and even expressed relief that immigrants were finally
being recognized for their contributions to society.

The single most dominant theme among students who read this cover
as sending a negative message about immigration focused on the Statue
of Liberty. Only this time, changes to her appearance were read as conveying a negative message. In chapter 4, I discussed the Statue of Liberty's power as an icon representing the nation. Any changes to this icon
can be viewed as implying changes to the nation's identity, people, and
culture. It's not surprising, therefore, that 55 percent of those indicating
that the cover sent a negative message about immigration explicitly referred to changes in the Statue of Liberty's appearance. They often used
the possessive "our" when speaking of the statue and frequently described
her new look with adjectives such as "ugly," "distorted," "messed up,"
"mad," "confused," or "mangled." For these students, the altered appearance of the Statue of Liberty was the magazine's way of countering
any positive message conveyed by the text about immigrants' economic
contribution. Some examples of students' comments:

> The statue's facial expression is not one of joy. It is saying immigrants will
> add more variety and eventually overtake what was once there.
>
> Irish/Native American/Italian/German/French female,
> U.S.-born student

> Our statue is defaced, i.e., immigrants are changing it.
>
> Hawaiian/Japanese/Filipino/German/Irish female,
> U.S.-born student

> It's basically blaming the immigrants for giving our Liberty Lady a
> distorted look. Everyone is giving her a patch from their country.
>
> Chinese/Mandarin female, foreign-born student

A second theme that emerges is a focus on the text "the immigrants."
For some students (18 percent of those who classified the cover as negative), this text marks immigrants as the "other," as separate and different from other Americans. Being different, or marked as different,

signifies that immigrants are not equal to other Americans, and are therefore inferior, or at least outsiders to society. Some comments:

> Although it's saying that immigrants help the economy, they're still a secondary group, "the immigrants," and never going to be Americans.
> Chinese female, foreign-born student

> It's good that they're helping the U.S. economy, but the fact that it starts out in large print "the immigrants" totally sets them apart from everyone else.
> German female, U.S.-born student

In sum, students were quick to attach well-known narratives about America and immigration to the images on the magazine covers. Narratives such as the "nation of immigrants," the "melting pot," and even "diversity is strength" affirmed positive aspects of America's relationship to immigrants. But there was also a wariness to accept these narratives at face value. This may not be surprising given that the students bring with them a multitude of positions—cross currents of gender, class, race, ethnicity, immigration history—to their readings of the covers. Their readings are also filtered through the high level of anti-immigrant sentiment in the public debate over immigration during the early and mid-1990s. Their cautiousness over reading these ostensibly affirmative covers as positive can be seen in the large number of students who classified them as neutral or balanced in their message.[11]

STUDENT READINGS OF ALARMIST IMAGES

Interestingly, students were less ambivalent in their readings of the seven ostensibly alarmist images that they viewed. Over 90 percent of the students classified two covers as negative, and over 80 percent classified two others as negative. In their readings, students focused on words with highly charged connotations, such as "invasion," "flood," and "mess." They were also sensitive to portrayals of race and symbols such as the Statue of Liberty and the American flag. And, once again, they were particularly critical when specific immigrant groups were singled out.

U.S. NEWS AND WORLD REPORT, 7 MARCH 1983

U.S. News and World Report's 7 March 1983 cover featured a photograph of a woman being carried by a man across a canal of water, with other people following, also being carried (see fig. 8.6). The text announced: "Invasion from Mexico: It just keeps growing." I read the cover, with its use of the word "invasion," as alarmist. Students had a similar reaction. Almost all of the students (92 percent) read the cover's image as conveying a negative message about immigration. This cover had the highest level of agreement among the students as to the intent of its message. There were no significant differences among the students in their classifications of the cover's message.

About half (51 percent) of the students reading the cover negatively focused explicitly on the invasion metaphor. Their responses included a number of associations with the term "invasion." Invasion equated immigration to a "war," "attack," "take over," threat," or a "struggle over power." The term "invasion" also called forth a message that immigrants are "unwanted," "unwelcome," "imposing," and "trespassers." Moreover, students associated "invasion" with a characterization of immigrants as "outsiders," "different," "aliens" (from outer space), "a burden," "bad people," "felons," "enemies," "criminals," and as persons with an "intent to do harm."

For eight students, the invasion metaphor called forth the image of a "disease," "cancer," "plague" that is infecting the United States. The negative interpretations of a disease metaphor are unmistakable. Some examples of the students' readings:

> Immigration from Mexico is an invasion. Mexicans are considered to be aliens, outsiders, different, coming into the United States. And the United States doesn't want any more. Directed toward Mexicans. Awful, shouldn't direct toward a particular group.
>
> Vietnamese Korean female, foreign-born student

> It is very threatening. The key word, invasion, is one that would make the reader feel as though Mexicans were threatening their way of life
>
> Italian American male, U.S.-born student

> Mexicans are evil, and they are going to do harm to the poor Americans. Mexicans are like a cancer.
>
> Hispanic male, foreign-born student

> The words call the immigrants' journey an invasion that keeps growing, as if it is a plague or something. The picture depicts the Mexican immigrants as animals or something crossing through the water.
>
> White female, U.S.-born

Of the 134 students who viewed the cover's message as negative for reasons other than having to do with the invasion theme, many (49 percent) focused on how Mexicans or Mexico were characterized in the image. Students found the portrayal of Mexicans "insulting," "hostile," "hateful," and designed to arouse "fear." Not surprisingly, Latino students more often (71 percent) focused on the presentation of Mexicans than the students generally. Students read the cover as "criticizing," "stereotyping," "degrading," and even "making fun" of Mexicans. It "oversimplifies" Mexican immigration. Other students read the cover as blaming Mexicans for "causing problems." They associated the image with issues of increased immigration, illegal immigration, and population growth. Students also commented on the cover's message of a "never-ending" flow of immigrants, as suggested by the visual metaphor of the infinityline, and the alarm sounded by the issue of reproduction. The cynical tone of some of the students' readings also came through clearly.

> This cover is very insulting. Immigrants aren't only coming from Mexico. Besides, all the states Mexican immigrants go to belonged to Mexico to begin with.
>
> Mexican female, U.S.-born student

> This portrays immigration in a very negative light. It suggests that all Mexicans, or people of Latino culture, came here illegally.
>
> English/German/Scottish male, U.S.-born student

> This shows a picture of overpopulation from the Mexican border. The problem of illegal aliens results in overpopulation, especially for California. It influences the high rate in crime, money, taxes, etc.
>
> Hispanic/South American female, foreign-born student

> Mexicans are breeding and infesting the world, build a big wall and keep them out. Everyone wants to live in the United States cause Mexico sucks.
>
> Jewish/European/Mediterranean/half Polish female,
> U.S.-born student

Other students (37 percent) who read the cover's image negatively took the message to apply to immigrants more generally. All immigrants, not just those from Mexico, were not wanted, or immigration in general was too large, out of control, or caused problems. Some of their readings as to the cover's message:

> It says to me that it [immigration] is out of hand situation. They want to stop or reduce immigration to save our country.
>
> Thai female, U.S.-born student

> It says that other races coming to United States from other countries is bad, wrong, and shouldn't be happening!
>
> Latina, U.S.-born student

> This cover brings up the issues of overpopulation in the United States in my mind, the question of how will we ever support so many people (esp. more

poor and uneducated) when we can't even take care of our own numbers
now.

                                                    Anglo female, U.S.-born student

In sum, students expressed a high level of agreement on the negative message of this cover's image. Their readings did not, however, lack variation. They read the image as conveying a negative message for a number of reasons. But the overall intent of the cover's message, as told through the use of alarmist imagery and text, was relatively transparent to the students.

TIME, 13 JUNE 1983

Time magazine's 13 June 1983 cover featured the headline "Los Angeles: America's uneasy new melting pot" (see fig. 4.5). Below the text were the letters *L* and *A* enmeshed in a twisting freeway system. A potpourri of Asian and Latino faces were in the space of the letters. I read this image as depicting a chaotic scene that combined with the adjective "uneasy," to convey an alarmist message about immigration. I also read the "new melting pot" as subtly referencing an "old" melting pot that was, in romantically induced memory, not "uneasy." The focus on Asian and Latino faces, and omission of white faces, contributes to the alarmist message about immigration. I also suggested that the assemblage motif was a particularly effective way to image social disharmony. Students noted these same elements of the image in their readings.

A majority of students (58 percent) read the cover as sending a negative message about immigration. Only 20 percent of the students read the cover as sending a positive message. White students (71 percent) were more likely to classify the cover's message as negative, compared to Asian Americans (56 percent), Latinos (50 percent) and other students (57 percent), although this difference was not statistically significant.

Among those few students reading the cover positively, the visual reference to "diversity" and the text to the "melting pot" were of prominent influence.

L.A. is a city in which many different faces can be found. L.A. is a melting
pot of all ethnicities.
                                        Mandarin Chinese female, U.S.-born student

The positive readings were dwarfed by the large number of negative readings. Ninety-five (55 percent) of the students reading the cover negatively focused on three sometimes overlapping themes: diversity, the "melting pot," and race. The cover's imagery, according to these students, represents Los Angeles's ethnic and cultural diversity as a "bad idea," "not good" and that it makes Los Angeles appear to be a "bad place," a place where people of different backgrounds "don't get along," "cause tensions," "cause problems," "put a strain on relations," are "hard to control," and "a revolution ready to explode."

> The cover is trying to convey an image that mixed people of different races cannot get along together, especially when there's too many living alongside each other.
>
> Korean American female, foreign-born student

> It seems that they're trying to state that since Los Angeles is racially diverse it is a revolution ready to explode.
>
> Mexican male, U.S.-born student

> There are tensions between all the different people in America (which wouldn't be the case if everyone was "American," not Asian American, Afro-American, etc.!).
>
> White female, U.S.-born student

The second theme had to do with a specific allusion to the "melting pot," as mentioned by the cover's text. Students commented on the negative connotation given to the melting pot concept by qualifying it with the adjective "uneasy." The image and text's message, according to these students, was that the melting pot "is not blending," "is not going right, 'mixing,'" and "cultures aren't assimilating." Here are a few examples of the students' readings of the cover:

> The word "uneasy" makes you think twice about the whole melting pot business. Usually it would be easy for things to melt together but there is some difficulty.
>
> Chinese American female, U.S.-born student

> Why is L.A. uneasy about being a melting pot? Do people want an all-white LA? Or is that just the politicians? Melting pot is good!! Not bad.
>
> Indian American female, foreign-born student

Race was the third theme. Some students focused on specific races or ethnic groups in the picture or omitted from the image. As in the students' readings of earlier covers, this singling out or omission of specific racial/ethnic groups connotes a negative message about immigration.

> Asian immigrants are contributing to a lack of social order in L.A. Does not even portray Europeans as immigrants anymore.
>
> Filipino female, foreign-born student

There still is this idea that nonwhites "pollute" white communities. There's still resentment toward immigrants.

Filipino American/Asian-Pacific Island-American
female, U.S.-born student

Another 31 percent of those reading the cover as sending a negative message focused on a message about "problems" associated with immigration. The cover's message, according to these students, "blamed" or "scapegoated" immigrants for overcrowding Los Angeles and cities in general, social tensions, crime, violence, overpopulation, and social chaos. They noted that the faces were crowded together, which was associated with overcrowding generally and conflict between the people. The faces themselves appeared "angry," "hostile," "disgruntled," "mean," "unhappy," "desperate," and even "funny looking," implying negative connotations. "Disharmony" was also suggested by the image. The yellow and hot pink colors suggested heat, which one student associated with a prediction of catastrophe and failure. The twisting freeways suggested "chaos" and that immigrants were "detrimental to cities."

It implies that immigrants are the blame for all of the problems in L.A.

Korean male, foreign-born student

The United States was once a chance for freedom and peace, but now it's so overcrowded that it is hard to find a good life—everyone's not as happy.

Caucasian female, U.S.-born student

The colors in the backdrop are indicative of a seemingly "simmering to boiling" melting pot. Almost predicting catastrophe and failure.

East Indian male, U.S.-born student

There are only two smiling faces out of ten. It's suggesting that immigrants are here, and they are mean and unhappy, almost desperate. This is quite unfair. This leaves me with a negative impression.

English/German/Scottish male, U.S.-born student

The students clearly read the cover's imagery as suggesting alarm, ethnic and racial conflict, and social disharmony. They saw the image as challenging America's identity as a melting pot demeaning the value of ethnic and racial diversity. Their comments suggest that their readings of these messages were not as cynical as the readings of the affirmative covers. Indeed, many of the students held that these values were important to America, and so criticisms of those values were also criticisms of their beliefs and their place in the nation. After all, many of the students are the subjects of this cover, the very ones who are allegedly not becoming American and are causing social disharmony.

NEW REPUBLIC, 1 APRIL 1985

The *New Republic*'s 1 April 1985 cover was intentionally ambiguous in its message (see fig. 4.10). Although I noted that it was alarmist in its use of imagery—a huge gate opening up to a mass flow of human heads, the text—"Open the Floodgates? The only honest solution to the immigration mess"—added a marked irony to the message. The text appears to advocate massive immigration, which is an image of alarm in the public discourse over immigration.

A majority (53 percent) of the students read this cover as conveying a negative message about immigration and only 13 percent read it positively. The remaining students classified it as neutral or balanced, reflecting the cover's ambiguous message. There were no significant differences in the pattern of classification among students based on gender, age, year in college, ethnicity, or where they were born (U.S. or foreign born).

Almost a third (32 percent) of the students who classified the cover as negative read the image as sending a message about the high number of immigrants coming to the United States. The metaphor of a "flood" for immigration contributed to the perception of the magazine's message about large numbers of immigrants and was explicitly mentioned by 26 percent of the students reading the cover negatively. The flood and the need for floodgates suggested to the students that immigration was so huge (an "excess") that it was something that "you can't control." Floods are also "natural disasters" and so equating immigration to a flood is equating immigration to a disaster or to the danger that floodgates protect us from. Floodgates can also refer to the "entrapment" or imprisonment of the people, immigrants, suggested by the image. Once released, that which was contained is free to wreck havoc or "absorb all resources." The image of the mass of heads pouring between the gates also contributed to the message of mass immigration. Students interpreted these signs as saying that immigration is "a bomb ready to explode," "a massive influx," "flooding," "inundating," "with no end in sight," and "needs to be stopped." For some, the "flood" metaphor and the little cartoon heads dehumanized immigrants, making them animal-like.

> It's definitely a negative image, even with the balloons. It's like there are way too many people coming here.
>
> African American female, U.S.-born student

Immigrants are coming to the United States in masses with the "gates" opening. There is no end as to how many are coming, and immigrants are overjoyed, celebrating.

> Mexican female, U.S.-born student

It states to me that the people who want to come here are in the thousands, posing an immense population increase. It depicts immigrants as cattle, flooding into our land like a stampede.

> Irish American female, U.S.-born student

It's as if people are unsure and unwilling to allow immigrants into the United States. Floodgates are used to keep dangerous floods away. In this way they are calling the immigrants dangerous in the United States.

> German female, U.S.-born student

Students (23 percent of the negative reads) also focused on the description of immigration as a "mess" as the reason, or part of the reason, they read the cover's message as negative. "Mess," for these students, was an unfair, pejorative, and demeaning way to characterize immigrants.

It suggests that we should let immigrants in but by using words like "immigration mess" and "floodgates" it's also saying that immigrants are a problem, a pain for the United States.

> Vietnamese female, foreign-born student

Immigration is not a "mess." It is the natural tendency of human beings wanting to better their lives. Instead of accepting fellow human beings, or even [helping] better their lives in their homelands, Americans are still being ignorant.

> Taiwanese/Asian American male, foreign-born student

This is sort of mean. The "mess" is a rude and slanderous word for people who are only making this country stronger.

> Persian/Iranian female, foreign-born student

A few students (16 percent of negative reads) read the cover as suggesting that all immigration should be stopped or restricted.

Shows we need to be more strict with immigration and regulate it more.

> Filipino/Swiss male, foreign-born student

Finally, students (29 percent of the negative reads) focused on the text suggesting a "solution" to the "immigration mess." Student readings underscore the way ambiguity results from the "solution" raised as a question and posed in contradiction to the metaphor of the flood. While a few students agreed with the solution of opening up the nation to increased immigration, others read the question as ironic, that is, as suggesting that it was not the solution. Still others read the "solution" as indicating that immigration is so difficult to control, or has gotten so large, that America has "given up" the attempt to control immigration. One student's reading suggested a contradictory logic in the "solution," that is, stop trying to control immigration as the only way to control immigration. Some examples of students' comments:

> Immigration is a problem but allowing everyone a chance to enter the United States legally will cause greater harm.
>
> Chinese American male, U.S.-born student

> Immigration is a problem. It is so out of control they might as well let everyone in.
>
> Muslim male, U.S.-born student

The minority of students (n = 39; 13 percent) who classified the cover as conveying a positive message about immigration did so largely for one reason. Four-fifths (80 percent) of these students focused on the positive message implied by the symbolism of opening the door to immigrants.

> This says to me that the United States is realizing that the best way to deal with immigration is to just let them in and welcome (balloons) them. Though it is a mess, it is still an open door.
>
> Vietnamese/Korean female, foreign-born student

> Immigration is fine, let everyone come in.
>
> Egyptian female, foreign-born student

> It is saying that immigration can be worked out, it doesn't have to be a problem.
>
> Irish-Native American-Italian-German-French female,
> U.S.-born student

In sum, students read this cover's signs and symbols in a way that was consistent with my reading. Although an ambiguous and contradictory message, the alarmist imagery was sufficiently powerful enough that most students read the cover as negative toward immigration. A major contribution to this negative reading was the use of the flood metaphor, which was repeated both visually and in the text, to suggest massive and destructive immigration.

TIME, 9 APRIL 1990

The following cover, which appeared on *Time* on 9 April 1990, was less ambiguous in its message, at least in the student's readings as well as my own (see fig. 6.2). The image is of an American flag, altered so that the stars are missing and the white stripes are covered over in black, brown, and yellow. The text reads: "America's Changing Colors: What will the U.S. be like when whites are no longer the majority?" I read the loss of white from the flag and the emphasis on "whites" in the text as an example of the use of alarmist imagery to racialize the immigration discourse.

Most students (72 percent) classified this cover as conveying a negative message about immigration for reasons similar to my reading. Only a few (11 percent) students read the cover as positive. Foreign-born students were more likely than U.S.-born students to classify the cover as negative.[12] Even though the cover "spoke" directly to a generalized white audience, few white students, only 3 or 5 percent, read the cover as positive, which was less than Asian Americans (14 percent) and Latinos (17 percent).

Students responded strongly to the way demographic change was represented on the magazine's cover. Students noted that the cover portrayed demographic change negatively, even with "hostility," as something "disliked" or to be "feared," especially by whites, as a "threat," a possible "takeover," or a possible "extinction of whites" by minorities and immigrants. The implications of the changing demographics implied by the cover, according to the students, were that Americans would "have to adapt to more diverse cultures," "that immigration should be stopped," that "immigrants will bring some sort of negative effect to the nation," that "America will amount to nothing when there are immigrants," and it will "upset the cultural hierarchy." One student even commented, facetiously, that "The magazine cover says whites are becoming an endangered species. Preserve the whites! Breed!" (Jewish-European-Mediterranean/half Polish female, U.S.-born student). Students overwhelmingly read these messages as constructing a negative discourse about immigration. Some examples of students' comments:

> I think it is saying that because America has so much immigration, America itself will change in some way that is bad or not as good as it was.
> > Irish/Native American/Italian/German/French female,
> > U.S.-born student

> It suggests that America is being conquered by the "others." Also saying "Let's get rid of them before they destroy us."
> > Asian Vietnamese male, foreign-born student

> This cover seems to be looking at the issue of immigration as something negative, like the issue of immigration will upset the cultural hierarchy in place.
> > African American female, U.S.-born student

That it is a scary, threatening occurrence. It actually shows two aspects of immigration—diversity and a loss of a racial group. A scare tactic for white Americans.

Greek/Turkish female, U.S.-born student

Students (23 percent of the students classifying the cover as negative) commented that the cover's text influenced their reading. The text "no longer a majority?" conveyed a number of negative messages to students. Students found the question itself objectionable, focusing too much attention on whites as a privileged group. The focus on proportionately fewer whites suggested that such demographic change is "a problem" that "assumes that the United States will not be as good," that the U.S. will "change dramatically," and that because of change "all hell will break loose." Students found that singling out whites as a group in this way is problematic in a multicultural nation, especially one with an ideology that all people are created equal. It also directly contradicts the ideology of the grand narrative of the melting pot since the cover clearly establishes an "us" (whites) and "them" (nonwhites) opposition.

It was never originally a country of white people. Why should the white majority remain? Or why should it matter?

Russian Jew female, foreign-born student

This seems to say to me that as more immigrants come into America that America will be a different nation. The words are what give this a negative connotation because it seems to imply a problem with whites not being the majority.

English/Irish/German male, U.S.-born student

It says the white race should be dominant. The U.S. constitution, however, states that all men are created equal. Our country was formed by immigrants in the first place.

Half Finnish, half Hungarian female, U.S.-born student

The United States is scared of the "melting pot." It gives out the message that they fear minorities overruling the majority.

Korean American female, foreign-born student

The picture seems to say that America is a blend of a lot of races. The words are so incredibly negative. I can't believe that this cover was published. The words seem to say that the United States will be at a loss when the majority is not white.

Mexican American/African American female,
U.S.-born student

Students also derived their negative reading from the changes to the image of the U.S. flag (24 percent of the negative readings). The new colors of the stripes, the loss of the white stars, and hardly any white in the stripes, and a general disheveled look sent a powerful set of related messages to the students. The flag appeared "damaged," "ugly," "sloppy," "shabby looking," "unprofessional," and "distorted." In short, "Immigration is making the country less attractive." A flag with "whites smothered out" meant, according to the students, that the cover was trying to convey that immigration equates with "conflict," "chaos," "pollution," "a takeover," "destroying a sense of unity," and "destroying the culture of the USA (flag)." Along these lines, immigrants are characterized as changing the " 'colors' of American identity" and "the traditions of America," leading to "a seeming degeneration of the U.S."

> By changing the flag's colors—the symbol that unites us as a country—it sort of destroys this sense of unity. By putting black and brown in the flag suggests races being described by color. It is as if immigrants will destroy a sense of unity.
>
>   German female, U.S.-born student

> Basically the cover does not regard the people from other countries as "created equal." The flag shows how the whites would be smothered or ousted out if immigration continues to grow.
>
>   Chinese/Mandarin female, foreign-born student

> It seems to me that the cover is saying that if whites are no longer the majority, our country is going to be in confusion and chaos (indicated by picture of flag). Why would the flag have to be mixed of colors to indicate mixed races in America? The flag stands for the country, not just whites.
>
>   Chinese female, U.S.-born student

> There's something off about this picture. Who is to say that the flag stands for courage, purity, and not the white majority?
>
>   Hispanic female, U.S.-born student

Because the cover speaks directly to whites about their loss of demographic, political, and cultural dominance, it casts whites as the victims and nonwhite ethnics and immigrants, the majority of the students, as the cause of the problems whites are experiencing. This relationship between victim and perpetrator undergirds a reading of the cover's message that whites "truly belong here" and immigrants and nonwhite ethnics do not. The imagined community of the nation as represented by the cover, is one that privileges whites and effectively excludes nonwhites. Students' readings are critical of such a representation and are sometimes tinged with a sense of resentment.

It says that we are not all Americans. It seems to separate us into
categories.

Caucasian/Greek female, U.S.-born student

It says immigration is a problem. Only whites truly belong here. Implies
America is getting worse and is threatened by colored people.

German/Irish female, U.S.-born student

I felt that the question of "majority" was stated in such a way that I felt
offended. I never thought that being white had anything to do with the
white stripes on our flag.

Filipino female, U.S.-born student

The overwhelming majority (88 percent) of the thirty-three students
who classified the cover as positive read the image, especially the multicolored flag, as imparting an affirmative message about ethnic and
racial diversity and that changes introduced by immigration were
"good." Seven students referred explicitly to the image as a representation of the melting pot narrative. The students read the cover as saying that America's new diversity was "okay," even though some students recognized that others might disagree with that or that the cover
also included less positive aspects. Interestingly, Asian American and
Latino students were thirty of the thirty-three students classifying the
cover as positive. Perhaps for these students the positive aspects
of diversity resonated with their own vision of America, which may
help explain why they discounted the alarmist aspects of the cover's
message.

Immigration is bringing different races and cultures to the United
States. Overall, I would think this is positive, but some might say
this is negative.

Korean female, U.S.-born student

The United States will become the race of the "melting pot." All races
combined.

Mexican American female, U.S.-born student

In sum, the changed image of the flag and the text engaged in an
alarmist discourse about immigration and the demographic change it is
bringing to the nation. Students easily read the intended message of the
magazine's cover. The transparency of the message was met with the students' critical stance toward the message. Few students were led by the
cover's message to become enraged about immigration and demographic
change. Rather, they perceptively deconstructed the elements of the message and their intended meanings about the relationship of immigration

to the (dis)unity of the nation and the racial privileging in this representation of the "imagined community" of the nation.

ATLANTIC MONTHLY, MAY 1992

The *Atlantic Monthly's* May 1992 cover had the words "the border" in large letters across its central area (see fig. 8.8). The words were torn in two, lengthwise, and were in slightly different font sizes, appearing mismatched. They were also in different colors. Little green bubbles flowed from the bottom half to the top half of the letters. The cover's text read: "The Border: In the tense, hybrid world along the U.S.-Mexican border, Mexico's problems are becoming America's problems." I read this symbolic rendering of the U.S.-Mexico border as using alarmist imagery and words to characterize Mexico as "a problem" for the United States. Problems flow only one way in the image, south to north. At the same time, the image characterizes the United States as a benign neighbor to whom "things happened" rather than as an active agent in the history and political economy of the two countries. Students picked up on these same aspects in their readings of the cover. They overwhelmingly (78 percent) classified the cover as conveying a negative message about immigration. Only four students (1 percent) classified it as positive. There were no significant differences in classification between U.S.-born and foreign-born students, by gender, age, or year in college.

Students overwhelmingly agreed that the cover's message was that Mexico and Mexican immigrants are the source of problems for the United States. Of the 233 students classifying the cover as negative, 189 (81 percent) explicitly indicated that the cover's message was that Mexico and Mexican immigrants created unwanted problems to the United States. Another 16.7 percent of the students commented that the message was that immigrants in general bring problems to the United States. In short, immigrants and external forces (Mexico) as the cause of problems for the United States were implicated in 98 percent of the students' negative readings of the cover's message. Although simple in design, the image, coupled with words such as "tense," "hybrid," and "problems," was quite effective in getting its message to consumers. A few examples of the students' comments on the cover's intended message:

> Mexican immigrants are coming into the United States in high proportion, bringing problems to our land and economy, and it should be stopped.
>   Laos/Chinese female, foreign-born student

> It says Mexico is bringing its problems over to us, inferring [implying]

immigrants (illegal and legal). Negative: it feels that the magazine is saying that if we stop immigration the problems would ease.

> European (Scottish) and Chinese male,
> U.S.-born student

Bad. It's showing how when we let Mexican immigrants into our country, we are also taking on their problems that we really can't afford to deal with.

> Caucasian female, U.S.-born student

The cover's image and text effectively underscored an "us"—"them" relationship between the United States and Mexico/Mexican immigrants. As the comments above reflect, students used "us," "we," and "our" to set themselves apart from the "them" causing the problems. By using such terms, students claim membership in the imagined "we" of the nation that the cover speaks to. One in five students (20 percent classifying the cover as negative) made such "us," "we," and "our" distinctions. As reflected in the comments above, foreign-born and nonwhite students just as easily made these distinctions as the white students. The negative association with Mexico and Mexican immigrants ("them") is constructed through the words, especially "problem," and the image of the words "the border."

Some students (19 percent of those classifying the cover as negative) specifically referenced the "border" in their comments. In their reading, the top half of the image is the United States, which is positive and morally "good," and the bottom half is Mexico, which is morally "bad" and flowing into the United States. They read the border itself as "torn," "weak," "not clearly defined," "split up and chaotic," and "a line between good and bad." Students interpreted this representation of the border as suggesting it "is being tainted by the Mexican side" and needs to be "defined," "enforced," and "walled up" to keep the Mexicans out. One student even noted that the bottom half of the words "the border" appears to spell "the burden," indicating how Mexico and Mexican immigration is represented by the magazine's cover.

> States definitely that Mexico burdens the United States with problems, as if that is all Mexico has to offer. "The border" is portrayed as a line between good and bad.
>
> Vietnamese American female, U.S.-born student

> Better wall up the border—strengthen the forces keeping Mexicans out of the United States. We have our own problems to deal with.
>
> Jewish/European/Mediterranean/half Polish female,
> U.S.-born student

The problems caused by the unique border situation we have with Mexico are causing a fracture in the "American" line. The broken words suggest a disruption of things.

> English/German/Scottish male, U.S.-born student

Immigration is seen as bringing problems rather than good to America. It is as if the border is between good and evil rather than two nations.

> White female, U.S.-born student

A number of students reading the cover as negative also voiced their criticism of the message. For example, twenty-four students commented that the cover "blamed" Mexico for the United States problems, using Mexico and Mexican immigrants as scapegoats. About half of these students (thirteen) were Latinos. Thirteen students also noted that the one-way flow of problems to the U.S. was a one-sided representation.

> That is so wrong. This government always has to point the finger at immigrants. They need a scapegoat.
>
> Mexican American female, U.S.-born student

As if America's problems don't become Mexico's! Mexico isn't the only country with problems. America has them, too. How America's problems affect other countries is not being addressed.

> Indian American female, foreign-born student

This seems to be insinuating that the migration of Mexicans into America will only bring problems and nothing good could come out of the fusion of Mexico and America. Why aren't America's problems becoming Mexico's?

> African American female, U.S.-born student

Only four students classified the cover as positive. All four were Asian American students, three of them foreign born. One student pointed out that Mexico was a problem for U.S. taxpayers. The others read the image as suggesting Mexico and the United States are neighbors and that they should help each other.

In sum, students easily associated the image of "the border" with its nationalistic colors with the U.S.-Mexican border. They picked up on various meanings implied by the uneasy fit between the two halves of the image and the flow of green bubbles. They also noted the negative association applied to Mexico and Mexican immigrants by the text and image working together to construct an overall message. The level of agreement was high among students that the cover sent a negative message about immigration. The next cover's message, however, was even more obvious.

NATIONAL REVIEW, 22 JUNE 1992

National Review's 22 June 1992 cover featured the image of the Statue of Liberty with arm stretched straight out, hand up, palm forward, in a symbol of "stop" (see fig. 6.5). The text read "Tired? Poor? Huddled? Tempest-Tossed? Try Australia. Rethinking Immigration." The cover leaves little doubt about the message it is attempting to convey about immigration. The use of the Statue of Liberty, the "Mother of Exiles," underscores the message that the nation is no longer automatically willing to accept immigrants.

Students overwhelmingly (86 percent) agreed that the cover sends a negative message about immigration. Few students (5 percent) classified it as sending a positive message. Perhaps because of the cover's lack of subtlety, the students were very uniform in their reading of the cover's message, that the United States "has had enough with immigration." The prevalence of this single theme helps to explain why there were no significant differences in how the students classified the cover. Some students noted that "liberty" and "opportunity for immigrants," core American values, no longer seemed to apply to immigrants. This irony, coming from a "nation of immigrants," was also noted by some students, as was the irony of using the Statue of Liberty to make such a statement. Some examples of the students' readings of the magazine cover's message:

> I laughed at first at the lines, but the imagery is sad. The Statue of Liberty trying to stop people from coming? What has our nation come to?
>
> Hispanic female, U.S.-born student

> Our Liberty Lady, who symbolizes what America stands for, is boldly holding up her hands and telling immigrants to stop coming.
>
> Chinese/Mandarin female, foreign-born student

> The U.S. does not want more immigrants arriving, assuming we are poor, tired, and storm-sick from the journey by boat, etc.
>
> Vietnamese female, foreign-born student

> It seems to imply that foreigners from other countries are not wanted. It is a powerful image since it draws upon an "American" symbol—the Statue of Liberty.
>
> Caucasian female, U.S.-born student

> This one boldly says "Stay out. You're not welcome." This is hardly a representation of what the "American spirit" should be.
>
> French/Russian/Scottish male, U.S.-born student

The fourteen students who classified the cover as positive did so for a number of reasons. Four commented that the cover was stating that something needs to be done about the number of immigrants coming to the United States. These students considered this move toward action—"taking a stand," "controlling," "rethinking"—as positive. Six other students commented on the "realistic view" of the cover. They found positive the cover's message that immigrants should be directed elsewhere. One student commented that "America is no longer a land of gold or jobs" (Chinese American female, U.S.-born student).

In sum, the cover's message left little to the imagination for almost all of the students. It was a blunt, direct, and simple message that sought to encapsulate the anti-immigrant sentiment in the country at the time. Perhaps because of the image's lack of subtlety, the students' comments were also relatively similar. The following, final, magazine cover also used the Statue of Liberty to convey a message that students overwhelmingly read as negative about immigration.

NEWSWEEK, 9 AUGUST 1993

The Statue of Liberty submerged in water up to her nose as little boats filled with dark-skinned people float around her was the image on *Newsweek*'s 9 August 1993 cover (see fig. 6.7). The text exclaimed "Immigration Backlash: A Newsweek Poll: 60% of Americans say immigration is 'bad for the country.'" I read this cover as using imagery and text to raise an alarm about immigration's deleterious effects on the nation. As a symbol par excellence of the nation, the Statue of Liberty's death by drowning in a flood of immigrants is a powerful statement. I also suggested that an alternative reading, perhaps a critique, of the public's anti-immigrant sentiments was possible. The inaction of the "Lady Liberty" on behalf of the immigrants circling her could be a way of suggesting that America and Americans are no longer willing to provide opportunities to immigrants and a safe haven to refugees, that is, a loss of principles.

Students overwhelmingly (91 percent) classified this cover as sending a negative message about immigration. A major reason for this reading had to do with the students' interpretation of the image as saying that the nation was in peril. Indeed, of the 270 students who read the cover as conveying a negative message, 145 (54 percent) commented on the nation and its impending doom. Students were clearly drawn in by the Statue of Liberty as a metaphor for the nation and the water/flood metaphor for immigrants, which combined to symbolize the United

States' death by drowning/immigration. Although "drowning" was the cause of death most often voiced by the students, they also read the cover as saying that the nation was being "flooded," "destroyed," "overwhelmed," "overpopulated," "overcrowded," "swamped," "invaded," "suffocated," and "smothered" by immigration. What the cover suggests is being destroyed or lost because of immigration are "American values and American culture," "the American way of life," "America's identity," the "country's institutions," and even its "history." Moreover, because of immigration, the country is "going down," "being brought down," or "sinking," which is metaphorically associated with "bad."

> It portrays immigration as if it is drowning the U.S.; implies it will soon kill the U.S.
>
> African American male, U.S.-born student

> It seems to say that immigration is drowning the American way of life, which is represented by Lady Liberty.
>
> Chinese male, foreign-born student

> The image disturbs me. The Statue of Liberty is drowning with the immigrants' boats all around her. It says that immigrants are corrupting and polluting the United States.
>
> Persian male, foreign-born student

> The image of the Statue of Liberty drowning among immigrant boats is one that says that immigration is causing our country's institutions to crumble.
>
> Filipino/German/Irish female, U.S.-born student

An interesting pattern that also emerged among the students' readings were the number (41) of what were clearly explicit critical commentaries on the cover's image and message. About a quarter of Latino students (13 or 24 percent) and the "other" students (8 or 27 percent) made explicitly critical commentaries, compared to few white (6 or 10 percent) and Asian American (14 or 9 percent) students. Students raised issue with the poll results, wondering who was polled and if it was done correctly. The reliability of the poll was questioned given that to some students the results seemed to be prejudiced against immigrants or that the respondents did not have their "facts straight." They questioned why immigration was "bad," raising the point that there are also good aspects to immigration. They also noted that "most everyone's" ancestors were immigrants and that immigrants "help build America's economy." Some examples of how these students read and responded to the cover:

> If Americans knew that immigrants make it possible for them to live in the middle class, they would not be so against immigration.
>
> Latino male, foreign-born student

It does not account for who "Americans" are; poll is not reliable, completely biased towards the magazine's views. "Americans" are the immigrants; every *white* immigrated to begin with.

> Taiwanese/Asian American male, foreign-born student

For those who know economics, immigration actually improves the economy, bringing in new ideals, tools, inventors from around the world.

> Korean/white male, U.S.-born student

It bothers me to know that 60 percent of "Americans" oppose immigration. Do they ever think about how they got here?

> White/Jamaican male, U.S.-born student

Only four students explicitly noted their agreement with the sentiments of the cover, which they classified as a negative message about immigration. Their comments included:

> The statue sinking is a good way to explain immigration. From this picture it shows what we really think about immigration. Most of us think that if we allow it to happen, we will sink as a country.
>
> Chinese female, U.S.-born student

> Immigration has become a burden on our country. In the beginning it is what made our country, but now we are paying for it.
>
> White/European American female, U.S.-born student

Three students—two Asian Americans, both foreign born, and a U.S.-born Latino—classified the cover as positive. One did so because the cover provided a clear focus on the issue of immigration. Another because "immigration needs to be controlled." And the third, the Latino, noted somewhat ambiguously that the message was that "Immigration seems to be increasing, so the multicultural society is somehow erasing the real U.S. image."

FINAL THOUGHTS

The students' readings of the magazine covers underscores that this is an important site for examining discourse on immigration and the nation. In their discourse, the national magazines construct the immigrant as a political subject, as marked and distinctive from the homogenized citizen audience. The national audience is implicitly constructed as culturally and racially singular, as a white, middle-class audience. Representations of "immigrants" and "citizens" are not fixed and static or without contestation by many of the students. Their contestation derives, in part, from the various intersections that position them in American society. The students do not fit what one might imagine was the profile for many, if not most, of the consumers the magazines originally anticipated for the covers. They do not reflect a generic, white, middle-class audience. Even the white students, as numerical minorities in the university, reflect the demographic changes hotly debated in the public discourse over immigration. The students, in short, mirror the "new demographics" that for the rest of nation are still not yet a reality. They are, if anything, the prototype of the consumers of national magazines in the future.

The students' readings are refracted through a prism of personal and family histories, diverse ethnic/racial backgrounds, and gender differences. Most of the students are not far removed from the immigrant experience. Most are also ethnic or racial minorities in a rapidly changing demographic environment. These students are not, therefore, objective bystanders, immune to the way immigration-related issues are played out in the public debate over immigration, especially the way "immigrant" becomes constructed as the "foreign" and "other" in society. Their reflections on the magazine covers are, in turn, reflections on how they imagine what it means to be "American" and their struggle over inclusionary and exclusionary cultural practices. Even when the covers affirmed aspects of America's immigrant narratives, students read them as affronts to, and moments of disjuncture with, the way many of them imagined their relationship to the nation.

Indeed, the students actively contested the representation of the immigrant as racialized and outside the imagined community of the nation. Their critique—their own cultural production—follows from a realization that the "them" that is outside and foreign to the nation includes many of the students themselves or members of their families, a representation they are unwilling to accept passively. Put another way, the images on the magazine covers force them to confront meanings that may conflict with their own experiences and subjectivities, that is, their unconscious and subconscious sense of self (Jordan and Weedon 1995, 15). Their resistance to what they perceived as negative characterizations of immigrants as low class, subhuman, dangerous, foreign, morally inferior, and without history is resistance to a misrepresentation of their own material existence and that of their meaningful social relationships. Student readers insisted on the inclusion of positive contributions of immigrants to American life and the historical roots of immigrants (e.g., references to particular immigrant groups having been in the United States for a long time and immigrants having "built this nation"). In so doing, students offered a critique of a discourse that excludes both immigrants and themselves from representations of citizenship.

The students, generally, were not receptive to the way immigrants were constructed or characterized on the magazine covers. They were extremely sensitive to the privileging of one racial/ethnic group (whites). They were just as wary of one group being singled out for negative attention. They held America up to its ideology of equality and were very critical of anti-immigrant discourse that contradicts that ideology. It is here that the relationship between ideology and practice emerges as central in the politics of the nation. By critiquing how immigrants and ethnic groups are represented in the magazines' discourse, the students also undermine, one would like to believe, unequal or discriminatory practices in general. It is in this sense that the students' views suggest the possibility that issues of race, ethnicity, and the nation will be transformed. Contestations and struggles over representations can be catalysts for change and the construction of new national identities. As Pierre Bourdieu and Loïc Wacquant (1992, 14) point out: "If we grant that symbolic systems are social products that contribute to making the world, that they do not simply mirror social relations but help constitute them, then one can, within limits, transform the world by transforming its representation." The student readers challenged the authority of cultural producers such as magazines to define the "immigrant" subject and to define which races or ethnic groups constitute the nation. In doing so, they contested the "common sense" version of immigrant characteristics and representations that magazines seemed to take for granted. Students subtly undermined the magazines' power as the legitimate voice of their social world. The magazines did not seem to speak on behalf of many of the students. Even when the covers appeared to be affirming immigrants as central to the nation's identity, students were wary and critical.

It should be emphasized here that white students were also often critical of the images and what they perceived were the images' messages. Perhaps they came to this perspective because they live and attend school in a diverse social environment. What about students in a place where whites are still a majority on campus? With the prospect of changing demographics still on the horizon, would their readings be significantly different? How critical, or supportive, would they be of negative representations of immigrants and ethnic/racial groups? It is beyond the scope of this work to answer these questions. What the students' readings examined here suggest, however, is that concepts of race, nation, and immigrant are not fixed and immutable. The challenge for the producers of cultural products such as magazines will be to develop a discourse on the nation that addresses "all the people" without privileging some and excluding others. Those "others" who were so easily cast as "them" are no longer so marginal or lacking in power, not the least of which is purchasing power, that they can be easily ignored. To fail to meet this challenge is to run the risk of alienating a generation of readers who are unwilling to support constructions of themselves and their families as outside the nation.

Epilogue

A central premise of the framework developed here for reading magazine covers is that magazines are sites of contestation. Rather than providing the public a uniform and monolithic, that is, hegemonic, view of immigrants, these magazines often differed dramatically in their perspectives. Even a particular magazine would sometimes present contradictory views in different issues, in one characterizing immigration and immigrants affirmatively and in another issue emphasizing problems. Such inconsistency reflects the larger society's ambivalence about immigration. And yet, magazines do not simply "report the news." They have editorial positions and points of view. They are active participants in a struggle over which view of immigrants—affirmative or alarmist—will inform the nation's discourse on immigration.

Throughout the last three and a half decades of the twentieth century both alarmist and affirmative characterizations of immigrants and immigration have been interwoven into the national discourse on immigration. As was found, however, alarmist images increased in frequency and came to dominate the covers during the early 1980s and 1990s. Both liberal (the *Nation,* the *New Republic,* and the *Progressive*) and conservative (the *National Review, Business Week,* and *U.S. News and World Report*) magazines as well as mainstream (*Atlantic Monthly, Time, Newsweek,* and *American Heritage*) resorted to alarmist imagery, which may or may not have corresponded with the tone of the accompanying article or articles. Despite this tendency to use alarmist imagery on their covers, the magazines did not present a consensus on immigration and its impact on the nation. Immigrants are both applauded as central to the identity of the nation of immigrants and at the same time are characterized as a threat to the nation.

The discourse of alarm has increasingly focused on immigration as a catalyst for race or demographic change, multiculturalism, assimilation problems, interethnic/racial conflict, and threats to the nation's territory and sovereignty. The rise of these issues occurred in conjunction with repeated attention to the change in immigrant origins. Proportionately fewer Europeans immigrated to the United States after 1965 than before that time. Warnings about the possible impact on the demographic makeup of the nation because of the decrease in European immigrants began appearing shortly after 1965 and has been a recurring theme in the magazines' discourse since that time. The metaphor of the "browning of America" captured the idea that changes were occurring as a result of immigration and high birth rates (compared to whites) among Latinos and Asian Americans. Demographic change raised further questions about an America that would no longer be predominately white. Would America still be America? This question about racial characteristics was not divorced from concerns over a national culture. Race and culture became intertwined in the question, Would the nation as an idea, as a set of principles, exist when whites were no longer the majority? As an anthropologist, I must state what is perhaps obvious. Race and culture are not isomorphic; they are independent factors. Race does not determine culture. Culture does, however, construct categories such as race and imbues them with meaning. In this sense, race as a culturally constructed category tells us more about how U.S. society thinks about people and their differences than it does about actual biological differences between people.

Questions related to demographic change, that is, race, led to an increasing sense of a crisis of national identity in the discourse examined in this book. The perceived crisis over the loss of "whiteness" among Americans necessitated the construction of an "Anglo-European ethnicity." America's "Anglo-European ethnics" were characterized as foundational to American culture and as the legitimate contributors to the maintenance of a national culture (see particularly Brimelow, Miles, and even Schlesinger in chapter 6). Some voices, mostly historians, pointed out that such a singular construction of the American people did not really exist historically, and that "European" as a classificatory term masks wide differences among peoples of different historical and cultural backgrounds. Despite such observations, the construction of an Anglo-

European ethnicity provided a subject, or more precisely, a class of victims of the crisis allegedly wrought by immigration. This crisis has been
exacerbated by broader economic changes during the late twentieth century, what Sassen (1988) and Harvey (1989) refer to as the "restructuring" of capitalist production, moving away from production in the Fordist
style to greater emphasis on "flexible accumulation." The ensuing challenge to the idea of the nation as having fixed borders, be they political,
cultural, or even racial, added to the crisis of national identity. These demographic and economic changes help explain the emphasis on a narrative about America as a singular culture/race/ethnicity that should be
longed for, whose supposedly imminent loss should be lamented, and
which is in need of protection from alien threats.

Immigrants surfaced in the discourse examined here primarily as objects of crisis. A number of immigration crises have erupted during the
latter half of the twentieth century. There has been public turmoil and
debate over boat lifts, boat people, illegal immigrants, legal immigration;
too many Asian and Latin American immigrants, too few European immigrants; immigrants' use of social services, education, health care; "radical" multiculturalism and immigrants; and race and ethnic mixings in
a variety of arenas, producing new bodies, new music, new cultures, new
foods, new everything. Not surprisingly, the public response has been to
target immigrants for "crisis management," which is the attempt to manage and control immigrants through public policies and laws. Among
the most prominent actions have been the Immigration Reform and Control Act of 1986, the 1990 immigration law, Proposition 187 in 1994,
and immigration and welfare reforms in 1996.

What contributed to the management and control of immigrants
"making sense" was, I would argue, the way immigrants were characterized in the media's national discourse. Since 1965, the magazines increasingly represented—imagined—immigrants as different, not-assim-
ilated, outside, and morally questionable Others to the community of
the nation. Moreover, immigrants also were represented as threats to the
nation in a variety of ways: by transgressing the nation's borders and
making claims on the nation's sovereign territory, by reproducing and
forming communities in the United States, by changing the racial composition of the nation and undermining the political unity of the nation,
and by adding to environmental/population pressures. Immigrants also
bring cultural differences that threaten "American" ways of doing things.
These threats were symbolized by changes to American icons such as the
Statue of Liberty or the U.S. flag. Interestingly, the discourses I have ex-

amined have been less concerned with the actual participation of immigrants in the labor force, although that did sometimes appear in discussions of their relative economic contributions and costs. But the costs were also intrinsically tied to these other social and cultural issues, especially reproduction, in both the biological and community senses. The message one comes away with is that immigrants need to be disciplined and subjected to surveillance technologies to ensure that their reproduction is kept within limits. The characterization of immigrants in the alarmist discourse also carries with it implications about where to focus control: at the U.S.-Mexico border and other points of entry to the nation, and at social services that may support immigrant reproduction, once again in both the biological and community senses, such as welfare, food stamps, education, and medical care. Discourse, as this analysis underscores, does not exist apart from practice. Discourse is a practice that helps produce the common-sense view of the world that legitimizes, affirms, and even rationalizes other practices.

Magazines are in the business of attracting consumers, but in a larger sense, they are also part of the national agenda of constructing subjects as citizens. That objective, however, is undermined by the representation of immigrants and their offspring as different, as Other, and as danger. These representations may not play well given the changing demographics of the nation, as reflected in the backgrounds of the students at the University of California, Irvine. It tells many of these students, who are immigrants themselves or the children of immigrants, that they and their families are outside the national community. As the students' readings suggest, this is not an acceptable message. The students represent America's new subjects. They come from myriad backgrounds and are constructing new identities based on a fertile ground of social interaction, rapid communication, the media, and all manner of cultural, social, and population hybridizations. Their diversity and their sensitivity to issues of race and issues of inclusion and exclusion suggest the possibility of new practices and coalitions. Moreover, their insistence on different representations of immigrants and their children may radically influence the national discourse in the future. This may also undermine the tendency to fix humans into immutable racial categories, a practice that may become as outdated as the concept of race itself. The national agenda of the twenty-first century will continue to be about constructing subjects as citizens. But a new tack may be required, one that is less concerned with the erasure of difference. Perhaps a national discourse for the next millennium would get more mileage out of stressing inclusion over exclusion, thus ensuring that all Americans are imagined as part of the national community. This would require a view of difference as permeable rather than formidable, creative rather than destructive, and engaging rather than threatening. It would also require a consideration of borders as bridgeable rather than as insurmountable barriers, or as the last defense against the "barbarians."

To accomplish these goals, we must foster cultural literacy. Reading images in a world of images is a skill that is often left uncultivated. And yet the culture industries—movies, television, music, art, and the print media—work their magic through images. We are often captivated, annoyed, or repulsed by these images, but we seldom contemplate how they play upon our assumptions about the world that we share as members of society, or how they help construct what is called "common sense." Images have the power to humanize and dehumanize, value and devalue, include and exclude, not in one particular instance but through their accumulation in a particular social and historical context. They become meaningful because of their position in elaborate webs of social and cultural understandings about the world. This book serves as an example of the importance and complexity of images. Reading magazine covers about immigration led to issues of history, identity, culture, demographic change, and debates over what constitutes "the nation" and "the people." These are quintessential issues to a society undergoing change, and how they are ultimately resolved in discourse and practice will determine the "America" of the future.

Notes

PREFACE AND ACKNOWLEDGMENTS

1. Gupta (1995) has noted that newspaper accounts, and by extension magazine covers and their accompanying articles, should be conceptualized as cultural texts and sociohistorical documents, comparable to oral interviews in that they offer a form of situated knowledge. He argues that such material can be seen as "a major discursive form through which daily life is narrativized and collectivities imagined" (385).

CHAPTER 1

1. The Chinese Exclusion Act of 1882 and the Gentleman's Agreement with Japan in 1907 had already severely restricted immigration from those two countries.

2. Such views have their historical antecedents earlier in the twentieth century when eugenicists argued that continued immigration of southern and eastern Europeans posed the possibility of "race suicide" because they lacked the superior qualities of the "Nordic race," who were a people of "rulers, organizers, and aristocrats" (Roberts 1997, 213). Moreover, immigrants reproduced faster than native Anglo-Saxon Americans and their children remained "foreign stock" (un-acculturated) despite their birth on U.S. soil (ibid., 212). As Francis A. Walker, superintendent of the census of 1870 and 1889, noted about the children of immigrants: "Although born among us, our general instinctive feeling testifies that they are not wholly of us. So separate has been their social life, due alike to their clannishness and to our reserve; so strong have been the ties of race and blood and religion with them; so acute has been the jealousy of their spiritual teachers to our institutions—that we think of them, and speak of them, as foreigners" (ibid.).

3. Assembling this collection of magazines involved extensive library searches. The library's computerized records provided information on the magazine covers' content only since 1990. The search based on this information turned up the ten magazines analyzed in this study. To find magazine covers before 1990, every issue that had an article on an immigration-related topic in each of the ten magazines had to be manually examined.

CHAPTER 2

1. Anthropologists have been particularly absent from studies of American popular culture (Traube 1996).

2. *Newsweek* (10 November 1997, 42) summarized these periods of economic recession.

3. Sources for Graph 2.1: Espenshade and Hempstead 1996; U.S. Bureau of the Census, *Statistical Abstracts of the United States,* various issues; Rosenblatt 1997; Walsh 1999.

4. Sources for Graph 2.2: Espenshade and Hempstead 1996; Simon and Lynch 1999; *U.S. News and World Report* 13 October 1980, 7 July 1986, 23 June 1993; *Business Week* 13 July 1992; *Newsweek* 9 August 1993; *Time* fall 1993; CBS/New York Times Poll September 1995; *Chicago Tribune* 3 April 2000.

5. I coded the covers first and then asked Juliet McMullin, an advanced graduate student at UC Irvine whose area of research is not directly related to immigration, to make an independent coding of the magazine covers. We agreed on all but three of the cover's classifications, an agreement of 96 percent. As social science graduate student and professor, we have, perhaps, learned to read in similar ways. Undergraduate students, as discussed in the final chapters, were more varied in their readings.

6. People on the cover were counted only if their characteristics were decipherable; partial heads or unclear features were not counted. The frequencies are, therefore, conservative.

CHAPTER 3

1. Massey (1994, 165) is critical of the uncritical perspective from which Harvey (1989) writes about the condition of postmodernity: "The point, however, is that much, if not all, of what has been written has seen this new world from the point of view of a (relative) elite. Those who today worry about a sense of disorientation and a loss of control must once have felt they knew exactly where they were, and that they *had* control. For who is it in these times who feels dislocated/placeless/invaded? To what extent, for instance, is this a predominantly white/First World take on things?"

2. See Banta and Hinsley (1986) for a discussion of the long history of using photographs in anthropological research.

3. See Stuart Hall (1973, 176) for a discussion of the "codes" of connotation and denotation, which make signification possible.

4. This view of photographs as "coded" contrasts sharply with Berger's

(1972) view of photographs as an "automatic record" of reality (see also Tagg 1988, 187).

5. For Walter Benjamin, the interaction of text and image results in allegory (Seyhan 1996, 229).

6. The source and point of emission might be best studied using interviews and observations among those producing the magazine and those consuming the magazine.

7. As Giddens (1987, 101–2) has argued: "The significance of cultural or informational objects is that they introduce new mediations between culture, language and communication. . . . Since language as 'carried' by cultural objects is no longer talk, it loses its saturation in the referential properties which language-use has in the contexts of day-to-day action. . . . Communication is no longer more or less taken for granted as a result of the methodological processes involved in the sustaining of conversations."

8. For readings on various views of immigrants in American history, see Kennedy 1986 [1958]; Sowell 1981; Segal 1994; Steinberg 1981; Perea 1997a; R. Simon 1985; Roberts 1997; Lamm and Imhoff 1985.

9. Renato Rosaldo (1994) has argued for a "cultural citizenship" that respects cultural difference. Aihwa Ong (1996) expands on this concept, arguing that cultural citizenship is "a dual process of self-making and being-made within webs of power linked to the nation-state and civil society." Ong's more complex formulation is applicable to the objectification of immigrants that occurs in the discourse found on magazine covers. See also Jonas 1996.

10. Jordon and Weedon (1995, 15) distinguish between "identity," the more or less conscious sense of self, and "subjectivity," the more or less unconscious and subconscious sense of self.

11. William S. Sax (1998, 294) has argued that this is a basic feature of how cultures construct both themselves and the Other: "Difference making involves a double movement, where the Other is simultaneously emulated and repudiated, admired and despised, and that the source of this ambivalence is the recognition of the Self in Other."

12. The Frankfurt School used the term *mass culture* in the 1930s and 1940s. See Lutz and Collins (1993) for a discussion of the Frankfurt School and popular culture.

13. Hall (1973, 179) has noted, "But behind the particular inflections of a particular new 'angle' lie, not only the 'formal' values as to 'what passes as news in our society,' but the ideological themes of the society itself."

14. Pierre Bourdieu (1982, 47) expressed a similar view more generally: "The conservation of the social order is decisively reinforced by . . . the orchestration of categories of perception of the social world which, being adjusted to the divisions of the established order (and, therefore, to the interests of those who dominate it) and common to all minds structured in accordance with those structures, impose themselves with all appearances of objective necessity" (quoted in Bourdieu and Wacquant 1992, 13).

15. Magazines have what Said (1978, 19–20) refers to as "authority." "There is nothing mysterious or natural about authority. It is formed, irradiated,

disseminated; it is instrumental, it is persuasive; it has status, it establishes canons of taste and value; it is virtually indistinguishable from certain ideas it dignifies as true, and from traditions, perceptions, and judgments it forms, transmits, reproduces."

16. As Bourdieu (1991, 236) has put it: "Knowledge of the social world and, more precisely, the categories which make it possible, are the stakes par excellence of the political struggle, a struggle which is inseparably theoretical and practical, over the power of preserving or transforming the social world by preserving or transforming the categories of perception of that world."

17. Foucault cited in Bhabha 1990, 301.

18. Research also suggests, however, that immigrants can, and often do, develop a sense of community in the United States. This is true even for undocumented immigrants who are not "imagined" as part of the national community by the larger society (Chavez 1991, 1994).

19. Rouse (1991) notes: "Some Aguilillans [from Aguililla, Mexico] have settled in Redwood City [California] for long periods, but few abandon the *municipio* forever. Most people stay in the United States relatively briefly, almost all of those who stay longer continue to keep in touch with the people and places they left behind, and even those who have been away for many years quite often return." The impression one is left with is that Mexicans such as those from Aguililla are really not interested in setting down "roots" in the United States. They are merely temporary residents waiting to return to Mexico.

20. Appadurai (1993, 424) goes on to say: "The politics of ethnic identity in the United States is inseparably linked to the global spread of original local national identities. For every nation-state that has exported significant numbers of its populations to the United States as refugees, tourists, or students, there is now a delocalized *transnation,* which retains a special ideological link to a putative place of origin but is otherwise a thoroughly diasporic collectivity. No existing conception of Americanness can contain this large variety of transnations."

21. Newt Gingrich's position on cultural meanings of being American is part of a larger debate characterized as the "culture wars" among American political leaders and intellectuals (Leonardo 1996).

22. As Ira Mehlman, West Coast representative of the Federation for American Immigration Reform, commented: "Is it in our national interest to have literally millions and millions of people who have this dual allegiance?" (McDonnell 1998a).

CHAPTER 4

1. "What is a lexicon? A portion of the symbolic play (of language) which corresponds to a body of practices and techniques" (Bathes 1977, 46).

2. As Barthes (1977, 22) has noted: "The photograph clearly only signifies because of the existence of a store of stereotyped attitudes which form ready-made elements of signification . . . A 'historical grammar' of iconographic connotation ought thus to look for its materials in painting, theatre, associations of ideas, stock metaphors, etc., that is to say, precisely in 'culture.'"

3. See Tagg (1988) for an extended discussion of the use of photographs as evidence in law.

4. See Marcus 1995 for a discussion of the use of montage in ethnographic film.

5. Harvey is commenting on the postmodern eclecticism of subcultural music such as reggae, Afro-Latin, and African American, as discussed by Chambers 1987.

CHAPTER 5

1. The "small is beautiful" philosophy, popularized by Jerry Brown, former governor of California, emphasized a high quality of life attained with fewer material goods, less waste, fewer people, less government spending, etc.

2. Better estimation techniques and the number who actually applied for legalization under IRCA suggest that the actual number of undocumented immigrants in the United States at the time was closer to the lower estimates that the higher ones.

CHAPTER 6

1. The poll was conducted by the Roper Organization and sampled one thousand adults, with a four-point margin of error.

2. In all, there were about 1.8 million applicants for legalization who had been in the United States since before 1982, and another 1.2 million applicants as special agricultural workers (CASAS 1989, 1). See Baker 1990 for an extensive review of the legalization programs established under the IRCA.

3. Although employer sanctions have been ineffective in curtailing undocumented immigration, evidence suggests that the law has increased discrimination against Latinos or Hispanics (U.S. General Accounting Office 1990).

4. Allan Bloom, author of *The Closing of the American Mind,* is quoted as saying: "Obviously, the future of America can't be sustained if people keep only to their own ways and remain perpetual outsiders. The society has got to turn them into Americans. There are natural fears that today's immigrants may be too much of a cultural stretch for a nation based on Western values" (31).

5. Brimelow's arguments are similar to those of early twentieth-century eugenicists who advocated immigration quotas based on census data predating the great immigration waves of the late nineteenth and early twentieth centuries. For example, Harvard professor Robert Ward explained that restricting southern and eastern Europeans was necessary, "[i]f we want the American race to continue to be predominantly Anglo-Saxon-Germanic, of the same stock as that which originally settled the United States, wrote our Constitution, and established our democratic institutions" (Roberts 1997, 213).

6. Micaela di Leonardo (1994) argues that the term "white ethnic" gained currency in the early 1970s.

7. On *This Week with David Brinkley,* an ABC News television broadcast, on 8 December 1991, Buchanan said: "I think God made all people good, but if we had to take a million immigrants in, say Zulus, next year, or Englishmen, and

put them in Virginia, which group would be easier to assimilate and which would cause less problems for the people of Virginia? There is nothing wrong with us sitting down and arguing that issue, that we are a European country" (Bosniak 1997, 297).

8. See Palumbo-Liu (1994) for a discussion of how images of Asian Americans, particularly Koreans, were used in the media to convey the meanings about race, violence, property, and justice in relation to the April 1992 Los Angeles rebellion.

9. According to the 1990 census, however, 8.6 percent of immigrant households received public assistance in 1989, compared with 7.5 percent of native-born households (Martin and Midgley 1994, 33).

10. Note the similarity between *Time*'s discourse about racial mixture and José Vasconcelo's (1948) writings about "La Raza Cosmica," or the formation of the Mexican people through the blending of Indian and Spanish (as well African) influences.

CHAPTER 7

1. Also see Olivas 1995 and Johnson 1995 for discussions of policies to restrict immigrants from education and social services.

2. Voting patterns in California over Proposition 187 suggest that attitudes toward immigration are polarized along racial and ethnic lines. Proposition 187 passed with 59 percent of the votes cast. But white Californians, in particular, appeared to be expressing sentiments of unease over immigration. Two out of three voting whites in California (about 67 percent) voted for the proposition, a significantly larger proportion than the vote among African Americans and Asian Americans (about half of each group voted for it) and Latinos (only about 23 percent voted for it) (McDonnell 1994; Martin 1995). The voting block provided by white voters ensured passage of Proposition 187. Importantly, even though whites accounted for about 57 percent of California's population, they accounted for about 80 percent of the voters. Thus their views take on tremendous political power. In contrast, while Latinos account for 25 percent of the state's population, they account for only 8 percent of those who voted (Johnson 1995). White voters in California appear to have sent a symbolic statement about their concern over immigration.

3. In 1997, the U.S. Congress adjusted the welfare law to allow elderly immigrants to continue receiving Medicaid and Supplemental Security Income (SSI) if they were living in the United States as of 22 August 1996 and were previously disabled or later became disabled (Sample 1997). Elderly immigrants who were not disabled but who received aid before 22 August 1996 will continue to get Medicaid and SSI. In June of 1998, Congress again adjusted the welfare law so that additional legal immigrants would be eligible for food stamps. Restored to food stamp eligibility were immigrant children, elderly and disabled legal immigrants, and noncitizens who had settled in the United States before 22 August 1996. Immigrants arriving after that date, which was the day the federal welfare law was signed into law, remain ineligible. Although approximately 250,000 legal immigrants are restored to food stamp eligibility, an additional 685,000 le-

gal immigrants, mostly ages eighteen to sixty-four, who lost their benefits under the 1996 welfare law continue to be ineligible (McDonnell 1998b, sec. A, p. 1).

4. See Durand and Massey (1995) for examples of the iconography left by Mexican migrants at the U.S.-Mexico border.

5. Foucault (1977, 218) observed that the formation of the disciplinary society that emerged in the eighteenth century corresponded to "an increase in the floating population (one of the primary objects of discipline is to fix; that is an anti-nomadic technique)."

6. Borjas's complaint of decreasing immigrant "quality" is challenged by Simon and Akbari (1995).

CHAPTER 8

1. See Shohat (1997) for a discussion of representations of "virgin" land in colonial and postcolonial image making.

2. See Dunn (1996) for an in-depth analysis of the escalating role of the military on the U.S.-Mexico border.

3. In response to the computer industry's claims of a dramatic shortage of computer programmers, the U.S. Congress is considering increasing by twenty-five thousand the number of foreign high-tech workers allowed into the country (Bunis 1998).

4. See Chavez et al. 1997 for data comparing immigrants and U.S.-born Latinas in Orange County, California. On almost all socioeconomic factors, U.S.-born Latinas are closer to Anglo women than immigrant Latinas.

CHAPTER 9

1. Introduction to Sociocultural Anthropology is a large class, but graduate-student teaching assistants lead smaller discussion sections.

2. Students not wishing to participate simply did not fill out the response sheet. I also advised students that if they did not wish to have their responses included, they could let me know at any time and their responses would be removed. Anonymity was also assured; students did not sign or identify themselves in any way. Preliminary questions solicited the students' self-reported ethnic identity and a few pertinent sociodemographic characteristics.

3. The composition of the students at UC Irvine and the other UC campuses shows signs of changing as a result of the UC Board of Regents eliminating all affirmative action considerations for admittance. UC Irvine, for example, admitted 19 percent fewer African Americans and 8.6 percent fewer Latinos to its 1998–99 freshperson class (Weiss and Curtius 1998). It appears, however, that the number of underrepresented minority students actually attending UC Irvine in 1998–99 was up 25 percent from the previous year.

4. There were, however, proportionately more females than males among the respondents (59.4 percent) than among UC Irvine students generally (52.5 percent). There were also more Latinos than found among students generally, but slightly fewer Asian American and white respondents. The "Other" category includes eight students from the Middle East, four African Americans, and

eighteen students who claimed mixed parentage across the major ethnic/racial identities.

5. The median age for all the students who responded to the covers was twenty. The proportions in each year at the university were: first year, 17.5 percent; second year, 35.7 percent; third year, 25.9 percent; fourth or more year, 20.9 percent.

6. Significance based on a chi-square test, which is a statistical test of the null hypothesis that there is no association between two nominal level variables.

7. Students' comments have been edited for typographical errors and minor grammatical errors.

8. Lutz and Collins (1993, 200) note that people who posed so that they are directly facing the camera, as are the people on this cover, have historically been associated with "the rougher classes."

9. Significance = < 0.05 for white students ($N = 58$) compared to all other students ($N = 240$), based on chi-square statistic.

10. Significance = 0.07 for foreign-born students ($N = 121$) compared to U.S.-born students ($N = 177$), based on chi-square statistic.

11. Students classified as neutral/balanced *Newsweek* 4 July 1977 (25.2 percent); *U.S. News and World Report* 9 July 1979 (24.8 percent); *Newsweek* 7 July 1980 (38.9 percent); and *Business Week* 13 July 1992 (17.4 percent).

12. Significance = < 0.05 for foreign-born students ($N = 121$) compared to U.S.-born students ($N = 177$), based on chi-square statistic.

References

Alien Children Education Litigation, Brief of the Appellants
    1980.   In Re: Alien children education litigation. *State of Texas and Texas Education Agency (Appellants) v. United States (Intervenor-Appellee) and Certain Named and Unnamed Undocumented Alien Children (Appellees)*. Case Nos. 80–1538 and 80–1934. Washington, D.C.: Supreme Court of the United States.

Allert, Beate, ed.
    1996.   Introduction to *Languages of visuality: Crossing between science, art, politics, and literature,* 1–25. Detroit: Wayne State University Press.

Alvarez, Robert R., Jr.
    1995.   Mexican-U.S. border: The making of an anthropology of borderlands. *Annual Review of Anthropology* 24:447–70.

Alvarez, Sonia E., Evelina Dagnino, and Arturo Escobar
    1998.   *Cultures of politics/politics of cultures*. Boulder, Col.: Westview Press.

Anderson, Benedict
    1983.   *Imagined communities*. London: Verso.

Andreas, Peter
    1988.   The U.S. Immigration Control Offensive: Constructing an image of order on the southwest border. In *Crossings: Mexican immigration in interdisciplinary perspectives*, edited by Marcelo Suárez-Orozco, 343–56. Cambridge: Harvard University Press, for the David Rockefeller Center for Latin American Studies.

Appadurai, Arjun
    1996.   Disjuncture and difference in the global cultural economy. In

Modernity at large: Cultural dimensions of globalization, 27–47. Minneapolis: University of Minnesota Press.

1993.   Patriotism and its futures. *Public Culture* 5:411–30.

Bailey, John

1989.   Mexico in the U.S. media, 1979–88: Implications for the bilateral relation. In *Images of Mexico in the Untied States,* edited by John H. Coatsworth and Carlos Rico, 55–87. La Jolla: Center for U.S.-Mexican Studies, University of California, San Diego.

Baker, Susan González

1990.   *The cautious welcome: The legalization programs of the Immigration Reform and Control Act.* Santa Monica and Washington, D.C.: The RAND Corp. and the Urban Institute Press.

Balibar, Etienne

1991.   Is there a "Neo-Racism"? In *Race, nation, class: Ambiguous identities,* edited by Etienne Balibar and Immanuel Wallerstein, 17–28. New York: Verso.

Banta, Melissa, and Curtis M. Hinsley

1986.   *From site to sight: Anthropology, photography, and the power of imagery.* Cambridge, Mass.: Peabody Museum Press.

Barken, Elliott Robert

1984.   Americans all? Well, some. . . : Immigrants, refugees, and California public opinion, January 1982. *Migration Today* 12:13–20.

Barthes, Roland

1977.   *Image—music—text.* New York: Hill and Wang.

1972.   *Mythologies.* London: Cape.

Basch, Linda, Nina Glick Schiller, and Cristina Szanton Blanc

1994.   *Nations unbound: Transnational projects, postcolonial predicaments, and deterritorialized nation-states.* Amsterdam: Gordon and Breach.

Baudrillard, Jean

1983.   *Simulations.* New York: Semiotext(e).

Bean, Frank D., Barry Edmonston, and Jeffrey S. Passel, eds.

1990.   *Undocumented migration to the United States: IRCA and the experiences of the 1980s.* Washington, D.C.: The Urban Institute Press.

Benjamin, Walter

1955.   *Illuminations.* New York: Harcourt, Brace and World.

Bennett, Tony

1986.   The Politics of the "popular" and popular culture. In *Popular culture and social relations,* edited by Tony Bennett, Colin Mercer, and Janet Woollacott. Philadelphia: Open University Press.

Bennett, Tony, Colin Mercer, and Janet Woollacott, eds.

1986.   *Popular culture and social relations.* Philadelphia: Open University Press.

Berg, Mary Helen

1992.   City of Orange approves "strict" occupancy law. *Los Angeles Times* 28 May 1992, sec. A, p. 1.

Berger, John
    1972.   *Ways of seeing*. London: BBC and Penguin Books.

Berlant, Lauren
    1997.   *The Queen of America goes to Washington, D.C.: Essays on sex and citizenship*. Durham: Duke University Press.

Bhabha, Homi K., ed.
    1990.   *Nation and narration*. London: Routledge.

Bloch, Maurice
    1989.   *Ritual, history and power*. London: The Athlone Press.

Bornemeier, James
    1995.   Clinton moves to curb illegal immigration. *Los Angeles Times* 8 February, sec. A, p. 3.

Bosniak, Linda S.
    1997.   "Nativism" the concept: Some reflections. In *Immigrants out! The new nativism and the anti-immigrant impulse in the United States,* edited by Juan F. Perea, 279–99. New York: New York University Press.

Bourdieu, Pierre
    1994.   Structures, habitus, power: Basis for a theory of symbolic power. In *Culture/power/history: A reader in contemporary social theory,* edited by Nicholas B. Dirks, Geoff Eley, and Sherry B. Ortner. Princeton: Princeton University Press.

    1993.   *The field of cultural production: Essays on art and literature,* with introduction by Randal Johnson, edited by Randal Johnson. Cambridge, Eng.: Polity Press.

    1991.   *Language and symbolic power*. Cambridge: Harvard University Press.

    1984.   *Distinction: A social critique of judgement and taste*. London: Routledge and Kegan Paul.

    1965.   *Un art moyen: Essai sur les usages sociaux de la photographie*. Paris: Editions de Minuit.

Bourdieu, Pierre, and Loïc J. D. Wacquant
    1992.   *An invitation to reflexive sociology*. Chicago: University of Chicago Press.

Boyarin, Jonathan
    1994.   Space, time, and the politics of memory. In *Remapping memory: Politics of time space,* edited by Jonathan Boyarin. Minneapolis: University of Minnesota Press.

    1992.   *Storm from paradise: The politics of Jewish memory*. Minneapolis: The University of Minnesota Press.

Brimelow, Peter
    1995.   *Alien nation: Common sense about America's immigration disaster*. New York: Random House.

Brownstein, Ronald
    1994.   Wilson proposes U.S. version of Prop. 187. *Los Angeles Times* 19 November, sec. A, p. 1.

Bunis, Dena
    1998.   Congress might raise cap on high-tech foreign workers. *Orange
                County Register* 3 March, News, p. 11.
Bunis, Dena, and Guillermo X. Garcia
    1997.   New illegal-immigration law casts too wide a net, critics say. *Or-
                ange County Register* 31 March, News, p. 1.
Calavita, Kitty
    1996.   The new politics of immigration: "Balanced-budget conser-
                vatism" and the symbolism of Proposition 187. *Social Problems*
                43:284–305.
    1982.   *California's "employer sanctions." The case of the disappearing
                law.* La Jolla: Center for U.S.-Mexican Studies, University of Cal-
                ifornia, San Diego.
Capps, Steven A.
    1997.   Lungren wants guest workers for California. *Orange County Reg-
                ister* 17 October, News, p. 4.
Cardoso, Lawrence
    1980.   *Mexican emigration to the United States, 1897–1931.* Tucson:
                University of Arizona Press.
Carrasco, Gilbert Paul
    1997.   Latinos in the United States: Invitation and exile. In *Immigrants
                out! The new nativism and the anti-immigrant impulse in the
                United States,* edited by Juan F. Perea, 190–204. New York: New
                York University Press.
CASAS (Comprehensive Adult Student Assessment System)
    1989.   A survey of newly legalized persons in California. Prepared for
                the California Health and Welfare Agency. San Diego: CASAS.
Chambers, I.
    1987.   Maps for the metropolis: A possible guide to the present. *Cul-
                tural Studies* 1:1–22.
Chavez, Leo R.
    1997.   Immigration reform and nativism: The nationalist response to the
                transnationalist challenge. In *Immigrants out! The new nativism
                and the anti-immigrant impulse in the United States,* edited by
                Juan F. Perea, 61–77. New York: New York University Press.
    1994.   The power of the imagined community: The settlement of un-
                documented Mexicans and Central Americans in the United
                States. *American Anthropologist* 96:52–73.
    1992   *Shadowed lives: Undocumented immigrants in American society.*
    [1998].   Ft. Worth: Harcourt, Brace and Jovanovich.
    1991.   Outside the imagined community: Undocumented settlers and ex-
                periences of incorporation. *American Ethnologist* 18:257–78.
    1988.   Settlers and sojourners: The case of Mexicans in the United States.
                Human Organization 47:95–108.
    1986.   Immigration and health care: A political economy perspective.
                Human Organization 45:344–52.
    1985.   Households, migration, and labor market participation: The

adaptation of Mexicans to life in the United States. *Urban Anthropology* 14:301–46.

Chavez, Leo R., Estevan T. Flores, and Marta Lopez-Garza

1990.   Here today, gone tomorrow? Undocumented settlers and immigration reform. *Human Organization* 49:193–205.

Chavez, Leo R., F. Allan Hubbell, Shiraz I. Mishra, and R. Burciaga Valdez

1997.   Undocumented immigrants in Orange County, California: A comparative analysis. *International Migration Review* 31 (2):88–107.

Chilton, Paul A.

1996.   *Security metaphors: Cold War discourse from containment to common house.* New York: Peter Lang.

Chock, Phyllis Pease

1991.   "Illegal aliens" and "opportunity": Myth-making in congressional testimony. *American Ethnologist* 18:279–94.

Coatsworth, John H., and Carlos Rico

1989.   Images of Mexico in the United States. La Jolla: Center for U.S.-Mexican Studies, University of California, San Diego.

Cornelius, Wayne A.

1980.   America in the era of limits. Working Paper No. 3. La Jolla: Center for U.S.-Mexican Studies, University of California, San Diego.

Cortes, Carlos E.

1989.   To view a neighbor: The Hollywood textbook on Mexico. In *Images of Mexico in the United States,* edited by John H. Coatsworth and Carlos Rico, 91–118. La Jolla: Center for U.S.-Mexican Studies, University of California, San Diego.

Cosgrove, Denis, and Stephen Daniels, eds.

1988.   *The iconography of landscape.* Cambridge: Cambridge University Press.

Coutin, Susan Bibler, and Phyllis Pease Chock

1995.   Your friend, the illegal: Definition and paradox in newspaper accounts of U.S. immigration reform. *Identities* 2:123–48.

Craig, Richard B.

1971.   *The Bracero Program: Interest groups and foreign policy.* Austin: The University of Texas Press.

Daniels, S.

1993.   *Fields of vision: Landscape imagery and national identity in England and the U.S.* Cambridge, Eng.: Polity Press.

De Leon, A.

1983.   *They called them greasers.* Austin: The University of Texas Press.

Devereaux, Leslie

1995.   An introductory essay. In *Fields of vision: Essays in film studies, visual anthropology, and photography,* edited by Leslie Devereaux and Roger Hillman. Berkeley and Los Angeles: University of California Press.

Dunn, Timothy J.

1999.   Military collaboration with the Border Patrol in the U.S.-Mexico Border region: Inter-organizational relations and human rights implications. *Journal of Political and Military Sociology* 27, no. 2:257–77.

1996.   *The militarization of the U.S.-Mexico border, 1978–1992: Low-intensity conflict doctrine comes home.* Austin: Center for Mexican American Studies Books.

Durand, Jorge, and Douglas S. Massey

1995.   *Miracles on the border: Retablos of Mexican migrants to the United States.* Tucson: University of Arizona Press.

Edwards, Elizabeth

1992.   *Anthropology and photography, 1860–1920.* New Haven: Yale University Press.

Elson, Robert T.

1968.   *Time, Inc.* New York: Atheneum.

Eschbach, Karl, Jacqueline Hagan, Nestor Rodriguez, Ruben Hernandez, and Stanley Bailey

1999.   Death at the border. *International Migration Review* 33: 430–54.

Espenshade, Thomas J., and Katherine Hempstead

1996.   Contemporary America attitudes toward U.S. immigration. *International Migration Review* 30:535–71.

Espinosa, Kristin E., and Douglas S. Massey

1997.   Determinants of English proficiency among Mexican migrants to the United States. *International Migration Review* 31:28–50.

Faegin, Joe R.

1997.   Old poison in new bottles: The deep roots of modern nativism. In *Immigrants out! The new nativism and the anti-immigrant impulse in the United States,* edited by Juan F. Perea, 13–43. New York: New York University Press.

Farnen, Russell R.

1994.   Nationality, ethnicity, political socialization, and public policy: Some cross-national perspectives. In *Nationalism, ethnicity, and identity,* edited by Russell F. Farnen. New Brunswick: Transaction Publishers.

Fernandez, Celestino, and Lawrence R. Pedroza

1982.   The Border Patrol and the news media coverage of undocumented Mexican immigration during the 1970's: A quantitative content analysis in the sociology of knowledge. *California Sociologist* 5:1–26.

Fitzpatrick, John C., ed.

1938.   *The writings of George Washington.* Vol. 27. Washington, D.C.: Government Printing Office.

Ford, James

1969.   *Magazine for millions: The story of specialized publications.* Carbondale: Southern Illinois University Press.

Foucault, Michel

1988.   *Technologies of the self.* Edited by H. Gutman et al. London: Tavistock.

1980.   *Power/knowledge.* Brighton, Eng.: Harvester.

1979.   *Discipline and punish: The birth of the prison.* Translated by A. M. Sheridan Smith. New York: Vintage Books.

1970.   *The order of things.* New York: Vintage Books.

Fox, Claire F.

1996.   The fence and the river: Representations of the U.S.-Mexico border in art and video. *Discourse* 18 (1, 2 fall, winter 1995–96): 54–83.

Gandelman, Joe

1986.   Wilson would back Marines on border if reform move fails. *San Diego Union* 6 April, sec. A, p. 3.

Geertz, Clifford

1983.   *Local knowledge.* New York: Basic Books.

General Accounting Office (GAO)

1990.   *Immigration reform: Employer sanctions and the question of discrimination.* Washington, D.C.: U.S. General Accounting Office.

German, Daniel B.

1994.   The role of the media in political socialization and attitude formation toward racial/ethnic minorities in the U.S. In *Nationalism, ethnicity, and identity,* edited by Russell F. Farnen. New Brunswick: Transaction Publishers.

Getino, Octavio

1997.   *La tercera mirada: Panorama del audiovisual latinoamericano.* Buenos Aires: Paidós.

Gewertz, Catherine

1992.   Appeals court voids Santa Ana occupancy law. *Los Angeles Times* 29 May, sec. A, p. 1.

Giddens, Anthony

1987.   *Social theory and modern sociology.* Stanford: Stanford University Press.

Gilman, Sander L.

1985.   Black bodies, white bodies: Toward an iconography of female sexuality in late nineteenth-century art, medicine, and literature. *Critical Inquiry* 12:204–42.

Gilroy, Paul

1992.   The end of anti-racism. In *"Race," culture and difference,* edited by J. Donald and A. Rattansi. London: Sage.

Glastris, Paul

1997.   The alien payoff. *U.S. News & World Report* 16 May, 20–22.

Goffman, Erving

1976.   *Gender advertisements.* Cambridge: Harvard University Press.

Goldman, Robert

1992.   *Reading ads socially.* New York: Routledge.

Gonzalez, Gilbert G.

1990.   *Chicano education in the era of segregation.* Philadelphia: Balch Institute Press.

Gordon, Larry
    1992.   Immigrants face fee hikes from Cal. state system. *Los Angeles Times* 9 November, sec. A, p. 3.

Gramsci, Antonio
    1971.   *Selections from the* Prison Notebooks. New York: International Publishers.

Gray, Steven
    1997.   Foreign-born citizens match natives in homeownership. *Los Angeles Times* 11 September, sec. D, p. 3.

Grimaldi, James V.
    1996.   Immigration reforms pass in the House. *Orange County Register* 29 September, News, p. 1.

Gupta, Akhil
    1995.   Blurred boundaries: The discourse of corruption, the culture of politics, and the imagined state. *American Ethnologist* 22: 375–402.

Gupta, Akhil, and James Ferguson
    1997.   Culture, power, place: Ethnography at the end of an era. In *Culture, power, place: Explorations in critical anthropology,* edited by Akhil Gupta and James Ferguson, 1–29. Durham: Duke University Press.

    1992.   Beyond "culture": Space, identity, and the politics of difference. *Cultural Anthropology* 7(1): 1–23.

Hall, Stuart
    1997a.   Introduction to *Representation: Cultural representations and signifying practices,* 1–12. Thousand Oaks, Calif.: Sage Publications.

    1997b.   The work of representation. In *Representation: Cultural representations and signifying practices,* 13–74. Thousand Oaks, Calif.: Sage Publications.

    1997c.   The spectacle of the "other." In *Representation: Cultural representations and signifying practices,* 223–90. Thousand Oaks, Calif.: Sage Publications.

    1996.   The question of cultural identity. In *Modernity: An introduction to modern societies,* edited by Stuart Hall, David Held, Don Hubert, and Kenneth Thompson, 595–634. Cambridge, Mass.: Blackwell Publishers.

    1990.   Cultural identity and diaspora. In *Identity: community, culture, difference,* edited by Jonathan Rutherford, 222–37. London: Lawrence & Wishart.

    1973.   The determinations of the news photographs. In *The manufacture of the news: A reader,* edited by Stanley Cohen and Jack Young. Beverly Hills: Sage Publications.

Handler, Richard
    1988.   *Nationalism and the politics of culture in Quebec.* Madison: University of Wisconsin Press.

Hannerz, Ulf
    1992.   *Cultural complexity: Studies in the social organization of meaning*. New York: Columbia University Press.
Harley, J. B.
    1988.   Maps, knowledge, and power. In *The iconography of landscape*, edited by D. Cosgrove and S. Daniels. Cambridge: Cambridge University Press.
Harvey, David
    1989.   *The condition of postmodernity*. Cambridge, Mass.: Blackwell.
Hayes, Linda B.
    1994.   Letter to the editor: California's Prop. 187. *New York Times* 15 October, p. 18.
Healy, Melissa
    1994a.   Gingrich lays out rigid GOP agenda. *Los Angeles Times* 12 November, sec. A, p. 1.
    1994b.   House GOP charts California agenda. *Los Angeles Times* 13 November, sec. A, p. 1.
Herman, Edward S., and Noam Chomsky
    1988.   *Manufacturing consent: the political economy of the mass media*. New York: Pantheon Books.
Higham, John
    1985.   *Strangers in the land*. New York: Atheneum.
Hobsbawm, Eric J.
    1992.   *Nations and nationalism since 1780: Programme, myth, reality*. 2d ed. Cambridge: Cambridge University Press.
Hobsbawm, Eric, and Terence Ranger
    1983.   *The invention of tradition*. Cambridge: Cambridge University Press.
Hoffman, Abraham
    1974.   *Unwanted Americans: Mexican Americans in the Great Depression, repatriation pressures, 1929–1939*. Tucson: University of Arizona Press.
Hollinger, David A.
    1995.   *Postethnic America: Beyond multiculturalism*. New York: Basic Books.
Hondagneu-Sotelo, Pierrette
    1995.   Women and children first: New directions in anti-immigrant politics. *Socialist Review* 25 (1):169–90.
    1994.   *Gendered transitions: Mexican experiences of immigration*. Berkeley and Los Angeles: University of California Press.
Hook, Janet
    1995.   Clinton moves to speed deportations. *Los Angeles Times* 7 May, sec. A, p. 1.
Hunter, Jefferson
    1987.   *Image and word*. Cambridge: Harvard University Press.
Jackson, Peter
    1989.   *Maps and meaning*. London: Unwin Hyman.

Jameson, Fredric

 1988. Cognitive mapping. In *Marxism and the interpretation of culture,* edited by Cary Nelson and Lawrence Grossberg. Urbana: University of Illinois Press.

 1983. Postmodernism and the consumer society. In *The anti-aesthetic: Essays on postmodern culture,* edited by Hal Foster. Seattle: Bay Press.

Johnson, Hans

 1996. *Undocumented immigration to California: 1980–1993.* San Francisco: Public Policy Institute of California.

Johnson, Kevin R.

 1997. The new nativism: Something old, something new, something borrowed, something blue. In *Immigrants out! The new nativism and the anti-immigrant impulse in the United States,* edited by Juan F. Perea, 165–89. New York: New York University Press.

 1995. Public benefits and immigration: The intersection of immigration status, ethnicity, gender, and class. *UCLA Law Review* 42 (6): 1509–75.

Jonas, Susanne

 1996. Rethinking immigration policy and citizenship in the Americas: A regional framework. *Social Justice* 23:68–85.

Jordon, Glenn, and Chris Weedon

 1995. *Cultural politics: Class, gender, race and the postmodern world.* Oxford: Blackwell.

Kanstroom, Daniel

 1997. Dangerous undertones of the new nativism: Peter Brimelow and the decline of the West. In *Immigrants out! The new nativism and the anti-immigrant impulse in the United States,* edited by Juan F. Perea, 300–317. New York: New York University Press.

Kearney, Michael

 1995. The local and the global: The anthropology of globalization and transnationalism. *Annual Review of Anthropology* 24:547–65.

 1991. Borders and boundaries of state and self at the end of empire. *Journal of Historical Sociology* 4:52–74.

Kellner, Douglas

 1992. Constructing postmodern identities. In *Modernity and identity,* edited by Scott Lash and Jonathan Friedman, 141–77. Oxford: Blackwell.

 1988. Reading images critically: Toward a postmodern pedagogy. *Journal of Education* 170:31–52.

Kennedy, John R.

 1986 [1958]. *A nation of immigrants.* New York: Harper & Row.

King, Peter H.

 1997. A welcome wagon for paradise. *Los Angeles Times* 8 October, sec. A, p. 3.

Kirby, John T.

1996.   Classical Greek origins of Western aesthetic theory. In *Languages of visuality: Crossing between science, art, politics, and literature,* edited by Beate Allert, 29–45. Detroit: Wayne State University Press.

Klahn, Norma

1996.   Writing the border: The languages and limits of representation. In *Common border, uncommon paths: Race, culture, and national identity in U.S.-Mexican relations,* edited by Jaime E. Rodríguez and Kathryn Vincent, 123–41. Wilmington: SR Books.

Krauss, Rosalind

1990.   A note on photography and the simulacrum. In *The critical image: Essays on contemporary photography,* edited by Carol Squiers, 15–27. Seattle: Bay Press.

Lacey, Marc

1996.   Toned-down immigration bill passes in House. *Los Angeles Times* 29 September, sec. A, p. 27.

Lakoff, George, and Mark Johnson

1980.   *Metaphors we live by.* Chicago: University of Chicago Press.

Lamm, Richard D., and Gary Imhoff

1985.   *The immigration time bomb.* New York: Truman Talley Books.

Leonardo, Micaela di

1998.   *Exotics at home: Anthropologies, others, American modernity.* Chicago: University of Chicago Press.

1996.   Patterns of culture wars. *Nation* 8 April: 25–29.

1994.   White ethnicities, identity politics, and Baby Bear's chair. *Social Text* 41:165–91.

Leppert, Richard

1996.   *Art and the committed eye: The cultural functions of imagery.* Boulder, Col.: Westview Press.

Lesher, Dave, and Patrick McDonnell

1996.   Wilson calls halt to much aid for illegal immigrants. *Los Angeles Times* 28 August, sec. A, p. 1.

Link, Jürgen

1991.   Fanatics, fundamentalists, lunatics, and drug traffickers—the new Southern enemy image. *Cultural Critique* 19:33–53.

Loefgren, Orvar

1993.   Materializing the nation in Sweden and America. *Ethnos* 48: 161–96.

Lowe, Lisa

1996.   *Immigrant acts: On Asian American cultural politics.* Durham: Duke University Press.

Lutz, Catherine A., and Jane L. Collins

1993.   *Reading National Geographic.* Chicago: University of Chicago Press.

Malkki, Liisa

1996.   Speechless emissaries: Refugees, humanitarianism, and dehistoricization. *Cultural Anthropology* 11:377–404.

1992.   *National Geographic:* The rooting of peoples and the territori-
               alization of national identity among scholars and refugees. *Cul-
               tural Anthropology* 7:24–44.

Mann, Jim
1995.   GOP candidates warm to anti-foreign policy. *Los Angeles Times*
               24 September, sec. A, p. 3.

Marcus, George E.
1995.   The modernist sensibility in recent ethnographic writing and the
               cinematic metaphor of montage. In *Fields of vision: Essays in film
               studies, visual anthropology, and photography,* edited by Leslie
               Devereaux and Roger Hillman. Berkeley and Los Angeles: Uni-
               versity of California Press.

Martin, Emily
1987.   *The woman in the body.* Boston: Beacon Press.

Martin, Philip
1995.   Proposition 187 in California. *International Migration Review*
               24:255–63.

Martin, Philip, and Elizabeth Midgley
1994.   Immigration to the United States: Journey to an uncertain desti-
               nation. *Population Bulletin* 49, 2 (September). Washington, D.C.:
               Population Reference Bureau.

Martin, Philip, and Jonas Widgren
1996.   International migration: A global challenge. *Population Bulletin*
               51, 1 (April). Washington, D.C.: Population Reference Bureau.

Martinez, Gebe, and Patrick J. McDonnell
1994.   Prop. 187 forces rely on message—not strategy. *Los Angeles Times*
               30 October, sec. A, p. 1..

Massey, Doreen
1994.   *Space, place and gender.* Cambridge, Eng.: Polity Press.

McBee, Susanna
1986.   Foreign roots on native soil: What we think. *U.S. News and World
               Report* 7 July, p. 31.

McDonnell, Patrick J.
1998a.   Mexico latest to grant rights to expatriates of other citizenship.
               Los Angeles Times 20 March, sec. A, p. 9.

1998b.   Food stamp eligibility restored for 250,000. *Los Angeles Times*
               5 June, sec. A, p. 1.

1997.   Prop. 187 found unconstitutional by federal judge. *Los Angeles
               Times* 15 November, sec. A, p. 1.

1994.   Prop. 187 heats up debate over immigration. *Los Angeles Times*
               10 August, sec. A, p. 1.

1986.   Hunter asks for National Guardsmen along border. *Los Angeles
               Times* 24 June, 2, 3.

Mehan, Hugh
1997.   The discourse of the illegal immigration debate: A case study
               in the politics of representation. *Discourse & Society* 8:249–
               70.

Meillassoux, Claude
    1975.   *Maidens, meal and money: Capitalism and the domestic community*. Cambridge: Cambridge University Press.

Mercer, Kobena
    1990.   Welcome to the jungle. In *Identity: community, culture, difference*, edited by Jonathan Rutherford, 43–71. London: Lawrence and Wishart.

Meyer, J. Stryker
    1986.   Sheriff urges posting Marines along border. *San Diego Union* 6 April, sec. A, p. 3.

Miller, Daniel
    1987.   *Material culture and mass consumption*. New York: Basil Blackwell.

Mills, Nicolaus, ed.
    1994.   *Arguing immigration: Are new immigrants a wealth of diversity . . . or a crushing burden?* New York: Touchstone.

Mitchell, W. J. T.
    1994.   *Picture theory: Essays on verbal and visual representation*. Chicago: University of Chicago Press.
    1986.   *Iconology: Image, text, ideology*. Chicago: University of Chicago Press.

Moore, Stephen
    1997.   *Immigration and the rise and decline of American cities*. Stanford: Hoover Institution on War, Revolution and Peace, Stanford University.

Mott, Frank Luther
    1938.   *A history of American magazines 1741–1905*. Vol. 2. Cambridge: Harvard University Press.

Muller, Thomas
    1997.   Nativism in the mid-1990s: Why now? In *Immigrants out! The new nativism and the anti-immigrant impulse in the United States*, edited by Juan F. Perea, 61–77. New York: New York University Press.

Muller, Thomas, and Thomas J. Espenshade
    1985.   *The fourth wave: California's newest immigrants*. Washington, D.C.: The Urban Institute.

National Research Council
    1997.   *The new Americans: Economic, demographic, and fiscal effects of immigration*. Edited by James P. Smith and Barry Edmonston. Washington, D.C.: National Academy Press.

Nochlin, Linda
    1989.   *The politics of vision*. New York: Harper & Row.

O'Barr, William M.
    1994.   *Culture and the ad: Exploring otherness in the world of advertising*. Boulder, Col.: Westview Press.

Olivas, Michael A.
    1995.   Storytelling out of school: Undocumented college residency,

race, and reaction. *Hastings Constitutional Law Quarterly* 22: 1019–86.

Omi, Michael, and Howard Winant

1994.   *Racial formation in the United States: From the 1960s to the 1990s.* New York: Routledge.

Ong, Aihwa

1996.   Cultural citizenship as subject-making: Immigrants negotiate racial and cultural boundaries in the United States. *Current Anthropology* 37:737–62.

Ortiz, Renato

1996.   *Otro territorio: Ensayos sobre el mundo contemporáneo.* Buenos Aires: Universidad Nacional de Quilmes.

O'Sullivan, John

1994.   America's identity crisis. *National Review* 21 November, p. 36.

Palumbo-Liu, David

1994.   Los Angeles, Asians, and perverse ventriloquisms: On the functions of Asian America in the recent American imaginary. *Public Culture* 6:365–81.

Parenti, Michael

1986.   *Inventing reality: The politics of the mass media.* New York: St. Martin's Press.

Passel, Jeffrey S., and Karen A. Woodrow

1987.   Change in the undocumented alien population in the United States, 1979–1983. *International Migration Review* 21: 1304–334.

Pedraza, Silvia

1996.   Origins and destinies: Immigration, race, and ethnicity in American history. In *Origins and destinies: Immigration, race, and ethnicity in America,* edited by Silvia Pedraza and Rubén Rumbaut, 1–20. Belmont, Calif.: Wadsworth.

Perea, Juan F., ed.

1997a.   *Immigrants out! The new nativism and the anti-immigrant impulse in the United States.* New York: New York University Press.

1997b.   The Statue of Liberty: Notes from behind the gilded door. In *Immigrants out! The new nativism and the anti-immigrant impulse in the United States,* edited by Juan F. Perea, 44–58. New York: New York University Press.

Peterson, Theodore

1956.   *Magazines in the twentieth century.* Urbana: University of Illinois Press.

Pollock, Griselda

1994.   Feminism/Foucault—surveillance/sexuality. In *Visual culture: Images and interpretation,* edited by Norman Bryson, Michael Ann Holly, and Keith Moxey, 1–41. Hanover: Wesleyan University Press.

Portes, Alejandro, and Robert L. Bach
    1985.   *Latin journey: Cuban and Mexican immigrants in the United
                 States.* Berkeley and Los Angeles: University of California Press.
Portes, Alejandro, and Rubén G. Rumbaut
    1990.   *Immigrant America: A portrait.* Berkeley and Los Angeles: Uni-
                 versity of California Press.
Portes, Alejandro, and Richard Schauffler
    1996.   Language acquisition and loss among children of immigrants. In
                 *Origins and destinies: Immigration, race, and ethnicity in Amer-
                 ica,* edited by Silvia Pedraza and Rubén Rumbaut, 432–43. Bel-
                 mont, Calif.: Wadsworth.
Prodis, Julia
    1997.   Texas town outraged at Marines over shooting of goat herder.
                 Orange County Register 29 June, News, p. 10.
Progressive
    1984.   *Two-thirds of a century: The story of the* Progressive. Madison,
                 Wis.: The Progressive Magazine.
Radcliffe, Sarah, and Sallie Westwood
    1996.   *Remaking the nation: Place, identity and politics in Latin Amer-
                 ica.* New York: Routledge.
Reimers, David M.
    1985.   *Still the golden door: The third world comes to America.* New
                 York: Columbia University Press.
Reza, H. G.
    1997.   Patrols border on danger. *Los Angeles Times* 29 June, sec. A,
                 p. 1.
Ritchin, Fred
    1990.   Photojournalism in the age of computers. In *The critical image:
                 Essays on contemporary photography,* edited by Carol Squiers,
                 28–37. Seattle: Bay Press.
Roberts, Dorothy E.
    1997.   Who may give birth to citizens? Reproduction, eugenics, and im-
                 migration. In *Immigrants out! The new nativism and the anti-
                 immigrant impulse in the United States,* edited by Juan F. Perea,
                 205–19. New York: New York University Press.
Rodriguez, Clara E.
    1997.   *Latin looks: Images of Latinas and Latinos in the U.S. media.*
                 Boulder, Col.: Westview Press.
Rodríguez, Néstor
    1996.   The battle for the border: Notes on autonomous migration,
                 transnational communities, and the state. *Social Justice* 23:21–37.
Rohrlich, Ted
    1997.   Latino voting in state surged in 1996 election. *Los Angeles Times*
                 31 December, sec. A, p. 1.
Romo, Ricardo
    1996.   Mexican Americans: Their civic and political incorporation. In

Origins and destinies: Immigration, race, and ethnicity in America, edited by Silvia Pedraza and Rubén Rumbaut, 81–97. Belmont, Calif.: Wadsworth.

1983.   *East Los Angeles: History of a barrio.* Austin: The University of Texas Press.

Rosaldo, Renato

1997.   Cultural citizenship, inequality, and multiculturalism. In *Latino cultural citizenship,* edited by William V. Flores and Rina Benmayor, 27–38. Boston: Beacon Press.

1994.   Cultural citizenship in San Jose, California. *Polar* 17:57–63.

Rosenblatt, Robert A.

1997.   U.S. jobless rate is 4.7%, a 24–year low. *Los Angeles Times* 8 November, sec. A, p. 1.

Rouse, Roger

1991.   Mexican migration and the social space of postmodernism. *Diaspora* 1:8–23.

Rumbaut, Rubén G.

1997.   Assimilation and its discontents: Between rhetoric and reality. *International Migration Review* 31:923–60.

1996.   Origins and destinies: Immigration, race, and ethnicity in contemporary America. In *Origins and destinies: Immigration, race, and ethnicity in America,* edited by Silvia Pedraza and Rubén Rumbaut, 21–42. Belmont, Calif.: Wadsworth.

1995.   The new Californians: Comparative research findings on the educational progress of immigrant children. In *California's immigrant children: Theory, research, and implications for educational policy,* edited by Rubén G. Rumbaut and Wayne A. Cornelius. San Diego: Center for U.S.-Mexican Studies, University of California, San Diego.

Said, Edward W.

1997   *Covering Islam: How the media and the experts determine how*
[1981].   *we see the rest of the world.* New York: Vintage Books.

1978.   *Orientalism.* New York: Random House.

Saldívar, José David

1997.   *Border matters: Remapping American cultural studies.* Berkeley and Los Angeles: University of California Press.

Sample, Herbert A.

1997.   Budget law would reverse assistance for legal immigrants. *Orange County Register* 30 July, News, p. 14.

Sanjek, Roger

1998.   *The future of us all.* Ithaca: Cornell University Press.

Santa Ana, Otto

1999.   Like an animal I was treated: Anti-immigrant metaphor in U.S. public discourse. *Discourse & Society* 10(2): 192–224.

Santa Ana, Otto, Juan Moran, and Cynthia Sanchez

1998.   Awash under a brown tide: Immigration metaphors in California public and print media discourse. *Aztlan* 23(2): 137–75.

Sassen, Saskia
    1988.   *The mobility of labor and capital: A study in international in-vestment and labor flow.* Cambridge, Eng.: Cambridge University Press.
Sax, William S.
    1998.   The hall of mirrors: Orientalism, anthropology, and the other. *American Anthropologist* 100:292–301.
Schlesinger, Arthur M.
    1992.   *The disuniting of America.* New York: Norton.
Schwab, Gabriele
    1996.   *The mirror and the killer-queen: Otherness in literary language.* Bloomington: Indiana University Press.
Segal, Daniel A.
    1994.   Living ancestors: Nationalism and the past in postcolonial Trinidad and Tobago. In *Remapping memory: Politics of time space,* edited by Jonathan Boyarin. Minneapolis: University of Minnesota Press.
Seyhan, Azade
    1996.   Visual citations: Walter Benjamin's dialectic of text and image. In *Languages of visuality: Crossing between science, art, politics, and literature,* edited by Beate Allert, 229–41. Detroit: Wayne State University Press.
Sforza, Teri
    1997.   Euphoria over O.C. *Orange County Register* 2 December, News, p. 9.
Shogren, Elizabeth
    1996.   Clinton's signature launches historical overhaul of welfare. *Los Angeles Times* 23 August, sec. A, p. 1.
Shohat, Ella
    1997.   Gender and culture of empire: Toward a feminist ethnography of the cinema. In *Visions of the East,* edited by Mathew Bernstein and Gaylyn Studlar. New Brunswick, N.J.: Rutgers University Press.
Simon, Julian, and Ather Akbari
    1995.   *The truth about immigrant "quality."* Arlington, Vir.: The Alexis de Tocqueville Institution.
Simon, Rita J.
    1985.   *Public opinion and the immigrant.* Lexington, Mass.: Lexington Books.
Simon, Rita J., and Susan H. Alexander
    1993.   The ambivalent welcome: Print media, public opinion and immigration. Westport, Conn.: Praeger Publishers.
Simon, Rita J., and James P. Lynch
    1999.   A comparative assessment of public opinion toward immigrants and immigration policies. *International Migration Review* 33: 455–68.

Siu, Paul C. P.
  1987.   *The Chinese laundryman: A study in social isolation.* New York:
              New York University Press.
Smith, Anthony D.
  1986.   *The ethnic origins of nations.* Oxford: Basil Blackwell.
Smith, James F.
  1998.   Mexico's dual nationality opens doors for millions. *Los Angeles
              Times* 20 March, sec. A, p. 1.
Smith, Valerie
  1997.   *Representing blackness: Issues in film and video.* New Brunswick,
              N.J.: Rutgers University Press.
Sontag, Susan
  1977.   *On photography.* New York: Farrar, Straus and Giroux.
Sowell, Thomas
  1981.   *Ethnic America: A history.* New York: Basic Books.
Spurr, David
  1993.   *The rhetoric of empire: Colonial discourse in journalism, travel
              writing, and imperial administration.* Durham: Duke University
              Press.
Steinberg, Stephen
  1981.   *The ethnic myth: Race, ethnicity, and class in America.* Boston:
              Beacon Press.
Steinfield, Melvin, ed.
  1970.   *Cracks in the melting pot.* Beverly Hills: Glencoe Press.
Stolcke, Verena
  1995.   Talking culture: New boundaries, new rhetorics of exclusion in
              Europe. *Current Anthropology* 36:1–24.
Stout, David
  1998.   Judges may review deportation orders, appeals court rules. *New
              York Times* 19 May, sec. A, p. 15.
Suarez-Orozco, C., and Suarez-Orozco, M.
  1995.   *Transformations: Immigration, family life and achievement mo-
              tivation among Latino adolescents.* Stanford: Stanford Univer-
              sity Press.
Swarns, Rachel L.
  1996.   Polish and Irish immigrants benefit from Visa lottery. *New York
              Times* 29 January, sec. A, p. 1.
Tagg, John
  1988.   *The burden of representation.* London: Macmillan Education.
Tatalovich, Raymond
  1997.   Official English as nativist backlash. In *Immigrants out! The new
              nativism and the anti-immigrant impulse in the United States,* ed-
              ited by Juan F. Perea, 78–102. New York: New York University
              Press.
Taylor, Lucien
  1994.   *Visualizing theory.* New York: Routledge.

Tebbel, John
    1969.   *The American magazine: A compact history*. New York: Haw-
                 thorne Books.
Traube, Elizabeth G.
    1996.   "The popular" in American culture. *Annual Review of Anthro-
                 pology* 25:127–51.
Turner, Victor W.
    1967.   *The forest of symbols; aspects of Ndembu ritual*. Ithaca, N.Y.:
                 Cornell University Press.
U.S. Bureau of the Census
    1991.   *Race and Hispanic origin, 1990 census profile*. Washington,
                 D.C.: U.S. Department of Commerce.
U.S. House of Representatives
    1986.   Immigration Reform and Control Act of 1986. Conference re-
                 port. 99th Congress, 2d Session. Report 99–1000. Washington,
                 D.C.: U.S. Government Printing Office.
U.S. Immigration and Naturalization Service
    1990–93.   *Statistical yearbooks*. Washington, D.C.: U.S. Government Print-
                 ing Office.
Vaillancourt Rosenau, Pauline
    1992.   *Post-modernism and the social sciences: Insights, inroads, and in-
                 trusions*. Princeton, N.J.: Princeton University Press.
Vasconcelos, José
    1948.   *La raza cósmica*. Mexico: Espasa Calpe-Mexicana.
Vélez-Ibáñez, Carlos G.
    1996.   *Border visions: Mexican cultures of the southwest United States*.
                 Tucson: University of Arizona Press.
Walsh, Mary Williams
    1999.   Soft growth in jobs makes markets jump. *Los Angeles Times* 4
                 September, sec. A, p. 1.
Weiss, Kenneth R., and Mary Curtius
    1998.   Acceptance of Blacks, Latinos to UC plunges. *Los Angeles Times*
                 1 April, sec. A, p. 1.
Williams, Raymond
    1980.   Advertising: The magic system. In *Problems in materialism and
                 culture*, edited by Raymond Williams. London: Verso.
Williamson, Judith
    1978.   *Decoding advertisements: Ideology and meaning in advertising*.
                 London: Marion Boyars.
Woo, Elaine
    1997.   Immigrants' children found to favor English. *Los Angeles Times*
                 16 June, sec. A, p. 1.
Wood, James Playsted
    1971.   *Magazines in the United States*. New York: The Ronald Press
                 Company.

Woodrow, Karen A., and Jeffrey S. Passel

1990.   Post-IRCA undocumented immigration to the United States: An assessment based on the June 1988 CPS. In *Undocumented migration to the United States: IRCA and the experiences of the 1980s,* edited by Frank D. Bean, Barry Edmonston, and Jeffrey S. Passel. Washington, D.C.: The Urban Institute Press.

Woodward, Kathryn

1997.   Concepts of identity and difference. In *Identity and difference,* edited by Kathryn Woodward. Thousand Oaks, Calif.: Sage Publications.

Zavella, Patricia

1997.   The tables are turned: Immigration, poverty, and social conflict in California communities. In *Immigrants out! The new nativism and the anti-immigrant impulse in the United States,* edited by Juan F. Perea, 136–61. New York: New York University Press.

Index

Page numbers in italics indicate tables and figures.

Compositor:	Integrated Composition Systems, Inc.
Text:	10/13 Sabon
Display:	Sabon
Printer and Binder:	Edwards Brothers, Inc.
Index:	Towery Indexing Service